Territory and Administration in Europe

Territory and Administration in Europe

edited by
Robert Bennett

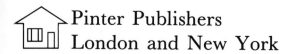

Pinter Publishers
London and New York

First published in Great Britain in 1989 by
Pinter Publishers Limited
25 Floral Street, London WC2E 9DS

British Library Cataloguing in Publication Data

A CIP catalogue record for this book is available from the
British Library

ISBN 0 86187 991 0

Library of Congress Cataloging-in-Publication Data

Territory and administration in Europe/edited by R.J. Bennett.
    p. cm.
    Includes index.
    ISBN 0-86187-991-0
    1. Local government – Europe. 2. Central-local government
relations – Europe. 3. Decentralization in government – Europe.
I. Bennett, R. J. (Robert John)
JS3000.3.A3T47   1989   89-3888
352.04–dc20   CIP

Filmset by Mayhew Typesetting, Bristol, England
Printed by Biddles Ltd, Guildford and King's Lynn

Contents

Preface

This book is concerned with the adaptation of local government administrative systems to economic and political change. It is argued that there is a specific European dimension to these issues: a dimension that because of its history in many ways transcends the different constitutional and political structures of the countries of Europe, the large trading blocks of the EEC and COMECON and the division of east and west. As a consequence much can be learnt from the presentation and interchange of individual experiences which can be compared. It is to the further encouragement and fostering of this collaborative and comparative research that this book is dedicated.

Many European countries are experiencing rapid economic and administrative change at the moment. In socialist Europe this has been given special stimulus by the economic and political reforms associated with Soviet *Perestroika* and *Glasnost*. In western Europe technological change and political development have tended to result in so-called 'crises': crises of representation, crises of financial resources or crises resulting from clashes of responsibilities between levels of government. The book seeks to reflect these rapid changes, recording developments up to June 1988, and directs attention towards likely future developments.

In editing a book such as this it has been important to ensure a common structure and approach, at the same time retaining the individual character of the contributions of each author and the specifics of their subject matter in each country. Thus although each chapter has been extensively edited to obtain good idiomatic English the original meaning has been maintained and checked by the authors, to whom I offer grateful thanks for their forebearance. As editor in the opening chapters I have sought to set the later chapters in a general context. There are also other contexting chapters by Bours, Perger and Maurel. I am sure that the contributors will not agree with all of these interpretations. Their own views are retained in their chapters and so, in this sense, the book seeks to represent an overall and coherent line of argument, yet retaining for the reader a good sense of the diversity of views.

It is inevitable, therefore, that the book has a mixture of messages: Europe is large, complex and diverse; economic change is rapid and unpredictable. The dominant editorial argument is that the only stable administrative response is, therefore, a means of achieving *flexible decentralization* and *flexible aggregation* of administrative territories. However, running through this argument, and through the diversity of views in the case-study chapters, are a range of other issues: of eastern Europe compared to western Europe, of different interpretations of administrative accountability, of public- as opposed to private-sector roles, of one party compared to multi-party representative politics, of voter representation versus participation and of political economic views in comparison with more restricted economic notions.

This book derives from the meetings of the 'Geography and Public Administration' Commission of the International Geographical Union (IGU) formed in 1984. Its aims have been to foster interdisciplinary research in practical policy analysis and administrative procedure. One key aspect of these aims has been developed through meetings in Europe which have sought to bring together interdisciplinary groups of researchers and administrators in a broad range of countries to confront the question of adapting current administrative procedures to changing economic and social circumstances. Two meetings in particular, in Poland and Hungary, were especially important in developing the work and many of the papers presented at those meetings are included in revised form in this book. A related book produced through the IGU Commission takes the concepts of decentralization further in the fields of finance and organization of competences: see Robert Bennett (ed.) 1989, *Decentralization, local governments and markets: setting a post-welfare agenda?*, Oxford University Press.

The preparation and publication of this book would not have been possible without the assistance of a great number of people and institutions, the chief of which I would wish to acknowledge and gratefully thank as editor. The IGU itself has provided essential support, both moral and financial through its Secretaries General Michael Wise and Leszek Kosinski, and through its Presidents Walter Marshand and Peter Scott. It has also been important to have the support of the sister body of the International Institute of Administrative Sciences (IIAS) which co-sponsored the meeting in Poland, as well as a number of other exchanges. The IGU and IIAS in turn are supported in part by the International Council of Scientific Unions (ICSU) and UNESCO. The meeting in Poland was organized by Maria Ciechocińska with the support of the Polish National Committee of the IGU, the Polish Academy of Sciences, the Polish Geographical Society and the Polish State Planning Commission; the meeting in Hungary was organised by Gyorgy Enyedi with the support of the Hungarian National Committee of the IGU and the Centre for Regional Studies of the Hungarian Academy of Sciences (Pécs). To all of these organizations this volume owes a major debt. I am also most grateful for the critical comments of Jerzy Regulski. The text has been prepared with the assistance of a large number of individuals but acknowledgement of the following is particularly important: Christine Gazely, Angela Barnes, Jutta Muller (typing); Jane Pugh, Kristina Ferris (cartography); Tom Elkins helped significantly in the translation of Joaquim Bräuniger's chapter.

Robert J. Bennett
Chairman, IGU Commission on Geography and Public Administration
London School of Economics

List of contributors

Gerhard Bahrenberg   Fachbereich 8/Geographie Universität Bremen
Federal Republic of Germany

Robert Bennett   Department of Geography
London School of Economics
United Kingdom

Hans Blaas   Universiteit van Amsterdam
Subfaculteit der Sociale Geografie
The Netherlands

Adriaan Bours   Bestuurskunde en Publiek Recht
Universiteit van Amsterdam
The Netherlands

Joaquim Bräuniger   Sektion Geographie
Humboldt-Universität zu Berlin
German Democratic Republic

Maria Ciechocińska   Institute of Geography and Spatial Organization
Polish Academy of Sciences
Warszawa, Poland

Z. Demerdjiev   Institute of Geography
Bulgarian Academy of Sciences
Sofia, Bulgaria

Petr Dostál   Universiteit van Amsterdam
Subfaculteit der Sociale Geografie
The Netherlands

Guy Gilbert   CREFAUR
Faculté de Sciences Economique
Université de Rennes
France

Alain Guengant   CREFAUR
Faculté de Sciences Economique
Université de Rennes
France

Zoltán Hajdú   Centre for Regional Studies
Hungarian Academy of Sciences
Pécs, Hungary

Boris Khorev — Institute of Economics
USSR Academy of Science
Moscow, USSR

Marie-Claude Maurel — Université Paul Valéry
Montpellier, France

Eero Nurminen — University of Tampere
Department of Regional Studies
Finland

Éva Perger — Geographical Research Institute
University of Budapest
Hungary

P. Popov — Institute of Geography
Bulgarian Academy of Sciences
Sofia, Bulgaria

Robert Sevrin — Laboratoire de Géographie
Facultés Catholiques de Lille
Lille, France

Joaquim Solé-Vilanova — Faculty of Economics
University of Barcelona
Spain

Igor Ushkalov — Institute of Economics
USSR Academy of Science
Moscow, USSR

Olga Vidláková — Institute of Public Administration
University of Prague
Czechoslovakia

Pavel Zářecký — Institute of Public Administration
University of Prague
Czechoslovakia

Part 1 Society and administration: the European context

1 Territory and administration
Robert Bennett

Introduction

Economic structures, the territory they cover and their administration are intimately intertwined. Not all fields of administration are concerned with economic structures and geographical space or territory, but most are. Systems of administration of economies, people and services that have ignored territory, such as that of the early Soviets, have usually had to encompass territory at a later date thus 'reinventing' the intimate link of territory, economy and administration.

This book examines the evolving interrelationship between the economics and geography of the space administered on the one hand and the administrative structure which occupies that space and influences its economic restructuring on the other hand. The relationship between territory and administration is dominated by the economic, social and political system. Europe is used as the context to examine this relationship. Europe offers a diversity but, as will also be argued, a unity of experiences. Europe is also an exciting area to study at present because of its rapid economic and administrative changes.

The concern of this volume is with administrative levels within countries and their interaction with each other and the central state. Most countries have a multiplicity of levels and agencies of government: some representative, some not representative. In simple terms these can be classified as in Table 1.1 according to their representativeness (elected or not elected), whether they have competence over a single function (such as water supply, education or housing) or are general-purpose governments. General-purpose government has competence over a range of functions which allows a level of political discretion and priorities to be developed between one function and another. Our chief concerns in this book are with the relation between economy and society, and the relation of political participation to governmental administration. Hence our key interest is with local representative government (perhaps over several tiers), in the upper left of Table 1.1. However, the other form of general-purpose administration shown in Table 1.1 is also important and we shall discuss non-representative local administrations such as French districts or the

Table 1.1 Types of local government

	Representative	Non-representative
General purpose	Local representative government	Non-representative local administration
Special purpose	Representative single-function districts	Decentralized agencies (usually of central government)

Source: Humes and Martin, 1961, p. 5

Kreis in Germany. However, we will generally exclude from discussion special purpose districts and decentralized agencies of central government.

Economy and administration in Europe

While economy, society and politics evolve relatively rapidly, it is often the case that administrative practice lags far behind. Indeed the obsolescence of administrative structures is almost a 'normal' phenomenon since it is difficult for administrative reforms to keep up with the pace of economic developments. This produces some surprising anomalies. Much of western Europe still retains important administrative characteristics dating from the Napoleonic reforms; and Napoleon himself drew heavily on the reforms introduced by the French revolution. In central Europe the legacies of the Habsburgs and Austro–Hungarian Empire are still present in its administrative structures. And in the USSR there is an administrative continuity of the *oblast* from the nineteenth-century *gubernia*. Of course in all cases, particularly that of the USSR, there is little or no continuity of objectives, functions, competences or financial arrangements. But bureaucratic structures have a marked resilience despite changes in their objectives! Thus Ridley (1979, p. 1) has noted that 'in France it used to be said that the republican order had merely been imposed on the imperial: the political institutions of democracy the visible, but relatively unimportant, eighth of the iceberg above the surface, the Napoleonic administration the effective seven-eighths below'.

Because of the different rates of change and restructuring of economies, society and politics on the one hand, and slower moving and frequently obsolescent administrative objectives and practices on the other hand, discontinuities frequently emerge over time. The discontinuities concern changing administrative needs, functions, financial and other resources, as well as the technologies for delivering them. To many of these changes administrations can and do readily adapt. Hence continuous modest reforms occur. However, over longer periods of time, major disjunctures can emerge between the administrative structures of a country and the needs of its economy and society as ·expressed through its political processes. When such disjunctures occur a root-and-branch reform of administration is usually required. It is often at this point that territory, because it is a reflection of economy, society and politics, becomes particularly crucial in shaping the reform debate.

It is argued in this book that because of the rapid rate of economic change and restructuring, the 1980s and 1990s are a time in which a major disjuncture is arising between administrative systems and the needs which they seek to satisfy. This disjuncture, it is argued, is the result of two chief factors: first an accelerated rate of evolution of economies mainly as a result of an increased pace of technological change and development; and second, a shift in the social structure and form of consensus which shapes the 'policy culture' and political priorities.

The disjuncture resulting from economic restructuring seems to be deeply affecting both socialist and west European systems, although of course in very different ways. But there is major common ground across the two systems which allows each to be compared, and for each to learn from the other. The common ground derives from the similar pressures of economic change and social development. The similarity of the disjuncture derives from the different, but parallel, phenomena of administrative form which create problems of adaptation. The similarities and common ground over distinct but parallel administrative systems leads to the arrangement of the following chapters.

Plan of the book

The book first examines the general pattern of interrelations of economy, society and politics with administrative systems over the span of recent European history. Phases of development deriving from feudalism, the emergence of nationalism and early capitalism laid in place systems of administrative structures which dominated Europe over different areas at different times. These gave rise to the major administrative structures for Europe which were laid out, in most cases, in the nineteenth century. The Russian revolution, and the administrative system established by the 1930s, then became a new and dominant force of political and economic development, with its attendant social provision, which has to greater or lesser extent been mirrored in much of central Europe in the late 1940s and 1950s. In western Europe the evolution of administrative systems in the twentieth century has mirrored the development of the 'welfare state'. In the 1950s and 1960s both socialist and west European administrative systems responded to the concept of functional regions and city-systems for service provision, although in many cases reforms to take account of these concepts were very partial.

The 1980s and 1990s, however, are presenting major new challenges both to socialist and to west European administrative systems. The territorial layout — the geography — of administration has often been nineteenth century in origin; enormous developments in the level of state provision accompanied by partial reforms and political compromises have only partially modified territory but have considerably modified competences and financial resources. At the same time economic restructuring and social development, and the related political priorities, have shifted at a rapid rate. Many reforms have already been undertaken in response to change, many in very recent years: for example in France in 1982, in Spain in 1982, in Belgium in 1988; in Bulgaria in 1987, in Hungary in 1987–8, in Poland in 1988 and in the USSR following the 1988 party congress. However, it is clear that most of these reforms are only tackling some aspects of current disjunctures. We are left therefore with a range of, at present, unresolved questions. How can administrative structures respond? What are the new territorial arrangements that should be put in place? How should competency be divided between central and other levels of government? How should the financial wherewithal be provided? What are the appropriate management structures? These are the questions which are presented in the current debate which this book seeks to answer.

The questions raised lead to the plan of this book. The next four chapters seek to give a synoptic overview of the challenges to administrative reform which are presented by economic restructuring. The following chief issues are tackled:

— the relation of economy, society and politics to the history of administrative evolution;
— the new challenges to administrative reform;
— divisions of competency and responsibilities within the state;
— social and public service provision and its effective management structure;
— provision of adequate financial resources.

This overview is then followed by two chapters which place the developments of socialist Europe into the context of, respectively, economic reform and the challenges to participation and community life. There then follows a set of detailed evaluations of reform structures and debates in thirteen countries. These countries do not include all of Europe, since the space available here is insufficient. However, the cases discussed do include the countries where major reforms of administration and territory are occurring, or are under active debate. Some significant omissions are Yugoslavia, Romania, Italy, Sweden, Norway, but these together with the remaining European countries are included in the overview chapters. Finally the book concludes with a systematic assessment of the future.

The future

The major editorial conclusion of this book is that a flexible approach is required to administrative questions. *Flexible decentralization* is argued to be the means of achieving a close relation of services and satisfaction of needs to local preferences and community requirements, as well as assuring a high level of participation and representation. This asserts a greater role for the smaller and basic level administrative units — the municipalities and communes. At the same time, however, technical arguments concerning economies of scale and internationalization of externalities, as well as the need to maintain a level of social and territorial equity and economic symmetry, require an aggregation of localities into larger units. It is argued that no one solution to the aggregation problem is possible: different public service functions have different optimal economic sizes, preferences vary over different spatial areas and there are important cultural and physical geographical differences between and within countries. As a result it is argued that *flexible aggregation* to different sizes of units is the only means of maintaining an adaptable but stable financial and administrative structure. This leads to arguments for different mixes of co-ordination, agency arrangements, 'associations' of local administrative units and ·different mixes of public administration, public finance and private (market) responses.

The different chapters confirm this view in different ways, as well as suggesting important contrasts. The editorial argument is not intended to impose an orthodoxy over the individual contributors. Other means of resolving current tensions in administrative systems are clearly possible, although they may be less enduring than flexible methods.

References

Humes, S. and Martin, E.M. (1961), *The Structure of Local Governments throughout the World*, Martinus Nijhoff, The Hague.
Ridley, F.F. (ed.) (1979), *Government and Administration in Western Europe*, Martin Robertson, London.

2 European economy, society, politics and administration: symmetry and disjuncture
Robert Bennett

Economic and administrative evolution

The development of administrative and territorial structures in Europe is immensely complex and varies considerably between countries. Thus generalizations are dangerous. Nevertheless an attempt is made here to approach European developments at a fairly high level of generality in order to provide the context for the detailed case studies of later chapters. The attempt to generalize is further justified by the fact that the historical development of administrative systems in Europe has included many similar and overlapping features.

The political development of Europe is fundamental to its administrative and territorial structure. European political development can be argued to be the result of three different sets of historical forces. The first was the shift from absolute government to a system of legal checks and balances. A major influence on this was the emergence of 'constitutionalism' following the French and American revolutions. A second force has been the attempt to bring government under popular control: to provide for *representative* government. This is the dominant political structure of western Europe in the 'liberal democracies'. The third force has been the attempt to introduce 'a state of the whole people' (*obshchenarodnoe gosudarstvo*),[1] a distinctive form of mass participation, which followed the Soviet revolution in 1917. The term 'socialist democracy' is used to describe this development which characterizes the USSR and eastern Europe.

At the same time the economic development of Europe has also had profound influence on territory and administration. The Roman Catholic ecclesiastical administrative divisions, particularly the commune (parish) has had an amazingly enduring structure. This, combined with feudalism, provided the economic system across the whole of Europe up to the end of the Middle Ages which then experienced a pattern of reforms and disjunctures at different times in different countries. These reforms introduced secularization during and after the Reformation, the development of administrative absolutism and nationalism associated with economic expansion and the growth of industrial capitalism. By the nineteenth century in most countries the feudal system had disappeared and with it the dominant power of the estates. In its place came capitalist economic systems which gave birth to the middle classes and increase of workers that laid the administrative foundations for the liberal and welfare state economies. In some parts of eastern Europe developments were much slower and in Russia and Bulgaria the transition from feudalism to socialist democracy was almost direct; in other parts of eastern Europe, for example Hungary and Czechoslovakia, a substantial development of capitalist economic and administrative systems took place before the development of socialist democracy and there is some legacy of historical administrative systems within their socialist democracies.

These developments of politics and economy were intimately entwined with administrative and bureaucratic structures, and no less so today. Thus the current tensions for administrative change are rooted in economic and technological changes. Since some major aspects of these changes are common to both eastern and western Europe it is not surprising that a common ground for discussion, and hence for generalization, is now emerging. At the same time tensions resulting from common aspects of history also allow generalizations to be drawn.

Constitutionalism

In Europe constitutional government is the underpinning concept of what are usually termed 'liberal democracies' which represent the dominant framework for administration of western Europe. Smith (1973) and Macpherson (1966) argue that their emergence was based first on liberal institutions which sought to prevent 'absolute' government (that is to limit government) and later these same institutions evolved into being representative, or democratic, as a means of asserting (and limiting) public collective power. Laski (1935, p. 217) sees them as more fundamentally class based: constitutional 'rules are respected so long as the class which is in power is broadly identified with those who evolved them'. Hence constitutions must and do change economic circumstances. However, they are intended to provide the basic set of rules, or rights, which are modified only infrequently. Constitutionalism emerged during the seventeenth and eighteenth centuries and was codified into the principle of *separation of powers* — of legislation, adjudication and administration — each with their own specialized institutions. Almond and Powell (1966) argue that constitutionalism is pre-eminently a functional theory which sought to establish the conditions for equilibrium between political forces that allowed a balance to be maintained which prevented absolute government. This structure, for a variety of reasons, became adapted to political representation for the population as a whole, not merely to balance institutions. This can be seen as exhibiting continuity, but also as introducing a tension. Smith (1973) following Bendix (1964) argues that the result is two systems of representation: direct or popular representation, which conferred equal status to all ('plebiscitarian'), and group or institutional representation, which is based on the affiliations of individuals (with business, trade unions, local government areas, etc.) and which conferred unequal power positions.

Because of its history the duality which exists between these two systems is particularly characteristic of western Europe. And, Bendix goes on to argue, the tension which arises from the duality is essential to the maintenance of liberal democracies:

> The two ideas . . . reflect the hiatus between state and society in an age of equality . . . the system of representative institutional characteristic of the western European tradition remains intact as long as this tension . . . endures, as long as the contradiction between abstract criteria of equality and the old as well as the new inequalities of the social condition is mitigated by ever new and ever partial compromises. [Bendix, 1964, pp. 101–4]

Almond and Powell (1966) take this further and argue that the constructive aspects of this tension are maintained by three processes: of *interest articulation* (the demands made through organization and representative bodies), *interest aggregation* (the conversion of demands into general policy alternatives as in party structures) and *communication* (socialization and administrative functions). These three processes together then lead to a *political conversion* process which transforms the demands and supports of the political system into a flow of extraction, regulation and distribution within any environment. In their later study Almond and Powell (1978) reinforce this argument with copious analysis of case studies, but the overall classification remains the same. In my use of their argument here, however, I extend their concept of communication to cover administration (which they restrict to governmental structures) since, as I shall argue below, administration, particularly at the local level, is an important aspect of two-way communication between people and the state.

Constitutionalism in the Bendix, and Almond and Powell interpretation is, therefore, a means of resolving the conflict of interest groups (including overall collective or 'public goods') and individual rights. This, Smith (1973, p. 125) argues, confers on liberal democracies in Europe a unified idea which has a general *normative* quality; that is the constitution itself speaks with authority as a higher form of law, irrespective of the issues or interest groups involved, as long as the whole structure is maintained by the political consensus which supports it. Smith goes on to argue that western European constitutions contrast with the more 'semantic' constitutions of eastern Europe. For example, Smith cites the Article I of the 1968 Constitution (GDR), which bases the leadership of the state on 'the Working Class and Marxist–Leninist Party', hence restricting the autonomy supposedly enshrined in Article 48 which gives the single-chamber Volkshammer full sovereignty. However, Smith's interpretation that the constitution is thus 'semantic' is not strictly correct, particularly at local level. In both east and west Europe the constitution performs the same 'normative' role, but clearly the forms of interest articulation, aggregation and communication differ greatly. Moreover developments in eastern Europe, with attendant reforms as in the West, are throwing new emphasis on the constitutional underpinnings of administrative practice.

Territory and administration

The division of power within the state and the geographical division of power between and within levels of government are interdependent. The interplay between the two dimensions can be described in various ways. One approach is to link the extent of division of powers territorially to the constitutional division of overall state powers. This was a key aspect of the Federalist writers (see Chapter 4) and is embedded in the American Constitution. In a different form it applies to the federal structures in Europe (chiefly West Germany and Austria). The 'original' granting of powers to sub-state levels (to state or *Land* governments) provides for a discretion and function separate from the central government which cannot be disturbed by the centre. A second approach is to treat geographical divisions and non-territorial divisions of power on an equal basis and examine their interplay in different contexts. This is essentially the approach developed by Maass (1959) and Fesler (1980) and provides the basis for many authors to classify administrative systems. These classifications, in Europe, normally range over four groups as shown in Figure 2.1:

(i) *Unitary* (or centralized), for example France, The Netherlands, Luxembourg, Portugal, Greece, East Germany, Poland, Romania, Bulgaria and Hungary;

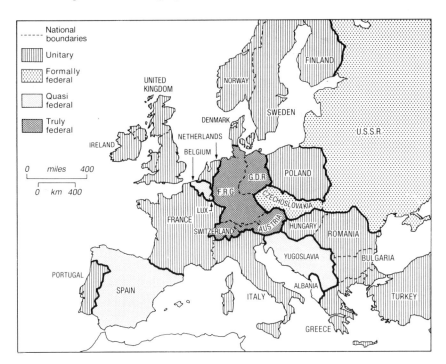

Figure 2.1 Constitutional structures in Europe in 1988: Unitary; formally federal; quasi-federal; truly federal

(ii) *Formally federal*, where a constitution provides for territorial autonomy, but where this autonomy is so limited in practice that they are almost unitary states, for example the USSR, Czechoslovakia;

(iii) *Quasi-federal*, where limited and formally autonomous areas have been combined or have lapsed through union (Britain which is now almost entirely unitary), or where a level of autonomy is exercised but is strictly limited (Italy or Yugoslavia), or where its development as yet is very limited (Belgium since 1988). A special case is Spain where an almost truly federal structure was instituted in 1982, but where central government still retains important powers;

(iv) *Truly federal*, where constitutional guarantees exist and are exercised for autonomy in certain major fields, for example West Germany, Switzerland and Austria (although Austria possesses important aspects of a decentralized unitary state and Switzerland retains characteristics of confederalism where central powers are limited by sub-state action) (see for example Duchacek, 1973; Ridley, 1979; Almond and Powell, 1978).

There is also the special case of the small states (Andorra, Liechtenstein, Monaco and San Marino). These classifications depict the formal legal structure of the territorial division of powers between national and state/regional levels, and not local government powers. Hence for our purposes here a more useful further classification is provided by Leemans (1970, ch. 4). He characterizes sub-state relationships in Europe as ones which follow either of three main models: *dual systems*, *fused systems* and *split hierarchy systems*. To these in Figure 2.2 we add the system of socialist democracy. To understand this classification fully it is first necessary to introduce something of the possible complexity in the number of levels of sub-state government and define a common nomenclature. In the discussion here, and as far as possible in later chapters, the following terminology is employed:

Central government: overall government of the state (often synonymous with national or federal government)
State government: in federal systems, for example *Länder*, Cantons
Regional government: within state, and groups of states or local authorities
Upper-tier local government: province, *département* (sometimes county)
Lower-tier local government: commune, municipality (sometimes district)

Between these five levels there may also sometimes be other administrative levels. There is also the complication of different uses of the same term. This is particularly a problem when state governments exist within the central state, and with the British term 'county' and 'district' which often varies from continental European usage.

Fused systems, in Leemans' terminology, are those characterizing most west European centralized and quasi-federal structures. The purest example is that of France before recent reforms. The *département* prefect is a career civil servant of the central government responsible to it, and not to local government, for local services (cf. Machin, 1977). Counterweights are provided by local councils, particularly in large cities, but these are limited since the local mayors, historically appointed by the *département* prefect but now locally elected, became closely associated with national policies through the prefect. The administrative order placed by Napoleon on much of Europe has evolved a similar system in Italy (but with a form of dual system at provincial level) and until recent reforms in Belgium and The Netherlands. Until recent reforms in states such as Spain, Portugal, Greece and Turkey the duality went beyond fusion to a total deconcentration in which only delegated powers from the centre were exercised locally: the mayors were centrally controlled. Recent reforms in Portugal and Greece have allowed a form of fused system to develop, while in Spain a quasi-federal structure is now in place.

The *dual system*, or detached hierarchy, of administration is represented by English[2] local government. This derives from a reliance on the dominance of 'government' by committee: the responsibility for the functions of local government are borne by the elected council as a whole, but within overall supervisory, legal and financial constraints set by central government departments. A major consequence is that it is difficult to have a unified executive, either politically or administratively. As a result the mayor is merely symbolic, and attempts at corporate management are limited by political and committee consensus. This has recently been modified by the British government's 1988 Local Government Finance Act and response to the Widdicombe Committee (1986) which has strengthened the importance of local collective political decisions, but has limited the financial freedom enjoyed.

Split hierarchy systems generally characterize the Scandinavian countries. Here the central government may hold considerable sway over the provincial level, including appointment of members, but localities have their own councils and autonomy with collective responsibility as in the dual system. The split hierarchy system is thus a mixture of fused and dual systems.

In the federal countries (West Germany, Austria, Switzerland, in major characteristics in Spain, and in some characteristics in Belgium) various blends of fused, dual and split hierarchy administrations also operate; but the operation is *within* each state (*Land* or Canton) and is supervised by the provincial level and not the central government. In addition there may be contrasts between states within one country, as in West Germany between north and south, and between city–states and other states (Hamburg and Bremen in West Germany; Vienna in Austria; Basel, Zurich and Geneva in Switzerland).

Socialist democracy is characterized by a special form of central–local interdependence. Although it differs in detail between different east European countries, and is evolving rapidly in some, its general structure emphasizes *mass participation* within local soviets (people's committees) and other organizations (production committees, trade unions and social organizations). Although elected, deputies to local soviets are strongly supervised by the party, the structure of which parallels that of the soviets

I Fused systems

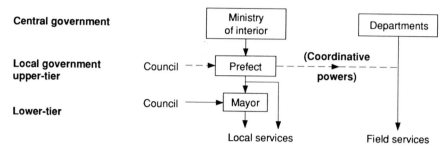

II Dual systems

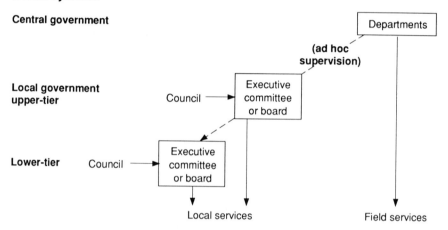

Figure 2.2   Forms of administrative structure based on an extension of Leemans' (1970) classification

at all levels. In addition the requirements of the economic plan, largely set centrally, keep the scope for local autonomy to a minimum. Party and plan also impose a strong sectoral (or departmental) view. This leads to two critical aspects which distinguish the Soviet administrative system from that in western Europe. First, is the character of local soviets which, as well as having a territorial focus, are also organized around the production process. This differs from the west European tradition of internal aggregation for area and hence for community. A second distinction derives from the role of mass participation on which rests the claim to socialist 'democracy'. The claimed participation has four chief aspects (see for example Churchward, 1975, pp. 269–70): public debate of policy and legislation; popular involvement in administration; participation in running

III Split hierarchy systems

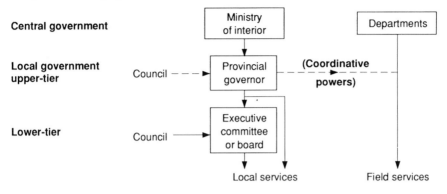

IV Socialist democracy

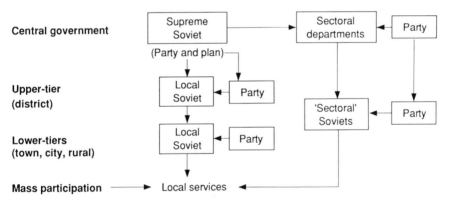

Figure 2.2 (continued)

social organizations; and socialist competition related to achievement of the economic plan. Mass participation is not spontaneous since, where it exists, it is closely supervised at all levels by the party, but it can involve large numbers of people in service delivery. This Soviet approach theoretically can resolve the tension between government power and popular representation, that is socialist authors argue that socialist democracies are simultaneously *direct* and representative democracies. This concept is often criticized by western commentators, and has been subject to internal criticisms as a force for nationalizing local government which stifles local initiative and enthusiasm.

The historical underpinning of modern territorial administration

The argument, that we can make generalizations in administrative structure over Europe as a whole, derives from its common history. This allows us to identify waves of reform established autonomously as well as by revolution and by conquest. Figure 2.3 brings out six broad stages. In a first stage, as early as the thirteenth century, but particularly in the sixteenth to eighteenth centuries, autonomous developments mainly in the cities, established a basis of local and personal rights. However the feudal system of estates survived largely intact. A second stage followed from the French Revolution. This, succeeded by the Napoleonic Empire, spread an administrative reform over extensive areas of western Europe. In turn this stimulated a third stage of both German federalism (as an accommodation to reform) and the Habsburg Empire (as a reaction against reform). A fourth stage resulted from the break-up of the Habsburg Empire after 1918 and the Russian Revolution in 1917. This was followed by stage five after 1945 — the establishment of 'socialist democracies' in many former Habsburg lands as well as other parts of eastern Europe. The sixth stage is represented by the amalgamation and reorganization of local government into 'functional regions' or 'city region' structures (which has occurred in both western and eastern Europe).

The generalizations presented in Figure 2.3 demonstrate that the political and economic history of Europe has ensured a degree of concordance of groups of administrative structures despite the range and diversity of its histories and peoples. Within each of these groups the basic unit since the Middle Ages has been the commune. Even in the exceptional cases of Britain and the socialist countries the commune (parish in Britain) still survives in some form, has significance and is vigorously defended against efforts at major reform. In countries like France, Switzerland and Belgium for example, the commune has an almost primaeval status: in Belgium the medieval granting of rights to the commune has the same status as Magna Carta or the American Declaration of Independence (see Weil, 1970, p. 77; quoted in Smith, 1973).

The commune derives from the administrative structure of the Catholic church and the government of its 'estate' within the feudal system. The commune had also acquired simple secular administrative functions such as registration of births, marriages and deaths, and a simple role in census. Church and state were also linked more formally: monarchies found their base through 'divine right'. The sixteenth-century Reformation and Catholic reaction (the 'Counter-Reformation') was responsible for one of the fundamental divisions of administrative structures which survives to this day (see for example Sack, 1986). This was codified in the Peace of Augsburg in 1555. The Thirty Years War in the seventeenth century and the 1648 Treaty of Westphalia retained the 1555 settlement and established the principle of 'cuius regio eius religio'. Henceforth the prince or ruler of a territory chose its religion and thus its administrative structure. The largely Protestant north and west of Europe disestablished the church and rapidly secularized its administration. The more Catholic south and east of

Europe retained the link of church and state, embodied in the Holy Roman Emperor. This survived in the Hapsburg hereditary possessions until World War I. The Hapsburg lands covered Austria and Hungary as a core, and also included Czechoslovakia, much of south Germany, part of Denmark, south Poland as well as links to the Balkans (parts of Yugoslavia, Romania), Italy and Iberia.

Whereas in the Protestant west the secularized state was able to develop strong 'national' governments and major territorial integration within the state, the Catholic east retained the tension between church and state, and most importantly between absolutism combined with the power of the estates and inadequate popular representation. As a consequence, while the west rapidly developed industrial capitalism, in the Habsburg lands there was a tension between nationalism and imperial centralization which was not resolved until 1918, and in Russia there was a tension between feudalism and capitalism which was not resolved until 1917.

Constitutionalism in the west

The western administrative structure that resulted was strongly influenced by the French Revolution and Napoleon in the south, and by Sweden and Britain in the north. The American Constitution and 1791 French Revolutionary Constitution brought the influence of constitutionalism to bear on all of western Europe and was extended to embrace local as well as central government. The 1791 Constitution established in France a uniform system of the *départements* and communes as the basic administrative units surviving to this day, although the intermediate level of districts (*arrondissements*) and Cantons were abolished by Napoleon except for Paris's districts. The Constitution also reflected the ascendancy of a centralized French 'Jacobin' view over that of the provinces, and this imposed a uniform structure everywhere. Napoleon replaced the 'excessive' decentralization of the Revolutionary Constitution by the 'fused' system in which the prefects, controlling the *département*, and the mayors, were central nominees. This largely retained the Jacobin emphasis of reforms; that is a centralized administrative state. Napoleon's reorganization of the rest of the administration also survived him. He reformed tax collection through new collection lists, new and reintroduced taxes and removed corruption and feudal privileges. The result was the establishment of a professional and fair allocation of taxes, which we would now recognize as the putting in place of the modern administrative principles of professionalism and dispassionate interest. Because of his territorial conquests the Napoleonic administrative order was imposed widely elsewhere and, despite the subsequent Napoleonic defeats, the administrative reforms were usually retained. As a result Napoleon can be seen as the founder of the modern territorial administrative structure of not only France, but also Italy, Belgium, The Netherlands, north-west Yugoslavia and Prussia, with profound influences elsewhere particularly in Spain, Portugal and Turkey, and indirectly on Austria–Hungary as well

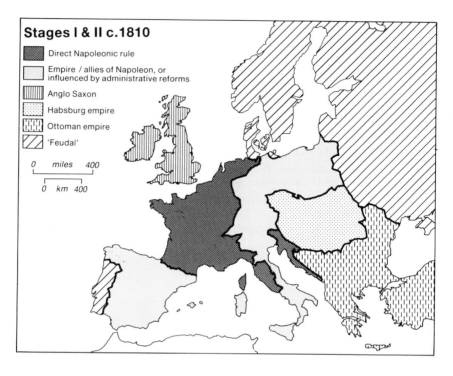

Stages I & II c.1810

- Direct Napoleonic rule
- Empire / allies of Napoleon, or influenced by administrative reforms
- Anglo Saxon
- Habsburg empire
- Ottoman empire
- 'Feudal'

0   miles   400

0   km   400

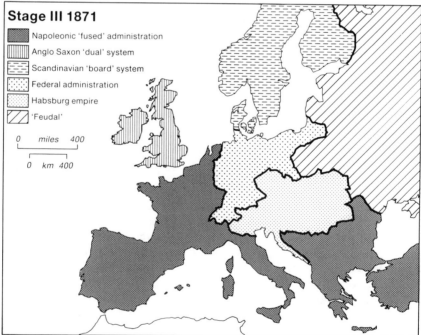

Stage III 1871

- Napoleonic 'fused' administration
- Anglo Saxon 'dual' system
- Scandinavian 'board' system
- Federal administration
- Habsburg empire
- 'Feudal'

0   miles   400

0   km   400

Figure 2.3   Stages of development of European administrative systems

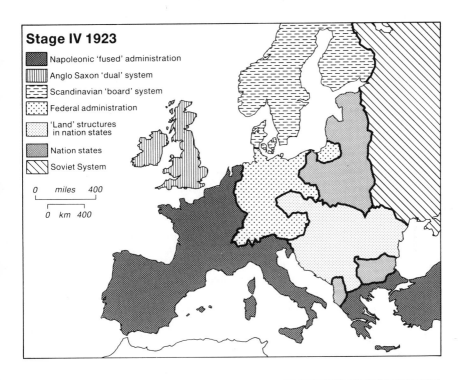

Stage IV 1923

- Napoleonic 'fused' administration
- Anglo Saxon 'dual' system
- Scandinavian 'board' system
- Federal administration
- 'Land' structures in nation states
- Nation states
- Soviet System

0   miles   400

0   km   400

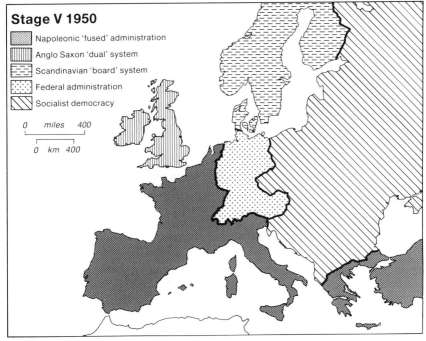

Stage V 1950

- Napoleonic 'fused' administration
- Anglo Saxon 'dual' system
- Scandinavian 'board' system
- Federal administration
- Socialist democracy

0   miles   400

0   km   400

Figure 2.3 (continued)

as Britain and Scandinavia whose administrative development was to be different.

Napoleon's communes were administered by a chief executive who was appointed by central government. By 1831 the council was directly elected, although it remained advisory until 1884 when the mayor was elected by the council which was granted a level of autonomy. Thus local government, although remaining a fused system, moved from being a local agency of central government to becoming a form of local representative government with strong central controls.

The dual system characterizes both Sweden and Britain. Both countries had enjoyed independence from foreign invasion since the Middle Ages and this allowed the development of 'constitutional' monarchies. The feudal estates were ended in Sweden in 1772 with the 1809 Constitution defining the powers of king and parliament. However it was not until the reforms of 1915 and 1921 that a final shift of power to parliament occurred. Local *self-governing* units were established in legislation of 1862 and this was directly copied in Finland in 1865. The local units were largely former ecclesiastical communes. This established a division of duties where the self-governing localities could act on their own, or were acting as agents of national government — a form of a dual model. Sweden gave the Scandinavian countries (except Denmark) the model of constitutional monarchy, but Norway provided the model of local self-government. The 1837 local government legislation in Norway was the first in the Scandinavian countries. It reflected both the strength of 'peasant' politics and the problems of central administration in a country with such difficult internal communications. This was a major influence on Danish and Swedish local legislation, and in turn on Finland.

The 'dual' system is strongly developed in all Scandinavian countries which all make extensive use of administering committees. They differ from England, however, in having a chief executive who also chairs a governing board. The board plays a key role in most actions, co-ordinates, supervises and develops major strategies.

The dual model evolved separately, but along similar lines in Britain except for the role of the board and chief executive. A very early form of elected representative government operated in chartered and incorporated towns which, from the Middle Ages had administrative and judicial functions. The electoral franchise was very limited until the nineteenth century. From the end of the seventeenth century a wide range of special-purpose authorities also grew up which were associated with the needs of rapid urbanization and industrialization — chiefly for water supply, sewers, roads and general improvement (including social services) (Webb and Webb, 1963). There were also parishes (communes) which, particularly in rural areas, had secular administrative significance. Local government in Britain is the creature of central government and the Municipal Corporation Act 1835 made the functions of cities uniform, extended the franchise and redefined competences. In 1888 the county councils were established for the rural areas within which a lower tier of urban and rural districts was established in 1894. In the former charter towns, re-established in

1835, however, the county did not exercise administrative power: these were re-labelled county boroughs in 1888. This system survived until 1974 when much larger units, based loosely on city regions, were established in a two-tier structure of counties and districts. The counties in metropolitan areas were abolished in 1986.

The English system displays a number of features unique in Europe, although copied elsewhere in former British colonies. One feature is the dominance of committees and the lack of real executive powers — the mayor is merely ceremonial; indeed local governments are normally referred to as 'councils' which emphasizes the collective responsibility exercised by a committee system. The committees prepare the major decisions and administer; the full council often merely offers approval. The profusion of committees prevents harmonization of activities within local government, although recent attempts at corporate management, 'local socialism' and financial pressures have increased the extent of co-ordination between services in local government. Nevertheless English local government still represents the purest form of 'dual' system. Its structure has recently been reaffirmed by the Widdicombe Committee (1986) and the government's response (G.B. Dept. of Environment, 1988). They state that the council is a corporate body, with no separate source of executive authority, with officers serving the council as a whole, and with no case for a statutory requirement for a chief executive.

Federalism in the centre

In Germanic central Europe, on to Napoleonic concepts of fused local government and professionalized administration, was grafted a very different federalized constitutional structure. Napoleon swept aside the Holy Roman Empire in central Europe and reduced its 1,800 principalities of imperial towns, townships, and dukedoms to thirty-three. In the German countries the principal of 'cuius regio eius religio' was swept aside at one level — princely national power was exchanged for land. Nevertheless the remaining states retained total independence and separation. On to this structure was grafted, in Prussia, a major constitutional and administrative reform with respect to representation and local government. Subsequently this administrative reform was integrated within the federal idea. The conquest and occupation of Prussia by the French under Napoleon in 1807 allowed the Prussian state to be reorganized under Stein and Handenberg. In twelve months Baron vom Stein abolished serfdom and other major feudal divisions. Local governments in the towns were permitted to choose their own councils and entrusted with services such as street maintenance and relief of poverty. The civil service was reformed and recruited on the basis of efficiency with competitive examinations and formal training in Law. In addition the professionalization of other administrative areas took place bringing engineers and other technical experts to senior posts. The reforms owed much to attempts to emulate British industrial and governmental successes, and to Napoleonic administrative influences. But it took a specific Prussian form in which many political matters were treated merely as questions of administration. As a result its bureaucracy became, at a later date, particularly under the Third Reich, a force which inhibited the scope for representation and self-governance.

On to these Prussian administrative reforms a federal structure was later grafted and the Prussian concept was extended to the rest of Germany. The key idea behind federalism, however, was the concept of bonding together a new German nation from the fragmentary and competitive dukedoms of the Holy Roman Empire, albeit more consolidated since Napoleon's reforms. Prussia proved to be the key to the development of German federalism. The Austrian empire in contrast retained a Catholic core, was subject to divine succession and was ethnically fragmented. Prussia and the other German states were predominantly Protestant and had a much greater development of local and civil liberties. However from the Congress of Vienna in 1815 until 1848 a German Confederation of the thirty-eight states was established which included the Habsburg empire. The individual states retained princely despotism and in only a few of these (chiefly Prussia, Hanover and Saxony) were internal constitutional reforms developed. An interesting case was Denmark. The Danish king, in his capacity as Duke of Holstein and Lauanburg, which were both members of the German Confederation, was forced to accept the principle of *Landesstädische Verfassungen* which introduced a mild form of representation (Andrén, 1964) and encouraged cautious reforms in the 1830s, culminating in the 1840–1 local government legislation and the 1849 Danish Constitution. However, Danish local government recognized the strong principle of self-government deriving directly from the former Danish territory of Norway.

The 1848 Revolution and attempt at a federal constitution rejected a *Gross-Deutschland* that included Austria and gave a basis for the subsequent North German Confederation of 1867 and the German Empire of 1871. Much contemporary thinking on federalism was strongly influenced by the United States Constitution particularly through von Mohl (1828) and de Tocqueville (1835). The Bismarck Constitution (1867) allowed substantial independence for the states, mainly to preserve Prussian independence, and after the acceptance of the federal structure by Bavaria, Baden, Hesse and Württemberg in 1871 the core of the German-speaking territories were all included (except Austria) (see for example Finer, 1961). The consequence was an extension of the vom Stein local administrative reforms to most of Germany but within a *federal* state structure, with major differences between north and south, and inside and outside Prussia. This federal balance was later revived and modified in the 1949 Constitution (see Chapter 17). The German adaptation of the American constitutional ideas also strongly influenced Switzerland's move from a confederal to federal structure finally embodied in its 1874 Constitution.[3]

Within the twenty-five independent states (*Länder*) in Germany in 1871, local government was determined by state constitutions and histories. The 1871 reforms determined the responsibilities of the *Länder* which they still hold: education, domestic order and police and cultural affairs. In their turn they allowed variable roles to the executive of the local governments. In general terms, within each *Land*, a Napoleonic two-tier structure obtains of *Kreis* (county) and *Gemeinde* (commune). Both the 'dual' and 'fused' models are present and became mixed-up with each other. To generalize from the historical legacy, however, we can summarize by noting three different structures: (i) a single council fusing legislative and executive functions and popularly elected. This now applies to Bavaria for both *Kreis* and *Gemeinden* councils and their chief executive, and to the *Gemeinden* mayors in Baden-Wüttenberg. It reflects the independence of the former south German dukedoms; (ii) a strong mayor system, in which an elected council appoints a chief executive (*Gemeindedirektor*), now applies in Niedersachen, Hesse and Nordrhein-Westfalia; in Rheinland-Pfalz and Saarland the council elects the mayor who is both chairman and chief executive; (iii) a bicameral (or *magistrat*) system, in which a lower house which is directly elected invests power in a council board that serves as an upper chamber (deriving from the vom Stein reforms), now applies to Schleswig-Holstein and Hesse and in a special form to Bremen and Hamburg.

These three structures were in place in 1871 and carried through into the Weimar Republic. They were revived in 1949 and derive from the individuality of the original historical states, even though only the present states of Bavaria, Bremen and Hamburg existed prior to 1949. In addition a group of city–countries (*Kreisfreie stadt*) combine *Gemeinde* and *Kreis* functions giving them a greater level of power and autonomy. Frequently this reflects their status more as medieval towns than as current urban centres and it applies particularly to the free-standing cities which formerly acted as the major ports, guild and market centres.

The original German federal structure has an important influence not only on modern German administration, but also retains some influence on the local governments of the modern states of East Germany which previously experienced Prussian influence. In Poland the Prussian system, which had been imposed on part of the country, was chosen for the whole state after its establishment in 1918. Although radically modified by socialist democracy, the *Kreis–Gemeinden* structure and power of the *Kreisfreie stadt* are particularly important influences.

Absolutism and empire in the east

The Catholic east developed differently. After the failed 1848 Revolution and the 1867 establishment of the North German Confederation, Austria and its empire became isolated from modernization. A high level of absolutism remained and the principle of divine right gave little concession to constitutionalism. The Habsburgs claimed to govern 'by God's grace' and the issue of popular representation was not tackled until after 1918. However, important developments of territorial representation did occur.

The fundamental base of the Habsburg administrative reforms in the mid-eighteenth century was laid by Maria Theresa who established a level of state (*Länder*) agencies with financial and administrative powers. These were fundamentally centralizing, as a means of effectively administering a monarchic bureaucratic empire. They also sought to defend the Habsburg Empire against the new representative movement of the nation–state. The multi-national empire was held together only by compromise with constitutionalism, not by meaningful reforms which accorded true representation to the people. The Habsburg state was a set of family territories, established largely by marriages and perpetuated by primogeniture which survived until 1918; its ending gave a crisis of legitimacy to the Austrian component in the 1918–48 period (see for example Hantsch, 1955; Steiner, 1972). The other components, particularly Hungary, Czechoslovakia, Poland and the Balkans (northern Yugoslavia and Romania) faced a different crisis of legitimacy. Since the Habsburg Empire had survived through compromise with the old estates, some elements of feudalism still remained in all these countries. Nevertheless a federal structure did become established and administrative reforms represented a compromise of nationalism with former imperial administrative structures. In the Austro–Hungarian core the Compromise (*Ausgleich*) of 1867 established separate dual monarchies with equal representation in parliament. This constitutional settlement applied to both Magyar-dominated areas (Hungary, plus parts of Czechoslovakia and Romania) and to German-dominated areas (Austria and parts of Czechoslovakia, Poland, Italy and Yugoslavia). However the compromise could not survive and the Emperor Karl's proposal in 1918 for a confederation was met by all the non-German nations declaring national independence. An Austrian rump with 13 per cent of the former population of the empire remained, precipitating a crisis of identity for Austria which was not resolved until 1948, after the German Anschluss.

In both Austria and in the independent non-German nations of Hungary, Czechoslovakia and Romania the nation–state *Länder* structure was retained from the former Habsburg Empire. Although with boundary changes, the modern states of Hungary and Romania derived from the cores of former *Länder*; and in Czechoslovakia, Austria and Yugoslavia former *Länder* of the empire became parts of federal or quasi-federal structures. Thus the divisions between federal and unitary states shown in Figure 2.1 disguise elements of common origin deriving from a larger former centralized empire.

Within the *Länder* the Habsburgs had instituted an administrative structure which used the existing *Land-tag*, which had survived from earlier reforms. Within each *Land*, the communes (*Gemeinden*) were derived from ecclesiastical divisions. There was also an upper tier of *Kreis*, and the civil charters granted to the towns allowed *Kreis* and *Gemeinden* to be combined as in Germany (in so-called charter cities or *Statutärstadt*). These retained the powers of local 'kingdoms' but there was no local autonomy at the commune level (see for example Hajdú, 1987). At the fundamental level the commune boundaries still largely follow the ecclesiastical divisions, but a variety of reforms under the systems of local Soviets in eastern Europe has repeatedly modified the upper tier. Austria, however, has retained the former two-tier structure and in addition, as in Germany, it retains a public law status for Chambers of Commerce (*Kammern*). This was granted originally in 1848 and confirmed in 1868. It creates a secondary set of territorial 'special interests' bodies with many powers equal to local government.

Socialist democracy

The approach to administration developed in the socialist democracies of eastern Europe represents a sharp discontinuity with earlier structures. In all cases they followed 'revolutions': in the Soviet Union in 1917, Yugoslavia and Albania in 1945, Bulgaria in 1946, Hungary, Poland and Romania in 1947, Czechoslovakia in 1948, and East Germany in 1949. Despite this discontinuity, however, there are some elements of administrative linkage to the past. The USSR is the most distinct since the economic system moved almost directly from feudalism to socialism in 1917. However there were elements of local populism in the Soviet Union in the autonomous development of village communities (*obschina*) in the nineteenth century (see for example Starr, 1972; Emmons and Vucinich, 1982); and this indeed formed the basis of Kropotkin's advocacy of an anarchist form of decentralized administration (see for example Stoddart, 1975). In contrast to the USSR, however, in former Prussian and Habsburg areas the large towns, but not the communes, had experienced a level of autonomy and had developed modern administrative procedures linked to a period of capitalism. These historical links left a tension between the basic territorial units at commune level, defined within personal activity spaces, and the higher level reorganizations which are normally given greater emphasis in socialist democracies. However, in general, in Habsburg areas the socialist revolutions replaced administrative empire by centralized socialism which still restricted autonomy.

The fundamental concepts of administration of socialist democracy were developed in the Soviet Union under Lenin, extended by Stalin and have undergone a variety of reforms since. There have also been a variety of adaptions to the local circumstances of the other socialist countries. Lenin's concept of socialist democracy was direct 'rule of the people' through mass participation, not through direct administrative work. 'The Soviet government, i.e. the dictatorship of the proletariat . . . is organised in such a way as to bring the masses of toilers closer to the apparatus of institution'. And the appropriate organizational structure should be through the economy of production. Hence economic and administrative structures are aligned. 'The same aim is pursued by the unification of the legislative and executive authorities under the Soviet organisation of the State and by the substitution of production units like the factories and works, for the territorial electoral constituencies' (Lenin, 1919; quoted in Churchward, 1975, p. 260). In addition Lenin regarded the administrative bureaucracy of the state to be only temporary; with the establishment of a true communist society the state would wither away since it would no longer be required for coercion to ensure observation of social rules — although it would still be required for economic and welfare administration, to administer the plan. The extensions by Stalin ensured the monopoly of political power by the party and replaced, in 1936, the functional or vocational structures of the soviets by territorial electorates. From 1936, then, a territorial structure was accepted for the soviets for 'welfare' and related 'services', but functional soviets and the primacy of economic objective remained (Churchward, 1975; Piekalkiewicz, 1975; Jacobs, 1983). This improved the potential for representation and participation in soviets in the USSR and has been the basic form applied in the rest of eastern Europe, but it created a tension, which still exists today, between territorial and economic administration.

The key aspects of socialist democracy today depend on the additional concepts of social ownership, the management of production by the workers, mass participation and 'direct democracy'. Adopting a class theory of politics it assumes that no social classes exist under socialist democracy; hence there is no basis for alternative political parties and the monopoly of power by the Communist Party confirms the democracy of the soviets (Churchward, 1975; Ross, 1987). A further aspect emphasized by Churchward is that of accountability. This allows soviet deputies and administrators to be removed from office (but not party deputies). This has also permitted periodic administrative reform. Indeed as later chapters show, administrative and territorial reforms in socialist countries have occurred very frequently compared to western Europe perhaps reflecting a greater capacity for administrative and territorial (but not functional) change.

Although undergoing many reforms at present (see later chapters), the basic concept of socialist democracy is derived from the USSR. Soviet administration has many levels, but at local level is usually a two-tier structure (see Figure 2.2). The upper tier is the main (District) soviet which characterizes the larger cities, towns and rural areas. Below these are numerous village soviets and a smaller number of urban settlement soviets. There are also a small number of town soviets subordinate either to city soviets or to rural district soviets (see Chapter 8). Legally the soviets of both tiers have extensive powers including supervision of the economic plan for their area; direction of industrial, construction, trading, housing, welfare, health and social amenity establishments; education; health; and a variety of other local services. There is, however, a lack of real autonomy because the principle of 'democratic centralism' subjects local decisions to the next higher level, and so on up to the supreme soviet (Figure 2.2). The extent of real power and autonomy thus depends on the degree to which it is permitted by central government and the party. Minor changes have occurred since the late 1950s in the USSR and at other dates in the rest of eastern Europe (see later chapters).

The councils in each of the socialist democracies have a large number of members. These are nominees from local factories and voluntary organizations which, after approval by the party, are then presented for election. In the USSR until 1987 there have been only as many candidates as seats on the soviets. Committees are used extensively and are responsible not only

Polish municipal government

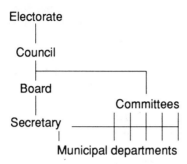

Yugoslav municipal government

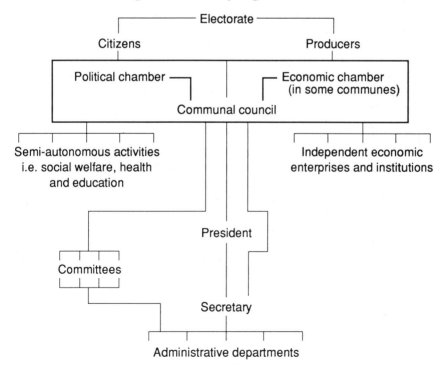

Figure 2.4   Polish and Yugoslav municipal administrative structures showing differences in Board and Committee Forms

Source: after Humes and Martin, 1961, pp. 295, 305

to the council or board, but also to the parallel committees at the next higher level. Their duties include services to people but also relate to economic enterprises. The members of the committees are mostly appointed from outside the council which further increases local participation. In most cases there is a centralized board which takes all decisions. This board will be large in urban areas, but may consist of only three people (chairman, vice-chairman and secretary) in small rural areas. Yugoslavia is the exception in eastern Europe using a bicameral system with no board; it uses a mayor and secretary as the overall managers. The contrast between the Polish administrative structure which is fairly typical of eastern Europe and that in Yugoslavia is shown in Figure 2.4. Humes and Martin (1961, pp. 198–9) note that there are close resemblances in these formal structures between the Soviet and Scandinavian systems, but they operate in very different ways: 'the forms of local representative government are present, but the important decisions are in many cases made by the Party organs outside of the formal government structure'.

The socialist democracies represent very different paths of administrative development from the liberal democracies of western Europe. They have attempted to develop mass participation but this has often led to a level of disillusionment. Moreover the soviet concept of administration as a whole has not ensured an efficient economy which can be compared to the rates of economic growth or material achievement in the west. Whether an increased autonomy for local soviets can improve this situation, and how far other reforms can be instituted, is one of the key questions in current debates which we address in the subsequent chapters.

Conclusion

Historical development of administrative structures in Europe has presented us today with seven groups of countries[4]: first, British and Scandinavian 'constitutional' self-government based on the dual model; second, the French-influenced constitutional models of France, Italy, Belgium, Greece and (with important differences) Spain, Portugal and Turkey; third, the German federal model; fourth, the former imperial Habsburg areas remaining in the west (chiefly Austria); fifth, the socialist democracies of eastern Europe where former Habsburg structures survived into the 1950s, to be replaced eventually by functional regions in the 1970s; sixth, the USSR; and seventh, Yugoslavia. Although historical continuities can be overemphasized these structures nevertheless serve to direct us to the chief problems of administrative adaptation today.

Notes

1. A term used since 1961; previously the term applied was 'proletarian dictatorship' (see Churchward, 1975, p. 257).
2. In this and all other discussion in this book the term 'English' is correctly

reserved to England; 'British' refers to Great Britain, that is England, Scotland and Wales.
3. See for example Wheare (1946) and Sawer (1976).
4. Note that this grouping differs somewhat from that of Humes and Martin (1961), but has a more logical structure than their primarily linguistic groupings.

References

Almond, G.A. and Powell, G.B. (1966), *Comparative Politics: A Developmental Approach*, Little, Brown, Boston.

Almond, G.A. and Powell, G.B. (1978), *Comparative Politics: System, Process and Policy*, Little, Brown, Boston.

Andrén, N. (1964), *Government and Politics in the Nordic Countries: Denmark, Finland, Iceland, Norway, Sweden*, Almqvist and Wiksell, Stockholm.

Bendix, R. (1964), *Nation-building and Citizenship*, John Wiley, New York.

Churchward, L.G. (1975), *Contemporary Soviet Government*, (2nd ed.), Routledge and Kegan Paul, London.

Duchacek, I.D. (1973), *Power Maps: Comparative Politics of Constitutions*, ABC Clio Press, Santa Barbara, California.

Emmons, T. and Vucinich, W.S. (eds) (1982), *The Zemstvoin Russia: An Experiment in Local Self-Government*, Cambridge University Press, Cambridge.

Fesler, J.W. (1980), *Public Administration: Theory and Practice*, Prentice-Hall, New Jersey.

Finer, H. (1961), *The Theory and Practice of Modern Government* (4th ed.), Methuen, London.

G.B. Department of Environment (1988), *The Conduct of Local Authority Business: the Government's Response to the Report of the Widdicombe Committee*, Cmnd 433, HMSO, London.

Hadjú, Z. (1987), *Administrative Division and Administrative Geography in Hungary*, Discussion Paper No. 3, Centre for Regional Studies of Hungarian Academy of Sciences, Pécs (also see paper in *Political Geography Quarterly*, 6, 1987, 269–78).

Hantsch, H. (1955), *Die Geschichte Österreichs*, Styria Verlag, Graz.

Humes, S. and Martin, E.M. (1961), *The Structure of Local Governments throughout the World*, Martinus Nijhoff, The Hague.

Jacobs, E.M. (1983), *Soviet Local Politics and Government*, George Allen and Unwin, London.

Laski, H.J. (1935), *The State in Theory and Practice*, Allen and Unwin, London.

Leemans, A.F. (1970), *Changing Patterns of Local Government*, International Union of Local Authorities, The Hague.

Maass, A. (ed.) (1959), *Area and Power: a Theory of Local Government*, Collier-Macmillan, London,

Machin, H. (1977), *The Prefect in French Public Administration*, Croom Helm, London.

Macpherson, C.B. (1966), *The Real World of Democracy*, Clarendon Press, Oxford.

Mohl, R. von (1824), *Das Bundes-Staatsrecht der Vereinigten Staaten von Nord-Amerika*, Erste Abt. Verfassungsrecht, Stuttgart.

Piekalkiewicz, J. (1975), *Communist Local Government: a Study of Poland*, Ohio University Press, Athens.

Ridley, F.F. (ed.) (1979), *Government and Administration in Western Europe*, Martin Robertson, London.

Ross, C. (1987), *Local Government in the Soviet Union*, Croom Helm, London.

Sack, R.D. (1986), *Human Territoriality: its Theory and History*, Cambridge University Press, Cambridge.

Sawer, G. (1976), *Modern Federalism*, (2nd ed.), Pitman; Carlton, Victoria, Australia.

Smith, G. (1973), *Politics in Western Europe: a Comparative Analysis*, Holmes and Meier, New York.

Starr, S.F. (1972), *Decentralization and Self-Government in Russia 1830–1870*, Princeton University Press, Princeton.

Steiner, K. (1972), *Politics in Austria*, Little, Brown, Boston.

Stoddart, D. (1975), 'Kropotkin, Reclus and "Relevant" Geography', *Area*, 7, 188–90.

Tocqueville, A. de (1966), *Democracy in America*, Wiley, New York.

Webb, S. and Webb, B. (1963), *English Local Government*, Cass, London (reprint of 1906 edition).

Weil, G.L. (1970), *The Benelux Nations: the Politics of Small-country Democracies*, Holt Rinehart and Winston, New York.

Wheare, K.C. (1946), *Federal Government*, Oxford University Press, Oxford.

Widdicombe Committee (1986), *The Conduct of Local Authority Business: Report of the Committee of Enquiry into the Conduct of Local Authority Business*, chaired by David Widdicombe Q.C., Cmnd 9797, 1985–6, HMSO, London.

Part 2 Territory and function: an overview

3 Stimuli to administrative reform
Robert Bennett

Pressures for change

The discussion of Chapter 2 has demonstrated that the territorial structure of western European administrative systems was laid down in the nineteenth or early twentieth centuries. Although adaptations of boundaries and adjustments of functions have occurred, there is nevertheless, in western Europe a tension created by an obsolescent administrative structure, attuned at its creation to the travel times of the horse, which is used as the basis for decision in an age of high technology and rapid economic change. In eastern Europe major reforms of local government introduced functional regions in the 1970s, but again an obsolescence has arisen because of their links to a planned economy which has been superseded by technological change.

Institutional frameworks should not be rigid entities. The assignment of territory, competency and functions between levels of government should not be a shibboleth to the past, nor to a particular economic or political theory. Most important, constitutional relations should adjust to new technologies and their consequent economic and social structure. Four main influences require changes to existing assignment structures. First, there are territorial problems resulting from continuing developments of urbanization and functional regions. Second, there are changes to the needs and the technology underpinning economic and public service provision which stimulates adjustment to the powers available at each level of government. Third, changes in social and cultural identity require reforms of methods of encouraging participation and interest articulation which may have consequences for governmental responsibility as well as for financial resources. Fourth, there are demands to rethink the total pattern of public service provision and its finance: in western Europe 'to rethink the Welfare State'; in eastern Europe radically to modify the political–administrative links, especially those to the party. These four sets of changes call into question the structure of government administration, its territorial base and place pressures upon it to evolve to satisfy new demands and criteria during a period of economic restructuring.

Urban change and activity spaces

In western Europe the two-tier structures of 'dual' or 'fused' local government based on the historical commune as the basic unit were the dominant structure until the 1960s. Even in eastern Europe this territorial structure remained in many significant aspects. This presented three difficulties for modern administration. One problem was the enormous range of sizes of territories and their populations. Some communes were as small as ten to twelve people while others, in the large cities, had a population of over half a million. Clearly common functional assignments and administrative competency was impossible; the result was a series of compromises which gave special additional powers to the large cities. However these did not always adequately recognize the administrative needs of smaller and medium-sized towns and cities, and introduced a great disparity between the basic communal units. It is clear that different units were undertaking very different tasks.

A second difficulty derived from the expansion of metropolitan areas. This created 'spillover' problems. People or enterprises located in one place would be making significant demands on the services and finance of other areas. This had the consequence that, in the absence of financial transfers, there were disparities in welfare burdens and benefits, as well as a hiatus of participation and political representation. Decisions made in one area could markedly affect residents of other areas without any consultation or representation of views, except in so far that an upper tier or central government provided co-ordination (which on many matters it cannot or does not do). There are thus urban and metropolitan boundary problems as well as functional assignments of competency and questions of political structure.

The third difficulty was associated with the viability of small communes in rural areas. Up to the 1960s, with few exceptions, at least 80 per cent of communes in western Europe had populations of less than 5,000 and at least 65 per cent had less than 1,000. In eastern Europe there was usually a similar situation although the administrative significance of these communes differed considerably. These communes were also often subject to rapid population depletion due to an adverse demographic structure and rural–urban migration. The smallness and rapid decline of these areas stimulated calls for reform — to achieve greater economic efficiency through economies of scale, or merely to retain viability.

Each of these difficulties is interlocked and derives from the tensions between activity spaces which form the basis of participation and technical and bureaucratic criteria for optimal administrative design. In geographical terms this relates to the question of how the administrative space is bounded (illustrated in Figure 3.1). The ideal is of an activity space which is precisely matched by administrative boundaries; that is 'truly-bounded'. In this case people's personal lives and contact patterns give a natural 'sense of community' which encourages in a direct way a high level of participation in administration: the two reinforce each other. More commonly, however, administrative structures are 'under-bounded': the

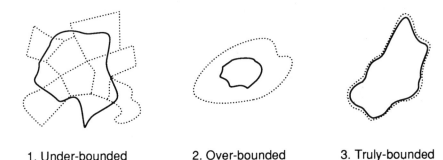

1. Under-bounded   2. Over-bounded   3. Truly-bounded

Figure 3.1 Forms of bounding of administrative spaces

Administrative spaces (dotted lines)
Activity spaces (solid lines)

activity space crosses over many local government boundaries with resultant 'spillover' problems and confusion of lines of representation which disrupts the possibilities of participation. 'Over-bounding' can also occur where the activity space is only a small part of an administrative division. This arises from over-large administrative areas and has often been an outcome of territorial reform of local government; for example in Britain and in many socialist democracies.

The 'bounding' concepts give an important means of approaching the territorial structure of administration, and particularly a means by which its reform can be developed. It should be a desired aim that administration as far as possible relates to and articulates realistic personal activity spaces since this is the most likely to produce administration decisions which are efficient and informed, and in which mass participation is most likely. As a result most reforms of local government have sought, in one form or another, to approach a more 'truly-bounded' structure. This approach has particularly dominated Britain, Sweden and eastern Europe where the city–region and functional–region concepts have been dominantly applied.

The bounding concept has interacted with a second concept, of size. Strong advocacy has been presented that administrative units are more economically efficient the larger they are since they will then be able to obtain maximum benefit from economies of scale. This argument has underlain administrative reforms to amalgamate the small communes in Scandinavia, Germany, Britain and eastern Europe. Activity spaces having rapidly expanded, largely as a result of developments in transport, the attempt more closely to approximate truly-bounded administrative structures interrelates with the objective of increasing size. Both, therefore, have induced pressures for reform to provide larger administrative units. In western Europe the major reforms following these concepts have taken place in many German *Länder* and in Belgium and The Netherlands in the 1960s and 1970s, in Norway in 1968, Denmark in 1970, Sweden in 1972 and in Britain in 1974 (England and Wales) and 1976 (Scotland). In eastern Europe recurrent reforms which have adjusted the local boundaries

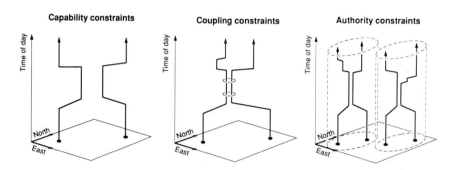

Figure 3.2   Time-space activity spaces and the potential for links between individuals subject to: A. capability constraints; B. coupling constraints; and C. authority constraints

Sources: Hägerstrand (1972); Pred (1974)

to changing economic and political concepts have occurred, with the city-region and size concepts being important to the reforms in the USSR in 1937, 1950 and 1971, Poland in 1973 and 1975, Hungary progressively through the 1970s and in 1984, Czechoslovakia in 1987, Bulgaria in 1959 and 1987 and in East Germany in 1952 (see later chapters).

There is much to be said in favour of increased size and a better approach to true bounding. This is perhaps nowhere better expressed than by Hägerstrand (1972) whose ideas concerning time–space budgets have underpinned the Swedish local government reforms. Hägerstrand argues that administration should be structured in relation to the overall time–space budget constraints operating upon the individual and upon society as a whole. Each individual or household is surrounded by an environmental structure of resource alternatives (food, shelter, services, society, etc.). These are unevenly distributed in time and space. In satisfying the needs of the individual, group or total society, therefore, there must be movement across space accompanying a particular time budget or time path. Each individual time path has two components: the daily-life environment describing the two-way interaction process to obtain goods, services, etc., and a life-perspective environment governing the birth and death points and describing the long-term migration process. The time paths are subject to the three overall constraints depicted in Figure 3.2. The aim of administration should be to adjust these constraints to improve the individual's range of choice. First, there is a capability constraint which limits the range of the individual's time–space path through the biological necessities of eating, sleeping and time spent travelling to obtain goods, services and work income. Secondly, there is a set of coupling constraints which govern the time path within each daily-life environment and determine where, when, how and for how long two or more individuals may join together in order to undertake some activity (work, leisure, etc.). Thirdly, there are authority constraints deriving from the administrative system which restrict the individual, or coupling of individuals, within certain spatial and temporal limits. These limits aim to protect resources, opportunities and efficiency of the individual or of society as a whole (Hägerstrand, 1972, 1975; Pred, 1974).

The improvement of administrative systems should therefore seek to increase the efficiency of the overall society, that is fewer journeys or less time is expended to satisfy given demands. This objective requires co-ordination and improvement of transport services, the better siting of service, job and leisure activities and adjustments to the overall administrative structure. In Pred's words the aims of administrative adjustments are, therefore, to determine:

How society should be organised and how any settlement pattern ought to be struc-tured so as to ensure a 'liveable' day-to-day existence for the individual, or, given the time restrictions on human movement and the fact that every economic and non-economic human activity is space consuming, how ought the system of human activities to be organised spatially so as to provide good accessibility to jobs, public and private services, and leisure-time activities for each individual. [1974. p. 4]

Despite these obvious advantages there are a number of problems in achieving 'truly-bounded' administrative structures. One problem is the level of aggregation, or generalization, of preferences and activity spaces that is required, and whose activity is to provide the definition of the administrative boundary. The American concept of the SMSA which has been applied in Britain and continental Europe, for example, is based on a commuting hinterland of 15 per cent of the working population (see for example Hall and Hay, 1980; van der Berg *et al.*, 1982). Although journey-to-work of that 15 per cent is important, it omits the working activity space of the 85 per cent in parts of the functional urban region who work elsewhere. Similarly the working population is only usually 40–60 per cent of the total population. The remainder may have totally different activity centres than the commuting workplace which is often a great distance away. The functional or city–region concept, therefore, tends to increase administrative size beyond the range of normal activities of the majority of people, and emphasizes work (or production) over social objectives.

A further difficulty arises from the hierarchy of different activities. Some journeys and activities are frequent, some infrequent and, although frequency often is related to distance of travel following some 'gravity' principle of interaction, this is not always the case. Which activities are therefore to be accorded priority in determining administrative boundaries? A hierarchical two-tier structure may allow two different types of activity principles to be followed (often commuting fields at the larger level, and personal services at the more local level), but this will still omit other activity principles, particularly at the most local level. As a result 'over-bounding' is a frequent outcome of those reforms which have been based on activity spaces. With this is also associated the problem of how to adapt the system to changes in activity spaces. Do we have to make administrative reforms every time the commuting field expands, or every time a new set of activities is introduced? There is an inherent instability in the activity systems approach. Although it has the advantage of seeking 'truly-bounded' structures which if achieved would assure strong participatory links of society and administration, it has the disadvantage that any such administrative regionalization is inherently ephemeral, becoming rapidly superseded or inequitable by excluding the activities of those groups which were not included when drawing the territorial boundaries.

The use of population size as an efficiency criterion is subject to even more criticism. Although frequently advocated, for example by the Redcliffe–Maud Commission (1968) in England, 'no objective basis exists on which to attribute any material significance to population size as a factor in any way influencing the performance of [local government]' (Senior, memorandum of dissent to Redcliffe–Maud Commission, Vol. 2, p. 268). Indeed no systematic correlates of size can be found. Bennett (1980), in reviewing the evidence, concludes that although major economies of scale are invariably present in 'technical' services, particularly those based on fixed networks such as supply of water, electricity, gas, sewerage disposal, district heating and sometimes road provision, for services in which people participate directly economies of scale seldom consistently operate. This is reflected in the very different sizes of local governments which have resulted from reform along these lines. In England Redcliffe–Maud advocated local government units of 250,000 people, and those actually implemented are normally over 100,000. In Sweden units of 8,000 resulted from reforms, and 5,000 in Denmark and Norway. Clearly size means different things in different contexts. The major difficulty, however, is that although administrative economies of scale to induce efficiency are theoretically possible, bureaucratic overload, distance from the consumer, the difficulties of participation and adaptation of decisions to needs has led to a dominance of practical inefficiency through diseconomies of scale with size and consequent alienation of the population served. This can be argued to be a local government example of Lammenais's (1848) adage of 'apoplexy at the centre and anaemia at the periphery'. It is a phenomenon of major importance to our discussion in this book and besets both western and eastern Europe alike. We suggest approaches to resolving the problem through public choice ideas in Chapter 4.

At the other extreme is the problem of rural communes. The rural communes in some west European countries as well as most of socialist Europe have experienced merger and amalgamation into larger units, with the loss of major administrative and other functions. The result has usually been the closure and concentration of schools and cultural facilities and a lack of infrastructure and other investments (including housing). This has undermined the viability of small rural communities giving them no future. Maurel (1982; and Chapter 7 of this volume) argues that the loss of a local administration profoundly destabilizes the local society, and villages have to look to external decision-makers to defend their interests. It remains to be seen whether new economic and administrative reforms reverse this trend. At present it appears that they will not do so, since new developments in decentralization in both western and socialist Europe are still dominated by concepts of amalgamation to achieve urban-dominated city region units much larger than the village (commune) level. Enyedi and Veldman (1986, p. 12), for example, argue that the adoption of urbanization concepts has created a form of 'mental urbanisation' which has 'paralysed' rural research. They particularly emphasize the need for administrative responses which differentiate between heavily urbanized city regions, 'peri-urban' rural areas which are within the reach of the housing and labour markets of the city region, areas experiencing suburbanization where non-agricultural forces are the main agent of change and peripheral rural areas outside the daily reach of urban housing and labour markets. This suggests the need for flexible administrative structures specifically attuned to rural areas and to differences in the level and form of rurality.

Economic change and technological development

Constitutional and jurisdictional structures tend to be relatively static. While the population and industry within a jurisdiction changes, their demands for services develop (quantitatively and qualitatively), their fiscal means and resources are modified and behaviour patterns evolve. The stimuli to such modifications are mainly changes in technology, especially in transport, communications, forms of factory construction, locational preferences and evolution in market supply and demand.

The earliest urban developments of railway settlements and tramway suburbs across Europe have been replaced in western Europe by a settlement structure linked to the motor car. Housing has become divorced from workplaces, areas of shopping, schooling, cultural activities and recreation. Similarly, the location of industry has been freed from central city locations. Suburban industrial developments, out-of-town shopping centres and hypermarkets, drive-in shops, technology parks and other commercial developments are growing and flourishing far from the central cities. In eastern Europe a different pattern of development has occurred since 1945 in which economic and territorial plans have bound industry to specific sectoral lines of development while changes in life styles and demands have evolved to create a tension of unfulfilled needs. This has been termed an economy of shortages by Kornai (1980).

Recent developments have therefore created two kinds of tensions. First, in western Europe economic evolution has washed across the territorial administrative structure like a wave across the beach. The result has been a tension between old systems and resource patterns and new needs which vary considerably from place to place: that is there is a fundamental problem of geographical equity to be addressed. Second, in eastern Europe territorial administrative structures have sought, but have failed to achieve, a high level of mass participation and equity, but have instead bound the economy and society in rigid lines, both territorial and social. This has, with few exceptions, been inefficient and has under-provided in comparison to the inherent level of resources in the economies. The result has been a level of disillusionment. A greater social and territorial equity has probably been achieved in eastern Europe than in western Europe. However, while individual local administrative systems in western Europe are experiencing tensions in a variable way, in eastern Europe the whole territorial administrative as well as the political system is experiencing a tension because of its interrelation with laggard economies.

Across the administrative systems of Europe, therefore, has developed a set of economic regimes which do not accord well with the layout of territory and function which, as we have seen in Chapter 2, is essentially nineteenth century in origin. A useful way of conceptualizing the range of tensions which has resulted is to examine how economic development in its various stages interacts with the administrative system. Berry (1976) and Hall and Hay (1980) provide a model of three main stages of spatial economic development: *urbanization, suburbanization,* and *counter-urbanization* or *decentralization.* In western Europe these stages can be related respectively to early capitalism, late capitalism and to 'post-industrial' economies. In eastern Europe only stages one and two have been fully developed, but the similarities of spatial development suggest a developmental character which extends beyond capitalist economies. This is confirmed in the comparative studies of east and west European cities by van der Berg *et al.*, (1982). Comparing 1960–70 and 1950–75 these studies demonstrate that eastern Europe is still experiencing a high level of urbanization, but with suburbanization already occurring. Southern Europe (northern Italy, Spain, Portugal, Greece) has had rapid urbanization and suburbanization of its major cities, but northern Europe (Scandinavia, Britain, Germany, the Benelux countries and France) has declining older and larger cities and a high degree of decentralization beyond to smaller towns and rural areas. More recent studies (for example in Britain by Champion and Green *et al.*, 1987) confirm the intensification of this trend. The European countries therefore accord with overlapping features of each of the three main stages.

The *urbanization* stage is one in which people and activities agglomerate closely together; there is a dominant central city focus for economic activity, retailing, cultural facilities and transport networks; and there is a major reduction of rural populations as a result of immigration to cities. In such a situation small administrative areas create immense difficulty for co-ordination. There are large spillovers of public service benefits and financial burdens, and there is a need for an integrated strategic planning perspective. Thus Leemans (1970, p. 13), writing twenty years ago, saw the main administrative problems to be those of obsolescence of local government structures as a result of excessive fragmentation of government in metropolitan areas, along with unviable communes in rural areas, neither of which could cope with life styles spread over extensive geographical areas or the needs of strategic planning. The main administrative problems of urbanized territories are therefore ones of co-ordination, amalgamation and integration. This leads to pressures for metropolitan-wide government or extensive coordination of competences (for respective local and metropolitan-wide functions) and for compensating financially, and otherwise, for spillovers of service benefits and fiscal burdens.

The urbanization stage was characteristic of the spread of industrial capitalism in north-west Europe, but is now developing in association with later capitalist societies in southern Europe (notably Spain and Italy), and in most of the socialist democracies of eastern Europe. However, the development of socialist democracies had differed fundamentally in starting from a primitive, often semi-feudal base with low levels of economic integration of industries, transport or governmental activity. Since the 1940s socialist economies have given primary emphasis to industrialization. For socialist planning urbanization offers the benefits of higher levels of services, education, cultural facilities and access to jobs, but in a context of capital shortages which have left urban infrastructure and housing often inadequate. As a result long-distance commuting is common. This led van der Berg *et al.*, (1982, p. 29) to conclude that, 'If urbanisation is measured by the number of people living in towns and by the degree to which towns are equipped with municipal services, then industrialisation can be said to have outpaced urbanisation' in eastern Europe. Nevertheless, the same pressures for metropolitan co-ordination and strategic planning result; and these demands have been more fully answered by administrative reform in eastern Europe than in the west.

The *suburbanization* stage of development is associated with continued growth of the physically contiguous built-up urban area, but with a shift of its major growth of population and employment to the cities' peripheral margins. With improved transport networks, a greater number of people are able to live at lower densities with continued increases in travel-to-work to city centres. In western Europe these developments are associated with the combined development of capitalist concentration of businesses which often require green-field sites and frequently employ large-scale assembly line methods — so-called 'Fordist' development. In eastern Europe the primacy of industrial growth objectives is also associated with the increasing size of industrial establishments which again often require green-field sites. This results in a similar pattern of suburban spread at the periphery of urban areas, but with very different processes operating. In particular there is a much closer tie of housing units to industrial plants especially in 'new town' locations (see for example Herman and Regulski, 1977). In both cases there is a major pressure for an extensive infrastructure for private and mass-transit transport facilities as well as for a social welfare network of public services. The administrative problems associated with urbanization (fragmentation, benefit and burden spillovers), are therefore exacerbated by suburbanization; and inequalities in service levels and fiscal burdens can become quite extreme.

The *counter-urbanization* stage is one in which the dispersion of people and workplaces further increases and there becomes established a settlement structure associated with the so-called post-industrial city. Its emergence is based on three features: first, the difficulty of keeping infrastructure investment up to the level of the demands placed upon it, with resultant congestion; second, the ability to satisfy greater desires for improved low-density, small-town environments; and third, an enabling technology which allows a substantial proportion of economic activity to be conducted in small dispersed units, sometimes located in houses, and with rapid telecommunication and high-speed data transmission capacities. It is a period of development associated with what Berry (1970) terms 'tele-mobility'. The most rapid rates of growth of population and economic activity now shift to small towns and those rural areas which are accessible to the main locations of economic activity. These growth areas are often distant and fragmented from the urban cores. The central cities and many suburbs experience economic and population decline. This stage is associated with late capitalism, often termed a period of 'flexible accumulation', in which smaller and dispersed economic activities become pervasive. This is becoming a dominant regime in most of western Europe, but has not been able to develop in socialist societies. What is the appropriate administrative structure for this stage of development? Area-wide co-ordination and strategic planning of extremely large, fragmented and non-contiguous areas is usually beyond the scope of administrative systems to cope. At the same time developments in methods of service delivery and 'post-welfare' policy cultures (q.v. below) suggest that extensive strategic co-ordination and administration is politically unacceptable. One approach includes a reassertion of smaller administrative units, greater central government links directly to the most basic administrative level (often the commune) or to service deliverers (for example to schools, hospitals, old people's homes) thus by-passing or abolishing upper tier local government. At the same time there is an increasing shift away from public administration to provision of services by private-sector businesses and non-profit associations and trusts. Hence with geographical dispersion an administrative focus on individual and 'consumer' responses also arises; thus there is a major pressure for decentralization.

Within administrative structures a similar tension develops between centralization and decentralization at each stage of economic and territorial development. Early capitalism and urbanization favours centralist administration, uniform powers and practices and the extensive provision of infrastructure requiring large-scale public investment and hence centralized co-ordination and strategic planning. These requirements are even more evident in the highly fragmented suburbanization stage. However, a regime of 'flexible' economic practices favours scope for decentralization with variable levels of powers, services and infrastructure suited to local needs, but with a strong centralized co-ordination to allow more readily a horizontal transfer of information between places and a vertical transfer between administrative levels. A major aspect of this is evident in the development of computing and other information technology (IT) systems which show an increasing tendency towards a centralized organization of dispersed information bases and administrative demands (see for example SOCITM, 1987).

Change in social and cultural identity

A major problem in many contemporary societies is that the areas in which there is a sense of community, which form such an important component of the collective identity necessary to support allegiance or loyalty to a given scheme of local administration, are not in accord with the existing boundaries of national, regional or local units. This may be especially marked when countries have undergone progressive centralization of finances in order to achieve a greater degree of equality of regional development as in eastern Europe. To sustain significant redistribution policies there must be a sense not only of identity, but of common economic and social linkage. Without this, areas and communities may feel that their individual needs or alternative forms of local identity are stronger. Hence they desire at least a level of separate development in order to find an independent economic and social focus, even if this can be achieved only at higher cost or a lower standard of general welfare.

There are three major geographical scales at which these issues are developing: one of enhanced regionalist or ethnic-nationalist consciousness; a second, of alienation of individuals from large-scale administrative units in favour of the basic neighbourhood or commune levels; and third, a redefinition of the interests of the individual in relation to public administration as a whole.

The first issue, of regionalism or ethnic-nationalism, has a long European tradition. It appears to have emerged as an Italian concept of regionalism to resist centralist state expansion and was later used by French writers to resist the dominance of Paris; but as noted by Hebbert (1987, p. 240) in the 1960s and 1970s the re-emergence of regionalism appears to have been mainly a defensive reaction of the periphery to the 'hegemonising and homogenising' pressures of both the modern state and the market economy (Poggi, 1978; Rokkan and Urwin, 1982). Marxist writers in particular, from Luxembourg and Gramsci, have seen regional alienation as part of an economic process of unequal exchange or 'internal colonialism' and regional exploitation (see for example Santos, 1975; Hechter, 1975). Others argue that this explanation overemphasizes one factor in regional development (see for example Orridge, 1981) and indeed regionalism seems to be as prevalent in socialist Europe, particularly in the USSR, as in capitalist economies (see for example Smith, 1985). Hence Bennett (1985) argues that a wider set of understandings is required of the mechanisms by which 'primary' nations come to dominate over 'secondary' ones.

'Primary' nations are argued by writers such as Lafont (1967), Heraud (1963, 1969), Conner (1973) and Smith (1979) to have the following three characteristics: (i) an ethnic-linguistic character, (ii) a sense of common destiny and (iii) an elite who articulate and 'manage' the desire to exist as a community. 'Secondary' nations lack the second or third characteristics: they have lost identity and/or leadership. The emergence of regionalism therefore depends upon the territorial politics of a country. Generally regional movements will be stronger (i) where the representation of local interests in the central state, (ii) the participation of local individuals and elites in central administrative decision-making, and (iii) the extent of local decentralized administration are weaker; (iv) the more specifically differentiated are the regional issues from the objectives of the central administration and (v) the more dominant are the economic and political activities of the central state (Bennett, 1985, p. 77). The greater the development of these characteristics the greater will be the 'territorial alienation' within the state (see Tarrow and Katzenstein, 1978; Crozier, 1973). It is interesting to note that these characteristics seem to be as prevalent in a socialist democracy, such as the USSR, as they are in western European countries such as Spain, Belgium or parts of Britain. For example, Smith's (1985, p. 50) conclusion, on the USSR, might equally be applied to western Europe: 'modernisation may have a disfunctional effect on political integration if the rate of social mobilisation proceeds at a faster pace than participation and cultural assimilation into the dominant state culture and its central institutions.'

The second focus of our discussion, the alienation of individuals from large-scale administrative units, has much in common with regional alienation, but may not have an ethnic focus. Again alienation is characterized by an absence of effective or appropriate: *representation*, *participation* and *decentralization* to relevant local characteristics, and resistance to bureaucratic *dominance*. Thus Almond and Powell (1966) and Barry (1965) argue that alienation results largely from the poor performance and ineffectiveness of administrative institutions; and from this flows the extent of their legitimacy. Barry argues that legitimacy, in liberal democracies, depends on the extent to which the relevant views of the people affected by given administrative decisions are taken into account. If bureaucracies are too large, or too distant, from the people affected by decisions, then not only representation and participation suffer, but so does effectiveness. Two key aspects which have depressed the legitimacy of modern administrative systems have been the reorganization of government into large units with the suppression of small communes, and the subjection of rural interests to central cities within city–region governments. It must now be recognized that many of the supposed economies of scale to be achieved by such reforms were illusory, that bureaucracies tend to become 'overloaded' and remote and that large-scale political tradeoffs within extensive local administrative territories are unpopular. Hence city–region concepts, which emphasize the functionality of 15 per cent commuting thresholds, have inevitably undermined the participation of the 85 per cent whose action spaces have been left out of account.

The third issue of our discussion, the redefinition of the interests of individuals in relation to administrative systems, follows, at a different scale, from the same processes which are associated with both regionalism and local alienation. In western Europe basic rights are usually encoded in constitutions. The problem of 'rights' is equally or more prominent in socialist democracies. There is something almost primaeval in the re-emergence of the issue of rights in current debates, and it interrelates with issues of changing policy culture outlined later in this chapter. Basic rights are the legally based ideals of most societies: socially recognized moral ideals. They are the fundamental and basic principles of social justice. But the concept of rights has come into increasing conflict with two other concepts of social justice: of deserts and needs. The term desert is applied to the judgement of the just 'share' of public service. Deserts are thus based on judgements after appraisal and evaluation, hence they rest fundamentally on ideology: 'when we make a judgement of desert, we are judging the appropriateness of this particular individual, . . . receiving a given benefit' (Miller, 1976, pp. 92–3). Such judgements are a daily aspect of administrative practice: the so-called principle of entitlement. Similarly needs are moral claims which exist within a set of administrative rules founded on established social practice or ideology (Bennett, 1980). In western Europe post-war state welfare systems, and in socialist Europe party–state organizations, have become dominated by claims for deserts and needs. To the extent that needs remain unsatisfied or deserts are unequally distributed, then major tensions and alienation are likely to result. In western Europe these tensions are, probably equally, ones between equity of deserts and claims by interest-groups to needs which are presently unfulfilled (or are not fulfilled to the level of desires). In socialist Europe the pattern differs: tensions of equity are usually lower, but tensions of unfulfilled needs are much higher than western Europe: socialist democracies have not yet found a way of overcoming the 'economics of scarcity' which Kornai (1980) and Winiecki (1988) argue is fundamental to the difficulties of socialist states (see also Chapter 6 of the volume). In both systems, however, the outcome is the same: an alienation of the individual from the administrative system. Because it is closest, this alienation is often targeted especially at the local government administrative level. Alienation is also often compounded by a further feature, again common to both western and socialist Europe, of increasing resentment by individuals of their dependence upon the administrative decisions of others. This further alienation is inevitable in a situation where individuals find themselves increasingly subject to administrative decisions about whether their desires are, or are not, a justified 'need'; this is fundamentally in conflict with individual rights and tends to be regarded as increasingly odious. These aspects draw us inevitably to questions of 'policy culture' which are addressed below.

'Rethinking' the administrative state

The pressures for rethinking the welfare state and its administrative structures is dominant in western discussions: in Europe led by Britain and the 'Thatcher revolution', and outside Europe by the United States, However, the issues raised are common not only to liberal democracies but also to socialist countries. The issues in each case are a result of the aspects of alienation noted above, which have led to increasing disillusionment with the extensive investments in social policy of the last thirty or forty years. While there is not usually any questioning of providing a basic welfare safety-net, there has been a growing demand for rethinking major aspects of the welfare state as a whole.

The motivation for this rethinking is six-fold: (i) too many programmes appear as political pork-barrels to buy the votes of particular interest groups, (ii) there is a growing cynicism with the effectiveness of administrators and politicians, (iii) too great a level of state intervention seems to have tended to generate and maintain dependency in the population, rather than encouraging self-reliance, (iv) dependency on the central state in particular has tended to suppress local community solutions, voluntary aid and self-help, (v) there appears to be a continuing escalation of the costs of state services, (usually because of lack of demand constraints and high elasticity with income) and (vi) there has been an increasing unwillingness to support the level of public expenditure that the welfare state now requires which derives in part from fears of public action 'crowding out' other activities, and in part from a shift in policy culture. The consequences of this political shift in views have been attempts to promote self-help schemes, 'neighbourhood' arrangements rather than local or central state action, reinvigoration of voluntary and church-sector activity and reduction in the level of dependency, for example by the linkage of welfare benefits to work (as in 'workfare' schemes).

The result of these developments has been a shift in the dominant 'policy culture': of western Europe with regard to the welfare state, and of socialist Europe with regard to the role of state bureaucracy. Policy culture is the dominant framework and beliefs within which administrative action finds legitimacy: the framework that mediates between political leaders, political parties, interest groups, administrative practice and state employees on the one hand, and individuals, families and business enterprises on the other. When a shift in policy culture occurs, it shakes the whole foundation of legitimacy of the state and its administration, including its territorial base.

The process of political socialisation imparts the values and beliefs of the prevailing culture and in doing this it underpins the legitimacy of the political authorities and the ruling groups. Yet the socialisation process also *generates a set of expectations* concerning how the political system *should* operate, and if these expectations are continually disappointed, then the whole edifice will become suspect; political socialisation works more than one way. [Smith, 1973, p. 9] (emphases in original)

In capitalist societies the original establishment of state welfare systems derived from the supportive ideology of the times. It was based pre-eminently on a concept of 'new liberalism' or social insurance (see for example Freeden, 1978; Weaver, 1982); it was not based on empirical investigation. Because of the failures of some parts of the resulting state edifice and because of the inability of welfare systems to keep up with expanding desires, alternative approaches to welfare provision are now being appraised. Some of the alternatives existed when state welfare was first being implemented: for example non-profit trusts; voluntary and charity organizations (see for example Roof, 1972) and Townsendism as in the United States (see for example Holtzman, 1963). Other approaches are now emerging in a wide range of different contexts (see OECD, 1987, for a review). Driving many of these developments has been the thinking of the so-called 'new political right' which proclaims emphasis on the individual rather than collectives and the state. As a result greater emphasis is placed on benefits and service objectives to individuals, and the response of provision to demand — a consumer-orientated public sector. This has stimulated reductions in the level of publicly provided services and an increase in privatization and contracting out. In fiscal terms it has stimulated reductions in tax burdens as a whole; a shift of taxation from direct to indirect sources where choice to consume is emphasized; and removal of tax 'distortions' or leverage to different types of behaviour.

The territorial effect of this change in policy culture has been to shift the emphasis of governmental action in two directions. First, there has been a shift from direct service delivery by the state to provision of an appropriate regulatory environment to stimulate individual action and provide checks and balances on market responses and the activities of non-profit organizations. This stimulates direct relations between the state, individuals and service deliverers which reduces the need for a territorial level of government as a whole. It certainly makes possible a major reduction in the need for strategic co-ordination and planning within metropolitan systems which in turn permits greater emphasis to be placed on smaller-size units at commune or similar levels. A second shift in policy culture has been from central to local or regional/province levels. In general, politically conservative periods (such as the late nineteenth century, the 1920s and the present) have seen the role of local government (state and local) being emphasized. Liberal or pro-government periods have seen greater accountability to the central government. This can, to some extent, be accounted for by the relative ease of political lobbying at the two levels in different ideological climates.

In Britain one expression of these phenomena has been the emergence of a 'fiscal conservatism' in the relations between central and local government (see for example Dunleavy, 1984; Bennett, 1989). Administrative bureaucracies of the state are increasingly seen as budget-maximisers which have crippled market power. To limit this requires a 'market discipline' to be induced into government at central and local level. At local government level market opportunities can even be encouraged by stimulating migration between areas to achieve better mixes of taxes and/or services in accord with preferences. Other methods of achieving a better relation between government and preferences are outlined in OECD (1987):

(i)   regulation of private-sector contractors
  — 'contracting out'
  — control of standards
  — competitive tenders;
(ii) co-operatives, associations, trusts, non-profit organizations;
(iii) voluntary and charitable bodies;
(iv) public-private partnerships;
(v)   para-state sectors.

In socialist democracies the development of state provision and its administrative apparatus is clearly very different. Yet similar tensions are emerging. Most notably a tension between 'general' provision and individual preferences, and a tension between the level of desires and the capacity of the state to provide. Both tensions mirror the patterns of capitalist societies. Indeed the tensions may be greater. At the individual level Heller (1988) argues the tension to be the result of state and party pressure to turn individuals into mere cogs in the production wheel through excessive centralization of education, culture and almost all activities; and Szelényi (1988) sees the secondary market in Hungary as a means of social and cultural survival of entrepreneurism as a resistance to bureaucratic order.

The tension of provision in comparison to desired service levels and qualities is evident in the often poor and declining levels of services: for example infant mortality in the USSR is officially 25.4 per 1,000, while in capitalist economies it is usually under ten; over 30 per cent of district hospitals have no hot water and over 27 per cent no sewerage; medicines are 30 per cent below requirements (Yevgeny Chasov, Soviet health minister 1987, quoted in *The Economist*, 21 November 1987); 50 per cent of schools in the USSR are without central heating, running water and sewerage, 25 per cent of schools are overcrowded with two or three shifts; and more than one million children cannot attend kindergarten because of insufficient places (Gennady Yagodin, Chairman of the Soviet Education Committee, 1988; quoted in *The Times Education Supplement*, 2 September 1988).

Additionally to these features, but related to them, there is also a tension between individual preferences and the dominant administrative-economic system which questions its overall capacity to provide. This goes beyond the tensions in capitalist societies and challenges the basis of the party–state structure. It is the basis of *perestroika* which, because it is so fundamental, creates the greatest difficulties for implementation. For example, Lukacs (1983) notes that in Hungary in 1977 planned 'necessities' in education exceeded by four times the planned 'possible' levels of investment: accordingly 'necessities' must be graded into priorities. This draws us to the interlinkage with the economics of shortage outlined below. Socialist democracies, therefore, have similar, but often more extreme tensions of provision between levels of 'desires' and 'needs'.

The reforms being contemplated in socialist democracies generally follow two main lines, one economic, the other political (see Aganbegyan, 1988; Gorbachev, 1987; and summaries by *The Economist*, 1988a,b; Hewett, 1988).

(i) *Economic Reform*: accelerated economic as well as social and attitudinal development (*Uskorenie*).

— creation of greater motivation by people through self-discipline and enthusiasm (*chelovecheskiifaktor*);
— economic and technical improvement, particularly emphasizing the machine-building, metal-working and chemical industries through foreign borrowing, domestic savings, (mainly) domestic restructuring

away from other sectors and an accelerated rate of scrapping of equipment;

— greater emphasis on the service sector (only 20 per cent of GDP in the USSR compared to 38 per cent in Hungary and 55 per cent in capitalist economies);

— decentralization of decision-making powers to enterprises and local soviets (including setting levels of outputs, inputs, customers, suppliers, wages, bonuses and investments), with associated rewards, risks and penalties (*khozraschet* and *samofinasirovanie*: enterprises must earn funds to cover current costs and have an investable surplus — this allows identification of inefficiency and insolvency);

— greater reliance on economic instruments (such as taxes, subsidies, interest rates, etc.) and less use of administrative orders and controls;

— greater activity at individual and co-operative levels including the possibility of bankruptcy, workers losing their jobs, plus legally sanctioned private enterprise (for example, in the first six months of 1988 14,000 new co-operatives with 150,000 members had been registered in the USSR, particularly in the service fields of restaurants, hairdressers, etc.);

— more flexible and responsive prices, and an increased role of money: contractual prices;

— a shift from obligatory targets to norms and indirect instruments (use of state orders for industrial output rather than planned targets);

— improved co-ordination between the socialist countries as a whole through the Council for Mutual Economic Assistance (CMEA).

The economic reforms follow principles enunciated by Aganbegyan (1988) and are related closely to the concept of the *Kombinate* System in East Germany. In East Germany these are large state companies with an average of 20,000 workers that have individual horizontal links to other enterprises and a level of independence of party and sectoral ministries. Price reform is the most difficult area to allow a genuine commodity, monetary, capital and labour market. While this is being openly discussed in Hungary, where an extensive secondary market and entrepreneurism have developed (see for example Szelényi, 1988; Batt, 1988), and to a lesser extent in Yugoslavia and Poland (Kuklinski, 1987), price freedom in the USSR is seen as a long-term reform. Aganbegyan, for example, notes that at present twenty-four million prices are officially set in the USSR; this should be reduced to about 1,000 for only key commodities. But this change is clearly well beyond 1990 which he suggests is the target. The studies of Kornai (1980) and Winiecki (1988) also show how far economic reforms have to go.

(ii) *Political and administrative reform*. This is one of the most difficult areas. Recent comments by Yakovlev (1988) and Zaslavskaya (1988) evidence the tensions that are present. However the reforms announced by Gorbachev at the July 1988 party congress show the extent of projected changes:

- limited terms for elected party officials (up to ten years);
- genuinely competitive ballots open to non-party candidates outside *nomenklatura*;
- replacement of part of the central committee between congresses;
- raising of the entry standards to the party;
- restoration of powers to soviets, particularly at city and region level;
- separation of the role of party and state, with party committees barred from issuing orders to factories or ministries;
- establishment of 'supremacy of the law', strengthening citizens' rights.

Political reform is the heart of *perestroika*; to create a new 'unity of socialism with democracy' (Gorbachev, 1987) and to move back to a purer Leninist concept and away from Stalinist excessive centralization. At the heart of political reform is administrative reform.

In terms of territorial structure, administrative reform is being targeted on increased decentralization to local soviets or People's Councils at the most basic level and to intermediate county or district levels. Because of the close interlocking of territorial administrative structure and economic planning, this development also means decentralization to the level of the enterprise and *Kombinate* (or to the territorial production complex — TPC). Kuklinski (1987) argues that the key reform is a shift to local self-government instead of worker self-government; that is to assert territory over economic structures. At present most local governments have relatively little autonomy, either in terms of administrative or financial discretion, even though the level of their expenditure and service provision is very significant. This is a result of centralized planning in which local budgets are part of the single unified state budget of the whole country. Moreover, it is the large cities which dominate expenditures, with little scope for small villages or other territorial levels. For example, in the USSR in 1975, cities accounted for 47 per cent of local expenditure, *oblasts* 20 per cent and *raions* 24 per cent, while workers' settlements accounted for only 23 per cent and villages 6.6 per cent (Lewis, 1983). The various ways in which decentralization can be increased varies considerably in both form and pace among different socialist democracies, being most advanced in Hungary and Yugoslavia, making modest advances in Poland, under active debate in the USSR and Bulgaria, but relatively static in Czechoslovakia and Romania (see later chapters, and Horváth, 1987; Vidláková, 1980; Le Grand and Okrasa, 1988; Batt, 1988). In East Germany economic reforms are advanced in some areas (for example the *Kombinate*), but political reform as well as wider economic reform of the price incentive systems are relatively static.

Conclusion

This chapter has sought to place administrative structures, and the pressures upon them for change, into the context of their changing environment: of evolving activity spaces and changing functional economic regions; economic change and technological development connected to the different stages of urbanization, suburbanization and counter-urbanization; developments of local and regional social and cultural identity; and changes in the 'policy culture' which are producing pressures for 'rethinking' the administrative state. What is being developed now as *perestroika*, or restructuring of the economy and administration in socialist countries, finds major counterparts associated with very different institutions in capitalist societies.

Territorial structures are crucial threads which run through each of these themes. Administrative systems are naturally subject to obsolescence: once the political will has been assembled to implement reform, it is almost always the case that society and the economic system have moved on to other levels of development. Hence attempts to restrain the economy to the characteristics of the administrative system inevitably lead to economic sluggishness. Because of the pace of current economic development, administrative obsolescence and reform are pressing problems. But, contrary to earlier periods, the major pressures are not towards greater geographical scales, but to both smaller scales and to the assertion of the importance of individuals over collectives. This suggests a reassertion of the basal administrative units (such as the municipality and commune) and of individuals and market stimuli, but with variations attuned to local territorial needs, that is a *flexible decentralization*. If flexible decentralization is to be the new reform agenda, it represents a reversal of most previous trends. It engenders the need for a fundamental rethinking not only of the scale of administration and the role of the state, but also for a reassessment of the distribution of competences, responsibilities and resources among the different levels of governmental administrative action. At the same time it is likely that if flexible decentralization occurs it must be matched to *flexible aggregation*, that is a means of linking small units and their competences and financial resources to gain economic/technical efficiency. We turn to these questions in the next chapter.

References

Aganbegyan, A. (1988), *The Challenge: Economics of Perestroika*, Century Hutchinson, London.

Almond, G.A. and Powell, G.B. (1966), *Comparative Politics: a Developmental Approach*, Little, Brown, Boston.

Barry, B. (1965), *Political Argument*, Routledge and Kegan Paul, London.

Batt, J. (1988), *Economic Reform and Political Change in Eastern Europe: a Comparison of Czechoslovak and Hungarian Experiences*, Macmillan, London.

Bennett, R.J. (1980), *The Geography of Public Finance*, Methuen, London.

Bennett, R.J. (1985), 'Regional movements in Britain: a review of aims and status', *Government and Policy: Environment and Planning*, C, 3, 75–95.

Bennett, R.J. (1989), 'Central and local taxes and responsibilities: the arguments for assignment and the demands for restructuring', in Italian Ministry of the Interior (eds), *Local Public Service and the Crisis of the Welfare State*, Rome.

Berg, L. van der, Drewett, R., Klaassen, L.H., Rossi, A. and Vijverberg, C.H.T. (1982), *A Study of Growth and Decline*, Pergamon, Oxford.

Berry, B.J.L. (1970), 'The Geography of the United States in the year 2000', *Transactions Institute of British Geographers*, 51, 21–53.

Berry, B.J.L. (1976), 'The counterurbanisation process: urban America since 1970', in B.J.L. Berry (ed.), *Urbanisation and Counterurbanisation*, Sage, London.

Champion, A.G., Green A.E., Owen, D.W., Ellin, D.J. and Coombs, M.G. (1987), *Changing Places: Britain's Demographic, Economic and Social Complexion*, Edward Arnold, London.

Conner, W. (1973), 'The politics of ethnonationalism', *Journal of International Affairs*, 27, 1–21.

Crozier, M. (1973), *The Stalled Society*, Viking, New York.

Dunleavy, P. (1984), 'Analysing British politics', in H. Drucker, P. Dunleavy, A. Gamble and G. Peele (eds), *Developments in British Politics*, Macmillan, London.

The Economist, (1988a), 'Survey of the Soviet economy', 9 April.

The Economist, (1988b), 'Soviet Union: before the battle', 4 June, pp. 53–4.

Enyedi, G. and Veldman, J. (1986), 'Key problems in rural settlement research and planning', in G. Enyedi and J. Veldman (eds), *Rural Development Issues in Industrialised Countries*, Centre for Regional Studies of the Hungarian Academy of Sciences, Pécs.

Freeden, M. (1978), *The New Liberalism*, Oxford University Press, Oxford.

Gorbachev, M. (1987), *Perestroika and the New Thinking*, Collins, London.

Hägerstrand, T. (1972), 'Tätortsgrupper Som Regionsamhällen: Tillgången Till Förvärsarbete Och Tjanster Utanför De Större Ständerna', *Regioner Att Leva i*, Allmann Förlaget, Stockholm, 141–73.

Hägerstrand, T. (1975) 'Space, time and human conditions', in A. Karlqvist (ed.) *Dynamic Allocation of Urban Space*, D.C. Heath, Saxon House, Farnborough.

Hall, P. and Hay, D. (1980), *Growth Centres in the European Urban System*, Heinemann, London.

Hebbert, M. (1987), 'Regionalism: a reform concept and its application to Spain', *Government and Policy: Environment and Planning*, C, 5, 239–50.

Hechter, M. (1975), *Internal Colonisation: the Celtic Fringe in British National Development 1536–1966*, Routledge and Kegan Paul, London.

Heller, M. (1988), *Cogs in the Soviet Wheel*, Collins Harvill, London.

Heraud, G. (1963), *L'Europe des ethnies*, Presses d'Europe, Paris.

Heraud, G. (1969), *Philosophie de l'ethnisme et du fédéralisme*, I.J.D. Malienneslez Charleroi, Paris.

Herman, S. and Regulski, J. (1977), *Elements of a Theory of Urbanisation Processes in Socialist Countries*, Vienna Centre, WD 3/77.

Hewett, E.A. (1988), *Reforming the Soviet Economy: Equality versus Efficiency*, Brookings Institution, Washington DC.

Holtzman, A. (1963), *The Townsend Movement: a Political Study*, McGraw Hill, New York.

Horváth, G. (1987), *Development of the Regional Management of the Economy in East-central Europe*, Discussion Paper No.5, Centre for Regional Studies of the Hungarian Academy of Sciences, Pécs.

Kornai, J. (1980), *The Economy of Shortage*, Magnetö, Budapest.

Kuklinski, A. (1987), 'Local studies in Poland: experiences and prospects', in P. Dutkiewicz and G. Gorzelak (eds), *Local Studies in Poland*, Institute of Space Economy, University of Warsaw.

Lafont, R. (1967), *La révolution régionaliste*, Gallimand, Paris.

Lammenais, H.F.R. de (1848), *Project de constitution de la République Française*, Bureau du Peuple Constituant, Paris.

Leemans, A.F. (1970), *Changing Patterns of Local Government*, International Union of Local Authorities, The Hague.

Le Grand, J. and Okrasa W. (eds) (1988), *Social Welfare in Britain and Poland*, Suntory–Toyota Research Centre, London School of Economics.

Lewis, C.W. (1983), 'The economic functions of local soviets', in E.A. Jacobs (ed.), *Soviet Local Politics and Government*, George Allen and Unwin, London.

Lukacs, P. (1983), 'On the central planning of education', *Educational Policy Research Papers 69*, Hungarian Institute of Educational Research, Budapest.

Maurel, M-C. (1982), 'Bureaucratie et contrôle territorial: le maillage de l'espace rural en URSS et en Pologne', *Heredote*, 25, 49–75.

Miller, D. (1976), *Social Justice*, Clarendon Press, Oxford.

OECD (1987), *Managing and Financing Urban Services*, Organization for Economic Co-operation and Development, Paris.

Orridge, A.W. (1981), 'Uneven development and nationalism: 1 and 2', *Political Studies*, 29, 1–15.

Poggi, G. (1978), *The Development of the Modern State*, Stanford University Press, California.

Pred, A.R. (1974), *An Evaluation and Summary of Human Geography Research Projects*, Statens Råd för Samhällsforskning, Stockholm.

Redcliffe–Maud Commission (1968), Royal Commission on *Local Government in England*, 2 vols, Cmnd 4040, HMSO, London.

Rokkan, S. and Urwin, D. (eds) (1982), *The Politics of Territorial Identity*, Sage, London.

Santos, M. (1975), 'Space and domination — a Marxist approach', *International Social Science Journal*, 27, 346–66.

Smith, A.D.S. (1979), *Nationalism in the Twentieth Century*, Martin Robertson, London.

Smith, G. (1973), *Politics in Western Europe: a Comparative Analysis*, Holmes and Meier, New York.

Smith, G.E. (1985), 'Ethnic nationalism in the Soviet Union's territory, cleavage and control', *Government and Policy: Environment and Planning*, C, 3, 49–74.

SOCITM (1987), *IT Trends in Local Government*, Society of Information Technology Managers, Warwickshire County Council.

Szelényi, I. (1988), *Socialist Entrepreneurs: Embourgeoisement in Rural Hungary*, Polity Press, London.

Tarrow, S. and Katzenstein, P. (eds) (1978), *Territorial Politics in Industrial Countries*, Praeger, New York.

Vidláková, O. (1980), 'Planning for the comprehensive economic and social development of regional and local authorities in Czechoslovakia', *Planning and Administration*, 8, 1, 35–41.

Weaver, C.L. (1982), *The Crisis in Social Security*, North Carolina University Press, Durham, NC.

Winiecki, J. (1988), *The Distorted World of Soviet-type Economies*, Routledge, London.

Yakovlev, A.V. (1988), 'Achieving qualitative change in Soviet society: the role of the social sciences', *International Social Science Journal*, 115, 149–62.

Zaslavskaya, T.I. (1985), 'The social sciences and the economic, political and cultural changes in the USSR', *International Social Sciences Journal*, 115, 137–47.

4 Assignment of competency and resources

Robert Bennett

Introduction

Considerable debate is now occurring around the issue of decentralization of competency, the responsibilities for functions and delivery of services and the financial resources to provide them. The previous chapters have argued that the context of this debate has two interwoven strands. First there is a disjuncture, of historically derived administrative systems, which have experienced only partial reform, with the needs of modern systems of state service provision and the economic and social system which creates service requirements as well as providing the technological and financial resources to supply them. Second, there has been a more recent shift in the 'policy culture', in both liberal and socialist democracies, which has called into question a 'rethinking' of the administrative state in Europe. The west European discussion is paralleled in eastern Europe by discussions of reform at two levels — one economic and the second political and administrative.

The previous chapter concluded that it was likely that new administrative reforms would be required to introduce greater *decentralization* to take account of the need for greater participation, improved relations of administrative action to people's preferences and real action spaces and greater *aggregation* of small units within administrative associations as well as some amalgamations which would permit greater economic and technical efficiency by internalizing externalities. However, to retain stability as well as adaptability over time, it was argued that these developments must retain a strong flexibility: a requirement, therefore, for *flexible decentralization* and *flexible aggregation*. Such a development points directly to the two issues of assignment of competences and allocation of responsibility and financial resources. These are taken as the core of the discussion of this chapter.

Assignment of administrative competences

The division of competence between levels of government determines the responsibility for different administrative functions and the degree of local political control over who receives what services as a function of which territory they live in. Various theoretical approaches to the determination of the assignment of competence over functions to different levels of government have evolved. The six most important of these are discussed here.

Sense of community

The 'sense of community' is an important overall constraint on the organization of competence for public goods and services, especially those programmes orientated towards social redistribution. This 'sense of community', or Thomas Jefferson's 'ward democracy', is a form of collective identity which requires a pattern of common history and culture, geographic inertia, social and economic conditions and previous distribution of administrative competence which have allowed a collective local cultural identity and loyalty to develop and survive. Often the smaller the size of the unit, the greater is this collective sense of communal values. This has led to the apportionment of competence to those levels at which particular community ties are evident. Thus, at one extreme, administrative competence can be organized on very wide geographical bases if they reflect loosely held, infrequently used but widely supported preferences for particular forms of government, ethnic or cultural institutions or for social and economic organizations. At the other extreme, competency over such functions as police, education and housing impinge on the daily lives of most people, are recurrent or continuous needs and relate to very strongly held local neighbourhood values which are most appropriate for communal or local government. Between the two extremes is a hierarchy of assignments of other competences. It should also be noted that the sense of community is a fairly slowly changing criterion; and is remarkably stable at the level of small rural settlements and urban neighbourhoods. It is a basic level condition for participation and a key to the need for decentralization.

Technical efficiency

A technically efficient criterion for apportionment of competences involves the determination of the level of government at which the output of administrative services can be produced at least cost in relation to economies of scale and distribution. This leads to ideas about optimum community size and density. Technical efficiency is most important where economies of scale are most significant (as in power generation, water and sewerage systems), or where distribution costs compose a large proportion of total service costs. This latter factor has led to a large literature on optimal districting, organization of bus and transport services for schooling, delimitation of police and fire protection districts and other optimal districting problems (Massam, 1975; Scott, 1971; Johnston and Taylor, 1978). However, these mathematical solutions have rarely been totally feasible in practice due to the constraints of political and preference factors. They represent broad indicia rather than rigid criteria for apportioning competences.

Each function performed by government administration has a different technically efficient size of population or area served. Moreover, each functional field is usually a composite of a group of sub-functions each of which also has different technically efficient sizes. In addition, there are seldom sharp discontinuities in the economy of scale cost-curve, suggesting that it will not usually be possible to find a unique hierarchical clustering of competences. In many instances, it must also be recognized that the level of government which provides a given service need not accord with the area in which consumption occurs. There are often significant spillovers and externalities. These can be overcome by methods of flexible aggregation: intergovernmental agreements and associations to overcome allocation problems. Moreover, technical efficiency is a rather static criterion which allows only slow adjustments of administrative institutions when technological changes induce shifts in economies of scale and distribution, again suggesting the need for a flexible approach.

Economic efficiency

The economic efficiency criterion for allocation of competence involves the technical issues of economies of scale and distribution, discussed above, but also raises three subsidiary features: first, the practical assignment of competency over questions of resource allocation, social distribution and economic stabilization; second, the extent of externalities and spillovers which determine the degree of 'publicness' of administrative functions; third, the price elasticity of demand for goods. With respect to the first of these features, the classical theory of public finance (see Musgrave, 1959; Oates, 1972) assigns the functions of distribution, stabilization and economic development to national level government, and the allocation function to local level, with some allocation and perhaps minor components of growth and distribution policies at regional level. While these lines of delimitation are generally appropriate, the assignment of competence must be sufficiently flexible to adapt to changing economic factors, as well as recognizing the requirements of reflecting local differences in preferences. In addition, in federal countries, there is a legal guarantee of rights to sub-state levels. It must be acknowledged, therefore, that decentralization of competences, combined with flexible aggregation (co-ordination of local and regional governments), allows a considerable degree of variation in fiscal burdens, distribution policies and growth incentives. This can accord local services and financial competence more closely with variation in local preferences and levels of demand, and hence encourage greater economic efficiency.

With respect to the second feature of economic efficiency, the degree of externality and 'publicness' of social goods, we are drawn back to the technical criteria discussed above as well as to technical attributes of jointness, non-excludability and non-rejectability. According to the degree to which a good possesses these public-good attributes, we may rank goods from an extreme of 'purity' (see Samuelson, 1954). Where a good possesses total purity (the same benefits are consumed by all, equally and at equal cost) this should be provided by national governments or international organizations (as shown in Figure 4.1). For a good which has no jointness aspects (a totally private good), economic efficiency requires that this will not be provided by government at all. Local, regional and other forms of public goods, as shown in Figure 4.1, are found between these two extremes where the degree of jointness defines the most appropriate geographical territory and hence the administrative unit over which to organize provision. Hence, the economic efficiency criterion gives rise to a hierarchical apportionment over the competency for the provision of public goods according to their degree of externality. Although such divisions are far from hard and fast, there is often a remarkable degree of relationship between the amount of joint externality of many goods and their territorial range. This arises from technical issues, for example in the cases of education, fire and police services, sewerage, water and street lighting; from supply constraints, in the case of education, police and fire services; and from political and community factors which relate to the degree of socialization or group identity of people (see for example Breton, 1965; Head, 1973; Forte, 1977; Musgrave and Musgrave, 1986).

The third element of the economic efficiency argument, the price elasticity of demand for a good, relates to the assignment of competence between the public and private sectors, and between government levels of the public sector, so as to allow a minimum distortion to the economically efficient allocation of economic resources. The normal demand for a private good, as shown in Figure 4.2a, induces a decline in consumption with an increase in price. Where other (social) criteria indicate that such goods should be provided publicly, the completely inelastic good is usually best assigned to the national or international level (Figure 4.2b). Where the price of a good exhibits a degree of decreasing marginal production cost with size of a producing unit, and/or external economies (Figure 4.2c), then Brownlee (1961) argues that it should be provided publicly, but that the level of government administration to which its competency is assigned will depend upon the degree of its externality and extent of its marginal savings. This argument is based on a situation in which it is desirable for the public sector to organize a service because it can only be run efficiently as a monopoly. Examples of such services are postal deliveries, telecommunications, radio and television, law, highways, railways, many utilities and water supply. They can also often be run on a private basis, but usually must be financed by user charges and subject to public regulatory controls.

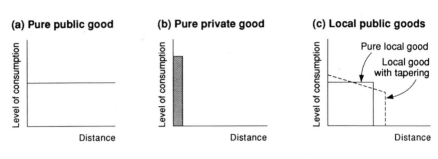

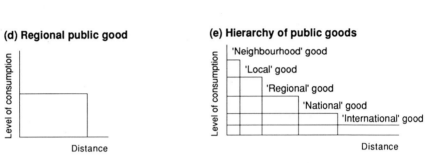

Figure 4.1

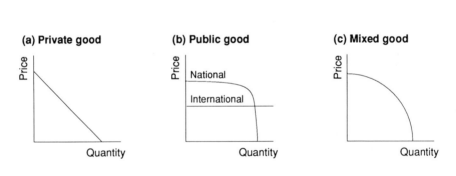

Figure 4.2

Preference structures

Preference structures present a fourth approach to assignment of administrative competence which is closely related to both the sense of community and to economic efficiency. This approach relies upon two arguments. The first argument derives from a basic decentralization theorem which is based on public choice arguments, especially from Buchanan: that smaller communities give a better accordance with preferences, a higher chance of consensus, minimize frustration and reduce the need for regulatory control. Hence, preferences form a major component of what Rothenberg (1970) terms the forces of administrative homogenization. The second argument is that there are benefits to be gained from collusion and collective action when there are joint externalities and spillovers. Indeed, much of the literature of the preference school is based upon a wide interpretation of the externality and spillover effects which is also so important in the economic efficiency approach. Authors such as Buchanan (1966), Breton (1965), Tullock (1969), Bish (1971), Ostrom (1973), Breton and Scott (1976) and Buchanan and Tullock (1969) have proposed that an optimal pattern of representative government administration can be based on determining, for each public good and service, the point at which the external costs resulting from collective provision of goods exceeds the external benefit to the individual. This so-called 'calculus of consent' can then be made the basis for allocation of functional competence between levels of government in which preferences are derived from the relative costs of involvement or non-involvement in collective decision-making.

Figure 4.3 shows typical graphs of costs and benefits hypothesized by Buchanan and Tullock to characterize the provision of public goods in groups of different sizes (N). The external cost-curve (Figure 4.3a) depicts how the costs to the individual resulting from the action of others decline as the group size increases, that is the group expands to the point at which no costs are external. The decision costs, depicted in Figure 4.3b, increase as the size of the group increases. This is the result of four factors: first, the need for larger administrative bureaucracies; second, more expensive consultation and participation processes; third, the costs to individuals from agreeing to decisions which are individually inappropriate in order to obtain gains elsewhere; and fourth, the costs resulting from lack of control over the bureaucracies of larger governments. Although these cost-curves will differ with different fields of competence, the combination of these two cost-curves (Figure 4.3c) allows the determination of an optimal group size for organization of each functional competence as that point at which the costs of participation in administrative divisions exactly equal the costs of non-participation. By combining the cost-curve for various goods, Buchanan and Tullock predict that a set of groupings of competence emerges which gives individual, neighbourhood/village, town, regional and national levels of administrative competence, as shown in Figure 4.3d. Hence, the hierarchy of group preferences reflected through costs determines a hierarchical apportionment of administrative competence as a form of what Buchanan terms an 'optimal constitution'. The main difficulty with this approach is that it is attractive more from a theoretical than a practical point of view. As noted by Bird and Hartle (1972) the social optimum, to which the public choice arguments of Buchanan and Breton lead, is subject to the same limitations as welfare economics; the optimum which is sought is defined with respect to the present distribution of real income, requires perfect knowledge by all actors, relies on a single set of values against which to judge optimality and hence requires a determinate

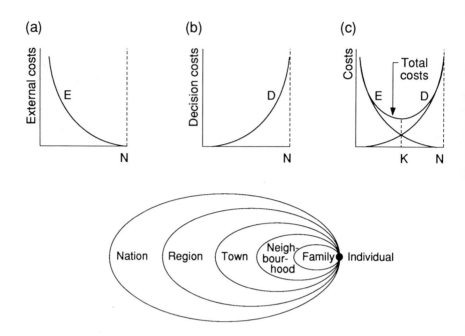

Figure 4.3

set of preferences (welfare function) which is shared without conflict by the majority of residents in any area. Nevertheless, preference structures represent an important indication for 'optimum' functional assignment of competency between levels of government; and they are particularly important in asserting the conditions for successful participation and relation to local community action spaces.

Administrative constraints

The fifth approach to apportionment of functions between levels of government is altogether less theoretical and more practical. It centres directly on the bureaucratic constraints on administrative practice. This places emphasis on the lines of vertical authority between levels of government, on horizontal co-operation between governments at the same level and on the creation of other such cross-linkages as may be necessary. The basic assignment of functional competence between administrative levels is therefore a task of appropriate departmentalization which involves one or more of the following principles: (i) *service principle*: this involves a separate administrative department for each group of people or problem (see Figure 4.4), for example a ministry for the economy, for the old, the unemployed, a Bureau of Minority Affairs and so forth. This is the dominant approach

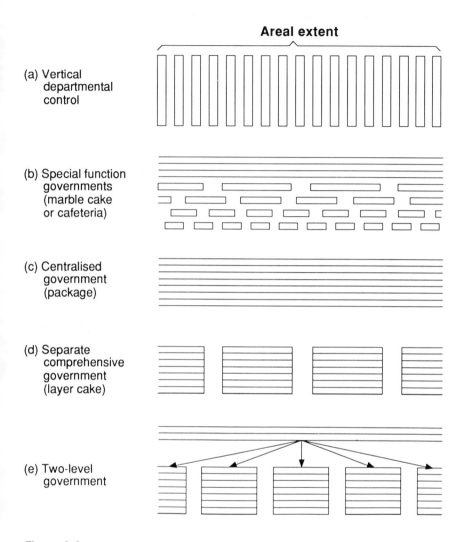

Areal extent

(a) Vertical
departmental
control

(b) Special function
governments
(marble cake
or cafeteria)

(c) Centralised
government
(package)

(d) Separate
comprehensive
government
(layer cake)

(e) Two-level
government

Figure 4.4

in 'socialist democracies'; (ii) *purpose principle*: termed by Sandford (1967) and Wright (1974) 'picket fence' federalism. A separate administrative department is defined for each administrative function. This is the usual governmental department structure in both western and eastern Europe; (iii) *process principle*: different administrative departments are defined for each type of administrative skill, for example engineers, architects, social care experts, economic planners and so forth. This is the normal method of division of labour and breakdown of decision-making in industrial companies; (iv) *areal principle*: (so-called 'layer-cake' federalism shown in Figure 4.4d). Administrative departments are evolved for each territorial unit with total devolution to lower geographical levels. Self (1972, p. 57), notes that this does not usually solve the departmentalization problem, and administrative competence will still need to be allocated at the new territorial level. This is one of the chief reasons for continuing tensions between territorial and sectoral administrative structures.

Mass participation and the arguments of socialist democracy

The discussion of administrative assignment thus far has been based largely on the literature and practice of western Europe and other liberal democracies. Although many of these principles also apply to socialist democracies, a further principle plays a more dominant role in eastern Europe: that of seeking 'democratic centralism', as outlined in Chapter 2.

The lack of a history of local autonomy in Russia, and in the Habsburg areas, except for the guild powers of the charter towns, has restricted the scope for administrative decentralization of competences and financial resources in socialist democracies. The approach that has been adopted has been vertical departmental structures with strong central controls. Thus the issue of territorial autonomy, or horizontal integration at a local level, has been largely circumvented. However the result has been a tension of territorial and sectoral/departmental planning, competence and resources. New developments seek to reassert the power of local soviets (people's councils) at the local level as a means of better targeting central investment tools. However, it is not yet clear that reforms to decentralize to *Kombinate* enterprises and local soviets will achieve the desired aim of increasing participation or economic efficiency. As yet a level of true decentralization of competence or resources to a local territorial level is awaited. However, there seems to be no a priori reason within socialist democracies to restrict the attainment of a much greater level of decentralization, which indeed would accord more closely with the original Leninist principles. Nevertheless, the dominant search for social and territorial equity clearly restricts the scope for autonomous action by local councils. Thus the main outcome for the assignment of responsibilities within socialist democracies has been centralized co-ordination and control, which is now being challenged by efforts to improve direct participation and increase 'localized' competency and resources at the most basic level.

Assessment

It is unlikely that any single administrative structure will serve all purposes; hence various mixtures of the different approaches will be necessary in practice. It may be that a 'little chaos' is a good thing (as suggested by Grodzins, 1966). Mixed assignments of functional competence have the benefit of allowing each service to operate at its efficient scale in accord with preferences. There are three main drawbacks. First, a high variety of local districts and fragmented control increases the cost

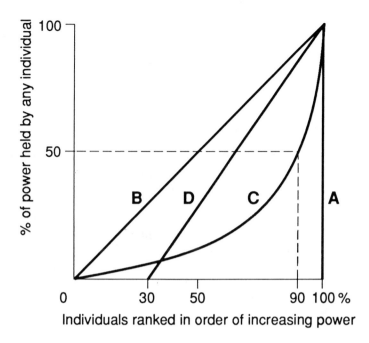

Figure 4.5 Relation between the power of individuals to make decision (0
= no power, 100 = total power) and the distribution of power
in society

Source: Neuberger and Duffy, 1976, fig. 4.3.

of co-ordinating decisions and restricts economies of scale in administration
at any level. Second, highly fragmented government administration
increases financial disparities by fracturing economic and geographical
space into very different areas of expenditures and revenues. Third, such
a 'marble cake' structure greatly confuses financial arrangements, leads to
overlapping and competition for local tax bases and confuses rather than
clarifies the lines of accountability. At the other extreme, the 'layer-cake'
or 'package approach', gives a single multi-purpose government for each
local area which administers all competences. This has the advantages of
easier co-ordination, reduction in operating costs and more obvious
administrative divisibility and accountability. However, it has the major
drawbacks of being relatively unadaptable to needs for changed boundaries; tends to ignore small-scale variations of needs, demands and
preferences within local units; induces a uniformity of taxation and other
administrative burdens irrespective of variation in local needs and ability
to pay, and often becomes uneconomically large and unresponsive.

Hence administrative structures that have evolved in most countries
contain elements of many approaches to government assignment of competence. Buchanan's concepts can be used to measure the actual concentration
of administrative power in administrative structures of different forms by
the Lorenz curve as shown in Figure 4.5. All distinctions of administrative

and political power in states are bounded by the two extremes of (a) complete concentration (curve A in Figure 4.5) in which one individual controls all administrative decisions, (b) complete dispersion (curve B in Figure 4.5) in which all individuals have an equal share of power. This latter is a form of anarchy, but also characterizes the perfect market economy. The curve C shows the more common situation in both socialist democracies as well as imperfect market economies in which all individuals have some power, but where most power is concentrated into the hands of administrators. In the case shown 50 per cent of the power is held by 10 per cent of the people. Curve D corresponds to a class system in which one group (for example slaves in classical Athens) have no power at all, in this case represented by 30 per cent of the population.

The variation of administrative organization to the specifics of different situations, as well as the difficulty of resolving the conflict between local participation and the economic efficiency of larger units, leads us to consider flexible, evolutionary or incrementalist approaches rather than the a priori design of administrative institutions. Each approach to the assignment of administrative competence discussed above specifies an ideal and cannot be applied to practice without blends of the other approaches. Economic and technical efficiency suggests a strong development of regional level administrative functions; functions with elements of distribution, stabilization and economic development require a strong development of national government administration; while political constraints, local knowledge and variation to take account of the needs, preferences and local community sense suggest a strong level of local government administration.

In practice also, the assignment of responsibilities is not the only method of overcoming the effect of spillover or confused preference structures. Two important alternatives exist: flexible aggregation, and transfers between governments to offset benefit-and-cost spillovers. In theory, at least, the concept of transfers has been used by Pigou (1928), Pauly (1970), and Sandler (1975) to suggest a method of optimal local finance using fees and grants. A further suggestion by Coons et al., (1970) is a 'power equalizing' approach in which financial competence is assessed over jurisdictions of wide extent (region or province), while the budget and administrative decisions are made locally. This keeps decisions locally based, but eliminates financial inequalities. It again throws emphasis on flexible decentralization and flexible aggregation through intergovernmental co-ordination and transfers of resources between administrative levels.

Assignment of administrative resources

The arguments concerning different forms of assignment of competence lead us to conclude that a flexible and co-ordinated system of territorially decentralized units is likely to offer the best form of administrative structure in practice. Similarly, the assignment of the resources for administrative action also leads us to favour the need for flexible decentralization and flexible aggregation.

Administrative resources cover a wide field of discussion, ranging from the extent of political power and autonomy, over personnel quality and quantity, through physical means (which are very significant in eastern Europe) to financial means (which are significant in both eastern and western Europe). We concentrate attention here on financial means — or revenue resources.

In the literature of market economies the normative theory of fiscal federalism provides the starting point for discussion of the assignment of revenue resources. This is based on the work of Musgrave, 1959; Musgrave and Musgrave, 1986; Oates, 1972, 1977; Scott, 1964; and Tiebout, 1956, 1961, with subsequent developments by Foster et al., 1980; Grewal et al., 1980; King, 1984; McLure, 1983; Mathews, 1977 and others. Its territorial implications are discussed by Bennett (1980, 1987). The normative theory can be broken down into the relation of the revenue system to four 'branches' of government activity: allocation, distribution, stabilization and economic growth.

Allocation

This concerns the use of the resources in the economy as a whole. Because it is expected that preferences, externalities and natural monopolies of publicly provided goods will vary from place to place, the theory of fiscal federalism argues that local administrative actions may have major impact on allocation, that is to say the most local levels may administer and provide many services and may raise considerable amounts of revenue; but only insofar as this helps to accord the allocation of resources more closely to the conditions of local preferences, since this will result in a more efficient allocation of resources in the economy as a whole. Hence local government activity is seen as mainly helping to improve economic efficiency; for example, in providing public goods 'whose benefits are limited to specific subsets of the population' (Oates, 1972, p. 11). This is an extension of the arguments of assignment of administrative competence outlined earlier.

The distribution function

This concerns social policy: the redistribution of goods and money to attain a desired final social distribution. The distribution function is reserved mainly to national level government in the normative theory of fiscal federalism. The main reason for this conclusion is the geographical mobility of factors of production in market economies. Unless differences in taxes or other revenue burdens are very minor, differences between localities affect residential and business location and result in efficient allocation of resources. Hence, it is argued, any redistribution policies at a local level produce distortionary taxes or benefits, which will be avoided by relocation.

Stabilization and economic growth

These policies concern counter-cyclical activity to reduce the effects of booms and slumps, and policies to promote long-term economic development. The normative theory argues that, since local economies are so open, local finance of counter-cyclical measures will mostly 'leak' outside the jurisdiction in which they are applied. This would not only nullify local actions, but also permit 'freeriders' in other areas to gain benefits at no cost, thus inducing inefficiencies.

The conclusion of the normative theory of fiscal federalism is therefore that, except for special circumstances, only the administration of, and collection of revenues for, services can have extensive local control — that is allocation function. As a result, localities should administer services in relation to preferences and can raise revenue, but only in a manner which is not distortionary or does not leak to other localities. The conclusion is that local public goods must provide benefits which are non-distributive; local taxes should be limited and must be flat rate or proportional taxes and the subjects taxed should not be mobile. In practice, therefore, the normative theory leads to only limited autonomous revenue powers granted to local government levels of administration.

However, the revenue systems of most countries do not fit this neat assignment of responsibilities. In practice most western European countries have evolved a mixture of separate, shared and overlapping revenue sources at different levels of government which allow a blend of local autonomy and central control. *Tax sharing* occurs when revenues are collected at one level, and then are made available to other levels of government on a fairly stable or guaranteed basis (usual in federal structures). *Tax overlapping* occurs when two levels of government independently compete to tap the same revenue source, often with different rates, tax bases, allowances and methods of assessment. Tax separation is not a prerequisite for local taxes. Intergovernmental transfers are a further method of revenue interlinkage between administrative levels.

In addition, the need to balance local preferences, participation and sense of community identity, with technical or administrative efficiency, leads to other requirements to interlock the revenue systems of different administrative levels. This is often presented as a constitutional argument (for example by Wiseman, 1987; Dafflon, 1977; Topham, 1983; Tresch, 1981; and Bennett, 1987). The constitutional argument is that any non-central administrative decision must be viewed in the context of the political and constitutional powers that form and maintain the relations between people and government, and between central and local levels of administration. For any tax proposal to be meaningful it must accept as a starting point that local government exists in part to choose revenue and administrative paths in accordance with its powers and preferences, and these may well differ from those of central government. As a result considerable activity in the fields of economic growth, stabilization and redistribution policies may result, and these cannot be criticized on a priori grounds as inefficient or inequitable, as suggested by the normative theory. Haller

(1965; quoted in Dafflon, 1977, p. 18), for example, states that 'it is misleading to label as "inefficient" state policies which modify the policy that the central governments may want to implement, if these policies are proposed with knowledge of the relevant facts and originate simply in the different weights being placed on different issues by federal and state governments'. Again, Peacock (1972, p. 94) states that 'the "inefficiency" argument makes a confusion between political ends and fixed means', that is if decentralization is an objective, then a particular assignment of central–local taxes cannot of itself be said to be inefficient just because it conflicts with centralized criteria. This emphasis throws into question the conclusions of the normative economic theory with respect to both equity and economic efficiency. As noted by Wiseman with respect to equity:

There is no reason why regions should agree upon what constitutes equity . . . and regions may well prefer to accept some differences in overall fiscal pressure, on particular groups, . . . there is no way to settle a priori what degree of equalisation is 'correct', and regions in different positions must realistically be expected to disagree about it. [1987, p. 402]

On efficiency Wiseman (p. 403) observes that 'it will usually be unrealistic to expect a region to acquiesce readily in its own depopulation, simply because it is believed elsewhere that economic efficiency requires that labour move'. Or as stated by McLure:

Citizens of states do develop loyalties to these states . . . Citizens of resource rich states will not gladly forego their rights to revenues . . . no matter how strong the theoretical argument . . . to reserve these revenue bases for the federal government. If they are not allowed access to these bases, they may be unwilling to participate in federation. [1983, p. xviii]

These arguments lead us to conclude that it is quite possible to utilize a wide variety of revenue resources at local administrative levels, although these may overlap and compete with higher levels. The resolution of conflicts is possible by tax sharing, intergovernmental transfers and other methods of co-ordination. Thus, as with assignment of competences, assignment of resources suggests the need for methods of flexible decentralization and flexible aggregation.

This discussion has not rejected normative theories such as that of fiscal federalism or of 'socialist democracy'; nor can these theories be rejected on their own terms. Rather the argument is that any one theory is limited in its applicability to practice. Theory must be seen, therefore, as a technical apparatus which may be useful for positive analysis within a given set of constraints, but the constraints which operate are political and cultural ones which require many additional factors to be included. First, there are political constraints which vest power at sub-national as well as central government levels; second, there are also geographical constraints in that the economy is not uniform, but exhibits strong variation in industrial and income concentrations and in the social or political consensus which derives from the variable location of different interest groups, and their power, as well as their potential or desire for mobility. As a result there will frequently be strong divergence between the objectives of different tiers of government, as well as between government units in the same tier. Third, there are participatory constraints which require the development of responsible administrative practice to changing preferences and needs.

The argument of this chapter has been that a strong case for both *localism* and *centralism* exists. Where possible localism should normally provide the more economically efficient outcome which also provides the best opportunities for participation and solidarity to local communities. Assignment of taxes to local level has most chance of administrative efficiency when based on benefit principles (charges); but for a large number of services which are redistributive, charging is impossible and taxes based on ability to pay are preferable. The objections derived from normative theory, to such taxes being assigned to local level, are important constraints but can be overcome provided that local taxes are implemented with care and supplemented by central financial transfers. The assignment of competence, like that of taxes, suggests the need for flexible co-ordination between levels of government and for blending 'efficiency' solutions with outcomes which assert a 'sense of community' and allow participation and revelation of preference structures. Emphasis on localism puts considerable pressures on co-ordination and association between localities as well as on central grant and transfer systems to provide the ultimate co-ordinative devices if local inequalities become extreme. A wide set of criteria can be built into programmes of financial transfers, but a localist emphasis leads to commending the dominance of shared-revenues as well as grants and the use of fees and charges where possible. The current period is one in which there are considerable pressures to rethink the assignment of taxes, competences and financial transfers. The emerging economic changes suggest the need to re-emphasize individuals as well as localities and local administrative discretion. Only increased responsiveness to people by public administration at all levels can create a sufficiently adaptable system to cope with the changing needs and demands of the future.

Conclusion: towards flexible decentralization and flexible aggregation

The development of the administrative state in Europe has shown a shift from concentrated to more dispersed forms of urban development — from an urban/rural dichotomy, to a form of integrated social development. The divisions between levels of government of competence and financial resources which were appropriate to times of urban concentration based on city regions as service centres to wide functional and rural hinterlands always created a tension between urban and rural as well as between central city and suburbs. In contemporary patterns of settlement development the tensions are in some ways greater, in other areas lesser, but the tensions are now as much the result of economic change as settlement change. Centralized city region administrations have strong characteristics of obsolescence for dispersed settlement patterns, decentralized economic development and modern communication technologies. There is a decreasing need for a 'strategic' view over regional or metropolitan areas. At the same time economic development has changed personal activity spaces, at one scale making them more extensive, but simultaneously reasserting the importance of the local. This is coinciding with the ability to co-ordinate strongly decentralized local delivery systems. As a result the capacity for representation and participation at the most basic (municipality and commune) level is now possible in a way which was previously inconceivable. Clearly co-ordination and association between these basic units will be increasingly necessary, but to avoid tensions between the administrative state and the individual, a reassertion of the basic levels seems essential.

The discussion of the assignment of both competence and financial resources between levels of government has reaffirmed that there are no fundamental theoretical or practical barriers to the decentralization of extensive responsibility to local levels, provided co-ordination and associations between areas are employed, aimed particularly at overcoming equity problems and allowing internalization of externalities. Thus the key conclusion of this discussion is the need to reconsider the questions of decentralization and co-ordination through more flexible methods of administrative practice. Ironically, in this context, those countries which have often been seen as most administratively backward in being tardy to amalgamate their numerous small communes (in areas of former Catholic and Napoleonic orders such as France, Spain and Portugal), which Leemans (1970) referred to as administratively obsolescent, may now be in the best position to respond to these changes. In contrast, those countries which have been most advanced in reforming their administration to large units, particularly those based on city regions, may have the greatest problems of adjustment. Again ironically, these problems may seem particularly to characterize Britain, which has the largest local authorities in Europe but historically was a leading country in developing the traditions of local autonomy. It is also a major problem for the socialist democracies of Europe, particularly the USSR, where mass participation should have assured the strongest accord between preferences and administrative outcomes, but where centralized economic planning and party control has disillusioned the incentives to participation.

Such statements remain at present at the level of speculation, but they do assert the significance of making a full reappraisal of the relations between territory and administration. Such speculations are developed further in the concluding chapter in this book after the detailed evaluation of case studies, and after the following chapter which develops the concepts of management within territorial administration.

References

Bennett, R.J. (1980), *The Geography of Public Finance*, Methuen, London.

Bennett, R.J. (1987), 'Tax assignment in multi-level systems of government', *Government and Policy: Environment and Planning C*, 5, 267–86.

Bird, R.M. and Hartle, D.G. (1972), 'The design of governments', in R.M. Bird and J.G. Head (eds), *Modern Fiscal Issues*, Toronto University Press, Toronto.

Bish, R.L. (1971), *The Public Economy of Metropolitan Areas*, Markham, Chicago.

Breton, A. (1965), 'Theory of government grants', *Canadian Journal of Economics and Political Science*, 31, 177–87.

Breton, A. and Scott, A. (1976), 'The assignment problem in federal structures', in M.S. Feldstein and R.P. Inman (eds), *The Economics of Public Finance*, Macmillan, for Institute for Economic Affairs, London.

Brownlee, O.H. (1961), 'User prices vs taxes', in National Bureau of Economic Research, *Public Finances: Needs, Sources and Utilization*, Princetown University Press, New Jersey.

Buchanan, J.M. (1966), *The Demand and Supply of Public Goods*, Rand McNally, Chicago.

Buchanan, J.M. and Tullock, G. (1969), *The Calculus of Consent*, University of Michigan Press, Ann Arbor.

Coons, J.E., Clune, W.H. and Sugarman, S.D. (1970), *Private Wealth and Public Education*, Belknap and Harvard University Press, Cambridge, Mass.

Dafflon, B. (1977), *Federal Finance in Theory and Practice with Special Reference to Switzerland*, (Schriftenreihe Finanzwirtschaft und Finanzrecht reo 21), Paul Haupt, Berne.

Forte, F. (1977), 'Principles for the assignment of public economic functions in a setting of multi-layer government', in *Report of the Study Group on the Role of Public Finance in European Integration*, Vol.2, EEC, Brussels.

Foster, C.D., Jackman, R. and Perlman, M. (1980), *Local Government Finance in a Unitary State*, Allen and Unwin, London.

Grewal, B.S., Brennan, H.G. and Mathews, R.L. (eds) (1980), *The Economics of Federalism*, Australian National University Press, Canberra.

Grodzins, M. (1966), *The American System*, Rand McNally, New York.

Haller, H. (1965), 'Wandlungen in den problemen foderativer staatswirtschaften', *Finanzarchiv*, 249–70.

Head, J.G. (1973), 'Public goods and multi-level government', in W.L. David (ed.), *Public Finance, Planning and Economic Development: Essays in Honour of Ursula Hicks*, Macmillan, London.

Johnston, R.J. and Taylor, P. (1978), *The Geography of Elections*, Croom Helm, London.

King, D. (1984), *Fiscal Tiers: the Economics of Multi-level Government*, Allen and Unwin, London.

Leemans, A.F. (1970), *Changing Patterns of Local Government*, International Union of Local Authorities, The Hague.

Massam, B. (1975), *Location and Space in Social Administration*, Arnold, London.

Mathews, R.L. (1977), *State and Local Taxation*, ANU Press, Canberra.

McLure, C.E. (1983), *Tax Assignment in Federal Countries*, Centre for Research on Federal Financial Relations, Australian National University, Canberra.

Musgrave, R.A. (1959), *Theory of Public Finance*, McGraw-Hill, New York.

Musgrave, R.A. and Musgrave P.B. (1986), *Public Finance in Theory and Practice*, McGraw-Hill, New York.

Neuberger, E. and Duffy, W.J. (1976), *Comparative Economic Systems: a Decision-making Approach*, Allyn and Bacon, Boston.

Oates, W.A. (1972), *Fiscal Federalism*, Harcourt, Brace Jovanovitch, New York.

Oates, W.E. (ed.) (1977), *The Political Economy of Fiscal Federalism*, D.C. Heath, Lexington, Mass.

Ostrom, V. (1973), *The Intellectual Crisis in American Public Administration*, Alabama University Press, Montgomery.

Pauly, M.V. (1970), 'Optimality, public goods and local governments: a general theoretical analysis', *Journal of Political Economy*, 78, 572–85.

Peacock, A.T. (1972), 'Fiscal means and political ends', in M. Preston and B. Corry (eds), *Essays in Honour of Lionel Robbins*, Weidenfeld and Nicholson, London.

Pigou, A.C. (1928), *Study in Public Finance*, Macmillan, London.

Pommerehne, W.W. (1977), 'Quantitative aspects of federalism: a study of six countries', in W.E. Oates (ed.), *The Political Economy of Fiscal Federalism*, D.C. Heath, Lexington, Mass.

Rothenberg, J. (1970), 'Local decentralization and the theory of optimal government', in J. Margolis (ed.), *The Analysis of Public Output*, Princeton University Press, New Jersey.

Samuelson, P.A. (1954), 'The pure theory of public expenditure', *Review of Economics and Statistics*, 36, 387–9.

Sandford, T. (1967), *Storm Over the States*, McGraw-Hill, Chicago.

Sandler, T. (1975), 'Pareto optimality, pure public goods, impure public goods and multiregional spillovers', *Scottish Journal of Political Economy*, 22, 25–38.

Scott, A.D. (1964), 'The economic goals of federal finance', *Public Finance*, 19, 241–88.

Scott, A.J. (1971), *Combinatorial Programming, Spatial Analysis and Planning*, Methuen, London.

Self, P. (1972), *Administrative Theories and Politics: an Enquiry into the Structures and Processes of Modern Government*, Allen and Unwin, London.

Tiebout, C. (1956), 'A pure theory of local expenditures', *Journal of Political Economy*, 64, 416–24.

Tiebout, C. (1961), 'An economic theory of fiscal decentralization', in NBER, *Public Finance: Needs, Sources and Utilization*, Princeton University Press, New Jersey.

Topham, N. (1983), 'Local government economics', in R. Millward, D. Parker, L. Rosenthal, M.T. Sumner and N. Topham (eds), *Public Sector Economics*, Longman, London.

Tresch, R.W. (1981), *Public Finance: the Normative Theory*, Business Publications, Plano, Texas.

Tullock, G. (1969), 'Federalism: problems of scale', *Public Choice*, 6, 19–29.

Wiseman, J. (1987), 'The political economy of federalism: a critical appraisal', *Government and Policy: Environment and Planning C*, 5, 383–410.

Wright, G. (1974), 'The political economy of New Deal spending: an econometric analysis', *Review of Economics and Statistics*, 56, 30–8.

5 Management by territory and the study of administrative geography
Adriaan Bours

Introduction: territorial management and administrative geography

Territory is an excellent tool of management and reform in the hands of governments. If other means fail, territory as an instrument of change will succeed. However, territorial change often arouses emotional reactions, including armed conflicts between and within countries. The international conflictual tensions and aspects will be excluded here. This chapter is restricted to the field of intra-national territorial structures and processes. The chapter has the aim of developing an administrative geographical theory which can be used both to provide understanding and as a practical tool of management.

Administrative geography follows concepts which date back to the ancient Greek world. In recent years an attempt to develop modern theory has been made by Whitney (1969, Chapters 1 and 7). He defines administrative geography as the study of the ways in which political power is expressed in areal terms. 'Territorial administrative areas from the national down to the local areas are part of the complex ecosystem comprising man, society and environment.' However, spatial policy as the geographical dimension of governmental processes is still underdeveloped. Therefore, in the following paragraphs attention is given to the development of spatial policy science within administrative geography.

Following Easton (1965), Whitney and others have applied systems theory to public organizations and management by categorizing demands and resources as an input to the system which are then converted into public policies within the organization. The outputs of the system then feedback via public and other governmental organizations, inside and outside the boundaries of the system, to influence new demands and resources.

Administrative geography is essential to government. No governmental unit or agent exists without a territory. This quality is basic in public administration, as basic as its powers and finance. Territory, powers and finance are interrelated. By changing the territory, both other factors are influenced as well. Either they are changed politically by receiving more or less power or money, or the new relation leads automatically to relatively better or lower credits. Creating new resources and enlarging old ones is often one of the main aims of territorial reforms in governmental management.

In the following discussion the study of territory and its applications is seen in the context of bridging the gap between territorial and administrative organizations: management for human scale by territorial flexibility. Deriving from this the elements of spatial and administrative organization are explained, with territory as a feature in common. This leads to the definition of the territorial congruency rule. Section two reflects upon the spatial aspects of the administrative and policy sciences, defining the spatial sciences involved and territory as a tool of management in administrative reforms. The main conclusion is that governmental structures should be flexible as to scale and the tensions of scale in policy-making. Solutions may be found in territorial assignments and relevant spaces. It is concluded that management of territory is an instrument of administrative reform, of structure as well as process. Examples are given of applications of these theories to underline the quality of management by territory. Also an 'early warning system' for managers in government is developed.

Administrative geography and public administration

In many countries administration as a science is part of the legal process, or is very closely connected to it. Even in those countries where this is no longer true, law provides an important framework. Nowadays public administration has emerged as a more or less independent scientific methodology. However in The Netherlands, for example, at the majority of the universities, public administration is incorporated in other faculties. In Amsterdam public administration is in the subfaculty of political and social sciences. Only at the universities of Rotterdam and Twente is public administration organized as a multi- or interdisciplinary science of its own. Exceptionally geography takes part in the development of public administration as a science. At the Amsterdam university, geography is one of the sciences involved in the multidisciplinary approach, although the accent is on public policy, management and law. None of these approaches however can reach its ultimate contribution without the input of the territorial dimension. This is true without exception, at all levels — global, continental, national, regional or local — and even between these levels.

In a multidisciplinary approach to public administration it may be the case that geography, or at least the territorial component, is a catalyst or synthesizing agent. Certainly in the scientific approach to administrative reforms this has been the case. For example, at the end of the 1960s, geography took the lead through the work of Hägerstrand. His research allowed him to draw up a new map of municipalities in Sweden; this map was then sealed and kept secret. The geographical criteria for administrative reform were then presented to the government. After their approval by parliament the map which had been prepared was then presented and accepted (Hägerstrand, in conversation with the author in 1973). In a number of other countries (Denmark, Germany, Belgium) new territorial boundaries were first agreed upon, then politically declared and legalized. Later, of course, they had to be brought to life by local policy-makers and politicians, but territorial principles of assignment prevailed.

In The Netherlands a similar development has taken place, but with other components of time and scale. New municipalities for larger parts of the country have not been developed as a whole. Instead reform was undertaken successively region by region, directed by the province involved, the central government and the National Physical Planning Board. However geographical criteria were eventually decisive.

In the 1970s two trends influenced political thinking about territorial reform in The Netherlands: democratization and integration (see Bours and Delmartino, 1983). Not only functional geographical areas were considered, but also demands for increasing the level of participatory policy-making, as well as attempts to restructure public services and their administration and management. The latest developments include financial criteria.

Management by territory

All examples of changing territories and administrative reform are concerned with the manipulation of the scale of the governmental organiza-tion. In society there exists a constant tension between the operation of government and the problems that have to be solved in its environment. This tension occurs within every society and may be defined as a strain between the operational capacity of government and the demands of society and its people.

The scale on which government has to operate is prescribed by the way in which society operates. Although constantly changing, the tensions of scale between the organization and its environment are intrinsic: the incongruency between the scale of societal needs and the scale of govern-ment organization seems to be permanent. Nevertheless the ongoing purpose of governmental management is to maximize the congruity of scale. Theoretically government bridges the gap between the individual and the state. Administration plays the important role of helping to fill the gap between large-scale public policy development in society and the human scale of living. It requires continual adjustment of governmental structures and processes, as society is constantly undergoing renewal and changes in scale.

There are two ways of achieving adaptation: one is to change to new processes and procedures, including centralization or decentralization of powers; the other is to change the whole structure of governmental organization or parts of it, as is the case with amalgamation and other means of territorial reform at the local and intermediate levels. Administrative geography has tended to emphasize structure, but processes and procedures within territory are equally important.

Territorial flexibility as a managerial quality

Governmental structure has the quality of flexibility as to scale. It can combine smaller and larger units or divide large units into smaller ones, whether these are involved in policy-making, decision-making and/or control, as well as execution of policy. This may be top-down, by regulation from higher levels of government, or bottom-up, by the initiative of lower levels.

Territory functions as a symbol of relative independence and autonomy. As Gottman noted: 'Territory is indeed a psychosomatic phenomenon of community' (1973, p. 15). In most countries, the alteration of boundaries is therefore prohibited. Alteration can take place only by law. This means that the concept of territorial integrity, in a spatial sense, is also a cause of inflexibility which is important as territory determines in a large measure the span of governmental processes and procedures of policy-making, decision-making, execution and control. However, at the same time, territorial integrity also provides a quality of flexibility. As government operates on different levels, each level is characterized by its own scale. Government in principle has the ability to handle each problem at an appropriate level. In countries like The Netherlands this ability is strengthened by a Joint Regulations Act, which provides extra facilities for lower governments to co-operate on a public base besides the possibilities of providing services by privatization. Working together functionally means the adaptation of the territory of individual governments to the function(s) concerned. This is a more recent and, especially, more flexible, adaptation to scale compared to amalgamation or restructuring the organization as a whole.

Thus one key feature in administration, which provides the means of adapting government to enlargement of the scale in society, is area or territory. Area is no neutral phenomenon, but is modelled by society, as well as modelling society itself. The spatial organization of society has a great influence on the territorial aspect of governmental organization and administration. Conversely the territorial division of governmental organization and administration has an influence on the spatial organization of society. Therefore, administrative and spatial organizations are to be considered as separate but closely interrelated features.

Spatial and administrative organization

Primitive government

Primitive government is firmly attached to the spatial organization of a tribe and within it to kinship and the family (Mair, 1962).

To ascribe the beginnings of government to force or to contract or to some particular conjuncture is to ignore the fact that already in the family, the primary social unit, there are always present the curbs and controls that constitute the essence of government . . . It is the continuation by the more inclusive society of a process of regulation that is already highly developed within the family . . . The family is the matrix of government. [MacIver, 1965, pp. 17,8]

If we realize that the span of a primitive family was limited, we understand that primitive government had jurisdiction over a limited scope of territory. Thus the 'political' space of control was actually determined by the activities of the family. In this regard, if activities can be viewed as a function of distance, then a clear distinction with respect to transport can be made in the activities of the primitive family. In a primitive society the dwelling was the nucleus of the family and the focus of all basic activities such as shelter, consumption of food, procreation, education and recreation, as well as the centre for all social and cultural life. To a certain extent the span in territorial occupation and control was increased through each activity mentioned. As a result the distance grew between the dwelling and the place of activity in the same order as listed. However these activities were all of a small-scale supportive type.

Quite different was the situation of activities such as hunting and defence. As functions of distance, these were large-scale activities, in accordance with the size of the area under control. In most primitive circumstances, the territory was determined by the one-day limit of a hunter or warrior on foot. As time went on this span of control was extended and was determined by a single day's journey on horseback. Curiously even Napoleon's administrative division of the state was based on the reach of a one-day's trip of the prefect travelling by carriage or coach. And these administrative divisions are still used in France, Belgium and elsewhere.

Many other examples of administrative areas determined by transport can be given. This appears to be a basic phenomenon in government and administration. However, gradually communication has become more a modifying than a dominant effect, resulting in administrative systems with distance as a function related to the span of control of government. Deutsch (1963) describes communication as vital to organization. Not all communications, in the sense of gathering and exchanging information, are linked to transportation bounds. However, transportation remains an essential phenomenon of administrative communication.

The essential categories of administrative systems

Even in our modern communication society we can still define nodal areas based on transportation criteria. This starts with basic activities that can be measured in frequency and span by travel distances. In principal administrative and spatial systems within a state are models of mobility which define the span of activities and policy-making. All basic activities are centred around the living habitat, the span of which is measured by migration and commuting to suburbs and satellite towns. Most of these activities are work-related ('production' in general), thus determining system areas measured by commuting distances from the habitat. However services ('distribution') are also important as measured by the catchment areas of shopping centres. There are also learning ('education') visits, measured by the catchment areas of high schools; relaxation ('recreation') trips, measured by Sunday picnic outings and social contacts, measured by sampling and social distance (Bours, 1976; Tornquist, 1970; Webster and McLoughlin, 1970, p. 389). All these basic activities need transportation; assessed and mapped, traffic patterns perform an excellent overview for determining functional and areal cohesion.

The activities which have been discussed determine patterns in the system of communication networks, which in turn form the spatial context of the social system. The mapping of these data shows the nuclei and the nodal areas of spatial organization. This provides a spatial hierarchy of central towns and regions that may then be compared with the existing hierarchical pattern of administrative organization, with the object of determining the degree of congruity between the two patterns.

On the same basis as the characteristics of the social and spatial system, the essential characteristics of the administrative system of government can also be 'mapped'. The process of communication within this system is the 'fluid' that makes the system work. Even the smallest governmental unit has its goals. The goals of governmental organizations are expressed by tasks to be performed and/or services to be rendered. Each complete unit is equipped to do this with powers, finance and other means, and a territory. All governmental systems are thus equipped. Territory and government cannot be detached, nor can its powers and finance. No governmental unit or agent exists without a territory.

The territorial congruity rule

The main hypothesis in territorial management is that there has to be a congruity between the spatial and the administrative organization which is assured by territory. If the area determined respectively by the spatial and by the administrative organization overlay, congruity is optimal. This might be illustrated by Figure 5.1: the territories of the two pentagons are seen to be the same.

In underdeveloped societies often a high degree of congruity exists between spatial and governmental organizations as long as the society is not disturbed by western ways of living and/or western models of governmental organization. However, even in developed areas, such as Europe, if disturbances to the territory through reforms have not ruined the traditional patterns, the relationship between spatial and administrative organization may reveal a high degree of congruity. The basic activities of work, services, learning, relaxing and social communication are still, for the most part, relatively short-distance activities, although the span has extended. For governmental purposes one of the main features that counts is the distance of people from the administrative offices.

However, it is a well-known fact that incongruities between the spatial

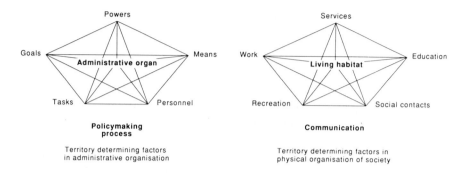

Figure 5.1 The 'pentagons' of the socio-spatial and the administrative systems in society. The left-hand diagram shows the factors which determine the space spanned by the administrative system. The right-hand diagram shows the social and spatial organization of society. In an optimal situation, from a managerial point of view, these two have to overlay in the same territory.

and administrative organization are emerging at lower and even at higher national levels. The main reason for this is the development of modern transport, but there are also new techniques of governmental management which play a role. For example, urban planning, even at the local level, may be wider in interest and span than the local community. Under these circumstances the planning tasks might be taken over by an administrative organization with a larger area under its jurisdiction, in an effort to maximize the effectiveness and co-ordination of proposed policies.

Spatial aspects of administrative and policy sciences

Public administration — spatial aspects

Public administration as a science is focused upon governmental functions, structures and processes. The tension of scale is one of its key problems, especially if the bridge-functions of government between large-scale and small-scale features in society are considered to be dominant. Figure 5.2 shows the tensions of scale in government for functions, structures and decision-making. The spatial dimensions of governmental organization and administration are the object of administrative geography as indicated in the figure. As outlined before, the present discussion is restricted to the internal organization of the state.

The spatial dimension of governmental policy-making is studied by what may be called geographical or spatial policy science. One of the main concerns of spatial policy science is how, in governmental policy-making, the gap between large-scale and small-scale developments can be bridged by determination of the areal span of a policy and by adjusting decision-making processes and procedures to an appropriate social and spatial level.

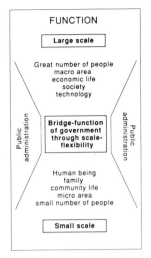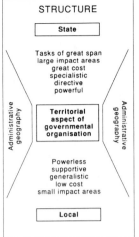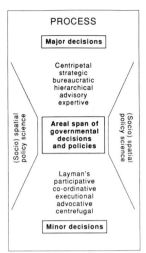

Figure 5.2 Tensions of scale in government. This figure is an illustration of the tension between large-scale and small-scale solutions in society and the bridge-function of government. The left figure expresses the tension between small scale and large scale, bridged by the functional scale, it demonstrates flexibility of the government. Such an approach is mainly studied by public administration as a science, in connection with administrative geography. The middle figure shows the tension bridged by territorial management of governmental units of various levels, and is especially studied by administrative geographers. The third figure concerns processes of policy-making in a similar field, where there are tensions between decisions of major and minor scale. This field is studied by (socio) spatial policy science, a special branch of administrative geography.

This is shown in the figure by the attempt to bring function, structure and process together at the different scales.

Geographers can contribute to analysis of governmental policies and to policy-making in various ways. They may be concerned with the impact of policies and policy-making in four dimensions:

(i) the impact on the landscape;
(ii) the impact on the spatial organization of society;
(iii) the reverse: the impact of landscape and spatial organization on policies; and
(iv) the impact on policy-making by the government.

An analysis of geographical impacts in connection with (i) concerns the spatial implications of the content of a given policy; that is to say, it studies the impact and implications of a policy on the physical and cultural landscape. It deals with artefacts and their location, as for example in physical planning. In connection with (ii) impact analysis focuses on the possible implications of a given policy for the spatial organization of a society. Thus the object of geographical impact analyses is either the land-scape or the organization of society within a given area.

The geography of policy and policy-making also explain the influence of, and the limits set by, geographical factors on governmental policies and processes of policy-making. These impact analyses deal with geographical factors influencing the content of a policy, case (iii). It is in this sense that the geography of policy and policy-making becomes a (spatial) policy science. For example: in mountainous areas government housing policy is influenced by the distribution of valleys and plains, habitation and accessibility. In other words the spatial structure of the physical world and of society determines to a great extent the content of a policy. Moreover, to a considerable extent, spatial structure also influences the systems of governmental policy-making. This is case (iv) in which geographical or spatial impact analyses are directed to the explanation of the geographical dimensions of policy-making, that is they attempt to explain policy-making from geographical factors. An example may be found in mountainous areas where, for instance, voting districts are determined by the spread of valleys and plains (physical factors) and habitation and roads (human factors). Cases (iii) and (iv) are examples of social and spatial dimensions of policy sciences, as described by Dror (1971).

Administrative geography and spatial policy science

In summary, geographical and spatial policy science may be referred to as the study of policy and policy-making in mutual relationship with spatial organization (spatial patterns and processes). Administrative geography refers to the geographical dimensions of the governmental and administrative system, within which policies are produced in the policy-making process. These dimensions can be analysed in two different ways: first, in terms of the impact of administrative structures and processes on spatial structures and systems; second, in terms of the impact of spatial organization on administrative structures and processes. Both approaches are aspects of administrative geography, which can be defined as the study of administrative organization in mutual relationship with spatial organization. Administrative geography also includes the study of policies and policy-making in mutual relationship with spatial organizations, their structure, functions and processes.

Thus defined broadly, administrative geography includes the study of the machinery of government and its operation from a spatial point of view. As such it may be viewed as a useful and important adjunct to the policy sciences, especially as the latter are organized to focus on administrative change and reform in a turbulent environment.

Territorial management principles and administrative reforms

Tensions of scale

Administrative reforms are necessary from a territorial point of view to bridge the gap between spatial and administrative organization; to restore congruency. Christaller (1966) developed theories on the hierarchy of central places, emerging from marketing, transport and other functions. Among these according to Morrill (1970), Abler, *et al.*, (1971) and others, general governmental functions demand a nodal region.

More specific functions demand specially adjusted areas, which in many cases are and have to be zonal. Examples are industrial zones, harbour areas, etc., where specific agencies operate which require the co-operation of local and other governments. Especially in metropolitan or urbanized areas these zonal functional districts are developing and are necessary because of the enlargement of the scale of society. To this category also belongs the determination of catchment, or service, areas of governmental functions. By defining desired functional areas the operation of government services can be organized more efficiently and more effectively. Thus indications of more functional boundaries of governmental units can be obtained and used in territorial reform (compare Paddison (1983) who introduces the notion of administrative regionalization).

However, the operation of the entire government and its administration is bounded by the territorial limits of the unit(s) involved. Enlargement of the scale of modern societies cannot be responded to by governments sufficiently and quickly enough. Hence the scale enlargement of society is a cause of constant tension between the operation of government and the problems governments have to solve, the tasks they have to perform and the services that have to be rendered to the public (Bours, 1976). Scale enlargement in society, especially caused by increased vehicle ownership and other technical developments in communications, hampers an optimal functioning of administration as long as the territories are not adjusted.

Territorial assignment and scale

Administration territory acts as an active force, functioning both as challenge and restraint. In a recent publication, Bours and van den Brink (1987) argue that new territories of multi-functional local governments in urban areas should be adjusted to the demands of local functional responsibility, especially physical planning tasks. This would lead to a spectacular shrinking of the number of municipalities, since in most cases planning requires larger areas which cross existing borders. It is argued therefore that not only scale enlargement is required, but also an accompanying scale reduction. This should be brought about by creating sub-units or metropolitan districts (area-government) within the urban municipalities, in order to meet the demands of public services which need face-to-face contacts and to support the accessibility and openness of government.

Territory and government have already been said to be inseparable. Both present demands of their own. The aim of administrative reforms is to bring these together. Although the necessary policy-making and decision-taking are, or at least should be, politically controlled, from a scientific point of view we know that there is an interdependence of public administration and social geography. Scale as a basic principle connects both. Scale is the key-word in reforms.

The relevance of scale in administrative geography and for administrative reforms may be defined as 'the size an administrative unit should take to accomplish its tasks in an effective, efficient and democratic way' (Verhoef, 1976). Size can be expressed as inhabitants and/or as surface area (square metres). Boundaries determine the number of inhabitants, the area and define the site. 'Bounded space' is a well-known concept in geography (Cox, 1972). Each municipality or any administrative district represents a bounded space, in a specific location and with unique qualities of its own. In geography as well as in public administration the number of inhabitants is a particularly important concept. In social geography it represents the human factor, the potential which rests with the people in that area. In an historical perspective, socio-economic development can be judged by the number of inhabitants in the past. The future is also often expressed in a series of pre-calculated population forecasts which reflect the potential and capacity of the area.

In administrative geography and public administration some things are alike. The quality of the administration bears the marks of the qualities of the people, in the past and in the future. In geography the number of inhabitants represents power, in this case administrative or bureaucratic power, but also governmental ability. Wagener (1969) developed a division of public tasks based on the idea of 'supporting regions', the minimum support needed expressed by numbers of inhabitants. In The Netherlands similar research applying Wagener's ideas has been developed by Brasz *et al.*, (1972). In The Netherlands, as in many other countries, population figures are a decisive factor in the flow of finance to local and regional governments and to their administrations. Even the salaries of the burgomasters depend on the number of inhabitants, as do the salaries of the officials and clerks in the civil service. Therefore administrative reforms often prescribe a minimum number of inhabitants for new units which is deemed to be a limit of viability.

In this discussion we must keep in mind the differences between scale and measure (Bours and van den Brink, 1987). The *measure* of an administrative unit expresses the quantity and quality of the equipment, which is determined by the number of inhabitants. It has to be sufficient to make an effective, efficient and democratic government possible. Not only the number of administrators but also the degree of specialization and even the number of representatives in the councils depends on the size of population. *Scale* is related to its size, expressed in population and territory. A unit should exercise its duties in an efficient, effective and democratic way. If it is too small in scale it has to be enlarged to make possible government which is sufficiently well equipped. A unit also should not be too big or it will have to be scaled down. It would be a misunderstanding to accept the idea that the 'bigger the better', from a bureaucratic point of view. In administration, smaller units often operate more efficiently and effectively. The concept of 'small is beautiful' is often put forward from a democratic point of view, although it does not always guarantee more democracy. The preferable solutions are those that bring congruity between spatial and administrative organization by a territorial synthesis. Administratively relevant space is a concept that can be used to achieve such a synthesis.

Administratively relevant space

Returning to our definition of scale as 'the size an administrative unit should take to accomplish its tasks in an effective, efficient and democratic way' we can interpret this definition normatively. It refers to the findings of Leemans, who stated that a governmental task should be performed at the lowest possible level (Leemans, 1969–70), the lowest level being defined by the span of the policy-problem to be solved, the task to be performed or the service to be rendered by the governmental unit involved.

The span of the governmental problem, task or service can be estimated by the 'impact area'. This is defined as the area where the living or working population are affected by the problem. Leemans called this the 'relevant space of the object of decision-making' (see also Delmartino, 1985). So this 'administratively relevant space for policy-making' should determine, or preferably not exceed the 'administratively relevant areas'. An example of such an administratively relevant area can be found in the impact or catchment area of air pollution. Polluted air spreads over much larger areas than the territories of municipalities, provinces or other local governments where the problems are caused. Hence in many cases governments at the larger regional, national or international level have to be involved. Geographers such as Massam (1975) and others have already provided studies of the impact or catchment areas of governmental services (for example fire protection, ambulances, hospitals etc).

According to the definition employed, the scale problem meets the democratic criterion: the population within the administratively relevant area should influence the decision-making; and this also meets the criterion for effectiveness and efficiency. Geographers have an important task in defining these administratively relevant impact or catchment areas and in searching for adequate administrative territories. Some applications of this concept are developed below.

An application of administratively relevant space to city government reform: Amsterdam

Scale is decisive in administrative reform. Most spectacular are applications at the local and regional levels, especially in urban areas with respect

to amalgamation of municipalities, the co-operation between local governments and the installation of sub-local authorities. An example of these
concepts is described below for Amsterdam.

In 1982 the City Council of Amsterdam passed a by-law on sub-local or
area government. Sub-units in metropolitan areas are not only required
because of necessary adjustments to the scale to achieve a better functioning of democratic policy-making. A more optimal functioning of the civil
service also requires scale reduction, as the Amsterdam experiment shows.
In this case, it was argued that the number of civil servants (32,000)
became too large for an effective and efficient functioning, and the
organization too complex to be kept under (political) control. Unlike most
other cities in the western world the Council of Amsterdam decentralized
not only advisory powers, but also effective policy-making and executive
powers, including financial resources and parts of the civil service. District
councils, directly elected by the people, are in political control although
their formal status is only a 'territorial committee of the city council'.
These district councils also choose Executive Boards of their own.

The experiment with area government in Amsterdam originated from
the intention of combining administrative enlargement of scale with reduction of scale. Scale enlargement was designed to meet the 'big-city
problems'. Although these problems originate in the city itself, quite a
number influence the conditions of surrounding municipalities, for instance
housing, (un)employment, drugs and crime. Planning problems are also
related to scale: for example public transport, industrial development, land
use and landholding. For these the central city needs the co-operation of
surrounding municipalities, unless it can control them by getting the 'in
control status' of a higher government level, in this case provincial powers.
Amsterdam failed in this intention.

Scale reduction, by creating sub-local districts of general government,
however, is now well on its way (Leemans et al., 1986). The aim is to adjust
the scale of local government to the smaller scale developments in society.
The span of the majority of the policy problems with which a local council
has to deal may be mentioned as a cause for the success so far. Some
empirical research for the Amsterdam Executive and Executive Boards in
the two experimental area governments brought to light the feature that the
great majority of problems concern very small scales, much smaller than
their territories. On only a few occasions did they involve problems of
policy-making which reached across the boundaries of the territories.

The findings of this research regarding the 'relevant space of the object
of decision-making' support scale reduction, but they do not take away the
necessity of scale enlargement to handle big city problems. Three conclusions can be drawn from this case:

(a) for big cities the span of control is underlain by the key aspect of
     scale in administrative reforms;
(b) the reform of local government in metropolitan areas demands scale
     enlargement and scale reduction at the same time;
(c) the best point of action in reforms is territorial.

Making use of scale comparisons by measuring administrative geographical distances

As mentioned earlier, there is a correlation between the number of inhabitants and the number of officials in most administrative areas. This means that in big cities their number can become very large. Especially where there are two governments in a metropolitan area at different levels, in a close hierarchical relationship to each other, which do not significantly differ in number of inhabitants, it is very likely that the relationship will be difficult and will cause malfunction of essential co-ordination, in public policy-making and in administration. The scale differences in this case are too small.

We may approach this problem by using the quotient of the number of inhabitants to measure the 'administrative geographical distance' between two units of government at different or equal levels. This is *ipso facto* a means for comparing scales. If the quotient approaches 1 then the distance has a 'critical' level. Empirical facts and theoretical considerations indicate that the factor should be 3 or more. An upper limit is hard to determine. Paddison (1983, p. 243) mentions between 20 and 25.

The comparison of population figures is a measure of 'administrative geographical distance', defined as the 'quotient of the population figures of the largest coinciding units in an administrative and territorial hierarchy' (see Bours, 1983). The measurement is explained in Figure 5.3 below.

An 'early warning system'

An illustration is developed here of the different 'administrative geographical distances' of several European and North American cities. Tables 5.1 and 5.2 show the quotients of geographical distances between existing or planned governments or administrations at different levels: (a) between the metropolitan (regional) and the urban (local) levels (Table 5.1), and (b) between the urban (local) and area government (sub-city) levels (Table 5.2).

Table 5.1 shows critical values for the metropolitan governments of Madrid and Barcelona which confirm experiences of local politicians and manager. In the case of Rijnmond (Greater Rotterdam, The Netherlands) the metropolitan government has been abolished. The resulting Greater Amsterdam administration (the Informal Agglomeration Consult) is more a debating club since the co-operation of municipalities is voluntary and without any decisive powers. Its quotient value is 1.6.

The cases of sub-city or area government, Table 5.2, are more favourable. Scale comparison does not show critical cases. Noteworthy in Germany are Dortmund, where the largest and smallest districts are compatible in scale (mean 50,000), and Bremen, where the largest district is ten times the size of the smallest (mean 31,000). In the case of Dortmund the districting is artificial, the scale is planned to be more or less the same for all units, in order to give a balance of equity and power. In Bremen, however, former municipalities of different sizes became sub-city

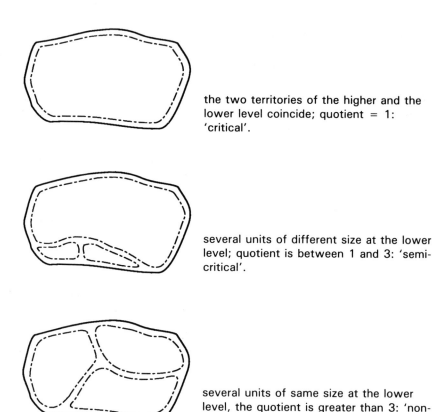

the two territories of the higher and the lower level coincide; quotient = 1: 'critical'.

several units of different size at the lower level; quotient is between 1 and 3: 'semi-critical'.

several units of same size at the lower level, the quotient is greater than 3: 'non-critical'.

Figure 5.3

An illustration of the first condition where the administrative geographical distance quotient equals 1 means that great difficulties can be expected in the co-ordination of administration in the same area. Competition on the basis of differences in governmental and political powers is not corrected by different territories. A second illustration, where the quotient is between 1 and 3, means a non-optimal condition for administrative co-ordination because of insufficient administrative geographical distance. A third illustration, where the quotient is 3 or more, yields territories at the lower level of compatible size. This is an optimal condition for co-ordination between units at the same and different levels.

Table 5.1 Administrative geographical distance between metropolitan government and its sub-divisions

Metropolitan area	Population ×1,000	Local authorities	Average population of local authority ×1,000	Population of largest local authority ×1,000	Population of smallest local authority ×1,000	Population divided by population of largest local authority ratio
Spain						
Metropolitan Barcelona	3,100	23	135	1,800	3	1.7
Metropolitan Madrid	4,000	23	175	3,400	5	1.2
England						
Greater London	7,800	32	244	329	145	23.7
West Yorkshire (Leeds c.a.)	2,022	5	404	697	190	2.9
Denmark						
Røbenhavns Amtskommune	1,197	20	60	488	9	2.5
USA						
Metropolitan New York	7,900	5	1,600	2,700	300	3.0
Metropolitan Minneapolis/St. Paul	2,000	7	286	960	35	2.1
Netherlands						
Rijnmond (Greater Rotterdam)	1,050	16	66	568	3	1.8
Greater Amsterdam (1)	1,190	23	52	718	0.3	1.6
Amsterdam divided into 16 subunits	1,190	38	31	128	0.3	9.3

(1) Informal Agglomeration Consult

Table 5.2 Administrative geographical distance between metropolitan city and sub-city governments

Municipality	Population ×1,000	Number of sub-city councils	Average population of sub-cities ×1,000	Population of largest unit ×1,000	Population of smallest unit ×1,000	Population divided by population of largest sub-city
Spain						
Madrid	3,400	18	189	311	115	10.9
Barcelona	1,800	12	150	300	60	6.0
Germany						
Bremen	590	19	31	49	5	12.0
Dortmund	605	12	50	57	36	10.6
Italy						
Florence	465	14	33	50	26	9.3
Pavia	88	9	10	23	3	3.8
USA						
Boston	638	17	38	80	4	8.0
Dayton	205	7	29	79	1	2.9
England						
Stockport	293	8	37	49	24	6.0
Poland						
Krakow	716	4	179	215	163	3.3
Yugoslavia						
Ljubljana	303	5	61	82	32	3.7
Kraljevo	789	15	53	133	13	5.9
Beograd	1,455	16	91	172	19	8.5
Netherlands						
Rotterdam	576	17	34	79	8	7.3
Amsterdam	718	16	45	87	22	8.3

districts. From this example it is clear that 'administrative geographical distance quotient' is also useful for 'horizontal' comparisons between units of one administrative unit.

From these examples of population figures an administrative geographical distances it is possible to develop an 'early warning system' for administrative reforms. If the planned reforms give quotients for comparisons between different administrative levels which are critical or semi-critical values, it may be preferable to seek alternative reform plans and design other territorial structures.

Summary and conclusions

Territory is an excellent tool of management which allows the adjustment of the scale of governmental organization to criteria of democracy, efficiency and effectiveness. Optimal conditions are fulfilled if the congruity rule is applied. This rule states that congruity between the spatial and the administrative organization is optimal if they overlay an area which is identical and which is determined by the essential characteristics of both administration and spatial functions. This rule is derived from the notion of the administratively relevant space: the span of the object of decision-making and the territory of the government taking the decision should coincide.

In reality the optimal conditions of the model are seldom fulfilled. Tensions of scale are widespread and governments are concerned to manage territories by scale adjustments. Administrative geographical distance may function as an early warning system as to whether present structures or proposed reforms contain irreconcilable tensions.

References

Abler, R., Adams, J.S. and Gould, P. (1971), *Spatial Organization*, Prentice-Hall, Englewood Cliffs, NJ.

Bours, A. (1974), 'Sociale geografie, stadsgewestvorming en gemeentelijke indeling' (Social geography, urban regionalization and local government reform), in A. Bours and J.G. Lambooy, *Stad en Stadsgewest in de Ruimtelijke Orde* (City and City Region in their Spatial Context), City Planning Department, Assen.

Bours, A. (1976), 'Towards a geography of public administration and policy-making', *International Geography*, 6, Moscow, 88–93 (also in Russian).

Bours, A. (1983), 'The ratio of territorial subdivisions for metropolitan government', in A.F. Leemans *Metropolitan Area Government and Decentralization of Large Cities: a Political and Administrative Approach*, Department of Public Administration, University of Amsterdam (IIAS Conference Paper, Berlin), pp. 26–36.

Bours, A. and Delmartino, F. (1983), 'Bestuurlijke reorganisatie in Belgie en Nederland, een vergelijking en evaluatie (Administrative reform in Belgium and The Netherlands)', in *Handboek Beleidsvoering voor de Overheid* (Handbook for Governmental Policy-making), Martinus Nijhoff, Alphen aan den Rijn.

Bours, A. and Brink, H. van den (1987), 'Schaal en taakverdeling, problemen van maat en schaal' (Problems of powers and tasks, measure and scale), in *De Grote Stad (de)Centraal* (The Big City, Centralized or Decentralized?), Department of Public Administration, University of Amsterdam.

Brasz, H.A. (1972), *Bestuursonderzoek Oost Nederland* (Search for Regional Government in Eastern Netherlands), Enschede.

Christaller, W. (1966), *Central Places in Southern Germany*, Prentice-Hall, Englewood Cliffs, NJ.

Cox, K.R. (1972), 'Bounded spaces', in K.R. Cox *Man, Location and Behaviour*, Maaroufa Press, New York.

Delmartino, F. (1985), 'The concept of relevant space for decision-making, as test and guide for territorial reforms', in L. Klinkers (ed.), *Life in Public Administration, who administers / how, where and with what does one Administer / how does one learn to administer?*, Free University, Amsterdam.

Deutsch, K.W. (1963), *The Nerves of Government: Models of Political Communication and Control*, John Wiley, New York.

Dror, Y. (1971), *Design for Policy Sciences*, Elsevier, New York.

Easton, D. (1965), *A Systems Analysis of Political Life*, John Wiley, New York.

Gottman, J. (1973), *The Significance of Territory*, University of Virginia, Charlottesville.

Leemans, A.F. (1969–70), 'The spatial hierarchy of decision-making', *Development and Change*, 1, 14–29.

Leemans, A.F. (1986), *Deelraden Nader Bekeken: Eindrapport* (Evaluation Research of Experimental Area government in Amsterdam, final report), Department of Public Administration, University of Amsterdam.

MacIver, R.M. (1965), *The Web of Government*, John Wiley, New York.

Mair, L. (1962), *Primitive Government*, Penguin, Harmondsworth.

Massam, B. (1975), *Location and Space in Social Administration*, Methuen, London.

Morrill, R.L. (1970), *The Spatial Organization of Society*, Prentice-Hall, Englewood Cliffs, NJ.

Paddison, R. (1983), *The Fragmented State, the Political Geography of Power*, Basil Blackwell, Oxford.

Tornquist, G. (1970), *Contact Systems and Regional Development*, Lund Studies in Geography, B., No. 35, University of Lund.

Verhoef, R. (1976), *Syllabus Openbaar Bestuur, thema I Decentralisatie* (Syllabus Decentralization), Department of Public Administration, University of Amsterdam.

Wagener, F. (1969), *Neubau der Verwaltung, Gliederung der Offentlichen Verwaltung und Ihrer Träger nach Effektivitat und Integrationswert* (Renewal of Government), Schriftenreihe der Hochschule Speyer, Bd. 41, Berlin.

Webster, J.N. and McLoughlin, B. (1970), 'Cybernetic and general systems approaches to urban and regional research', *Environment and Planning*, 2, 369–408.

Whitney, J.B.R. (1969), *China: Area, Administration and Nation Building*, Rand McNally, Chicago.

Part 3 Present and futures: case studies of socialist democracies

6 An overview of East European developments

Éva Perger

In each East European Socialist country a range of similar problems and phenomena have emerged since the 1960s, and have continued in the 1970s and 1980s. These developments evidence aspects of an economic and administrative crisis. Often these developments have necessarily been accompanied by regional tensions and have gradually made us aware that, despite significant differences between countries, the contradictions hidden in the common system come from the same source. It is also clear that such crisis-phenomena follow from the nature of the model of organizing society, and that the more extreme 'crisis' reactions are merely the consequences of the way that problems are handled. Explanations based on traditional 'Marxist' ideology are inadequate to disclose the deeply hidden interrelations of mechanisms which, in many cases, function contrary to declared targets.

Hungarian scientists have achieved remarkable results in uncovering the nature of these interrelationships. Particularly important is the work of the internationally acknowledged Hungarian economists (above all Kornai, 1980, 1983; Bauer, 1975, 1982; Soós, 1986; and Antal, 1980) who explain the background of investment cycles experienced in the socialist countries by such new concepts as, for example, the 'flexible budget limit', 'campaign', etc. But also important is the work of a group of Hungarian lawyers, political scientists and sociologists who have revealed, among other things, the phenomena of simultaneous over- and under-regulation, 'organized irresponsibility', informal efforts for centralization and informal ways of gaining advantages (particularly note among others, Bihari, 1982, 1984; Berényi, 1978a, 1978b; Hegedüs and Rozgonyi, 1969; Laky, 1980; Lengyel, 1987; and Sárközy, 1986). Economists have dealt less with regional processes, while political scientists and sociologists have more frequently referred to the regional aspects of power and of interest-relations (see for example Szegö, 1974, 1976, 1977; Wiener, 1987 and Szoboszlay, 1980a, 1980b, 1985). Geography has also provided important insights by revealing the problems of backward regions as well as the consequences for regional and settlement development (see for example Enyedi, 1979, 1983, 1986; Barta, 1987 and Vági, 1982, 1987). There is, however, the need for a line of comprehensive research which, by combining the results of each discipline, could summarize the regional aspects. This task should be solved by social geography. This would be a major advance compared to that line of approach in socialist geography which endeavours to comply with the requirements of centralized management based on the traditional notion of the planned economy, for example by studying the factors of locating industry in specified regions. In this chapter I cannot deal with the whole of this task of integration in a comprehensive way. However, relying primarily on the Hungarian scientific literature, I shall endeavour to raise some general suggestions concerning the relation between reforms of economic planning and public administration, and reforms of regional development policy and the possibilities and roles of regional and local organizations in the socialist system. The cases of Hungary, Romania and Yugoslavia will be used primarily, but generalizations for the whole of eastern Europe will be drawn as far as possible.

Economy — public administration — regional development

The interdependence of the economy and public administration in socialist states is well reflected in the fact that important socialist theories exist which have considered, and still consider, that companies are part of the public administration system (see Lörincz, 1981). This is based on the concept of the sphere of proprietory role. However amazing it may be for a western research worker today, this concept still exists in the practice of some socialist countries (particularly Romania, Bulgaria and Czechoslovakia). In these countries the traditional concept of the planned economy has survived in which, in the spirit of legal decentralization, part of the administrative control of plan implementation has been transferred to big economic organizations (such as trusts, unions, etc.). This concept also survives in a less obvious way in those countries, such as Hungary and Poland, where the so-called 'controlled market economy' has been the chosen development route.

In the latter countries the first steps have been taken to separate the administration of the state and the economy, and this is the process which has become generally known as the 'economic reform'. The essence of this is, first, the deliberate limitation of centralized state economic management; second, the recognition of the independence of economic organizations; and third, the acceptance of the existence of the market (that is of a 'self-moving' economic sphere). In such a system the relevant state executive agencies which we consider are threefold: central agents, local officers of central agents of economic management, and regional agents. These three agents are the basic concepts of public administration. They are concerned with the regulation and control of the 'self-moving' economy and the 'self-moving' actions of the citizens.

In the literature on this subject it is a recurring theme that changes in the economy and in society induce changes in the system of public administration. Though this interpretation is in general correct, it does not provide sufficient understanding for a complete interpretation because the system of public administration is a sub-system of the political system. As such, public administration cannot be understood unless analysed in the context of the entire political system. While the Marxist thesis, which states that the economic base determines the superstructure (including both the political system and public administration), is correct in the long run, in the short run this relation is the other way round. Thus there is a reversal of dependent and independent variables. The Polish sociologist Jerzy Wiatr (1980, p. 196) states that 'politics in socialist society to some extent plays the same role as does the capitalist market in classical capitalism: it provides the terrain of social integration which dominates the nature and progress of the course of events, including other "non-political" fields of social life.' Or, in the terminology of Károly Polányi (1976, p. 294): 'In the redistributive economic system the economy is institutionalized not in an isolated way but embedded in the political administrative conditions, which results from the fact that the fundamental economic decisions are made by political administrative institutions.' In this approach the relation between public administration and the economy is mainly dominated by the development of the relation between the economy and politics. Hence the progress of substantial reforms of the economy, and at the same time of public administration, can be measured by the extent to which politics 'withdraws' from the economy, and the extent to which the influence on economic management of public administrative organization is diminished.

The other substance of the reform of public administration takes place within the system of political relations, but it also has important influences on economic management. Political democratization increases the influence of representative agencies on the political system, therefore public administration will also become more subordinated to the representative agencies. The other changes taking place within the public administration system, such as changes in the regional distribution of public administration, modification of the structure of the organizations, staff and public administration technology, are purely formal, however important they may be in themselves and in their effect on the development of the processes described above.

The extent of centralization of politics and the relation between economy and politics are of course reflected in regional developments. The various groups of society, whose relative power positions determine the above relations, are connected to certain regions and settlements. Hence the ranges of interests always have a 'regional character'. However, in a highly centralized political system, central power takes into consideration the interests of the 'periphery' only to the extent that is absolutely necessary for it to maintain its power. A lesser degree of centralization requires a wider group of interests to be taken into account. This makes possible a higher degree of representation of regional interests and also allows a greater opportunity for regional differentiation of administrative policy.

The process of economic reform, administrative reform and regional development

Before starting to analyse the reform process in eastern Europe, it is first necessary to give a brief overall picture of the main features of the traditional system of politics, public administration and economic management which is undergoing change, and their influence on regional development. Major aspects of this traditional system still have important influences today.

In the stage of development characterized by the traditional centralized planned economy, management was hierarchical and based upon two principles of organization: namely sectoral and regional principles. During earlier periods more stress was laid on sectoral management since the aims of economic policy were dominated by rapid industrialization which could be achieved only in a centralized manner. From the regional point of view, the main task of the organ of regional public administration was to implement the aims of the highly centralized political power. A chief regional administrative level is the county. Councils of the counties were in this period directly subject to the sectoral ministries. Most industrial enterprises were also directly subject to the sectoral ministries. Agriculture was also subject to sectoral ministries but used the lower administrative level of the districts to a greater extent. This strongly hierarchical organization ensured the redistribution of incomes in favour of large-scale industry. Politics entirely dominated the economy, which was also supported by frequent and direct intervention by the party.

The regional question was also treated unilaterally by both economic political practice and the scientific literature. The role of geography was principally to serve planning, that is to help to plan the location of large economic projects. The policy of rapid industrialization ignored wider social issues, as well as structural and regional distortions to the economy. The results of this period are well known from a geographical point of view: centralized political will, without any control by society, 'systematically' produced over-industrialization of cities and some other areas, while leaving other parts of the economy under-developed. It also produced single-function big 'socialist' villages and towns, in which the single industrial plant fundamentally predetermined the development of the settlement in question and the life of its citizens. This laid the foundations for under-development of infrastructure and encouraged either excessive commuting or extensive migration.

The geographical irrationality of the system manifested itself at two levels: from the economic point of view the transport distances were irrational and there was a complete lack of co-operation between the plants operating in the same area. From the political point of view there remained considerable differences in living standards between the various territories.

Practically all of the eastern European socialist countries have started to 'reform' this system, although at different times and to different extents. In the following I shall draw chiefly from the Hungarian example which is best known to me. But I shall also introduce the two extreme cases of

Romania, where reforms of the political, economic and public administrative systems have so far been rather limited, and Yugoslavia, where the reforms have been most advanced.

The Hungarian case

In Hungary the possibility of an economic reform was raised as early as 1957 (see for example Sárközi, 1986; Gálik, 1987), but until the mid-1960s reforms were characterized rather by the improvement of planning, and the attempts by the central administration to eliminate the regional disparities. Hence, 'owing to exaggerated centralization, local conditions cannot be efficiently taken into account for the purpose of disaggregating improvement programmes to regions' (Bartke, 1979, p. 416). The so-called Council Act II, enacted in 1954, concerning the public administrative system, proved to be purely a political declaration which promised a wider range of authority for representative organization; but it failed to be implemented (Bihari, 1984). Hence until 1965 only internal structural changes took place within the administrative system.

From the mid-1960s a preparatory process was begun which paved the way for an economic reform. A key aspect was the abolition, in 1965, of the direct subjection of local administration to the sectoral ministries. This was followed by an elaboration of the main principles of regional development, regional planning and settlement policy. In this way regional policy was given the rank of a central policy. However, 'phantom' elements of the traditional redistributive economic planning began to show up, particularly in the methods of regional planning and settlement policy (for example, in the classification of settlements). After a little delay, the Council Act III of 1971 laid the foundations for reform of the regional public administration system. The main point of this can be summarized as follows (Bihari, 1984, p. 70): 'the activities of the local councils (districts) include both state-governed and self-governing elements, while the councils of the counties and their organs perform primarily governmental tasks'.

The most significant change for the relation between the economy and public administration was of course the declaration of the independent existence of the economy. This introduced the principle of the 'self-reliance' of enterprises. The relation between the state administration and the enterprises will be changed to a major extent as this principle is implemented. Within the central administration the direct disaggregation of the aims of economic plans from centre to region is replaced by normative regulation, the sphere of activity of the functional ministries is widened, that of the sectoral ministries is modified. The county councils lose their right to intervene directly in the activities of the enterprises in their areas and are limited to tasks of inspection, organization and information work, as well as participation in the infrastructure development of their region.

It is my hypothesis that the relation between the reform of public administration and the economic reform in Hungary is characterized by a special form of independence. On the one hand, the reforms of public administration were delayed until after the reform of the economy, and on the other hand, the unfolding of the two reform processes and their slowing down were closely in parallel.

With the measures introduced in 1968 the economic reform process was started. This began to weaken in the early 1970s as a result of an 'informal counter attack' noted by a number of commentators (see for example the economic analyses of Antal, 1980; Bauer, 1975; Kornai, 1980; Nagy, 1978; Sipos and Tardos, 1986; and the sociological research of Hegedüs and Rozgonyi, 1969; Laky, 1980; Gombár and Lengyel, 1986; Csepeli, 1987). The economic reform measures were not followed by a full-scale public administrative reform. The agencies of central economic management hardly changed at all, nor did the structure of regional public administration. Although the sphere of activity and jurisdiction of the regional agencies was modified, this took place in 1971 which was too late to counteract the tendencies for recentralization which had by then begun. The authors of the 'reform literature' agree that the main reason for the recoiling from economic reform was that it was not combined with an institutional reform either in the economic or in the administrative spheres. Research in both spheres reveals attempts to 'recentralize' decisions, 'expectations' and preliminary approvals (for example Laky, 1980; Sárközy, 1986, Verebélyi, 1987), and informal assertion of self interests (for example Bihari, 1979; Bogár, 1983; Berényi, 1978a). Apparently the key reason behind the whole process was that the economic reform was not supported by a political reform. Highly centralized political power was not replaced by a more democratic distribution of power. This avoided the risk of open confrontation among the various groups of society. The concept of the 'all-knowing' paternalist state survived, but instead of overt instructions it was asserted through more complex informal channels which made use, among other things, of the same traditional structure of administration.

Among the aims of the reform, the main effect realized was perhaps the 'separation' of the agencies of regional administration and the economic sphere. Although the development decisions of the regions were taken over in part by the enterprises, nothing was fundamentally changed because the development of the regions remained determined by central administrative agencies through both the county councils and the management of the enterprises. A group of conflicts always recur in the argument about reform, for example between plan or market centralization and decentralization. From the regional point of view these arguments oppose 'development forced from outside' to regional self-development. However, this is a false opposition since increases in the independence of either the enterprises or of the regions would result in a real decentralization. Thus administrative decentralization and economic decentralization are processes which do not contradict but complement each other. If the regional distribution of industry is determined within the enterprise sector, the role of a more independent regional public administration, which also has access to economic resources, would be to provide support by indirect means, among other things, by developing infrastructure. In spite of their widened range of powers the regional councils are inadequate for this, since, as economic organizations, they belong to the tertiary sector (Wiener, 1987). Thus their range of actions is subject to national appraisal, for example as in the case of infrastructure investments.

The practical advantage for existing authorities of postponing infrastructure investments is that the resources thus released can be used centrally without delay, while the effects of the postponement will be dispersed across the regions and will not be evident until later (Kornai, 1980). Therefore the regional councils never received the required resources, and infrastructure was always left behind. What is more, the resources available were reduced even more by restrictions of economic policy (Wiener, 1987). The fight for a better share of the distribution of scarce resources made the counties enemies of each other, and from 1971 when the counties themselves also became the centres of redistribution owing to their increased possibility of retaining certain taxes, the settlements within the counties also became enemies of each other (Szegö, 1976). And since any significant infrastructure investment still could be obtained only on the pretence of a large industrial investment, the same rivalries continued between areas to obtain industrial investments. So it is no surprise that, under these circumstances, the counties and the settlements did not seek co-operation with each other (Vági, 1982; Bogár, 1983).

The regional aspects of central administration, and the sectoral and functional aspects of the regional system, could be asserted only through informal channels (Berényi, 1978a, b). The relations between the enterprises and the district and county councils were also organized informally. In most cases the enterprises were the 'stronger' actor in this relationship since they did not rely exclusively on central resources, but could transfer a part of their cost increases on to their customers (Wiener, 1987). So the economy and regional administration were formally separated, but the general influence of state administration on the economy was not significantly reduced. The future of settlements was still decided in Budapest or at best in the county administrative centres. The increased influence of self-governing agencies in public administration was not realized at all, notwithstanding the regulations that were issued (see the sociological analyses of Bihari, 1979; Lörincz, 1981; Wiener, 1987). As a consequence 'the revelation of the alternatives of decision-making, the acquaintance with or ranking of alternative interests either failed or was transferred up the hierarchy of administration' (Bihari, 1979, p. 110). The very form in which the regional councils and the enterprises could 'find each other' again could not be other than a 'horizontal' co-operation based on the self-government of councils and the independence of enterprises.

Thus in spite of some improving characteristics, regional development was still burdened with serious problems which were the necessary consequences of the contradictions of the economic and administrative reforms. In the course of these reforms some counties obtained a better position through informal routes, while others were left behind (Bogár, 1983; Vági, 1982; Enyedi, 1986). However, the 'stronger' counties did not improve their position because the industries which showed deficient investment were concentrated in their territories. Today, neither an elaborated theory, nor a strategy, exists to determine what should be the future of these one-sided heavy-industry districts and settlements. Only separate 'fire-fighting' measures have been introduced (Cséfalvay, *et al.*, 1986). Tensions developed also within the counties themselves. The nationwide redistribution usually favoured Budapest and the county-wide redistribution usually favoured the administrative centres of the counties. The opportunities of the smaller settlements were thus restricted. They were further reduced by reforms which amalgamated the communities and also introduced amalgamation of the agricultural co-operatives into larger units (Vági, 1982; Enyedi, 1983).

By the beginning of the 1980s, the distortions caused by this lack of balance affected the Hungarian economy so seriously that the idea of further reform, or as others put it, of introducing a second reform, inevitably had to be put back on the agenda. Since economic reserves were not available (these might have been available in the 1970s) institutional reform seemed to be the most applicable (Sárközy, 1986). The measures taken in 1984 aimed primarily at the reform of the system of economic organization. However a major territorial reform also took place by abolishing the districts and by terminating the rigid rules by which the counties were administered. It is too early to evaluate these changes comprehensively. In addition the new taxation system introduced in 1988 will further modify the relation between economy, administration and regional development. Nevertheless I will express some conjectures.

I would argue that the wider range of legal independence which has been introduced since 1984 will not provide a real independence either for the enterprises or for the councils. This is because vestiges of the traditional highly redistributive policy of central planning still survive. Without independent resources no independence exists. The regional bodies and enterprises have succeeded in maintaining part of their previous hierarchical state administration structure even in the so-called 'competitive sector'. The so-called 'social debates', as well as the invitation to regional councils to take part in the meetings of the agencies of the central economic administration, seem to be more a new means for having central ideas accepted rather than introducing real debates or changes. Political decentralization is still awaited. The statement by Gombár and Lengyal (1986, p. 115), that 'the political technology of reform measures is of a technocratic and bureaucratic nature in the case of economic change which systematically and deliberately ignores democratic solutions' is true today. In any case, in spite of every economic and administrative reform measure, the accumulation of severe tensions continues. As a consequence of the process of economic restructuring Hungary also has had to face problems of employment, at least after 1987. Such problems affect mostly the 'traditional' backward areas (for example the county of Szabolcs-Szatmár) and counties where in the past heavy industry was located (for example the county of Borsod-Abauj-Zemplén). Since 1986 government agencies have allocated financial funds to develop backward regions or ones having structural difficulties (the Central Fund for Regional Development). However, the budget of this fund envisaged for the whole five-year plan period is so very small (3,000 million Hungarian Forints) that the aim of diminishing regional imbalance cannot be taken seriously or achieved. (An up-to-date workplace today costs approximately 1 to 1.5 million Forints in Hungary.) Consequently, the counties and settlements are left to use their own meagre resources. Their traditional sources of income have decreased, at least in real value, due to high inflation. Thus it is to be feared that the inequalities and backwardness of infrastructure will become greater. The only favourable process generated by this situation is that the regional administrative units are being forced to seek co-operation with the economic units within their region.

Traditional sectoral planning: the case of Romania

In Romania until the second half of the 1960s the system of centralized economic management showed no signs of change and the question of economic reform was not even raised. In the administrative area, however, several changes were introduced which affected mainly the regional distribution of public administration. The outline which follows is based, in particular, on Hunya (1982, 1987). Following the Soviet theory in 1950 *rayons* or territorial production complexes for planning and public administration were organized to serve as the basis of the administrative system. From groups of *rayons*, provinces were formed. The reorganization in 1950 was followed by repeated 'improvements' in 1952, 1956 and 1960. In this period some regions were amalgamated and some areas were connected to other *rayons*. These processes cannot be considered as real reforms of administration since they were driven mostly by political motives and served to strengthen centralized management. The frequent reorganizations made 'regional interests' impossible to develop, provided opportunities for replacing leaders, made the system more manageable by reducing the number of the territorial units and had the additional advantage of presenting a picture of diminishing regional differences. The aim of diminishing actual regional inequalities was not among the targets of that era, and moreover, the existing tensions were increased further by the policy of locating industry primarily with respect to raw material resources.

The objectives of explicit regional planning and regional policy gained ground in the mid-1960s in Romania and, like Hungary, ran parallel to the declaration of economic reform. However, here again the term 'reform' has to be treated with circumspection, since the declared programme was in itself very moderate. Actually, it did not set a target of shifting towards a real 'market' economy. The purpose was rather to declare a link with other east European reform processes. Thus it is understandable that 'reform measures' were delayed or not taken, since in the spirit of the 'policy of independence' the secretary-general of the party continued to be a follower of centralization and of an upwards revised industrialization policy. The only significant change was the organization of so-called industrial centres (of nationwide, large-scale enterprises). These did diminish the share of authority of sectoral ministries and strengthened medium-level management. At that time the policy of industrial development gave preference to the processing industry, while its territorial conception was a 'concentrated decentralization', that is the development of a few local centres. The 1968 administrative reform complied with these conceptions. The reform abolished the system of *rayons* and provinces and introduced a system of counties. By an extensive process of uniting villages, in 1972 communities became the smallest units of public administration. It was at that time that the system of 'systematizing' was elaborated: namely, some settlements were classified as ones to be developed, others to be neglected, the main object being to develop an artificial hierarchy of towns. By administrative measures the practice of regional development distorted not only the historically developed system of settlements but its inner structure as well. For example, strict regulations restricted the selection of building sites. Urbanization was given special preference and emphasis. However in practice this meant an actual 'ruralization' of the towns, both because of the large numbers of people who migrated to towns from rural regions and also because of the low standard of infrastructure in these towns. The most favoured type of settlement of that era was the medium-sized town consisting of an industrial plant and a housing estate. This was the cheapest way of providing infrastructure facilities.

These reforms were dominated by political objectives: the main purpose was to suppress regional or national minority interests. For example, following regulations introduced in 1971, the same person is to serve as first secretary of the Romanian Communist Party and as president of the council's executive committee in order to keep regional interests 'well in hand'. Economy and politics, economy and public administration are not separated. The majority of the enterprises operate in dual subordination, that is subordinated to the industrial centre and to the county council. Overlapping and unclear spheres of authority are frequent phenomena. The state of the entire Romanian administration is well illustrated by the following quotations:

The organization of the Romanian state is characterized by institutionalized organizational and legal insecurity . . . the paralysis of the state organization, which is the consequence of its own structure, erects the management structure of the legally unregulated party to be an organizational structure of the state . . . the agencies, which consist of representatives elected by the subjects of the country, are at best allowed merely to implement party decisions. [Hunya, 1987, p. 36]

In Romania, as in Hungary, the answer to the crisis phenomena of the 1970s was to intensify the previous reform. However, the reform measures remained within the scope of the system of plan directives. What is more, such measures either were not actually implemented or often served to screen other objectives or problems. In 1980 the interpretation of the reform which granted enterprises certain rights to independent decision-making was declared by Ceauşescu as 'entirely mistaken'. Instead he ordered state management agencies not to leave partial problems to be solved at lower levels and demanded from them a 'lot more active role' in solving 'concrete issues'. In addition to making the categories of commodity and money active to a certain degree, the 'new economic and financial mechanism' was designed to increase the role of the hierarchical disaggregation of central plans. This reinforced central planning. The principle, according to which the presidential functions of the leading collective agencies were to be performed by leaders of the competent party agencies, was extended to economic organizations as well. This reinforced the party. The economic management role of the counties was intensified and, according to the resolution of the 12th Party Congress, each plan was elaborated in its territorial projection as well. The party committees in their respective counties were made fully responsible for complying with all of the plan figures prescribed for the economic organizations operating within their region. Thus the party became the main administrator of the economy.

After 1982 Romania tried to recover from its serious economic situation by exhausting its reserves, further limiting consumption, strongly restricting imports and by a forced increase of exports. The means for implementing this economic policy was the renewed strengthening of direct management of operations. Romania tried to reach its unmet economic targets by stricter administrative measures such as detailed plan figures, compulsory self-support of the villages, plan obligation for household plots, obligatory public works, limiting numbers of children, etc. Centralization became complete in 1985 by placing energy supply under military control. In a sense, regional differences diminished in this era. The whole country, and each individual territorial unit, was forced to strict autarky. Due to difficulties in food and energy supply, the towns lost their previous relative advantage. However, it is difficult to be pleased with such an 'equality'.

Advanced reforms: the case of Yugoslavia

In Yugoslavia a centralized planning and economic management system was introduced rather early, in 1945, but it operated only up to the beginning of the 1950s. After that time an uninterrupted reform process was initiated. From the very beginning this was interpreted not as a mere economic reform but also as a political and social reform. The reform aimed at a continuous decentralization of political and economic decision-making by means of strengthening the regional powers of self-administration of enterprises, diminishing the role of central planning and intensifying the role of the market.

The first wave of this reform was introduced at the beginning of the 1950s. A system of workers' administration was organized in the economic units at that time. Simultaneously, several changes were introduced in public administration as well. Yugoslavia is a multi-national country and this was recognized in the six republics and two autonomous provinces of the mutli-national Yugoslavia created in 1949. Within the republics or provinces, regions were organized which were further divided into districts, towns and communities. However, in 1952 the regions were abolished and by 1955 the communal administration system, organized by amalgamating settlements, became the basis of administration. The aim was to develop real social, economic and political communities from the settlements. The sphere of authority of the local representative agencies was extended and a two-chamber system was introduced. This consisted of councils of electors and of producers. The dual subordination of the administrative organs was terminated at the same time.

Between 1961 and 1965, a new reform was initiated by reorganizing, in the first place, the institutional structure. The new constitution of 1963 introduced administrative change and made the system of communal self-administration complete by abolishing districts. It also replaced, at the communal level, the producers' councils by working teams' councils, members of which could be other than workers of the producing units.

In the commune units, the executive had only such rights as were laid down by law on the basis of the principles of the constitution. Economic reforms followed the 1963 administrative reform from 1965 on. The aim of these was to make the market more active and to allow independence in enterprise management. This resulted in modification of the price structure, prices of the majority of commodities became decontrolled and foreign trade was liberalized. Decisions regarding state investments were made at the respective republic or community levels. State intervention in the respective regional administration or enterprises was normative and was based on supports and other financial means.

Yugoslavia inherited considerable regional inequalities from the past. Efforts were made to diminish regional differences by financial means, for example by means of allocating a development fund for 'economically underdeveloped regions'. This federal fund mainly aimed at promoting the infrastructure and development of the backward republics. However, the pace of economic progress of the economically advanced republics remained faster, thus making existing regional differences greater. In a peculiar way, this process was supported by the extensive decentralization, since it established the basis of regional division.

Formally, the 1965 reform in Yugoslavia strongly curtailed the hierarchy of administration. In the 1970s, however, Yugoslav economists and sociologists revealed, as in Hungary, that the hierarchical system continued to exist in many informal ways (see for example Soós, 1986). In their opinion state and economy remained in practice unseparated. The regional principle and not the sectoral principle had become the main line of state administration. But despite a level of autonomy, the regional level still acted within the hierarchical setting of tasks, for example, by the appointment of leaders, and through its responsibility for employment and the state of the market. In practice, credit banks were no more than subsidiary bodies of the regional administration. The power structure within enterprises remained dominated by the managing director and professional staff, with frequent personal interdependence between enterprise leaders and the state administration. Co-operation between the various regional units and other agencies within the regions was planned to be strengthened by a complex system of contracts, but in practice the reforms merely strengthened lobbying.

The reforms of the constitution in 1974 increased decentralization further. A system of communities within enterprises was formed by the centre. However according to many commentators, this measure introduced processes which encouraged recentralization. This arose because the self-administration agreements combined the principle of market relations with both the principle of solidarity and the political line of control of the enterprise leaders, increasing the power of the settlements but mainly at the level of the republics and provinces. In the 1970s the efforts of the republics to gain autarky intensified, and this hindered federal decentralization policy and encouraged additional regional tensions.

With respect to the crisis-phenomena of the 1980s the targets set in Yugoslavia have been to diminish territorial divisions and to strengthen federal macro-economic management. A policy of retrenchment has been introduced. The investment programmes of the republics are now more closely supervised, regional prices have been abolished and imports have been restricted. Now the former reform concepts have been recalled because according to many economists the economic problems can be interpreted as the consequence of an inconsistent implementation of the previous reforms, particularly the lack of a capital market and the continuation of a dominant central price control.

Conclusions

This chapter has briefly outlined the practice of economic and administrative reforms and their impact on regional development in three east European countries. The differences between countries are striking. In Yugoslavia, as a result of an early reform process, public administration was formally entirely separated from the economy, and extensive regional autonomy was developed for both administrative and economic organizations. The spheres of authority granted to the regional level made it possible for the administrative agencies in each of the republics to become the major redistributional centres.

In Romania the 'reform measures' were limited to a decentralization of decision-making authority within the hierarchical structure of state administration. However even this decentralization was quickly swept away by a new wave of centralization, and the 'reform' of the 1970s almost entirely eliminated any tendencies to decentralization. As a result ideology and politics continues to dominate the economy, the party and the state administration are independent; hence the economy operates in close subordination to state administration. Moreover the subordination is often to both regional organs and to industrial centres. The main method of distribution of material goods continues to be a strict state control mechanism.

In Hungary the separation of the administration of the state and the economy was carried out in a peculiar, contradictory way. Economic management by the regional administration diminished, while the authority of the centre increased. Distribution policies were hardly changed. Instead direct decentralization was replaced by indirect means hidden within the regulations and informal networks.

Yugoslavia provides the best example of the increased importance of representative bodies. Hungary is today at the beginning of this process, while in Romania any increase in the level of real representation is excluded both by the prevailing legal uncertainty and by the central prescription of the composition of the representative bodies. In Hungary the reform was limited for a long time to the economy, and the delay of reforms of the socio-political institutional system (within the administration) often hindered further reforms. In Yugoslavia the institutional and administrative reform was introduced in parallel to the economic reforms, and in many cases even preceded it and laid its foundations. In Romania the 'reform steps' were often limited to organizational changes without any real economic reforms.

Despite significant differences, we can see several points of similarity between the three countries. Moreover these characteristics are representative of situations which can be identified in the rest of socialist eastern Europe. In this sense the examples of Yugoslavia and Romania represent the two extreme cases. However, it can be observed in all three countries that the waves of declared reform measures coincide with the intensification of economic problems and periods of economic stringency. This has been followed in each country by a later recentralization process, although this has not resulted in a withdrawal from the previously declared targets. This process is driven by conflicts of power and politics. In an informal way central powers have generally succeeded in taking advantage of shortcomings and gaps of legal regulation. The result is that formal legal decentralization regulations do not reflect the reality.

As a result centralized management based on the hierarchical principle has remained firm in each country, but is organized in different ways. In Romania centralization has remained through formal and sectoral lines; in Yugoslavia on regional lines and often informally; while in Hungary centralization is strong through co-operation, to different extents, between the centre and sectoral, functional and regional bodies, partly formally and partly informally. In each of these countries politics still dominate the economy, as witnessed for example by the continued importance of 'mobilization campaigns'. As a result, peculiar 'administered markets' have developed. In such 'markets' not only commodities and money are subjects of the bargain between party bodies, administrative bodies, enterprises, institutions and social organizations, but so also are official decisions, information, regulations, monopolistic rights, subventions, allowances, etc. Hence the political party, the state and the civil sphere cannot be separated within the exchange process.

Regional political objectives and a form of regional planning appeared in each of these countries in the mid-1960s. The chief target was to diminish the main regional inequalities, but less attention was paid to the other regional tensions, for example urban-rural relations or the social segregation phenomena in large towns. As a result of their strong central distribution policies, Romania and Hungary tried to solve regional problems mainly by central administrative measures; for example by the grading of settlements, by the location of central investments, etc. In Yugoslavia, it was planned that the poorly developed republics would catch up mostly in an indirect way, by means of economic supports, but within the republics and autonomous provinces administrative support was not unknown. In practice, however, regional and community development targets in all countries were only partially implemented, and the interventions in regional autonomy produced new regional tensions. Ironically, regional units are forced into a position of autarky by this exaggerated centralization in Romania, while in Yugoslavia they are forced into centralization by the independence of the regional bodies. As a result Yugoslavia has something of the character of a feudal state broken up into petty monarchies, while Romania is a strongly centralized state lacking the traditions of market and democracy.

The central distribution practices in each country have frequently functioned contrary to declared regional targets because regional equalization is contrary to the interests of the most powerful social groups. This has been further encouraged by the weak bargaining position of the more backward areas where the negative effects of centralization are felt only after the elapse of time. As a result regional infrastructure and social investments have fallen into the background in each of these countries.

References

Antal, L. (1980), 'Fejlödés Kitérövel' (Development with a 'Bypass'), *Gazdaság*, 1980/2, Budapest.

Antal, L., Bokros, L., Csillag, I., Lengyel, L. and Matolcsy, Gy. (1987), 'Fordulat és reform' (Turn and reform), *Közgazdasági Szemle*, 1987/6, Budapest.

Barta, Gy. (1987), 'A termelés térbeli szétterjedése, és a szervezet területi centralizációja a magyar iparban' (The spatial diffusion of production and the spatial centralization of managerial function in Hungarian industry), *Tér és Társadalom*, 2, Pécs.

Bartke, I. (ed.) (1972), *Területfejlesztési Politika Magyarországon* (Regional Policy in Hungary), KJK, Budapest.

Bartke, I. (1979), 'Az ágazat és területfejlesztés kapcsolatának változásai' (Changes in the relationship between planning the development of sectors and regions), *Közgazdasági Szemle*, 4, Budapest.

Bartke, I. (1981), 'A területfejlesztést megalapozó kutatások társadalmi — gazdasági szerepe és hosszutávu feladatai' (Socio-economic role and long-term research tasks for direct foundation of regional development), *Közgazdasági Szemle*, 6, Budapest.

Bauer, T. (1975), 'A vállalatok ellentmodásos helyzete a magyar gazdasági mechanizmusban (Contradictory situation of the enterprises in Hungarian economic management mechanisms), *Közgazdasági Szemle*, 6, Budapest.

Bauer, T. (1982), 'A második reform és a tulajdonviszonyok' (The second reform and ownership relations), *Mozgó Világ*, 11, Budapest.

Beck, B. (1975), *Jugoszlávia Gazdasága* (Economy in Yugoslavia), KJK, Budapest.

Berényi, S. (ed.) (1978a), *Az Urbanizáció Hatása a Közigazgatásra az Európai Szocialista (KGST) Államokban* (Influence of Urbanization on Public Administration in European Socialist (CMA) Countries), KJK, Budapest.

Berényi, S. (1978b), 'Az államigazgatasi reformok elméleti kérdései' (Basic theoretical problems of the public administrative reforms), *Állam és Igazgatás*, 3, Budapest.

Bihari, O. (1979), 'A döntési mechanizmus szervezeti, hatalmi és érdekkörnyezete' (Sphere of organization, power and interest in the decision-making mechanism), *Társadalmi Szemle*, 3, Budapest.

Bihari, O. (ed.) (1982), *Dolgozatok a Területi Irányitás Eszközrendszeréről* (Studies on Means of Regional Management), MTA Dunántúli Kutatóintézet, Pécs.

Bihari, O. (1984), *A Területi Decentralizáció. A Területi Autonómia és a Politikai Regionalizálás* (Regional Decentralization. Regional Self-government and Political Regionalization), MTA RKK Közlemények/31, Pécs.

Bogár, L. (1983), *A Fejlödés Ára* (The Price of Development), KJK, Budapest.

Bokor, K. and Bora, Gy. (1985), *A Termelési Szerkezetváltás Fejlesztés és Településfejlesztés Összefüggései* (Relationship between Changing Economical Structure and Settlement Development), (Kézirat) Közgazdasági Egyetem, Budapest.

Constantinescu, M. (ed.) (1974), *Urban Grown Processes in Romania,*, Meridiane Publishing House, Bucharest.

Compton, P.A. and Pécsi, M. (eds) (1976), *Regional Development and Planning*, Akadémia, Budapest.

Cravero, R. (1987), 'A területfejlesztés és a gazdálkodás uj vonásai a VII. Ötéves tervidöszakban' (New feature of the territorial development and management in the period of the VIIth five-year Plan), *Állam és Igazgatás*, 4, Budapest.

Cséfalvay. Z., Perger, É. and Pomázi, I. (1986), 'Túl kis lyuk ez ahhoz . . .' (It is a too small hall for . . .), *Mozgó Világ*, 7, Budapest.

Cséfalvay. Z., Perger, É. and Pomázi, I. (1987), 'Rudabánya 1985', *Forrás*, 5, Kecskemét.

Csepeli, Gy. (1987), 'A reform akarata, az akarat reformja' (The will of reform, the reform of will), *Társadalomkutatás*, 1, Budapest.

Enyedi, Gy. (1979), *Economic Policy and Regional Development in Hungary*, Akadémia, Budapest.

Enyedi, Gy. (1983), *Földrajz és Társadalom* (Geography and Society), Magvetö, Budapest.

Enyedi, Gy. (1986), *Település és Társadalom* (Settlement and Society), MSzMP KB Társadalomtudományi Intézet, Budapest.

Farkas, Z. (1986), 'Egyes szám harmadik személyben, Portré-interjú Nagy, T. közgazdász professzorral' (In third person with T. Nagy, Professor of Economic Sciences), *Mozgó Világ*, 11, Budapest.

Gálik, M. (1987), *Vállalati Válság, Reformválság* (Crises of Enterprises, Crisis of the 'Reform'), Közgazdasági Egyetem, Mikrogazdasági Kutatások/1, Budapest.

Gombár, Cs. and Lengyel, L. (1986), 'A társadalmi reform kérdéseihez' (To questions of social reform), *Társadalomkutatás*, 1, Budapest.

Hegedüs, A. and Rozgonyi, T. (1969), 'Döntési rendszerünk a szociológus szemével' (Our decision-making system as a sociologist sees it), *Valóság*, 5.

Horváth, Gy. (ed.) (1984), *Területi Összefüggések a Gazdaságirányitásban* (Regional Inferences in an Economic Management System), MTA RKK Közlemények RKK, Pécs.

Hunya, G. (1982), *Románia Iparositásának Regionális Kérdései* (Regional Problems of Industrialization in Romania), MTA Világgazdasági Kutatóintézet, Budapest.

Hunya, G. (ed.) (1987), *Románia — a Szélsöséges Eset* (Romania — an Extreme

Case), MTA Világgazdasági Kutató Intézet, Budapest.

Kara, P. (1987), 'Gondolatok a kétszintü gazdaságirányitásról' (Ideals on the two-tier council administration), *Állam és Igazgattás*, 5, Budapest.

Knight, P. (1983), *Economic Reform in Socialist Countries: the experiences of China, Hungary, Romania and Yugoslavia, World Bank Staff Working Papers*, No. 579, Washington, DC.

Kornai, J. (1980), *A Hiány* (The Economy of Shortage), Közagazdasási és Jogi K., Budapest.

Kornai, J. (1983), *Ellentmondások és Dilemmák* (Contradictions and Dilemmas), Magvetö, Budapest.

Korodi, J. (1974), *Regional Development Policy and Regional Planning in Hungary.*

Laky, T. (1980), 'A recentralizáció rejtett mechanizmusai' (Hidden mechanisms of recentralization), *Valóság*, 2, Budapest.

Lengyel, L. (1987), 'Végkifejlet' (Final dénouement), *Valóság*, 12, Budapest.

Lörincz, L. (1981), *A Közigazgatás Kapcsolata a Gazdasággal és a Politikával* (Relationship between Public Administration and Economy and Politics), Közgazdasági és Jogi, K., Budapest.

Mandel, M., Pappné, Gáspár, L. and Sághi, G. (1987), *Infrastruktura-politika* (Infrastructural Investment Policy), Közgazdasági és Jogi Könyvkiadó, Budapest.

Nagy, T.Gy. (ed.) (1978), *Közigazgatási Döntés és Városfejleztés* (Decision in Public Administration and City Development), ELTE Államigazgatási és Jogi Tanszék/6, Budapest.

Polányi, K. (1976), *Az Archaikus Társadalom és a Gazdasági Szemlélet* (Archaic Society and Economic Attitude), Gondolat Kiadó, Budapest.

Ronnas, T. (1983), *Urbanization in Romania*, The Economic Research Institute at the Stockholm School of Economics, Stockholm.

Sárközy, T. (1986), *Egy Gazdasági Szervezeti Reform Sodrában* (In the Wake of a Constitutional Reform in Economy), Magvetö, Budapest.

Schmidt, P. (1979), 'A bürokratizmus forrásai az államigazgatásban' (The origins of bureaucracy in the state administration), *Társadalmi Szemle*, 2, Budapest.

Sipos, A. and Tardos, M. (1986), 'Gazdaságirányitás és szervezeti rendszer a reform második évtizedének végén (The economic management and constitutional system at the end of the second decade of the reform), *Gazdaság*, 3, Budapest.

Soós, K.A. (1986), *Terv, Kampány, Pénz* (Plan, Campaign, Money), KJK, Kossuth Könyvkiadó, Budapest.

Szegö, A. (1974), *Területi Érdek, Területi Igazgatás és Fejlesztési Politika* (Regional Interest, Administration and Development Policy), Tanácsakadémia, Budapest.

Szegö, A. (1976), 'A területi érdekviszonyok, a központositott ujraelosztás és a területi igazgatás' (Regional interest relations, the centralized redistribution and regional administration), *Szociológia*, 3-4, Budapest.

Szegö, A. (1977), 'A redisztribució tispusai és az érdekviszonyok' (Types of redistribution and interest relations), *Szociológia*, 3, Budapest.

Szelényi, I. (1973), *Regionális Fejlödés, Gazdalkodás, Igazgatás* (Regional Development Economy, Administration), Tervtanulmány, MTA Állam és Jogtudományi Intézet, Budapest.

Szoboszlay, Gy. and Wiener, Gy. (1980a), 'Az állami terület beosztás politökonómiai kérdései' (Political economic questions of national regional distribution), *Jogtudományi Közlöny*, 6, Budapest.

Szoboszlay, Gy. and Wiener, Gy. (1980b), 'Önkormányzat és gazdaságirányitás' (Autonomy and economic control), *Közgazdasági Szemle*, 1980/7-8, Budapest.

Szoboszlay, Gy. (ed.) (1985), *Politics and Public Administration in Hungary*, Akadémia, Budapest.

Tatai, Z. (1980), 'A gazdaság irányitásának regionális tényezöi' (Regional factors of economic management), *Állam és igazgatás*, 5, Budapest.

Településfejlesztésünk kérdéseiröl (Vita) (1980), (Questions of settlement development in Hungary, exchange of views), *Társadalmi Szemle*, 12, Budapest.

Tóth, L. (1985), *Településfejlesztés és a Tanácsi Gazdaságirányitás Rendszere* (Regional Development and the System of Council-level Economic Management), Gazdaságirányitás, KJK, Budapest.

Toldy, F. (ed.) (1977), *Az Európai Népi Demokratikus Országok Területi Beosztása és Tanácsi Szervezete* (Territorial Division and Council Organization in a European People's Republic), MTA Állam es Jogtudományi Intézet, Budapest.

Vági, G. (1982), *Versengés a Fejlesztési Forrásokért* (Competition for the Resources of Development), KJK, Budapest.

Vági, G. (1987), 'Egy új tanácsi gazdaságszabályozás körvonalai' (Outlines of a new economic regulation in the councils), *Állam és Igazgatás*, 5, Budapest.

Vasovic, Z. (1971), *A Hegyvidéki Körzetek Fejlesztési Problémái Szerbiában és Montenegróban* (Development Problems of Mountainous Regions in Serbia and Montenegro), IGU European Regional Conference, Budapest.

Verebélyi, I. (1987), 'A tanácsi önkormányzat kibontakozásának irányai' (Directions in the development of council-level self-government), *Állam és Igazgatás*, 5, Budapest.

Wiatr, J. (1980), *A Politikai Viszonyok Szociológiája* (The Sociology of Political Relations), Kossuth, Budapest.

Wiener, Gy. (1987), 'Az infrastruktura és a tanácsi gazdálkodás fejlödése' (The development of infrastructure, and council-level economic management), *Állam és Igazgatás*, 4, Budapest.

Zala, Gy. (1972), *A Területfejlesztés Nemzetközi és Hazai Tapasztalatainak Rendszerezése és Értékelése, Jugoszlávia* (Systematization and Valuation of International and National Experiences in Territorial Development), Kézirat, Yugoslavia.

Zagar, M. (1971), *Problémák és Folyamatok Jugoszlávia Viszonylag Fejlett Köztársaságának, a Szlovén Szocialista Köztársaságnak Gyengén Fejlett Körzeteiben* (Problems and Processes in the Underdeveloped Regions of the Slovene Socialist Republic; Comparative Development in the Republic of Yugoslavia), IGU, European Regional Conference, Budapest.

7 Administrative reforms in eastern Europe: an overview

Marie-Claude Maurel

Introduction

The desire for restructuring (*perestroika*) now declared as a priority in eastern Europe has led to renewed activities of administrative reform. Such reforms are not new. The history of most east-central European countries since the end of the Second World War has been punctuated by many reorganizations in the system of territorial management, and has been marked by the relative instability of administrative networks. However, current changes are a sharp contrast to previous reforms. The changes now being introduced into the territorial structure and into the institutional functioning of state institution can be explained only within the context of an enlarged process of management reform. The concerns they address represent a major break with the aims of previous reforms, which in the 1950s emphasized the political imperative of controlling territory through hierarchical structures, and in the 1960s and 1970s emphasized the functional principle which led to technocratically-based reorganizations.

In comparison with earlier reforms, it seems that we have now entered a new period of change in the administrative actions of government in which changes in administration are intimately tied up with reforms of the economic and social system. This is likely to lead to a real restructuring supported by a flexible regulation by economic mechanisms and a democratization of social and political life. Most reforms in progress have the intent of decentralizing powers and functions to lower administrative levels, and to different economic agents, seeking to reinforce social participation and to stimulate initiatives. The main focus has been particularly at the local level. A key question is: to which extent are these adjustments, which have been introduced mainly because of the need to manage the economic crisis, synonymous with a change in the management of east-central European countries?

This chapter first describes aims and principles being applied to implementing the administrative reforms carried out during the last decades in east-central Europe. The discussion then examines the impact of territorial restructuring on the functioning of local societies. Finally the consequences of the reforms in progress are assessed.

Administrative reforms: aims and application

The fact that the reforms of territorial administrative structures are accompanying change in the power system are a clear sign of the close relation between the political–administrative structure and the political plan in eastern Europe. The ability to govern a state depends not only on the cohesion of common procedures, it also requires the support of a territorial system. The restructuring and strengthening of power logically require the reorganization of territorial networks. The establishment of an administrative division calls for a compromise to be struck between two different principles: first, a principle of 'visibility' which derives from the necessity of asserting control over territory (to gather all information, in order to know everything, to plan anything); and a second principle, of identification which is based on 'territoriality'. The implementation of the first principle leads to a regular partition of territory, so that the state machinery can have a hold over all the cells in society. In this way, central power seeks to make homogenous what is not because its authority can be exercised in a similar way in every area. The implementation of the second principle leads to taking account of the territories with which people identify as a result of their history and socio-cultural solidarity.

When the principle of 'visibility' dominates over the principle of identification, there is a risk of defining an 'artificial' network that can disrupt permanently the relationship between society and territory. This tends inevitably to reduce the ability for self-organization and autonomy of local government by communities. The history of administrative reforms carried out in eastern Europe provides many examples.

The system of power introduced immediately after the Second World War was characterized by a territorial system of government based on the Soviet model. Based strongly on the principle of 'visibility', like the USSR it had three levels (region, district and commune) and divided the surface of the states by a tight administrative network. This instituted control over people and allowed implementation of a plan for industrial development of the economy. In the rural districts, the party's machinery (executive committee) and the state administration were used to ensure the fulfilment of the programmes of agricultural collectivization. 'Bringing closer administration to the population' at the scale of local administrative units, allowed the necessary pressure to be introduced in order to impose a new mode of production on a reluctant peasant society.

From the 1960s the territorial imperative of control gave way to precedence for the functionality principle. The progressive introduction of economic reforms, and even more the emergence of new objectives for regional planning, emphasized the increasing inadequacy of a territorial system which was strongly centralized and hierarchical. In particular the increased number of administrative levels produced a bureaucratic heaviness. In contrast, economic regionalization became the dominant objective which, by means of territorial reform, central powers used to make the functional economic regions and administrative boundaries coincide. The concept of a functional region came to dominate research on

Table 7.1   Administrative divisions in 1986 in eastern Europe

	Bulgaria	Czecho-slovakia	Hungary	East Germany	Poland	Romania
State level						
Area (km²)	1,109	127	93	108	312	237
Population (000s)	8,949	15,534	10,622	16,659	37,340	12,724
Counties[1]						
Name	*Okrag*	*Země*	*Megye*	*Bezirk*	*Voïvod*	*Judet*
Number	*28*	*12*	*20*	*15*	*49*	*41*
Average area (km²)	*3,961*	*10,658*	*4,651*	*7,222*	*6,381*	*5,792*
Districts						
Name	Sup-pressed in 1959	*Okresy*	*Jaras* (Sup-pressed in 1984)	*Kreise*	Sup-pressed in 1975	Sup-pressed in 1968
Number		112		227		
Towns						
Number of town councils	*Obchtina* 300		*Varos* 139	1,013	*Miasta* 812	*Municipiul* 237
Rural communes		*Obce*	*Közseg* 1,345	*Gemeinden* 6,537	*Gmina* 2,121	*Commune* 2,705

[1] Includes capitals: Sofia, Prague, Bratislava, Budapest, Warsaw, Bucharest.
Source: National statistical yearbooks

national and regional development. The objective thus became to model administrative units on the factors which structured economic space. The detailed specification of territorial plans was carried on in parallel with the drawing-up of administrative reforms so that administrative regions became the basis for the management of economic activities and for the implementation of territorial planning.

Following these aims, the reform process in each country tends to show strong similarities, mostly because of the importance given to the functional criterion. But they differ in the timing, the extent and the conditions of their implementation. The overall structure in 1986 is summarized in Table 7.1.

Bulgaria did not hesitate radically to modify its territorial structure several times. In 1959 it was the first country to carry out a reform which reduced from one to two the number of territorial levels. This introduced administrative and economic division into twenty-seven departments (*okrag*) which replaced the fifteen regions established in 1949. At the same time, the districts were abolished. At the local level, the communes (*obchtina*), managed by local councils, were grouped together and their number was reduced to one-half. The economic regionalization, launched soon after the

Soviet reform of the *sovnarhoz*, attempted to introduce the territorial principle into the management system of the economy. The experiment was abandoned and a strongly centralized mode of planning and management system quickly resumed. In 1979 a new administrative reform changed the territorial areas and boundaries of the smallest administrative units. The previous communes (1,374 in number) were grouped together within 291 'settlement systems' (*selichni sistem*). The reform came within the scope of a policy of national and regional economic development. The desire was to promote a more balanced regional development by strengthening the network of urban centres. The officials in charge of land planning tried to base the administrative division on social and economic facts, for example, the functional region and size of central places. The unity of the political and administrative system coincided with a 'settlement system' which was a kind of territorialized organization of people each with its own economic base. The reform recognized local organs of state power, and enlarged their responsibilities in the fields of culture, social and economic management and their co-ordination. Territorial reorganization accompanied the introduction of a 'new economic mechanism' which tended to substitute for purely administrative management a management based on the action of economic instruments.

Polish and Romanian administrative reforms were also radical. At the end of the 1960s, Romania carried out a complete reorganization of its administrative structure as a part of its actions to reform regional development policy (law of December 1967). In 1968, the law about the 'administrative distribution of the territory' replaced the three-level structure by two administrative levels: the department (*judet*) and the commune. The new departments (numbering thirty-nine, plus the city of Bucharest) were supposed to be based on a unity of the links between geography and community. The purpose of the administrative reorganization was to favour both the partial decentralization of management and investments, and to develop a more equal distribution of production between areas. Several partial reforms have followed, but the system remains a highly centralized one based strongly on the principle of 'visibility' and control.

In Poland, administrative reforms implemented in 1973 and 1975 restructured the territorial divisions and changed the functioning of the local organs of state power. The 1973 reform, inspired both by the desire to reinforce the role of the local administration in the co-ordination of social and economic activities, and by the conception of an integrated development at the micro-regional level, enlarged the responsibilities of the lower-rank administrative communities and changed their number (*gmina*). Operational management was entrusted to an official (*naczelnik*) appointed by the regional administration. At all territorial levels, the reform changed the functioning of local administration: it separated the control functions, which were exercised by the people's councils, from the executive functions, which were given to a state employee (the *naczelnik*) who was subordinate to central power. The 1975 administrative reform abolished the intermediate level of the district (*powiat*) and increased the number of *voivodies* (from seventeen to forty-nine). This introduced a real administrative 'departmentalization'. The purpose was to create smaller administrative units, which were easier to manage and could form complete economic regions organized around urban centres which played the role of integration. This notion corresponds to one of the main principles of spatial organization based on the urban network: the principle of 'moderated polycentric concentration'. The administrative reorganization which was followed by E. Gierek had specific political objectives, reduced the influence of the secretaries of *voivodies* and renewed political–administrative staff. But these immediate concerns cannot veil the fact that the reorganization of the territorial structures was framed within a voluntary policy of national and regional development.

Hungary has pursued a continuous process of remodelling territorial structures. The territorial system established in 1950 continued to a large extent an inherited administrative division (*megye, jaras, közseg*), the country level (*megye*) of which proved to be poorly adapted to the realities of the new economic structuring of space. Reforms were limited to reducing the number of districts (*jaras*) from 150 in 1950, to eighty-three in 1984, and to the grouping during the 1970s, of the local councils into joint councils. This procedure was applied primarily to the regions where the population was spread out in small villages (Transdanubia), while the councils of large rural localities of the Alföld remained independent. In 1984, of the 1,381 local councils, 681 had independent councils, 700 had common councils embracing several villages, but 1,576 villages had no administrative councils for their services at all. The 1984 reform thus represented a considerable reduction in powers of the very small villages in rural areas. In Hungary the recent evolution is also marked by the abolition of the role of the intermediate level (*jaras*). The law of 19 February 1971 suppressed district councils, only permitting district offices as administrative relays of central decisions not representative organs. The disappearance of the district met with strong resistance from the party's machinery at that level. The decision finally to abolish the districts, which came into effect in 1984, was justified by a concern to eliminate a bureaucratic level. In addition the reform introduced the possibility of an intermediate link between the county councils (*megye*) and local councils. The local councils located in the most important urban centres took on the function. There are 139 of these intermediate regional centres. They were selected taking into account various functional factors, (for example historical solidarity, the functional regions of the central places, transportation networks, etc). This has resulted in a network of 'town regions'. In order to ensure an optimal and uniform territorial pattern, because the urban centres were insufficient in number, thirty-four large villages were also recognized as administrative centres and given the same powers as the towns. Local councils in these towns and 'large villages' received part of the previous powers of the district offices. In practice this has meant that a simple legal control (*a posteriori*) of the activities of the village councils (*közseg*) has taken the place of the traditional link of subordination. The autonomy of local councils should therefore be reinforced.

Until recent years the reorganization of the administrative and territorial structure of Czechoslovakia has remained very limited. Since 1960 administrative regroupings had reduced the number of regions (*kraji*) from nineteen to ten, and the number of districts (*okresy*) from 286 to 112. The extreme dispersion of the rural settlements has limited the possibilities for administrative reorganization and improvement of the rural services. However a major reform of local government has been introduced by constitutional amendments of 1982 and 1983. This has set up 'central communes' with a broader range of responsibilities.

The general direction of the territorial reforms which have taken place in eastern Europe have tended to give greater importance to the functional principle over the visibility principle in the delimitation of administrative units. Either through a full-scale reform, or by a more continuous process of reorganization, each of the countries discussed has introduced this principle, either at one of the levels of the territorial structure (and generally at the most local), or at all levels as in Poland. These changes in the territorial system indicate that, besides a simplification and reduction in number of levels in the hierarchy, there has been a common tendency to enlarge the size of the basic administrative unit. A change has been instituted, from a fragmented network composed of a large number of small community-level administrative units, to a network where the basic lattice has been markedly increased in size (for example, to an average 379 square kilometres and 30,000 population in the Bulgarian communes, and to 120 to 130 square kilometres and about 10,000 population in the Polish communes). Today, these elementary administrative areas are generally disassociated from the territory of social action and hence from local culture in the settlement units.

Administrative reforms and the restructuring of rural areas

For the rural areas it can be argued that the reform process has undermined local autonomy. The relationship between local society and territory has been deeply modified and has led to a breaking-up of the traditional pattern of rural communities and a loss of the council institutions that previously gave them cohesion. A first break occurred in the 1950s with the establishment of the local councils, then a second break occurred in the 1970s with the redefinition of their administrative boundaries. The reshaping of the territorial system has defined new areas in which rural societies must develop. The chief centres have important new functions in the management of production activities (such as the administrative headquarters of socialized farms) as well as managing services. These have become the nodes of the new administrative areas which have often been formed by arbitrary enlargement and administrative merger. These shifts in administrative and political power, as well as shifts in the centres of social life, have been mostly imposed from above on local society — a kind of manipulation of their territory. This change of relationship between people and territory is a significant aspect of a general political change as well as a change in the mode of local government. In this sense the rupture of the territorial link is contributing to a destruction of local communities.

The transfer of power

The remodelling of the rural territorial system has been carried out with two chief objectives: centralization of power structure and concentration of the seat of power. These effects act simultaneously and both deprive the rural local societies of the very institutions which previously ensured their relative autonomy. The merging of small village co-operatives within larger units, has led to the transfer of certain management and production functions. This represents the end of economic independence for these localities — not only for the organization of their production but also because they are deprived of any kind of socio-cultural administrative infrastructure. The logic upon which the administrative reorganization was based has also been applied to the merger of agricultural enterprises, as well as to the restructuring of service delivery and collective facilities. The reformers wished to put an end to the dispersion of social life by strengthening local central places and mobilizing investments to their advantage.

The transfer of administrative functions is often a consequence of the disappearance of economic functions. Whatever method is adopted (the creation of joint councils, or the redefinition of administrative boundaries), the loss of the local administration profoundly destabilizes local societies. After these reforms the management of their affairs and the defence of their interests depends upon external decision-makers. In spite of the presence of elected representatives within local councils, the representation is formal, without any real ability to intervene. It is often reduced to a purely symbolic representation (a walk-on) since the local community cannot choose the candidates; they are appointed by the political authorities. The direction of economic, social and cultural activities by the local administration is carried out by professionals, selected by the party, who respect the orders from the superior level to which they are subordinate. Hence local officials usually represent a power which is external to the local community and are not part of it. The present generation of local officials in particular has lost the contact previously present because they no longer come from the local population. In these conditions, the participation of the local society is purely formal and has no real meaning.

Local society in decay

The reorganization of the functional centres has accelerated the drift from the land. The politics of restructuring the settlement pattern condemned the existence of small villages by putting them in the category of built-up areas 'without future'. This implied that infrastructure development, as well as building or restoration of housing by private individuals should not take place. If the improvement of services implied the concentration of investments in some centres, as well as the grouping of infrastructure and services, it also called for an effort to improve their accessibility. The improvements offered were generally insufficient to make up for the under investment in rural areas. The discrimination was particularly harmful for peripheral localities which were victims of a whole range of other processes which were in any case hastening their social disintegration. The drift from the land is not only the consequence of the loss of jobs directly linked to the transfer of administrative responsibilities, it also weakened in a general way, the economic basis and the opportunities for employment. These trends were further amplified by the offputting image of villages 'without future'.

The resulting drift from the land leads to a selective decay of local society in the small villages. Active workers employed in services are few, with the exception of commuters. Specialists in agriculture and administrative employees have gone. In the depopulated villages, only unqualified workmen and aged couples without children are left. The result is a 'residual' structure, where the village has a 'truncated' and incomplete society which has been deprived of its most dynamic social groups. In some areas of Transdanubia, in Hungary, marginalized social groups have settled in empty villages as a consequence of the drift from the land after the reorganization of co-operatives.

The decline of local society is a consequence of the weakening of social relationships. Founded traditionally on close social interrelationships, social support and mutual help have decreased, the primary life has disappeared and the system of values has fallen into ruins. With the closure of public places where people can meet (such as schools, cultural centres and sometimes bars), the feeling of belonging to a community vanishes. Deprived of its elite and its institutions, atomized by the weakening of its social links, the local society in the small rural villages has lost its collective identity.

Local societies and self-government

The rediscovery of the values of the locality

In the 1980s there are many signals that a change, which may be called a movement of political and economic 'relocalization', is taking place. As a result, and deriving from the period of destructuring marked by a strong tendency to delocalize, local societies have now tried to re-establish their links with their territory. The movement is not an attempt to go back to the past or a withdrawal into a narrow local area. It is a rediscovery of the values of locality, and of its significance as the right place to manage work and resources, with the aim of mobilizing latent energies.

The 'relocalization' movement has been developed as one part of more general management reform. The process is now taking place in most east European countries but is developing unequally. 'Decentralization' and 'democratization' are the key-words employed in the new political discourse. They mean a rehabilitation of the local and a breaking-off with previous authoritarian and centralized practices. This favours a rebirth of the local as the right place where economic and social actors may have influence. This movement is not unambiguous nor without contradictions. Two different principles meet. The first emanates from people who are trying to gain more autonomy; the second derives from the attempts by central powers to find more efficient economic mechanisms through a controlled integration of local government and local actors.

People do not escape the necessity of rediscovering the local, all the more because they have lived through the destabilizing effects of the previous movement of delocalization (or 'de-territorialization'). As private initiative is encouraged, it opens up new opportunities to people who want to create or develop small enterprises. At this level, their capacities of initiative can be easily carried out. At this level too, the informal networks of a parallel economy can be established and the constraints of legislation can be more easily bypassed. People are encouraged by a desire for independence and the local is the appropriate level at which they can act. The stakes and power struggles are personal and clearly apparent to everyone.

At the local level, self-management in all its forms (economic, social, territorial) is possible, at least, theoretically, but it is not always desired by the people who live and work in an area. There is a tendency to passivity by local societies who reject any kind of social participation because they expect to be swindled, as in the past. As a result individual and family strategies, which seek social status and material improvement, have predominated over common initiatives for local development. This is natural since it has been the case that, up to now, the power and means to promote local development have remained limited. The new concerns, which are now appearing, raise the prospect of decentralization in various fields of the economic, social and political life and may change these attitudes. The present period of economic crisis is reducing available resources, and hence central powers are tempted to release themselves from part of their financial burden. There are thus more grounds for confidence that real decentralization may now occur. The logic of decentralization applies to both local administrations, which receive more important decision-making powers, and to organizations and economic enterprises which receive more autonomy. In both cases, the image of the local level has changed and it is possible to hope that the impact of the new mechanisms will introduce a new social dynamic and economic progress. Romania, for reasons which are linked to the personality of its ruler, is the chief exception to this reform process which is occurring to variable degrees in each of the other socialist countries.

Towards self-government of local societies?

The promotion of local initiatives is now publicized as one of the key aspects of *perestroika*. This derives from the reform process in each area of economic, political and social life. In most of the countries concerned, significant changes to encourage local initiatives have been made by legislators, or are in the process of being introduced. These reforms seek to strengthen the role of local authorities by giving them more powers and more resources in order to allow them to boost local economic development. In the political discourse, as well as in the law, the notion of self-government is strongly asserted. The people's councils are to have a double status: as 'state power organs' and as 'self-government organs' to represent the people's interest.

It is interesting to conjecture about the changes in progress. Are they a genuine transfer of decision-making powers, or just a simple deconcentration movement to restore the efficiency of administration? Will these changes really increase the participation of society? In the present transition period it is premature to offer complete answers to these questions; hence it will be possible here only to point out the most significant elements.

In Bulgaria, the 1977–8 reform introduced a new territorial framework which supported management and control by the state administration. The territorial reorganization carried out in 1987 grouped together twenty-eight intermediate units (*okrag*) into nine regions (*oblast*), indirectly implying recognition of the fundamental role played by the smallest administrative units (the *obchtina*) which were recognized as having a self-government status. The principle of self-finance, which is an essential part of the logic of the 'new economic mechanism', implies that their rights and responsibilities should be widened (for example to cover the creation of small- and medium-sized enterprises, the production of goods and services and the improvement of infrastructure). The official discourse advocates an extension of the responsibilities of 'the manager–citizen', but it does not introduce the new rights for citizens which would be necessary to reverse the apathy which is now so generally widespread.

In Hungary, the will to decentralize the power system is particularly favourable to the establishment of meaningful local initiatives. The decision-making powers of local councils have been extended: they can now create new enterprises, build socio-cultural infrastructure and rent buildings and land. Until now, the financial support of local councils has been weak, and the development of infrastructure has been slow. The 1971 law gave a decisive role in the distribution of financial resources to the county councils. They kept for themselves a major part of the available financial resources while the villages received only a very small part. With the emergence of the economic crisis, the drying up of resources has forced the central powers to transfer the responsibilities for financing infrastructure to the local level. The granting of greater economic and financial independence to local councils is one means of reducing the burden on the central budget. As a result of a new law introduced in 1986, the local communities' budget is also now partly supplied by local resources. The local administration must develop good relations, on a partnership basis, with the enterprises and co-operatives that operate in their territory. But they must also encourage the small contractors in the parallel economy that constitute an economic elite, in order to mobilize their resources and experience for local development. These developments are not all. Local initiatives can also be channelled through associations which take charge of various infrastructure works. The role played by associations has rapidly increased and is an example of the movement of 'relocalization' of society.

In Poland, the law of 20 July 1983 introduced important functions to be exercised by local people's councils: territorial co-ordination, planning and management of economic and social activities. New arrangements of local finances give a relative independence to local councils for the drawing up and management of their budget. The budget can be adopted without the intervention of the regional authority. However, in practice, the autonomy is limited because of the relatively small resources of local communities. In Poland the realization of self-government is more a problem of resources than of rights. As a result when the responsibilities were transferred to the lower administrative level, the margin of initiative of the local population was not significantly increased, nor was their control of local government strengthened, and local power remained subordinate to higher authorities. The administrative network is still used as the chief basis for a bureaucratic mode of government within which local societies have little power.

The participation of local societies might be stimulated more in other ways. The reactivization of institutions which traditionally ensured the autonomy of the local communities is another sign of the tendency to rediscover the value of the local level. The present policies are trying to remove most of the negative effects of the neglect of the natural territories of local societies. The desire to return to meaningful territories, which the legislators had tried to erase, is expressed for example in the terms traditionally used to name the local representative (*kmet* in Bulgaria, *elöljaroszag* in Hungary, *soltys* in Poland). In Bulgaria the 1978 reform introduced, at the level of the village, the *kmetstvo* represented by a mayor (*kmet*) who was elected by the people and who had the duty to manage public services and to organize the social and cultural activities. However this institution is an administrative agency, which although decentralized to the village level, had no real decision-making power and no proper budget until the new administrative regulations were introduced in 1988. In Hungary, the concern to revive local democracy was sought by the introduction of a new representative organ (*elöljaroszag*) in those villages that had lost their administrative functions during the merger of councils. These self-government organs are composed of the elected representatives to joint councils. They play the role of a mediator with a double mission: defence of local interests and mobilization of local initiatives. In Poland a new institution was established in 1984 to function at the level of the *solectwo*, an area which corresponds to the village. An assembly of inhabitants undertakes self-management within the limited field of competence of village affairs: the improvement of infrastructure (water supply, maintenance of roads and by-roads) and stimulation of social activities. The executive functions are wielded by the *soltys*, a representative elected by the population. Today he is supported by a small council. The establishment of this institution in 1984 demonstrates the desire to boost territorial self-government by associating the population with the undertaking of voluntary infrastructure works such as pavements, lamp-post setting, road maintenance etc. However the resources available to finance these investments remain very poor.

The attempts to rehabilitate traditional forms of organization of local societies are expressions of the movement of 'relocalization'. These are largely limited to the realization of voluntary works and rarely extend to a collective will to ensure wider local development. The premises on which the 'relocalization' movement is based are that it will lead to the creation of new economic initiatives and the encouragement of certain kinds of community associative life. The realization is often weak and we must not be too optimistic that the reversal of the decline in traditional local activities has been achieved. The decline is still present in most cases. However, the authorities that are alert to the effects of the drift from the land are trying to find solutions, and in Bulgaria and in Hungary specific measures of assistance to marginal areas have been adopted.

Generally speaking, the economic crisis has considerably reduced the resources available, and this has led to a shift towards other sources in order to finance the provision of amenities. Individuals and collective initiatives are required which provide clearly seen incentives and benefits to individuals and to local communities. Such incentives are essential in order to stimulate local societies to participate more actively. The increased responsibilities of local authorities are not sufficient as long as they are subordinate to upper levels, and as long as the local society remains passive. But the reconstruction of local society in an associative mode seems to be difficult as long as the reforms continue to dislocate social links. Reformers have realized this. As a result the new reforms give priority to the process of democratization of political life as the basic prerequisite for further developments. Without doubt the real power is going to remain at the centre, but the assertion of the principle of local democracy reveals an important change in the image and importance accorded to the local level.

References

Berezowski, S. (1976), 'Les Poles d'attraction dans l'aménagement du territoire en Pologne', *Espace Géographique*, 1, 39–48.

Enyedi, G. (1987), *Y a-t-il un Pouvoir Local en Hongrie?*, Communication à la IVE Table ronde du Groupe de recherches sur les pays de l'Est, INALCO, Paris.

Hajdú, Z. (1987), *Administrative Division and Administrative Geography in Hungary, Discussion Paper No. 3.*, Centre for Regional Studies, Pécs, Hungary.

Maurel, M-C. (1982a), 'La commune rurale polonaise entre l'ordre bureaucratique et l'autogestion territoriale', *Revue d'Etudes Comparatives Est-quest*, 3, 105–28.

Maurel, M-C. (1982b), *Territoire et Stratégies Soviétiques*, Economica, coll. Géografia, Paris.

Maurel, M-C., Rey, V. and Volle, J.P. (1982), 'Planification et gestion du territoire en Bulgarie', Rapport de mission, 1982, Résumé, *Courrier des Pays de l'Est*, No. 269 (1983), 40–5.

Maurel, M-C. (1983), 'Réformes administratives et gestion locale en Europe de l'Est', *Notes et Etudes Documentaires*, l'URSS et l'Europe de l'Est', 1983–4, La Documentation Française, 37–50.

Rey, V. (1972), 'Organisation régionale et structure urbaine de la Roumanie', *Annales de Géographie*, 711–29.

Vidláková, O. and Zářecký, P. (1989), 'Czechoslovakia: the Development of Public Administration', in R.J. Bennett (ed.), *Territory and Administration in Europe*, Frances Pinter, London.

8 The USSR: territorial and administrative structure

Igor G. Ushkalov and Boris S. Khorev

Introduction

According to its Constitution, the Union of Soviet Socialist Republics is an integral, federal, multinational state founded on the principle of socialist federalism. It is the outcome of the free self-determination of nations and the voluntary association of equal Soviet Socialist Republics.[1] Each Union Republic retains the right to secede freely from the USSR. The sovereignty of the USSR extends throughout its territory.

The jurisdiction of the Union of Soviet Socialist Republics, as represented by its highest bodies of state authority and administration, covers among other items:

— The admission of new republics to the USSR; endorsement of the formation of new autonomous republics and autonomous regions with Union Republics.
— Determination of state boundaries of the USSR and approval of changes in the boundaries between Union Republics.
— Establishment of general principles for the organization and functioning of republican and local bodies of state authority and administration.
— Ensuring the uniformity of legislative norms throughout the USSR and establishment of the fundamentals of the legislation of the USSR and the Union Republics.
— Pursuance of a uniform social and economic policy and management of the country's economy.
— Determination of the main lines of scientific and technological process and the general measures for rational exploitation and conservation of natural resources; the drafting and approval of state plans for the economic and social development of the USSR, and endorsement of reports of their fulfilment.
— The drafting and approval of the consolidated budget of the USSR and endorsement of the report on its execution; management of a single monetary and credit system; determination of the taxes and revenues forming the budget of the USSR; and the formation of prices and wages policy.

— Direction of the sectors of the economy, amalgamations and enterprises under Union jurisdiction; and general direction of industries under Union–Republican jurisdiction.
— Issues of peace and war, defence of the sovereignty, safeguarding of the frontiers and territory of the USSR, and organization of defence; direction of the armed forces of the USSR.
— State security.
— Representation of the USSR in international relations; the USSR's relations with foreign countries and international organization; establishment of the general procedure for, and co-ordination of, the relations of Union Republics with foreign states and with international organizations; foreign trade and other external economic activities on the basis of state monopoly.
— Ensuring that the USSR Constitution is observed and ensuring the conformity of the constitutions of Union Republics to the USSR Constitution.

A Union Republic is a sovereign Soviet socialist state that has united with other Soviet Republics of the USSR. It has its own constitution conforming to the Constitution of the USSR, with the specific features of the Republic taken into account. A Union Republic ensures comprehensive economic and social development in its territory, facilitates exercise of the powers of the USSR, implements the decisions of the highest bodies of state authority and administration of the USSR. The territory of a Union Republic may not be altered without its consent and the mutual agreement of the other Republics concerned; it is also subject to ratification by the USSR.

A Union Republic determines its division into territories, regions, areas, and districts, and decides other matters relating to its internal administrative and territorial structure. It has the right to enter into relations with other states, concludes treaties with them, exchanges diplomatic and consular representatives, and takes part in the work of international organizations.

An Autonomous Republic is a constituent part of a Union Republic. It has its own constitution conforming to the constitutions of the USSR and the Union Republic with the same objectives, but taking the specific features of the Autonomous Republic into account. In matters within its jurisdiction, an Autonomous Republic co-ordinates and controls the activity of enterprises, institutions and organizations subordinate to the Union or the Republic (Union Republic). The territory of an Autonomous Republic may not be altered without its consent.[2]

An Autonomous Region is a constituent part of a Union Republic or Territory.[3]

Levels of government and territorial structure

At present the USSR has four levels of administrative territorial units.

The first level comprises 42,312 rural soviets, 3,961 settlements of cities and 1,181 cities which have a district rank (in total 47,454 units). The number of rural soviets has steadily declined as a result of enlargement due to the concentration of production and population in rural areas, as well as other factors. Between 1951 and 1985 the number was reduced from 74,500 to 42,000.

The second level comprises 3,224 administrative districts and 982 cities with the rank of region, territory or republic (ASSR or SSR) or area — in total, 4,206 units. The number of districts shows a slight tendency to decrease through enlargement, and the number of cities to grow.

The third level comprises the 149 ASSRs, territories, regions and eight Autonomous Regions as constituent parts of territories, ten autonomous areas as constituent parts of regions, and seven cities of the jurisdiction of SSRs in major SSRs; in total 174 units.

The fourth level comprises the fifteen SSRs of which seven have no regions.

The changes in administrative and territorial structure of the Soviet Union 1917–87 are summaried in Table 8.1. The detailed structure of the administrative units differs considerably. Thus, for example, within the cities with the rank of regions (territory, republic, ASSR or SSR, and area) there is a group of cities which do not have direct jurisdiction. There are seventy-two in republics which have no regions. In republics comprising regions the regional cities as a rule are the capitals; there are fifteen of these. From the formal point of view these should be attributed to the third hierarchical level, but their functions are considerably greater. Eighty cities are attributed to the second level.

The number of third and fourth level units has stayed rather stable mainly as a result of the stability of the national regions. At present there are more than forty large cities of non-regional jurisdiction which have been transformed into regional centres because of their development, geographical position and population. Therefore the process of regional dispersion may continue.[4]

Evolution of government and territorial structure

In place of the *guberniyas* and regions of pre-revolutionary Russia (the territory of modern RSFSR, except the Kaliningrad region) there now exist seventy regions, territories and ASSRs of which fifty-four formally correspond to the former units (except the Kaliningrad regions constituted after World War II). This is a vivid illustration of the inertia of administrative and territorial structure.

The regions, territories, ASSRs and local districts differ from each other markedly in the size of their territory, population and economic potential. In many economic units the difference between the constituent regions, territories and ASSRs is so great they cannot be associated with the same administrative level. Even within the limits of an homogeneous economic

Table 8.1   Changes in administrative and territorial structure of the Soviet Union 1917–87

	1917	1923	1937	1941	1950	1971	1980	1987
SSRs	—	4	11	16	16	15	15	15
ASSRs	—	13	22	20	16	20	20	20
Autonomous regions	—	16	9	9	9	8	8	8
Autonomous areas	—	—	9	10	10	10	10	10
Territories	—	—	5	6	6	6	6	6
Regions	—	—	42	101	126	114	121	123
Guberniyas	74	75	—	—	—	—	—	—
Areas	—	—	26	8	13	—	—	—
Uyezds	605	766	—	59	54	—	—	—
Districts	—	—	3,307	4,007	4,285	3,031	3,176	3,225
Volosts	13,913	13,659	—	1,023	553	—	—	—
Cities	—	—	755	1,241	1,424	1,949	2,074	2,176
Settlements of city type	—	—	616	1,711	2,243	3,596	3,864	3,992
Rural Soviets	—	—	62,585	70,034	74,866	40,915	41,374	42,411

district such as the Central district, the range is rather great. For example, the Orlov region is 24.7 thousand square kilometres, the Kalinin region 84.1 (four times more). The population range is even greater: the Kostroma region has 797,000 people and the neighbouring Gorki region 3,698,000 (five times more). The differences between regions within the economic districts are even more striking.

The local administrative districts differ from each other substantially. Let us consider three main characteristics: the type of centre, its area and its population. In the RSFSR the district centres are represented both by cities (39 per cent) as well as settlements of city type (27 per cent) and villages (34 per cent). The major differences in population may be observed between the cities which are district centres. These are minor cities with a size several times less than the official census standard for cities in the RSFSR, which is 12,000. In Russia there are twenty-seven city-district centres with less than 5,000 inhabitants. In parallel there exist major cities with more than 500,000 inhabitants, that is more than 100 times greater.

The rate of fluctuation in the population of the administrative districts is also considerable: from a few thousand up to several hundred thousand. Twenty-seven per cent of all districts of the RSFSR each contain up to only 20,000 inhabitants. Meanwhile in the main districts of Non-Chernozem zone (North-West, Centre, Volgo-Vyatka), there are 31.8 per cent (1979 census). These small population areas result in the local administration having little influence on the development of productive forces in their regions.

It should be noted that the average population of a RSFSR district now constitutes only 31,900. For a rural district the population is altogether insignificant (average 3,200). Only in three major economic districts (North Caucasus, Central Chernozem and Povolzhye) does the level of rural population exceed the republican average. In the Non-Chernozem zone, characterized by complicated agricultural conditions, more than 60 per cent of the districts have less than 20,000 rural inhabitants, and 15 per cent of the districts have less than 10,000 inhabitants. The economic development problems of this zone are aggravated by low population. The area of the districts is even more variable: from several hundred thousand square kilometres down to a few hundred square kilometres. At the same time there are considerable gaps between the administrative levels: for example in the RSFSR the highest (fourth) level can be compared with the seventy-three third-level units. The range of size of territories and regions between the third and second level is between 1:70 and 1:90.

The concentration of production and integration between economic sectors sometimes contradicts the administrative and territorial structure. The existing network of administrative units is often misaligned with the present and prospective hierarchy of territorial production complexes (TPCs) and economic planning regions. At present economic planning is practiced in nineteen major economic regions in the USSR, including fourteen intrarepublican (in the RSFSR and the Ukranian SSR), two republican (in the Byelorussian and Kazakh SSRs) and three interrepublican regions (Baltic, Transcaucasian, Centralasian SSRs). In addition, there is the Moldavian SSR which is too small to constitute an economic region. The modern network of major economic regions, in its main features, has been very stable with a close relation to economic and historical centres.

Functions of state administration

The territorial and political organization of the Soviet society is founded on a hierarchical structure of elected soviets, ranging from the local soviet up to the supreme soviet of the USSR. The highest level of the state administration, the government of the USSR (Council of Ministers of the USSR), emphasizes a series of ministries for different sectors of activities (foreign relations, defence, foreign trade, interior, justice, education, culture, health, finance), as well as ministries for the different economic sectors (production, construction, distribution and exchange), as well as functional state committees. Among the committees with the greatest economic importance are the following: the State Planning Committee of the USSR (Gosplan), the State Construction Committee (Gosstroi) and the State Scientific and Technical Committee of the USSR (GKNT).

According to the Constitution of the USSR, the economy is an integral economic complex comprising all the elements of social production, distribution and exchange in its territory. The economy is managed on the basis of state plans for economic and social development, with due account for sectoral and territorial principles, and by combining centralized direction with the managerial independence and initiative of individual and amalgamated enterprises and other organizations.

At the highest level of the USSR state, the administrative jurisdiction covers the following economic matters: pursuance of a uniform social and economic policy; direction of the country's economy; determination of the main lines of scientific and technological progress and the general measures for rational exploitation and conservation of natural resources; the drafting and approval of state plans for the economic and social development of the USSR and endorsement of reports on their fulfilment; the drafting and approval of the consolidated budget of the USSR and endorsement of the report on its execution; management of a single monetary and credit system; determination of the taxes and revenues forming the budget of the USSR; the formulation of prices and wages policy; direction of the sectors of the economy, and enterprises and amalgamations under Union jurisdiction and general direction of industries under Union–Republican jurisdiction.

What place does the territorial principle of administration occupy in this system? The federal system and political structure of the USSR determine the territorial principle of organization. For the organization of the economic sectors the level of the Union Republic is clearly stressed (not only by the existence of a Union, but also by the Union–Republican ministries and institutions). Each Union Republic ensures comprehensive economic and social development in its territory. In matters that come within its jurisdiction, a Union Republic co-ordinates and controls the activity of enterprises, institutions and organizations subordinate to the Union.

The territorial principle is also manifest at the next lower level of sectoral administration, on the level of production amalgamations formed within ministries and other institutions. Many of these are territorial production amalgamations (that is sectoral territorial systems) situated within a given region, a minor Union Republic or even a big city. The formation of a wide network of production, scientific, and productional industrial amalgamations began in the USSR in the mid-1970s although production units of this type existed before. By the end of 1972 there were 1,101. At present the production amalgamations are the basis of the two-tier and three-tier general schemes in the industrial sectors. Many amalgamations are almost 'sectoral territorial systems': for instance, enterprises with a high level of concentration of production. The territorial amalgamations which combine enterprises located in the same region are regarded as particularly effective. Experience suggests that such complexes are more manageable, they use regional labour and natural resources more fully and they better co-ordinate their activities with local party and soviet bodies.

At the same time the existing system of sectoral administration manifests certain drawbacks. Being rather dispersed, some sectoral and intersectoral problems are not being solved effectively enough. Therefore we see the need to strengthen the territorial administration by groups of interrelated sectors (or subsectors) of the national economy.

Functions of local administration

During the whole period since the Revolution the local soviets have occupied the main place in state administration, their rights and obligations being stipulated in the Constitution of the USSR. At each level the soviet is responsible for the principal functions of administering the territorial development of society, from the supreme soviet of the USSR, to the soviets of people's deputies in the districts, cities, city districts, settlements and villages. These constitute a single system of bodies of state authority. Local soviets of people's deputies deal with all matters of local significance in accordance with the interests of the state as a whole and of the citizens residing in their area: they implement the decisions of higher levels, guide the work of lower soviets of people's deputies, take part in the discussions of the Republics and Union. Their chief functions are to direct state, economic, social and cultural development within their territory; endorse plans of economic and social development and the local budget; exercise general guidance over state bodies, enterprises, institutions and organizations subordinate to them; ensure observance of the laws, maintenance of law and order and protection of citizens' rights. Within their powers, the local soviets ensure the comprehensive, all-round economic and social development of their area; exercise control over the observance of legislation by enterprises, institutions and organizations subordinate to higher authorities and located in their area; and co-ordinate and supervise activity as regards land use, nature conservation, building, employment of manpower, production of consumer goods and social, cultural, communal and other services and amenities for the public.

The 1918 RSFSR constitution defined the main functions to be fulfilled by the local soviets: to develop the territory economically and culturally, to solve all questions of local importance and to guide the economic and cultural activities of their territory. The regional administrative structure established in 1920 strengthened the position of local soviets and ensured the unity of economic and political guidance and provided them with substantial powers in comparison to the former territorial administrative bodies. Special attention was paid to strengthening the local administrative district. Besides enlarging the city and district soviets, much attention was paid to the rural soviets which played a big role in the collectivization of agriculture. The local soviets developed their role rapidly and this was codified with laws defining their rights and obligations. Such were the 1971 Law of City and City District Soviets of People's Deputies, the 1971 Law of District Soviets of People's Deputies, and the 1968 Law of Rural and Settlement Soviets of People's Deputies.

By the time these laws were adopted, the local soviets had accumulated vast experience in guiding the national economy, and in planning, calculation, budgetary-financial activity, etc. However, simultaneously a series of deficiencies appeared in their functioning. For example, parallel to the enterprises and institutions of social infrastructure managed by the local soviets, there existed (and still exist) a considerable number of bodies not subordinate to them. Their creation often takes place without the knowledge and direct guidance of the local soviets. In fact, many infrastructural projects are not guided by local soviets and capital investments are made by institutions and enterprises controlled by higher levels which are not accountable to the soviets. This has hampered the administration of the economy in a given territory and undermined its optimal development.

Deficiencies in planning also came to light. Within a given territory the complex planning was inadequate; in addition the co-ordination and linkage between the plans of the separate enterprises, organizations and institutions was unsatisfactory. Over a long period of time the local planning commissions planned the development of the whole city or district economy, but not of the separate sectoral elements (enterprises of local industry, agriculture). The absence of comprehensive planning hampered the rational use of territory. All this reduced the efficiency of local use of resources. To overcome this the role of the soviets should be increased, since they could then adopt the role of comprehensive planning.

A substantial change in the principles of combining sectoral and territorial administration took place after the late 1960s, and was settled in the articles of the new 1977 USSR Constitution. This gave to the Union Republic and the soviets the role of ensuring and planning the comprehensive economic and social development of their territories. This requirement reflected a long process of enhancing the role of the soviets at all levels in the development and guidance of the economy. First of all, this ensured a tight linkage between economic and social development, a correct correlation between sectoral and territorial principles of administration and the establishment of co-operative links between enterprises, institutions and organizations of different sectors situated in a specific territory. All this provided the main objective of comprehensive economic and social development of the territories for which the soviets are responsible.

A substantial role in enlarging and defining the rights of the soviets of different levels was played by reforms of the laws regulating their activity adopted in the late 1960s and early 1970s. These reforms improved local administration, enforced the role of the soviets in developing and accommodating the production enterprises and helped in using territorial resources efficiently. At present the functions of the local soviets comprise the following: all-round planning of economic and social development of their territory, guidance of the separate economic sectors and budgetary and financial activity. The administration of the national economy controls the production sphere as well as the sectors of public service. The functions of the city, district and rural soviets are analogous. The difference lies only in the material basis of their administrative functions (in cities, industrial production and a higher level of public services are present; in rural areas agricultural production is the main function).

At present the local soviets are expanding and strengthening their material and financial foundations. They have received into their jurisdiction a series of enterprises which are of importance at the regional and republican level. This provides an increase in their revenues. These enterprises assign a part of their profits to the budget of cities and districts, and this provides their chief financial resource. Therefore, the wider the basis of the city, the larger the profits of the local soviets. Similarly, agricultural enterprises are important sources of profits for the districts. The rural soviets receive their financial resources from local industry. They also retain the whole level of profit after calculation of the revenues required to match expenditures. Nevertheless, further increases in the level of resources of the local soviets are necessary.

Especially wide rights are now given to the upper levels of the soviets within the Union Republics, that is to the soviets of people's deputies of territories, regions, Autonomous Republics and autonomous areas. Their rights in economic management have been substantially enlarged with the endorsement of the new 1980 Law of the USSR on their Basic Rights. The Law obliges ministries and institutions to ensure that the main draft of the industrial plan be submitted to the relevant soviets of the territory, region and area. They must also consider the resolutions of the soviets while drafting plans in order to stimulate the interests of the soviets in the development of industrial and agricultural production. The Law also provides for the assignment of part of the profits of the enterprises and organizations to the budget of the relevant territories, regions and areas. This is a new step which enlarges the capacity of the local administration bodies.

The soviets are also responsible for the administration and control of the exploitation and protection of land, water, forests, soils, atmospheric air and wildlife and for environmental protection. In 1982 a substantial restructuring in the country's managerial system of the agro-industrial complexes took place. This further enlarged the role of the soviets in the area of economic administration. In accordance with the 1982 Decision of the CPSU Central Committee and Council of Ministers of the USSR, district agro-industrial agglomerations (RAPOs) were formed within local administrative districts (as well as regions, territories, and Autonomous Republics). These include collective farms, (kolkhozs), Soviet farms (sovkhozs) and other agricultural production and processing enterprises as well as organizations in services related to agricultural production and processing. All retain their economic autonomy, juridicial person and institutional affiliation. The council of the RAPO is formed by the soviets of the district, and its president is simultaneously the head of the agricultural department of the soviet and vice-president of the executive committee. This represents a reassertion of the 'double jurisdiction' principle drafted and implemented during the managerial economic experiment of the first years of Soviet power (1921–4).

The restructuring of social and economic life in the USSR has introduced some radically new features into the functional structure of local administration as well. The process of democratization of social life is strengthening the political significance of the local level, not only as executor of common national economic interests, but also in pursuing its own detached territorial interests. The structure of functions of the local soviets has hence been greatly developed and enriched.

Territorial planning and territorial-production complexes (TPCs)

Since the USSR is a planned socialist economy, regional social and economic policy is realized through planning (be it sectoral or territorial). Territorial planning is based on the principles of comprehensive economic and social development of the territories (Union Republics, regions, cities); the rational allocation of production to primary sources and consumers; a more uniform allocation of production between the territories of the country; the development of the economy and culture of the Union Republics; achieving a rational combination of specialization and comprehensive development of the economic regions; and efficient division of labour between the socialist countries and their economic integration into the Council of Mutual Economic Assistance (CMEA).

In order to include the territorial aspect of development in sectoral economic planning, it is necessary to ensure a territorial aspect of economic planning. The main tasks of economic development in some five-year plans are set not only in the plans for economic sectors, but also for all Union Republics. (This amounts to two-thirds or more of the national income of the USSR.) The extension of economic competence of Union Republics has allowed new developments and use of productive assets to be found which have improved sectoral planning while serving a more comprehensive process of economic development in economic regions of the Union Republics. An important link between sectoral and territorial planning is the allocation of new industrial enterprises. This is mostly orientated towards industrial displacement into the eastern regions of the USSR. A further aspect is the production of consumer goods and social organizations. The overall objective of this co-ordination is to achieve the principle of democratic centralism, that is local characteristics and local initiative are to be combined with central planning of the national economy. This allows sectoral plans to be co-ordinated into a comprehensive territorial plan aimed at co-ordination of all economic sectors in Union Republics and economic regions.

Regional social and economic policy is executed not only through planning. An important role is played also by budgetary policy, tax policy, the policy on wholesale prices and the regional aspects of demographic policy. The major problem to which these policies are directed is the more equal social and economic development of the USSR among its different regions. Many of the differences in the level of social and economic development in the USSR (apart from natural and geographic conditions) may be explained by the considerable demographic differences which exist, particularly the different rates of increase of population and average family size. The major factor affecting the redistribution of income among the Union Republics is demography. As a result, produced income may differ considerably from the used income in the Union Republics. The latter is greatest in the Republics with the highest birth rates and the largest average families (the Uzbek SSR, the Turkmen SSR, the Kazakh SSR and others). Some of the annual subsidies from the social fund in favour of these Union Republics amount to 40 per cent of the national income used in them. The difference between the income produced and used in a Union Republic is often counted as the balance between the production volume transported in and from it. But the mechanism of redistribution is far more complicated and requires further research. Certainly, the budget distribution is the main source of financing the development of a Union Republic, including the distribution of tax and state social security revenues, and this promotes a considerable redistribution in favour of the least developed regions.

The basic object of territorial planning in the USSR is an economic region formed from a network of territorial production complexes (TPCs)[5] which are used as a means of achieving an efficient combination of natural, material and labour resources. One of the most important aims of modern territorial policy in the USSR is to regulate the conflicts between the TPCs (which demand an adequate mechanism of territorial administration) and the established structure of territorial boundaries and administration division. At the local level, there is also the regional production complex (RPC). This has four main characteristics:

1. The economic integrity arising from the regional specialization of division of labour and the interrelated character of its economy. This makes it possible to outline common development policies for a region;
2. The interrelation of the development of all complexes in the economic framework of the country;
3. The level of production and technological specialization due to natural, economic, national and cultural features of the region;
4. The level of development conditioned by the process of economic assimilation of different territories in the USSR.

The TPCs ensure the unity of economic regions and their efficient interconnected development. Each large economic region, in principle, must be formed on a TPC. If practical life diverges from the rule, the territorial structure of the state network of economic regionalization must be adjusted. In turn, the single territorial links of TPCs may be separated. Their functional elements participate in ensuring specialization and comprehensive development, as integral parts and main nuclei for economic and geographical modelling and planning the territorial allocation of production.

The planning of new TPCs is very important at present. These are being developed at Bratsk–Ust–Ilimsk, Sayani as well as elsewhere and are founded on the exploitation of hydro-electric resources of the rivers Angara and Yenisei. There are also the Kansk–Achinsk lignite and power complex (KATEK), the KMA, Orenburg, South–Tajik, South–Yakut, Pavlodar-

Ekibastuz TPCs and others. In 1976–80 the new TPCs ensured the increase in oil production, almost the whole output of natural gas extraction and a considerable proportion of the increase in production of electric power, iron ore, coal, automobiles and tractors.

The new TPCs now occupy a separate line in the state plan. They are planned as comprehensive structural territorial formations and have different bodies to administer them (such as the interinstitutional commission in West Siberia made up of a council of the directors of the enterprises). All this makes it possible to regard the TPCs as a form of planned regional policy in two ways. In a narrow sense, TPCs are a kind of territorial economic formation which allow comprehensive regional development of territories particularly through concentrating new construction. In a broader sense, TPCs are a method of socialist territorial organization of production allowing a wider approach to planning the territorial social and economic system which facilitates more efficient resource allocation.

Problems of perfecting the functions of territorial and administration structures

The present period in the USSR is characterized by the initiation of structural changes in order to accelerate scientific and technical progress and intensify access to social production. This is the process termed economic restructuring (*perestroika*). Economic restructuring introduces a series of important theoretical problems within the territorial organization of society which require changes to the underlying goals, criteria and functions of territorial economic development. The increased mobility of resources results in the need for a new look at the structure of territorial development, the regional isolation of economic and social processes of economic reproduction and the openness of territorial systems. Simultaneously, the possible paths for regional development diversify, the interconnections between regions at differing hierarchical levels grow and a more decisive role is played by the human factor; all this moves the social and political aspects of territorial development to the forefront.

The emphasis on scientific and technical progress introduces the following new aspects into the territorial organization of Soviet society. First, in seeking to transform the scientific and technical revolution into a scientific and production one, there is an increasing emphasis on the effect of economic policy in general, and on territorial economic policy in particular. The ecological impacts of social and economic development are in essence regional. At the same time, they are strongly connected with the human factor. As a result, ecological factors are more and more important in affecting local political issues. This affects the comprehensive territorial structure of the country, and its form depends on how local interests are combined with the territorial structures. As a result there is a growing need for a political-geographic foundation to territorial policy which introduces new mechanisms of administration that can respond to the main criteria of economic restructuring: through making the relationships closer between the system levels.

A complex set of problems derives from these developments which have not yet been resolved. The first of these is the definition of which factors should determine the efficiency and stability of the territorial and administrative structure. This leads to the need to understand the mechanisms for the development of new functions which allow the fields of competence of the administrative bodies at the different territorial and administrative levels to be defined.

With respect to the structure of the local economic administrative units, the following defines some basic ideas of the developments in the territorial administrative system which are feasible. These developments can be as:

1. Objects administered automatically;
2. Objects administered with the sanction of higher bodies;
3. Objects of a higher jurisdiction for which there is the right of being the sanctioner;
4. Objects administered absolutely by higher bodies;
5. Objects whose function lies in maintaining the object's development.

In the USSR there are three ways of increasing the competence of the regional administration:

1. Enlarging and activating the rights of the existing regional administrative bodies. This is one of the main trends in developing socialist democracy. It has the effect of enlarging the rights and competences of the soviets at all levels, but especially at the local level;
2. Creating new administrative bodies in the existing administrative units. This trend was and still is rather popular in economic practice but in many cases it is not fully effective because it does not take sufficient account of the real territorial interests;
3. Changing the existing structure of economic and administrative regions with the aim of making their boundaries coincide with their functions, by broadening their administrative rights but without creating new bodies. We consider this to be the chief trend but stress that in the past two decades it has not gained sufficient attention in practice. The broadening of rights and competences of the existing territorial bodies undoubtedly serves as the necessary preliminary step. Naturally it must not be isolated from those territorial fields where genuine comprehensive economic and social development is possible, but the existing limits do not always permit this to be realized.

Notes

1. Russia, the Ukraine, Byelorussia, Uzbekistan, Kazakhstan, Georgia, Lithuania,

Moldavia, Latvia, Azerbaijan, Kirghizia, Tajikistan, Armenia, Turkmenistan and Estonia.

2. The Russian Soviet Federative Socialist Republic includes the Bashkir, Buryat, Daghestan, Karbardin-Balkar, Kalmyk, Karelian, Komi, Mari, Mordovian, North Ossetian, Tartar, Tuva, Udmurt, Chechen-Ingush Chuvash, and Yakut Autonomous Soviet Socialist Republics (ASSRs). The Uzbek SSR includes the Kara-Kalpak ASSR. The Georgian SSR includes the Abkhasian and Adzhar ASSRs. The Azerbaijan SSR includes the Nakhichevan ASSR.

3. The Russian Soviet Federative Socialist Republic includes the Adygei, Gorno-Altai, Jewish, Karachai-Chircassian, and Khakass Autonomous Regions. The Georgian Soviet Socialist Republic includes the South Ossetian Autonomous Region. The Azerbaijan Society Socialist Republic includes the Nagorno-Karabakh Autonomous Region. The Tajik Soviet Socialist Republic includes the Gorno-Badakhshan Autonomous Region. An Autonomous Area is a constituent part of a Territory or Region. The law on an Autonomous Area may be adopted by the Supreme soviet of the Union Republic concerned.

4. The present share of city population in the USSR exceeds 65 per cent: in the RSFSR it is more than 73 per cent, in Estonia 71 per cent, in Latvia 70 per cent, in Lithuania and the Ukraine 66 per cent, in Byelorussia 63 per cent. In the Asian Republics it is always less than 50 per cent, for example Tajik (33 per cent), Kirghiz (40 per cent), Turkmen (47 per cent).

5. Up to now the definition of the TPC in the USSR is a point of scientific debate which reflects different opinions as to territorial structure of society and the primacy of production. As an example the territorial production complexes may be defined as a multisectoral combination of production types situated on limited territory, having a comprehensive political and social infrastructure; a system of settlement aimed at comprehensively exploiting the natural resources of its territory, ensuring comfortable conditions of life for attracting and settling the labour forces and for environmental protection.

9 Poland: searching for increasing economic effectiveness

Maria Ciechocińska

Introduction

A wide range of circumstances and events, which Poland experienced in the early and middle 1980s, has revealed the obvious necessity of reforming the overall functioning of central and local administration at all levels of planning, management and control. Such reforms were necessary to tackle economic difficulties related to a deep crisis, which the former structures had not been able to overcome. What is more, the majority of troubles which the country was going through seemed to result from the strong centralization of authority as well as the powerful influence of bureaucratic administrative structures. The power exercised by the latter was so great as to impede effectively all attempts at reforms made in the years 1957–87. The mechanisms of failure have been presented in the literature (see for example Graham and Ciechocińska, 1987).

Apart from economic breakdown, among other factors prompting political and economic reform of the system, conventionally labelled as a centrally planned socialist economy, were the economy's stumbling due to low management efficiency, lack of interest in introducing new technologies, petrification of status quo and public apathy. For example, Reykowski (1987) has analysed factors ensuing from the functioning of the doctrine, Koźmiński (1982) has drawn an analysis of inadequacy of the measures taken, and Pajestka (1983) and Müller (1985) have explained the economic processes affecting the weird circle of the Polish economy's impuissance.

Noteworthy in this context are changes which have affected regional and local administrative bodies, the activities of which have been frequently modified. In view of the limited space in this chapter, chief attention will be concentrated on evaluating the functioning of administration at the regional level emphasing their budgets in relation to the central budget (this accords to a maxim, which is more and more commonly circulated in Poland, that the authority of an administration is in proportion to the funds at its disposal).

Evolution of the territorial organization of the state

Since 1975 Poland has had a two-level administrative division, including the *voivod*ship level (regional), and the local level (municipal, municipal–rural, or rural). At each of the management levels, there is a basic body of state administration and a people's council, being a body of local self-government, both of which were established by the Law on the System of People's Councils and Local Self-government, dated 20 July 1983.

Under the Polish constitution and other legislative acts, local self-government is prescribed to play a leading role, yet in practice the position of the state administration has always been stronger, in spite of the repeal of the Law on People's Councils as Local Agencies of Uniform State Authority, dated 20 March 1950. 'People's councils, as agencies representing the state authority . . ., are at the same time agencies of local self-government of people in rural communes, towns, districts of cities, and *voivod*ships' (Art. 1 of the Law of 20 July 1983).

The changes introduced in the 1950s were later assessed, especially in the perspective of the subsequent experiences of the 1980s, as deeply degrading the system of councils through the dismantling of democratic mechanisms, reducing the activities of council sessions, commissions and the councillors themselves to a ritual which was necessary only to enforce decisions which had already been at a much higher level, most frequently the central level (Zawadzka, 1981, pp. 4–5). Thus it was considered that local authorities should be fully self-governing, yet people's councils should be part of the state machine. The idea was typical of the Stalinist period, when a conviction was prevalent that the greater the level of control, uniformity and subordination the state had in the regions, the more socialist it would be. The abandonment of that policy has taken the form of a slow evolution. Gradually, the range of responsibility of local administrative bodies has been expanded, as well as their powers and the financial means at their disposal (Ciechocińska, 1984).

However, expansion of the range of tasks and competences of the people's councils has proceeded very slowly. In the 1970s, for example, a reorganization of local administration was carried out. This reduced the economic activities of the councils by centralization of public spending resources. The councils operated as both state-authority and self-government bodies, since they were fully subject to higher-level state administrative bodies. However, the legislative acts lacked a division of assignments, and did not state clearly enough which tasks should be realized only by local self-government bodies, without the influence of other, particularly central bodies.

An amendment to the law on the system of people's councils and local self-government, dated June 16, 1988, has strengthened the position of the people's councils compared to the state administration. It has also increased their economic autonomy, and has introduced, with an enforcement date of 1 January 1989, communal property. Property had been nationalized in 1950 under the law on uniform state authority bodies mentioned earlier. Communal property had practically ceased to exist as a collective property of a particular local community. This gave rise to the subordination of the economic benefits to be obtained for satisfying public needs in a given locality, to the realization of national goals set up by the central-level authorities according to their own criteria.

The amendment has provided the foundations for economic and financial self-dependence of the regions, increased the range of local competence and it may become an important step forward in the process of territorial and functional decentralization (Lange, 1962).

Territory and administration: management aspects

The management aspects of the relationship of territory and administration are of major importance when dealing with the basic administrative units at the local and regional level. Depending on the adopted model, that is centralized or decentralized management, the relations are different and they greatly affect the functioning of the national economy as a whole. This thesis will be explicated with reference to the experiences of Poland.

In the centralized model of management, powerful hierarchical, vertical structures are created which serve the implementation of quantitative economic tasks. Local self-government, which is subordinated to state administration bodies, ceases to play any significant role. Division within the centre into departments which are headed by different cabinet members, leads to the primacy of sectoral branch structures over horizontal ones, such as regional or local structures. Owing to its autonomy, vertical administration is far more powerful than the horizontal levels. Geographical studies have demonstrated that centralized models of management inevitably lead to increasing conflicts between regions and branches. Furthermore, the centralized system of management is liable to encounter obstacles, such as information barriers (for example Bennett, 1980, p. 70), because the central apparatus is not able to digest all the information which flows to it and this results in an increased number of erroneous decisions pertaining to the allocation of financial means, the localization of new investments and the like. Attempts to improve the centralized model of management by expanding and rationalizing the techniques of command and distribution based on economic coercion have not brought about the desired effects.

The reasons for the inefficiency of the centralized system are well known. An illusory convergence of the non-market and non-monetary economy model of utopian socialism with the command-distribution organization of the war economy resulted in the latter being adopted as the *only* socialist model: it excluded any alternative possibilities. Such a context gave rise to an ideology of extreme state control over the economy, promoting centralization of decision-making and demonetization of the economy, the side effect of which was a specific economic education.

The theoretical difference between the centralized and decentralized models of management boils down to the fact that the former uses methods of compulsion and takes advantage of market and monetary categories only for record-keeping and control purposes, while the latter uses these categories as an active instrument in the decision-making processes, to aid reliable cost-benefit studies and the application of economic parameters.

The decentralized model helps towards consolidating ties between administration and society, favours public initiatives and enterprise and accelerates the increase of economic effectiveness. It also eases the co-ordination of developments of settlement units and areas. Local bodies are reinforced and this shapes the horizontal ties necessary for the development of a given town or rural commune. For example agreements are facilitated in such fields as the co-operation in the construction of factories with houses for workers, technical infrastructure, health centres, shops and the like. These agreements contrast with the difficulties of co-ordinating regional interdependences in the centralized management system, which almost entirely lacks means for respecting horizontal ties (see Ledworowski, 1988).

Increasing the economic effectiveness of multi-level administrative structures requires decentralization of decision-making. The essence of decentralization lies in giving a degree of autonomy to a lower level. This entails non-interference from a higher level. There are two forms of decentralization: territorial and functional. In Poland efforts are currently being made to widen both of these forms as part of economic reform.

Functional decentralization consists of increasing the autonomy of particular economic agents (carriers of rights) regardless of their organizational subordination in the system of multi-level management. In 1981 the rule for functional decentralization in Poland was formulated as 3xS: enterprises should be self-dependent, self-financing and self-managing.

Territorial decentralization applies to state administrative units which gradually take over enterprises, real estate, equipment, material and financial tasks. The economic autonomy of local authorities does not extend to some fields, for example railway transport, airlines, the post and telecommunications, mining and so on, which remain within centrally governed structures (Sochacka-Krysiak et al., 1986, p. 32).

There have been cases of seeming decentralization, grounded on depriving hierarchical structures of in-between bodies, and seizure of their competences by other existing or newly created agencies. This happened in Poland when a three-level territorial organization of the country was replaced by the two-level one. The missing element, namely the district level, was then recreated within the new structures.

Normally the most frequently occurring model is a mixed one which combines elements of both centralized and decentralized systems in various configurations of local and regional concepts which vary with respect to the intrinsic features of each part of the country. Empirical studies and the development of events indicate that not every form of decentralization consisting in the passing down of competence is approved. The interested party often makes efforts to prevent decentralization occurring in order to preserve its power. This has been the case of some public works enterprises which are governed by *voivod*ship authorities whose workers do not want to be subject to the lower-level administrations. This has not been the rule,

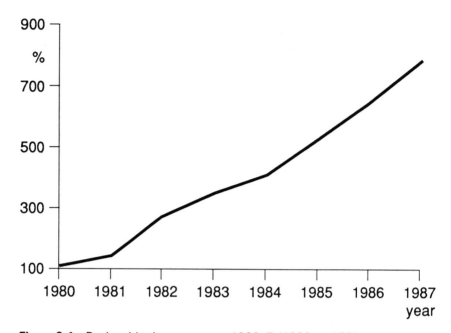

Figure 9.1 Regional budget revenues 1980–7 (1980 = 100)

Source: author's elaboration based on Rocznik statystyczny (1987, p. 113, Table 14/159) and Ministry of Finance data

however, for one can quote many opposite examples. The accepted options in a particular instance are always the outcome of the contending of the particular interests which come to play in amending the aims of legislation which define the range of competences in decentralized systems of state territorial administration.

The structure of regional and local budgets

Regional and local budgets can be used as an indicator of the dependence of regions upon the central administration. The degree of interrelation of the local and central budgets may be analysed for both revenues and expenditures. The 1980s saw sharp inflation in Poland which was related to the social and economic crisis and a broad programme of reforms. Owing to the rapid changes in values that resulted, the percentages of these two particular items in the budgets were subjected to analysis. Absolute proportions of regional budgets' revenues in the years 1980–7 recorded a sevenfold increase, as shown in Figure 9.1.

Changes in the share of the central contribution to the revenues of regional budgets are shown in Figure 9.2. It can be seen that central contributions have fallen due to the gradual implementation of reforms of the financial system. Taxes on wages and salaries were introduced in 1982 as a source of reinforcing local budgets' prime revenues. This made it

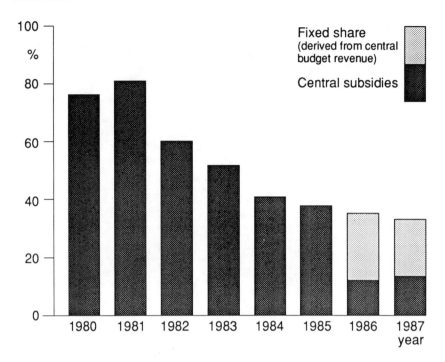

Figure 5.2 Share of central contribution to regional budget revenues in 1980–7

Source: as Figure 9.1.

possible to compensate localities for a gradual reduction in the level of finance which was derived from the central budget. This can be seen in Figure 9.2. Another important change took place in 1985, when a new budget law secured for regional funds a fixed share of the central budget revenues. This allowance was granted earlier from the so-called 'compensation funds'. Nevertheless, one-third of financial means necessary for compensating regional and local budgets is still derived from the central budget. As a result the central administration can still maintain a tight supervision of the local economy and its administration, as well as making changes to some decisions. This allows, on the one hand, for levelling out of social development between areas and counteracts the particular interests of better developed areas. On the other hand, this power considerably reduces the autonomy of decisions of regional and local administration and self-government (Jaworski and Sochacka-Krysiak, 1982).

Conclusions of the same character can be drawn from analysis of the structure of the expenditure side of the regional budget. Figure 9.3 shows that this is dominated by routine expenses. Few resources are left for major repairs and investments. In such a system, investment policy is largely determined by the central administration and financed accordingly from the central budget. A favourable phenomenon, however, from the point of view of local interests, can be observed in the gradual increase in the

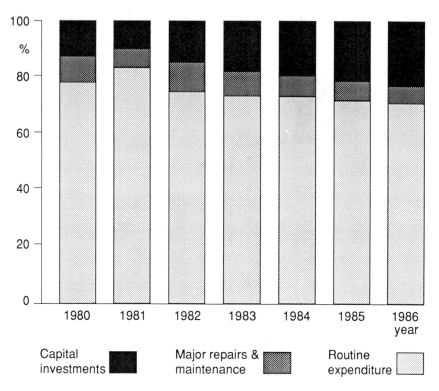

Figure 9.3   Structure of regional expenditures, 1980–6

Source: as Figure 9.1

proportion of the investment expenditure in regional budgets: from 10.1 per cent in 1981, to 22.3 per cent in 1986. There is a comparatively small share, as yet, of expenditure on major repairs. Given the considerable physical depreciation of fixed assets and infrastructure, this appears to be a barrier to development of the economy.

It should be made clear that in a centrally planned socialist economy negligence in the field of routine and major repairs may result not only from shortages of money, but also from the lack of material means and operational capacities of the specialized enterprises concerned with maintenance and repairs. The long-term preferences that have existed for heavy industry in the investment policy have led to a considerable abandonment of the broadly defined sphere of services.

Routine expenditures dominate the regional budgets, and this is not likely to change radically in view of their structure. As shown in Table 9.1, about 90 per cent of the total routine expenditure is devoted to three groups of expenses: enterprises and other socialized economic units, education, health care and welfare. Of special significance here is a systematic decrease in the percentage of funds used to support health care and welfare. This has occurred in spite of a dramatic increase in population. At the same time there has been a comparable growth of expenses for

Table 9.1 Structure of routine expenditure of regional budgets in the years 1980–6 (%)

Year	Enterprises and other socialized economic units	Education	Culture and art	Health care and social welfare	Physical education, sport, tourism	Administration
1980	24.0	28.0	3.1	38.4	1.4	5.1
1981	25.0	28.5	2.9	37.5	1.5	4.6
1982	34.1	26.4	2.7	32.1	1.2	3.5
1983	32.2	29.1	0.4	33.0	1.3	4.0
1984	31.4	32.0	0.3	29.4	2.0	4.9
1985	31.9	32.1	0.2	28.8	1.7	5.3
1986	31.6	31.0	0.5	29.3	2.3	5.3

Source: the author's elaboration based on Rocznik Statystyczny (1987, p. 113, Table 14/159)

enterprises and other socialized economic units. This reflects the level of financial difficulties which are faced by regional budgets.

The tenets of economic reform envisage an intensification of local initiatives and an enlivening of the regional economy. Yet, the slow implementation of the reform has led, at the initial stages, to the increase of expenditures for enterprises and other socialized economic units, as well as increases in spending on local administration (see Table 9.1). Expanding competences have entailed the need to raise employees' salaries in order to increase effectiveness and to stimulate improved personnel selection.

At the same time, some other solutions have been sought. For example the establishment of the National Foundation for Development of Culture in 1983 has allowed a partial relief for local budgets as far as expenses for culture and art were concerned. Decisions on the utilization of these funds are subject to public control, but are taken at the central level.

One can infer from the considerations presented here that, despite the drive to make regional and local administration and self-government more autonomous, the central administration is still in possession of powerful financial means which enable it to have important effects on local economies.

Spatial variations of central budget contributions to regional and local budgets

Regional and local budgets vary considerably in the proportion of both general and allocated subsidies, and their participation in central budget revenues. This wide variation is shown in Figure 9.4. Poland's *voivod*ships have been classified into five groups with regard to the total funds which are derived from the central budget. The *voivod*ships are also divided into

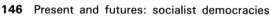

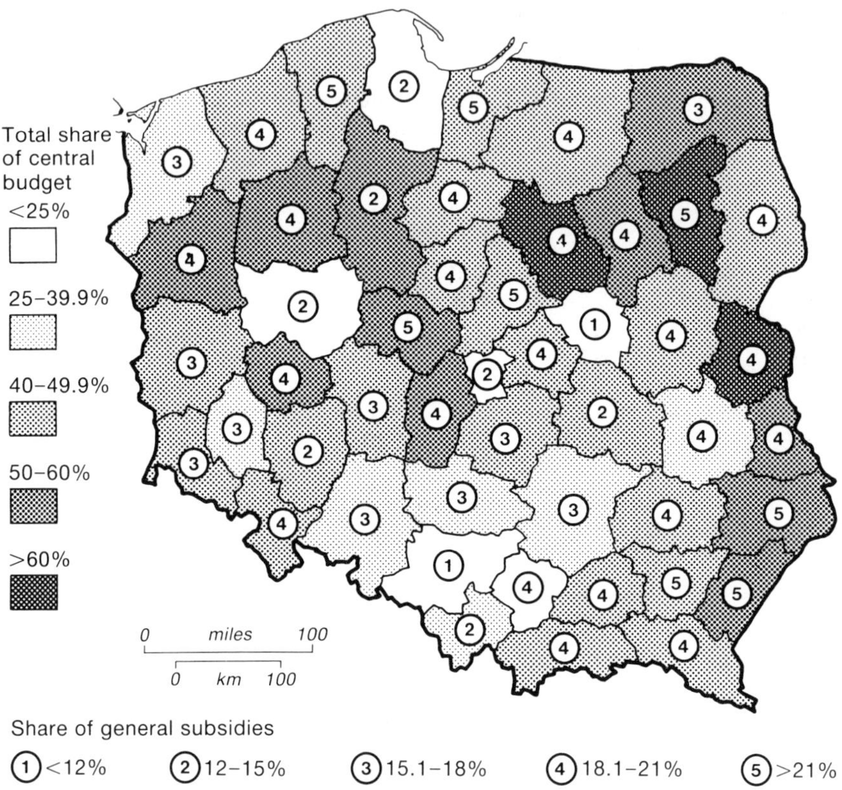

Figure 9.4 Spatial distribution of the proportion of central budget contributions (subsidies and share in central budget revenues) in the regional budgets of *voivod*ships in 1987

Source: the author's elaboration based on Ministry of Finance data

five classes with regard to the share of allocated central subsidies, but their scope is so small in the regional budgets, amounting to 1.6 per cent in national terms, that an indistinct picture of differences emerges. Figure 9.4 shows that the largest degree of financial autonomy (as measured by a proportion of less than 25 per cent *voivod*ship funds derived from the central budget) occurs in Warsaw, Gdańsk, Katowice, Cracow, Lódź, and Poznań. The location of the *voivod*ships is shown in Figure 9.7. These are regions attached to large urban agglomerations and industrial districts, which are the areas of the country with the largest local resources because of the size of their economies. Another group having a relatively small share of funds from the central budget is constituted by eight *voivod*ships which have comparatively strong industry (Bielsko-Biala, Bydgoszcz, Czestochowa, Kielce, Legnica, Lublin, Opole and Szczecin).

The highest proportion of central budget funds is located in the *voivod*ship budgets of Ciechanów, Biala-Podlaska, and Lomza, which are typical agricultural *voivod*ships which have poor soils and large forest areas. This

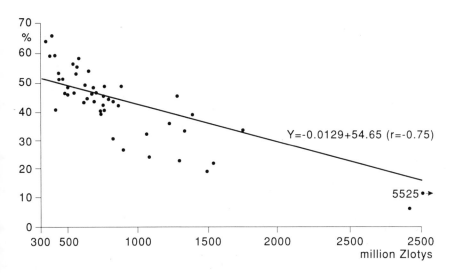

Figure 9.5 Percentage contribution of the central budget to regional
budget revenues in 1988 according to the value of fixed assets
in 1986 in current prices

Source: the author's elaboration based on Ministry of Finance data and
Rocznik Statystyczny (1987, LI Table II)

indicates a clear relationship between the proportion of central budget
contributions to regional budgets and the level of economic development of
the region. This thesis is confirmed by Figure 9.6, which compares the
central contributions to the value of *voivod*ship's fixed assets (defined by the
prices on 31 December 1986). This value gives a measure of the region's
investment level, which in a sense indicates its economic development.
Despite an apparent dispersion of the values, connected with the fact that
relations within the economy are usually fostered by many parameters, a
clear correlation emerges between the two variables (a high correlation
ratio of $r = -0.75$, assuming straight-line regression formula). One can
infer from Figure 9.5 that the correlation would be even higher if the relations were approximated by means of curvilinear regression formula.

This correlation indicates a tendency for the influence on regional
budgets by the central administration to be mainly a reduction of the
differences inevitably existing in the economic development of particular
regions; that is it seeks a regional equity. This influence is evident only for
the total contribution of the central budget. For the study of general
subsidies to regional budgets, one obtains a much less distinct picture of
the relation of the allocations to each region and its level of its economic
development (see Figure 9.4).

The influence of the central administration on regional budgets cannot
eliminate differences in the economic situation of particular regions, of
course. It can only diminish them. Figure 9.6 displays the 1986 differences
in regional budget revenues per capita. Considerable differences exist

Figure 9.6 Regions (*voivod*ships) in Poland according to the territorial organization put into effect in 1975

despite the receipt of central budget funds. Comparing Figure 9.7 and Figure 9.4 one can see that different groups of *voivod*ships occupy particular classes. This is because social and economic differences are historically conditioned; the varying level of pre-existing local investments entails different financial requirements; regions have different economic functions; and there are different levels of urbanization as well as other factors. These all occasion specific consequences. For example in the large urban agglomerations, city transport is aided by the regional budget, while in the rural areas centrally financed transportation prevails (for example the railway and buses).

The balancing of the country's social and economic situation calls for much more intense activities by the central administration, using central budget funds and aiming them at the economic development of particular regions. The activities of economic enterprises using bank credits and their own funds following from the newly implemented economic reforms will be of considerable importance in this respect.

The analysis presented here has concerned regional budgets at the level of *voivod*ships. A further differentiation appears when dealing with the

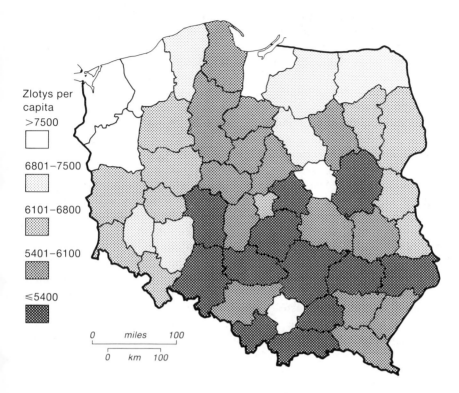

Figure 9.7 Spatial distribution of the regional budget revenues per capita in 1987

Source: the author's elaboration based on Ministry of Finance data and Rocznik Statystyczny (1987, XLVI–XLVII Table II)

budgets of the basic administrative units (municipalities, etc.). Their revenues depend upon a complex distribution among the various levels. This thesis was confirmed by research inquiries conducted in 1986 by Sochacka-Krysiak and Bolkowiak (1987) in 242 communes across the country. The results of their research indicate that the financial situation of the communes is largely determined by the prime revenues from socialized economy. These are based mainly on income from the real property tax to which they are entitled. The average share of income from this source, in the prime revenues of the 73 communes which exhibited a surplus of their prime revenues over expenditure, amounted to 40.7 per cent, while in the 169 communes which showed a deficit of prime revenues in relation to expenditure, the share amounted to 22 per cent.

At the same time, a considerable differentiation of this share was observed. In almost 78 per cent of communes the share of revenues contributed by the property tax was lower than 40 per cent and in only 11 per cent of communes was it higher than 60 per cent. This means that the spatial distribution of socialized enterprises and their concentration in towns is the chief reason why rural communes lack an efficient source of revenues (Sochacka-Krysiak and Bolkowiak, 1987, p. 9). This research also proved that agriculture alone cannot provide sufficient revenue for commune budgets, indicating that the local budgets of communes cannot be found solely from their own funds. Hence it is necessary to provide external sources of financing, although as a consequence the autonomy of local administration and self-government is limited. However, the need for financial aid for local budgets is a common phenomenon in countries under all political systems, and Poland is not exceptional in this respect.

The implementation of economic reform will trigger mainly the operation of economic parameters. This will make taxes a new and efficient source for financing local budgets. A new situation is likely to appear, therefore, in which local sources of revenue will determine, to an increasing extent, the scope of local expenditure. The contrary situations, which have previously obtained, has been that a given *voivod*ship, or even a particular person, could obtain funds from central authorities regardless of objective needs. Such arrangements are disappearing.

Previously, the local administration did not feel responsible to the citizens for satisfying their needs. As an apology it was enough to quote an argument that 'those at the top' did not provide the means for the required undertakings, instead allocating them elsewhere. All in all, this led to a highly ineffective utilization of finance, promoted favouritism, incited public dissatisfaction and provoked apathy and social inactivity by the people.

Conclusions: the tendencies of future changes

It was assessed that out of 2,404 administrative bodies at the lowest level (the total of municipal, municipal–rural and rural people's councils), only 222 councils in 1987 had their budgets balanced by their own revenues. Among the forty-nine people's councils at the *voivod*ship level, only the People's Council of Warsaw did not take advantage of a general subsidy. All the others needed aid in the form of a central budget subsidy. Out of these forty-eight *voivod*ships, fifteen received over half of their budget revenues from a general subvention and from shares in the tax revenues of the central budget. Some *voivod*ships, with economies based mainly on agriculture (such as Łomża and Bielsko-Biała), received as much as 68 per cent of their revenues from the central subvention, leaving less than one-third of their expenditure to be based on their own revenues.

Activating new revenue sources for local budgets at the municipal level requires a lot of effort and takes much time. It is not easy to agree on how the income of socialized enterprises should be allocated. This is now the prime revenue of a local council budget but had previously belonged to a *voivod*ship budget.

The 1988 amendment to the law on councils has made it possible for people's councils to acquire bank credits. This is an important move which leads to new situations: one must wait till the budget opens for a subsidy to be granted and this must be realized during a given budget year. For a credit one goes to a bank, makes a repayment pledge, accounts for its realization, but otherwise can proceed independently. Also, the introduction in 1989 of communal property, whose good old traditions in many regions of Poland were broken in 1950, is considered as promising.

With the creation in 1988 of new powers of regional and economic autonomy, eliminated during the 1970s, a process has been started of taking over some enterprises by local or *voivod*ship administrations. Under the resolution of the Council of Ministers of 8 February 1988, the State Planning Commission made a list of over 1,800 enterprises which will be passed over to the regions within the frame of decentralization. The bargaining and jockeying procedures which accompany the whole business are very interesting. The People's Council of Cracow, for instance, made it quite explicit that, instead of receiving the enterprises scheduled to be transferred to their supervision, they would rather take over others which would better suit the city's needs and be more profitable. On the other hand, the council would prefer to give away some of the enterprises now under its control.

The regional distribution of the decentralized enterprises ranges from a few to more than a dozen in some *voivod*ships. Single transfers will also occur, as in Piła *voivod*ship. The transfer procedure will last until the end of 1988. At the time of writing only two initial lists have been made public and further decisions are expected in the course of the campaign. Therefore any geographical analyses would be premature. However it is clear that the new decentralization should improve economic effectiveness in the regions, help towards creating attitudes of local identity, promote local economic development and increase the revenues of regional and local budgets.

The 1988 reforms give an opportunity for real, not theoretical, reintegration of society, village, commune, town, or region despite the shortage of financial means. The capacity for practical action is as important as the psychological change of attitude. A saying has appeared in popular discussion which depicts a councillor as 'counsel-less'. This was really true to life. According to statistics, only 10 per cent of the basic-level councils contributed to their budgets with their own revenues, while over 40 per cent only confirmed, by voting, the distribution of subsidies, half of which was absorbed by maintenance of educational institutions. As a result most initiatives were impossible because of the shortage of financial and material means, and this made the capacity to manage a given locality illusory.

The decentralization reforms are being paralleled by making the *voivod*ship level the main element in territorial administration. The local municipal, municipal–rural and rural bodies are to perform auxiliary and executive functions. As a result, over 70 per cent of total revenues and expenditures of territorial budgets is attributed to the *voivod*ship people's councils' budgets. In this way, the powers over investment expenditure will be even more concentrated at the *voivod*ship level, which absorbs some 90 per cent of all funds allocated to it. In the budgets of communes, for example, investment expenditures presently constitute only about 3 per cent and in municipal public works and related branches about 6 per cent. One can speak then about a new dimension to the phenomenon of centralization which appears between the local and regional level. At the same time, the prime revenues of people's councils at the basic level of the commune are actually ceasing to be their revenues. This is occurring because the basic levels are dependent on the *voivod*ship authority. No provisions were enacted in the 1988 amendment concerning the change in the share of *voivod*ship budgets in the communes' prime revenues. Hence the *voivod*ships have to derive more revenue from the commune level. The extent to which recentralization will occur at *voivod*ship level is, of course, a question which has to be resolved.

The changes introduced by the amendment to the law on the system of people's councils and territorial self-government have expanded the prime revenue sources of councils and have created conditions for the gradual elimination of central subsidies: by making the system of distributing territorial budget revenues among particular council levels more flexible, and by introducing legal guarantees of non-infringement of budget surpluses. Moreover, some taxes, such as those paid by co-operatives, and an 85 per cent tax on wages and salaries, have been passed to the control of local budgets. These moves have started a process of withdrawing from economic paternalism and reducing the extent of non-profitable enterprises. While seeking means to increase economic effectiveness, out-dated ideological and political dogmas, which affected the form of activities of all levels of state administration, are being gradually repealed. New concepts are also being sought, which will be tightly connected with Poland's economic development and should enable it to find a satisfactory balance between the competences of central and local administration as well as regional self-government.

References

Bennett, R.J. (1980), *The Geography of Public Finance*, Methuen, London.

Bennett, R.J. (1988), 'Economic restructuring, urban administration and state resources allocation', *Geographica Polonica*, forthcoming.

Ciechocińska, M. (1984), 'Local authorities in towns in Poland', *Bundesforschungsanstalt für Landeskunde und Raumordnung*, Seminare, Symposien, Arbeitspapiere, Bonn, Heft 14, 236–50.

Ciechocińska, M. (1988), 'Remarks on the geographical nature of social infrastructure provision in a centrally planned economy', *Environment and Planning C: Government and Policy*, 6, 349–57.

Graham, L.S. and Ciechocińska, M. (eds) (1987), *The Polish Dilemma: Views from Within*, Westview Press, London.

Jaworski, W. and Sochacka-Krysiak, H. (1982), *Finanse krajów socjalistycznych* (Finances in the socialist countries), PWE, Warsaw.

Koźmiński, A.K. (1982), *Po wielkim szoku* (After a great shock), PWE, Warsaw.

Lange, O. (1962), *Niektóre zagadnienia centralizacji i decentralizacji* (Some issues on centralization and decentralization), Warsaw.

Ledworowski, B. (1988), 'Problem własności komunalnej' (Problem of communal ownership), *Biuletyn Informacyjny Instytutu Gospodarki Przestrzennej i Komunalnej*, forthcoming.

Müller, A. (1985), *U źródel polskiego kryzysu* (By the spring of Polish crises), PWE, Warsaw.

Pajestka, J. (1983), *Polski kryzys i jak do niego doszło* (The Polish crises and how they are approaching), KiW, Warsaw.

Reykowski, J. (1987), 'Czy socjalizm jest psychologicznym nieporozumieniem?', (Is socialism a psychological misunderstanding?), *Nowe Drogi*, 6, 50–70.

Sochacka-Krysiak, H. and Pietrewicz, M. (1986), *Gospodarka terenowa* (Territorial economy), PWE Warsaw.

Sochacka-Krysiak, H. and Bolkowiak, J. (1987), *Dochody wlasne budżetów terenowych stopnia podstawowego. Próba oceny sytuacji, perspektywy, wnioski* (Revenue ability of the basic level territorial budgets. An attempt at evaluation, perspectives and conclusions), (mimeo).

Zawadzka, .B. (1981), 'Jakie chcemy mieć rady' (What councils we want to have), *Prawo i Zycie*, 15, 4–5.

10 Hungary: developments in local administration

Zoltán Hajdú

Introduction

Hungarian public administration, particularly the administration of territory by local government has always been an issue closely bound up with state power and policy-making. The content and functioning of the territorial system and the extent of centralization or decentralization have always been the outcome of the prevailing political relations and power ambitions. Hungarian administration has also a number of distinctive historical and national characteristics. The development of administration has been closely connected with the historical conceptions of the ideal state and it cannot be sharply separated from the major changes which have occurred in state structure and national boundaries.

General-purpose territorial units are a major part of the framework of political power in Hungary. These are multiple-purpose administrative organizations upon which are based the activities of representation, administration and judiciary which constitute the most important activity of the state. To perform special functions, such as water conservation, transport and mining, a number of *specific-purpose territorial units* have also been created.

There are two chief levels of territorial organization: (i) *local, settlement administration* (village and town); and (ii) *territorial administration* (district, town-regions,[1] county, and administration embracing several counties). Of these local government units the most important has been the county. The system of counties is a major national peculiarity of Hungarian administration which is nearly as old as the establishment of the Hungarian state. It has provided an anchor of great territorial stability. The county attained great independence in certain periods and was always important in its effect on new administrative procedures, determining the practical activity and level of reforms of administration which could be implemented. The functioning of the system of counties was characterized by great adaptability and flexibility, and proved itself able to adjust itself to everything from feudalism to socialism. The county became the chief area for discussions concerning territorial politics and equity. And, particularly important, in contrast to the central administration under foreign influence, it played a key constitutional and legal role as a stronghold of the Hungarian nation. Thus over the centuries its mere functioning has greatly restrained the independent administration of settlements.

The extent of decentralization or decentralization of administration has varied in Hungary over time with major reorganizations affecting local government administration in the 1870s, in 1949–50 and later in the 1970s and 1980s. These changes arose because of internal economic, social and political transformations and because of major changes in the national boundaries. Each period is summarized below as a pre-requisite to understanding the context of the current reform process.

The 1870s reforms

The Compromise of 1867 regulated the relations of Hungary and Austria with regard to public law. Within the Austro–Hungarian Empire, Hungary was granted a level of relative independence. By means of this arrangement a complicated state structure came into being which can be regarded as an outcome of external and internal compromises. The Communal Act of 1871 set up three categories of local community administration: (i) corporate towns; (ii) large villages able to perform from their own financial resources the duties conferred on them by law; (iii) villages with limited financial resources which co-operated with other villages in performing their administrative tasks. In the villages which formed a notarial district an independent body of representatives was set up but they had only one administrative organization.

In matters of public administration the appellate authority of villages became the county in the first instance and the national government in the second instance. The managing activity of the county was assisted by the districts. The district acted as an agency of the county at local level but it had no autonomous authority. The villages intercommunicated with the county through the district.

In 1876 the position of the county and municipal authorities was established. Only a few of the former so-called free royal boroughs retained the character of the municipality; most were degraded into boroughs and some were reclassified as large villages. The county reform of 1876 aimed at abolishing the feudal character of local governments in order to form a unified territorial system. In Transylvania and the Great Plain radical changes took place, while in the rest of the country territorial reorganization was more minor.

After the implementation of the reforms in 1880 the local government administration of historical Hungary was carried out within the framework of eighty counties or military districts, forty-six towns of county rank, 137 other towns, 483 districts, 1,914 large villages and 16,177 villages. As has been stated the counties were the most powerful unit but they varied considerably in size of territory and population.

After the defeat of the Austro–Hungarian Empire in World War I historical Hungary disintegrated. After the Trianon Treaty in 1920 only

28.5 per cent (92,833 square kilometres) of the former territory (325,411 square kilometres) of the country remained under Hungarian jurisdiction. This reduced the number of local administrative units, in 1921, to thirty-five counties, twelve towns with county rank, thirty-six other towns, 162 districts, 985 large villages and 2,425 villages (the last group were integrated within 712 notarial districts). The changes of the national boundaries aggravated the previous inequalities in size of the administrative divisions. Thus reform of the system of territorial administration became imperative. In 1923 the parts of the counties along the national boundaries were united in the spirit of 'provisionality', that is with claims to be revised if the national boundaries were ever increased. As a result the number of the counties decreased to twenty-five but there were no effects on the internal divisions of the counties.

Between the two world wars there was a legal continuity of the pre-1918 laws. However significant changes were introduced by the so-called nationalization of public administration and its subsequent drift towards Fascism. This significantly centralized administration and resulted in a narrowing of the range of activities of local governments and their freedom of action.

Administrative reforms 1949–50

In 1944–5 a major transformation of administration was initiated. Under a coalition-government the different political parties advocated reform concepts of a widely varying character in accordance with their political ambitions and ideologies. In this period it became clear that the state structure, and the experiments aiming at its reform, were inseparable from the struggle for political power. This was manifest in the debates about the form of government, the transformation of the representative system and in the form of administration.

The Constitution of 1949 laid down the socialist economic, social and political state and gave an outline of the new administrative system of the country. It established a system of councils copied from the practice of the soviets established in the USSR, but taking into account the previous experience of the Hungarian Soviet Republic of 1919. The Constitution and the Council Act (1950) laid down the main characteristics of the councils. They were to be regarded as local executives and the traditional duality of self-government and state administration was to be eliminated. The party-guidance of the councils was codified and the main principle to underlie their organization and functioning was to be democratic centralism. Within the system of public administration hierarchical relations became predominant: the main task of the local councils was to implement central decisions. There were no substantial changes to the historically developed structure of administration, but the counties, districts, towns and large villages received new functions and forms of organization. The whole administrative system was assigned new tasks and duties. The political role of administration, together with its scope, duties and content, was re-arranged; its spatial organization was partly changed; and its permanent staff were replaced.

One major reform was the reorganization of the system of counties. A new system of nineteen counties replaced the former twenty-five. However, because of political considerations a level of territorial stability was sought, and reforms were only partial. By abolishing parts of the counties and dividing the county of Pest into two parts the inequalities in size and population of the counties were eliminated, with the result that a system of medium-sized counties was established. In forming the new counties account was taken of natural resources, economic and transport conditions, settlement-network relations and long-range planning requirements.

After the reorganization of the counties a new system of districts was defined. Substantial changes also took place in district functions. The districts were provided with a complete council apparatus, which created a new relationship with the administration of the large villages. The number of districts was decreased from 150 to 140. Before the reform, extensive investigation of the area of influence of each settlement was carried out. As a result the majority of the main central places of the settlement-network became district administrative seats. Of the new district seats forty-two were towns, and ninety-eight villages. Most of the districts were relatively homogeneous geographically and well balanced from the point of view of economy, transport and administrative hinterland.

New principles were also established for the management of towns. An outstanding role was played by the reorganization of the administrative area of Budapest. Here seven suburbs and sixteen large villages were united to form Budapest. In other towns earlier administrative solutions were abandoned. Three categories of towns were established: (i) a city under the direct government of the Council of Ministers (Budapest); (ii) towns subordinate to the county councils (twenty-four in number); (iii) towns subordinate to the district councils (twenty-nine in number). The towns and villages thus became separate in their management. The subordination of the towns to the regional councils allowed the possibility of co-ordination at regional level, either within counties or within districts but exploitation of this possibility was limited by the economic and political situation.

The reforms established 3,169 villages in Hungary: 1,190 large villages and 1,979 villages (the latter were co-ordinated by 662 notarial districts). The 1950 Act transformed these into 2,978 Community Councils, 2,808 of which were autonomous, and 361 villages administered by 170 Joint Councils. This comprehensive network of community councils served the purpose of directly imposing the objectives of the central government in pursuit of its transformation of society. Formally it implied decentralization, but in reality it served the objective of centralization.

The administrative reform was adjusted in detail to fit the needs of the reform of the political system and the method of economic management. Local administrative reform was seen as contributing to the introduction and implementation of the planned economy. The councils had a role in disaggregated implementation of the plan, but centrally confirmed plans and budgets were provided only to the County Councils. The counties also controlled the revenues and expenditure of the subordinate councils (districts and villages). The scope for autonomous management and investment activity and the freedom of action of the councils was restricted within very narrow limits.

Administrative reforms 1950–80

Administrative developments after the reform of 1950 must be analysed in the light of the political, economic and social changes which occurred. There is a close relationship between the two even if some administrative changes occurred only after considerable delays.

After the establishment of the system of councils it soon turned out that their functioning was not economically well founded: they had too few economic resources and lacked the necessary degree of independence to allow proper execution of functions. Over-centralization of the administration of both the state and the economy imposed serious constraints on independent initiatives. Administrative and bureaucratic solutions dominated council decisions and their relationship to the population deteriorated.

The Second Council Act of 1954 sought to eliminate the discontinuity between administrative structure and its responsibilities. The responsibilities of the councils were increased and their sphere of activity was extended. Several thousand institutions and enterprises moved under the direct government of the councils with the effect of increasing both their resources and responsibilities. The 1954 Council Act was characterized by centralization at the county level; that is the process of decentralizing responsibilities for decision-making generally stopped at the level of the counties. From 1955 the local councils were given legal power to impose limits and targets for communal development which allowed them to obtain significant population resources. Thus activities connected with the development of towns and villages became prominent. The economic responsibilities of the councils gradually extended so that they became interested in increasing their revenues and were entitled to take up bank loans.

The extent of administrative reforms which had developed up to 1966 raised the question of the needs and responsibilities of economic management and planning, and also raised the question of reorganization of the system of political institutions. The result was a reform of economic management introduced in 1968 which allowed a switchover from direct to indirect management. This in turn was followed by reform of public administration and council management. The result was the Third Council Act of 1971. This modified the former conception of the councils. The councils were defined as representative self-governing and administrative organs of the socialist state. The reinforcement of the self-governing character and independence of the councils became a declared political objective. The district councils were abolished by the 1971 Act diminishing

Table 10.1 Administrative divisions of Hungary, 1950–80

Year	Counties	Districts	Town-regions	Towns	Villages	Villages with independent councils	Villages with common councils
1950	19	140	—	54	3,169	2,808	361
1960	19	128	—	63	3,210	2,857	353
1970	19	107	2*	73	3,151	1,711	1,440
1980	19	83	49	96	3,026	715	2,311

*Town administration

the hierarchical character of the administrative system. But the districts continued to exist as offices of the County Councils.

The economic and management activities of the councils were still regulated. The economic duties of the councils included, on the one hand, the local and regional organization and co-ordination of the economic objectives of the state, and on the other hand, the implementation of the specific local tasks of the councils. As a result of the 1971 Act the chief responsibility of the councils became provision of services to the population and the improvement of the local infrastructure. The greatest problem for the functioning of the councils was the fact that their finance and their responsibilities were sharply separated from each other. This resulted in considerable inefficiency, waste of resources and irrational investments. Substantial change also took place in the allocation of functional responsibilities. The responsibility for decisions shifted downwards. The communal councils received some 200 new functional responsibilities; altogether 80 per cent of the official matters were shifted to the local councils.

The administrative territorial structure established in 1950 was also transformed. The main pattern of change up to 1980 is shown in Table 10.1. The main trends can be summarized as follows:

1. The counties retained their historical importance and remained the most powerful element of local-territorial administration. The number of counties remained unaltered, only the boundaries of one county and a few villages changed from the pattern established in 1950. The role of the counties became greater in territorial economic development: mainly to assert regional interests. As a result the counties obtained an important role in redistribution policy in the 1970s.
2. The administrative weight and role of the districts was substantially transformed. Up to the 1960s their importance increased, but after the collectivization of agriculture their importance decreased. The number of districts also gradually decreased after 1950 with a progressive switch of district seats from villages to towns. Most important, however, the districts without real centres were abolished. In 1971 all the district councils were abolished as representative

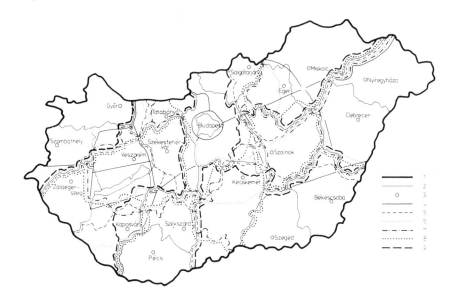

Figure 10.1 Proposals for the economic regional division of Hungary

Key: 1 = state borders; 2 = county boundaries; 3 = county seats; 4 = proposal by Markos (1952); 5 = proposal by Láng (1959–1960); 6 = hypothetical proposal by Karl Marx University of Economics (1960); 7 = proposal by Karl Marx University of Economics (1960); 8 = proposal by Karl Marx University of Economics (1963); 9 = proposal by Krajkó (1969)

    governments and became merely offices or agents of the county councils.

3. After 1969 the possibility of the management of villages by the towns was established. As a result the number and size of town-regions rapidly increased in the 1970s. In the earlier period these hinterlands encompassed only a few settlements in the immediate suburbs. In the 1970s large town-regions were established and replaced the districts. In the management of these hinterlands a form of co-ordination was established between the town councils and communal councils.

4. The settlements which played a role in the administration of districts and town-regions in Hungary between 1950–80 resulted in a very complicated organization (see Figure 10.1 and Table 10.2). During this period there were many towns which had no administrative role either as districts or as town-regions.

5. The main tendency of this period was an increase in the number of towns. The settlements functioning as towns and the towns which had a form of legal status became more equal in number. At the same time the position of the town managers was rather contradictory. The structure of town management established in 1950 did not work. In 1954 the towns were removed from the control of the district councils

Table 10.2 Formation of settlements playing a role in the administration of districts and town-regions in Hungary, 1950–80

Year	Number of districts	From the seats of districts town	village	Number of town-regions	Number of towns only with districts	Number of towns only with town-regions	Number of towns with both district and town-regions	Number of towns playing no roles in the administration of districts or town-regions
1950	140	42	98	—	42	—	—	12
1960	128	44	84	—	44	—	—	19
1970	107	50	57	2*	50	2	—	21
1980	83	61	22	49	39	21	27	14

*Town administration

and were put under the county government. Debrecen, Mickolc, Pécs and Szeged were granted rights equal to those of the counties, but in 1971 they were returned to their former status within counties. The normative basis for declaring towns was established in the first half of the 1970s. This period saw the development of settlements and declaration of towns based upon the National Conception of Settlement Network Development.

6. The overall tendency since 1950 has been for a continuous decrease in the number of communities as a result of fusions, town declarations and the depopulation and abandonment of some villages. As a result the system of communal councils has become highly concentrated, the number of independent councils has decreased, the number of joint community councils has increased and a large number of communities have been deprived of their own council organizations. The fusion of the community councils contradicted the spirit and nature of self-government which was imposed upon them from above. A great many communities were left without a governing organ or body of representatives. However, after 1971 the category of large villages was reintroduced and the communities belonging to this category received greater independence.

The administrative reform of 1984

On 1 January 1984 the district administrations were abolished altogether. They were replaced by uniform territorial division into town-regions. A major part of the functions and responsibilities of the district offices was decentralized and taken over by the communities. In the course of this reform the general aim was to introduce a two-tier administration. However it was accepted that the right conditions did not yet exist for this. Thus the towns and the newly established large villages with town rank[2] were temporarily to take part in the county administration and supervision of communal councils. In addition the towns, and large villages with town rank, took over from the districts the administration of secondary matters. They were also to handle some primary functions where a specialized knowledge is required. A strong centralization of policy in the main settlements occurred since only 5 per cent of the administrative services of towns and villages with town rank falls on the villages in the hinterlands.

In the determination of the town-region two factors were used: (i) the relation of the functional regional hinterland to settlement geography, economic and social characteristics of the area; and (ii) the administrative, political and technical infrastructure of the hinterland. Of these two factors the latter was often the primary determinant; thus the system of the functional regions was often subordinate to the considerations of administrative policy.

In the course of the reform 139 town-regions and large villages with town rank were created. Apart from four exceptions the towns came to play a major role in the new territorial administration. In general the result

Table 10.3 Administrative divisions of Hungary on 1 January 1984

Capital, Counties	Area (hectares)	Population	Town-regions	Surroundings of municipalities with town rank	Towns	Villages	Village councils of various rank (total)	Independent councils among the village councils	Common councils among the village councils	Villages without local councils
Budapest	52,507	2,064,307	—	—	1	—	—	—	—	—
Baranya	448,701	433,788	5	—	5	291	77	11	66	214
Bács-Kiskun	836,170	566,066	6	4	6	105	98	91	7	70
Békés	563,193	431,291	6	3	6	68	58	50	8	10
Borsod-Abaúj-Zemplén	724,784	803,956	9	1	9	339	151	62	89	188
Csongrád	426,268	454,633	5	2	5	54	41	31	10	13
Fejér	437,367	423,377	3	3	3	103	69	45	24	34
Győr-Sopron	401,222	429,987	5	—	5	160	75	35	40	85
Hajdú-Bihar	621,161	553,036	4	2	5	74	42	21	21	32
Heves	363,755	347,763	4	1	4	114	83	63	20	31
Komárom	225,052	323,256	6	1	6	68	45	30	15	23
Nógrád	254,438	238,319	3	3	3	117	52	18	34	65
Pest	639,414	983,200	7	6	8	171	122	89	33	49
Somogy	603,630	358,283	5	3	5	233	63	4	59	170
Szabolcs-Szatmár	593,809	587,784	6	1	6	219	108	48	60	111
Szolnok	560,756	443,375	7	1	8	67	45	28	17	22
Tolna	370,391	268,237	5	—	5	103	56	33	23	47
Vas	333,682	284,504	6	1	6	209	65	8	57	144
Veszprém	468,888	388,625	8	1	8	212	66	12	54	146
Zala	378,440	316,368	5	1	5	250	65	2	63	185
Hungary (total)	9,303,628	10,700,155	105	34	109	2,957	1,381	681	700	1,576

Figure 10.2 The division of public administrative areas of Hungary in 1984

Key: 1 = capital; 2 = county seats; 3 = towns and municipalities with a town right to participate in the government of counties; 4 = towns without 'town-surrounding'; 5 = municipalities under county government; 6 = boundaries of 'town-surrounding'; 7 = non-attached territory.

has been a system of uniform medium-sized units with only small variations in area or population. Among the 139 units 105 had towns as their centres, while thirty-four had large villages with town rank as their centres (see Table 10.3 and Figure 10.2).

In order to experiment with the desired two-tier structure thirty-four developed villages were placed directly under the county government. Only eleven out of the nineteen counties experimented with this direct county government.

The limits and scope of the territorial reform of 1984 were determined by the prevailing economic and political conditions. The greatest obstacle to the reform, which was the result of various compromises, was the unchanged structure of the counties. Without radical corrections of the county boundaries it is impossible to establish a reform of local government based on functional regions. As a result of this internal contradiction, the territorial structure carried within it a necessity for further reforms.

Issues in the future improvement of local government administration

The continuing crisis of the Hungarian economy has again posed the question of the need to resume reform of the economy, society and political institutions. New processes have been begun and the preparation of a new constitution is in progress. This will affect both the system of political institutions (the party) and the methods of economic management, planning and public administration including the representative and electoral system.

The main directions of these movements are democratization and decentralization. From these far-reaching issues I wish to emphasize the processes that have an impact on local territorial administration. The main direction of these changes can be summed up as follows:

(1) In the new system of elections the value of representation and assertion of interests will be increased at all levels.
(2) Decentralization is meant to increase the duties and responsibilities of the local-territorial councils.
(3) Instead of the former 'plan-bargaining' a system of norms has begun to be established for the distribution of resources between the counties, each county getting its share of investment resources from central funds in proportion to its number of inhabitants.
(4) In the administration of the communities an important measure has been to set up local boards in those villages that did not have local councils. These represent the interests of the associated villages in the joint councils and were set up by the elected members of the councils.

In 1986 a new system of local economic management by the councils was introduced. A feature of Hungarian government is that the central government's budget share of GDP is high, about 60 per cent while local government's share is only about 15 per cent. Resources are distributed between the counties in proportion to their numbers of inhabitants. But they are distributed between settlements within counties in a different way. The local council can receive resources by two routes: (i) they compete for subsidies by implementing key programmes announced by the county council; (ii) they increase their own revenues. In addition a uniform system of financial budgeting has been introduced. This has been long demanded and allows recurrent and investment expenditures to be less rigidly separated. (About 75 per cent of the local council budget is expended on maintenance and recurrent expenditure; the resources available for capital investments and economic development are substantially lower.)

Within the objectives of modernizing economic management and state administration, taxation and the administration of taxation have also changed since 1988. A personal income tax and general turnover tax have been introduced, and a new system of central and local tax administration has also been established. The organization of the tax affairs of the population (such as tax assessment and checking) is managed by a new taxation administration not at local but at central government level.

Only some of the personal taxes are available to the local councils. The main local taxes are the tax on houses, levies paid on buildings used for purposes other than dwellings, levies on automobiles, taxes of complementary farm plots, taxes on land, purchase tax on wine, etc.

Half of the financial resources of the councils for the 1986–90 period is to be derived from direct state subsidy (or grants); 29 per cent is to be made up from the budget-receipts from the profit and income taxes of firms and organizations which are under the councils' control; 11 per cent will derive from the operating revenues of the council institutions and from the personal taxes and fees; 10 per cent will come from other sources.

In the light of the experience of the first year we can say that because of the continuous reductions in the level of resources, some of the councils have had to face a difficult situation with their investment activities. They have even had to cut back on their recurrent expenditures. The councils have been bridging this deficit by issuing shares and taking up bank loans. (There are precedents for this in the past, but these resulted in financial reorganization.)

From 1 January 1988, four counties (Fejér, Komárom, Vas, Szolnok) switched over experimentally to a pure two-tier administration. This resulted in an end to the mediating role of the towns and large villages of town rank. The counties drawn into the experiment are representative of most of the problems and peculiarities of Hungarian local government administration. The experiment is to last three to four years. The changeover to a country-wide two-tier system will be carried out on the basis of the experience of this experiment.

The importance and responsibilities of local government are likely to increase in the future. It will continue to remain the most important agent in achieving economic, political and social objectives. Hence over-hasty organizational and functional changes based on short-term political ideas should be avoided. Territorial organization has to be handled with due consideration, with the co-operation of the population affected by the changes, and taking into account their interests. This is the only guarantee of the existence of an essential component of administrative organization — its general acceptability to the people.

Notes

1. Town regions are similar to the city regions used in British discussions, although usually smaller in size. They are based on the same criteria of a threshold size and a functional hinterland.
2. The tasks and level of responsibility of the villages with town rank coincide with those of the towns but their special administration department is divided.

References

Alsó, L. (1935), *A községszervezés alapelvei* (Fundamental Principles of Organization of Villages), Magyar Közigazgatástudományi Intézet, Budapest.
Andrási, J. and Kekesi, L. (1987), 'A lakossági adóigazgatás szervezeti változásai'

(Changes in tax administration of citizens), *Állam és Igazgatás*, 37, 12, 1057-61.

Beluszky, P. (1980), *A közigazgatási területi beosztás földrajzi-térszerkezeti alapjai* (The Geographical and Spatial Structural Basis of Regional Administration), Államigazgatási Szervezési Intézet, Budapest.

Fonyó, Gy. (1970), *Községi igazgatás* (Administration of Villages), Közgazdasági és Jogi Könyvkiadó, Budapest.

Gulácsi, G. (1985), 'Irányitási reformok és müködési problémák a tanácsi gazdálkodásban I' (Management reforms and operational problems in the council-level economy I), *Állam és Igazgatás*, 35, 6, 553-64.

Gulácsi, G. (1985), 'Irányitási reformok és müködési problémák a tanácsi gazdálkodásban II' (Management reforms and operational problems in the council-level economy II), *Állam és Igazgatás*, 35, 7, 604-19.

Hajdú, Z. (1982), 'Területrendezési törekvések a magyar földrajztudománban a két világháború között' (Endeavours of the territorial redivision in Hungarian geography ˙between the two World Wars), *Földrajzi Közlemények*, 30, (106), 2, 89-106.

Hajdú, Z. (1987), 'Administrative geography and reforms of the administrative areas in Hungary', *Political Geography Quarterly*, 6, 3, 269-78.

Hajdú, Z, (1987), *Administrative Division and Administrative Geography in Hungary*, Discussion Paper No. 3, p. 79, Centre for Regional Studies, Pécs.

Hencz, A. (1973), *Területrendezési törekvések Magyarországon* (Endeavours in County Planning in Hungary), Közgazdasági és Jogi Könyvkiadó, Budapest.

Kara, P. (1987), 'A helyi–területi tanácsigazgatás továbbfejlesztése' (Improving local and spatial council administration), *Tér és Társadalom*, 1, 4, 3-14.

Kara, P., Kelényi, G. and Verebélyi, I. (1983), *A városkörnyéki igazgatási rendszer müködése* (Functioning of the System of Town Regions), Államigazgatási Szervezési Intézet, Budapest.

Kovács, T. (1985), 'A helyi–területi igazgatás szabályozása a felszabadulás óta I' (Regulation of the local-territorial administration since the liberation I), *Állam és Igazgatás*, 35, 2, 97-108.

Kovács, T. (1985), 'A helyi–területi igazgatás szabályozása a felszabadulás óta II' (Regulation of the local-territorial administration since the liberation II), *Állam és Igazgatás*, 35, 3, 193-209.

Lettrich, E. (1975), *Településhálózat — urbanizáció — igazgatás* (Settlement Network — Urbanization — Administration), MTA Állam — és Jogtudományi Intézet, Budapest.

Madarász, T. (1971), *Városigazgatás és urbanizáció* (Town Administration and Urbanization), Közgazdasági és Jogi Könyvkiadó, Budapest.

Schmidt, P. (1985), 'Negyven év alkotmányfejlödéséhez' (On the development of our Constitution), *Állam és Igazgatás*, 35, 4, 289-99.

Szamel, K. (1981), *A megyerendszer fejlödésének története Magyarországon*, (The History of Development of the County System in Hungary), Államigazgatási Szervezési Intézet, Budapest.

Szoboszlai, Gy. and Wiener, Gy. (1980), *Településfejlesztés, települési vonzásfunkció és közigazgatás* (Development of Settlement, Function of Attraction and Administration), Államigazgatási Szervezési Intézet, Budapest.

Szoboszlai, Gy. and Wiener, Gy. (1980), 'Az állami területbeosztás politökonómiai kérdései' (Political economic questions of state territorial division), *Jogtudományi Közlöny*, 35, 6, 355-66.

Vági, G. (1987), 'A helyi kormányzatok (tanácsok) pénzügyei a nemzetközi tapasztalatok tükrében' (Financial matters of local self-governments [councils] compared to international experiences), *Állam és Igazgatás*, 37, 2, 143-53.

11 Czechoslovakia: the development of public administration

Olga Vidláková and Pavel Zářecký

Introduction

In most European countries, local government is an essential part of their political, economic, social and cultural life. Yet a great many scholars investigating public administration, be they lawyers, economists, sociologists, politicians or others, write or speak of local government as if it is facing problems which might lead to its decline or even abolition. For most commentators a radical change is now indispensable in order to reorientate the traditional model of local government on a modern basis. In this period of transition it is primarily the most basic level of local government that has to undergo the greatest changes; (that is, the administration of municipalities and rural communes).

There are a number of different reasons for this development. First, there is the growing role of central government, which is seeking to limit the autonomy of local government, especially at its most local level. Second, as some authors point out, there is a disadvantage of scale; modern society asks for large-scale solutions, whereas the local community operates in a relatively small area and has strong limitations in its human and material resources.

A further reason for criticisms may lie in a conflict in the way in which geographical and functional principles of organization have been applied to local government. Conflict is in part one between 'control' functions and economic functions. It is also reflected in the replacement of a society of communities by a society of associations. This may have its roots in a process of disintegration taking place within people themselves. This disintegration encourages people's interests to be shifted to the sphere of professional functions. Simultaneously with this process of disintegration, there is strong pressure for integration into professional groups and associations. This means that people have been integrated into associations, but have been disintegrated from local government because government has been so highly integrated into administrative control that people feel alienated from it.

There are also other reasons for the contraction of influence of traditional local government: particularly the increased mobility of the population and the new and diverse possibilities of communication among people, and between people and institutions. All these phenomena have brought about a change in the quality of local government and in its relationship both in horizontal and vertical directions.

In spite of all these differences and problems a renaissance of local government can be observed, particularly in the larger cities. However, the essential problem remains of how to adapt local government to the increasing physical integration of people in a given territory. In Czechoslovakia, as in many socialist countries a solution is being sought in reforms of the territorial-administrative system at the most basic level of local government.

Administrative developments in Czechoslovakia since 1945

In 1945 a new type of local authority was created in Czechoslovakia: the National or People's Committees (*národní výbory*). The National Committees are representative bodies of self-government which simultaneously act as central government's field agencies. They are entrusted by law with the execution of state administration in the widest sense which means in practice that the National Committees carry out all the tasks connected with the development of the territory under their jurisdiction. This has been the character of the National Committees ever since their inception in 1945.

The system of local government of 1945 comprised three tiers: large regions (*země*),[1] districts (*okresy*) and municipalities (*obce*). In 1948 a new constitution established a People's Democracy based on a new arrangement of decentralized public administration. This was based on a regional system whereby the whole territory was divided into nineteen regions (*kraje*), 286 districts (*okresy*) subordinate to the regions, seventeen large cities excluded from the districts' jurisdiction, and nearly 12,000 municipalities subordinate to the appropriate district. This 1948 territorial-administrative structure suited the geographical character of the country better than the present structure which dates from 1960.

In 1960 a law on territorial-administrative structures was enacted (Act No. 36/1960 CoL) with the aim of integrating small administrative units into larger ones. Superseding the nineteen former regions were ten new regions: seven in the Czech Socialist Republic (CSR) and three in the Slovak Socialist Republic (SSR). There was a reduction in the number of districts from 286 to 112 (seventy-five in the CSR and thirty-seven in the SSR), and in addition there was the inner division of both capital cities into districts. Despite the aim of obtaining a more equal sized distribution, the new regions differed greatly both in size (for example the South Moravian region is three times as large as the North Bohemian region) and in population (a range of 200–300 per cent) as well as in the structure of their communities. Also, the character of the regions differed especially with respect to the presence or absence and structure of industry. Indeed, the only similarity between the regions was their lack of homogeneity.

Further changes subsequently occurred, but were restricted to the Slovak

Table 11.1   Intermediate regional units and big cities in Czechoslovakia 1960–87*

	1 Jan. 1960			1 July 1960			1 Jan. 1987		
	CSSR	CSR	SSR	CSSR	CSR	SSR	CSSR	CSR	SSR
Regions	19	13	6	10	7	3	10	7	3
Districts	270	179	91	103	71	32	107	71	36
Capitals	2	1	1	2	1	1	2	1	1
Non-district cities	17	12	5	4	3	1	5	4	1
Districts in the capitals and in non-district cities*	—	—	—	47	35	12	39	29	10

*The so-called 'statutory cities'

Republic and to a limited period. In 1969, the regions in Slovakia ceased to exist and a two-tier structure of districts and municipalities was introduced. This system existed, however, only from 1 July 1969 until 1 January 1971 when the regions were re-established (see Table 11.1).

A specific feature of Czechoslovakia, and especially of the Czech Socialist Republic, is the scattered arrangement of settlement and localities. This creates the problem of finding a suitable administrative pattern. The very nature of the territory invites attempts to integrate communities. There is practically no area without continuous scattered settlement. Czechoslovakia ranks as one of the most highly fragmented and dispersed settlement structures. The fragmentation is a consequence of the historical development of the territory which as a whole has been devoted to intensive farming. This development means that independently of administrative units there is a large number of so-called localities or settlements (*sídla*). These are used as statistical units in population censuses but are not independent *de jure*. The (*sídlo*) unit is used by geographers and physical planners who define it as the 'topogeographically rounded-off and separate smallest unit of the settlement structure, representing a unity of people's collectives, housing estates and production buildings, public facilities and utilities, production activities and services'.[2] In the last census of 1980 there were 21,199 such localities in Czechoslovakia, of which 15,291 were in the CSR and 5,908 in the SSR. This illustrates the extremely high fragmentation of settlement.

A tendency towards administrative amalgamation was introduced as early as the late 1960s. The trend varied from region to region, being more intensive in those cases where there were the highest densities of small and very small settlements. There are also differences between the Czech and the Slovak Socialist Republics. Amalgamation particularly affected the smallest settlements, where the necessity for integration was not only most urgently felt, but also where it was geographically easiest to achieve. This was true especially of regions with a high density of settlements, where the distance between individual localities was less than two kilometres and communications were unsatisfactory. Unfortunately, in general, the degree of amalgamation of settlements was relatively low and the result was often the maintenance of a pattern of small communities.

In the Czech Socialist Republic, where the dispersion of localities was extreme, the government set long-term guidelines for the development of the settlement structure in 1971. According to these guidelines the core of the settlement network was to be district centres (numbering 163) which would serve as cultural and economic focal points. From these, seventy-one centres were selected for priority concentration. A further 859 local centres were selected by the regional level national committees as the approved and defined settlement structure.

Five years later, in 1976, a prognosis of the future development of settlement structure was endorsed by the government of the Czech Socialist Republic. The prognosis stemmed from the assumption that the concentration of settlement was a natural, continuing process. Thus, the main goal of the prognosis was to define the areas where concentrated urbanization could take place, and where the population and economic activities should be established. The prognosis was intended to serve as an instrument for achieving an optimal balance — if possible — between economical use of land and the shaping and protection of the human environment in a broad sense. The result was an integrated project consisting of twelve regional residential agglomerations and twenty-nine important centres, with account being taken of the previous historical development. In the official prognosis no radical changes in the settlement pattern up to the year 2000 were proposed and, unfortunately, the territorial-administrative structure as well as that of local authorities was left untouched.

In the late 1970s, the need for a more radical change to the administrative pattern of the municipalities and rural communities made itself strongly felt. The result was a series of documents which sought to improve the work of the national committees in the political arena. It was launched by the highest level of the Communist Party. In the legislature, the process was completed by the enactment of two amendments to the Act on National Committees (Act No. 69/1967, CoL), followed by a series of governmental decrees.

The reform of local government in the 1980s

Recently a series of reforms of the administrative structure have been introduced. The amendments consist of the so-called 'minor amendment', valid from 1 July 1982 (the Act of the Czech National Council No. 49/1982 CoL and the Act of the Slovak National Council No. 52/1982 CoL) and the so-called 'great amendment', valid from 1 January 1983 (the Act of the Czech National Council No. 137/1982 CoL and the Act of the Slovak National Council No. 139/1982 CoL). There are no differences between the Czech and the Slovak laws.

The rural areas

In the early 1980s Czechoslovakia was still characterized by a great number of rural communities, most of which had few inhabitants. Growing demands for rationality and economy of local state administration had led to a process of creating 'central communes'. These have local-level national committees with relatively wide competence. In the other rural communes the local-level national committees have been left with more limited competence. The minor amendment increased the competence of the local-level national committees only in the 'central communes'.

The central communes in rural areas have been chosen as natural economic, political, cultural, trade and educational centres which satisfy the needs and promote the interests not only of their own population but also of a hinterland. They are designated by the regional-level national committees. In the creation of the central communes account was taken of existing integration and co-operation in the economic field, of plans for the development of the settlements, the size of their population (a minimum of 2,500–3,000 inhabitants), of transport conditions (the distance to the centre should not exceed ten kilometres) and of the economic and social infrastructure of the commune. The creation of central communes and granting a wider competence to national committees was not a single act, but is a long-term still unfinished process. By 1 January 1987, 464 local-level national committees in central communes had been established from a total of 5,501 local-level national committees in CSSR (407 in the CSR and fifty-seven in the SSR).

At the same time, neighbourhood units, or so-called citizens' committees, have been created in both urban and rural areas as a link between the national committee and the citizens. These have responsibilities in the fields of public order, reporting gaps in services and organizing voluntary work teams. In the CSR there are 17,008 citizens' committees of which 11,017 are in towns, 3,800 in rural communes and 2,191 in central communes or rural communes with a joint local-level national committee with increased competence. In the SSR there are 3,184 citizens' committees. The citizens' committees are directly elected by the citizens at public meetings for a period of five years.

The increase in the level of competence of the national committees in the central communes has enhanced their opportunities to ensure the comprehensive economic and social development of their territories. The central communes are gradually becoming a basis for provision of services to the inhabitants of both the commune proper and its hinterland. For this purpose the national committees can create and administer services, organize the management and maintenance of housing property, make use of all local resources for setting up workshops and establishments providing minor craft jobs and repairs, run personal services, etc. They establish and administer various types of schools and school facilities, social care establishments, libraries and other cultural facilities.

Central communes are still very varied with respect to the size and density of their population, their area, the number and size of the formerly independent parts, their distance from the seat of the local-level national committee and the level of their public facilities and utilities. Important differences also derive from whether a centrally controlled production unit and co-operative organization operates in their area, and the extent of its contributions to the financial resources of the commune. The level of development and standard of services achieved prior to the creation of the central commune is also bound to affect the possibilities of those local-level national committees with increased competence.

The resulting central communes can be classified into three groups from the point of view of the conditions in which they function:

(1) the optimum cases are those where the creation of the central commune is the result of the preceding economic, social and urban development and is a logical outcome of the operation of geographical, demographic and economic factors.

(2) there are different cases where the creation of a central commune is expected to accelerate economic and social development and increase infrastructure. Achieving a uniform and desirable standard of utilities in these communities is a long-term process.

(3) there are also central communes which are the result of seeking to overcome unfavourable factors, such as a wide dispersal of settlements, a long commuting distance or an orientation towards other settlement centres which were formally independent.

Particular problems are bound to arise with the amalgamation of those smaller communes which possess public facilities and utilities into larger units. There are also considerable differences between communes in the use by local-level national committees of their wider competence. This derives from the varying political and professional abilities, especially of the full-time functionaries of the national committees and staff, as well as from the different levels of management control exercised over the communes by the higher tiers of national committees. Some of these developments have not been entirely successful and future policy in the creation of central communes should more consistently respect the actual conditions of each commune.

The towns and cities

The problems connected with municipalities and their administration required a different approach. In Czechoslovakia 55 per cent of the population live in the municipalities (71 per cent in the CSR and 53 per cent in the SSR). In the Act on National Committees the term 'town' is not defined, rather the term 'town national committees' is used. According to the law, only those municipalities in which a town national committee operates have the status of town. The decision as to which municipalities should have a town national committee has been determined by the government of the Republic since the legal amendment of 1 January 1983.

However, all town national committees established before 31 December 1982 maintained their status in the amended law.

The hinterlands of the towns and cities are an important aspect of the administrative and economic structure. In the CSR 943,000 and in the SSR 493,000 persons commute to towns every day. This is inevitable since the large municipalities concentrate the chief economic functions, cultural facilities, education, social care and other services. They are also the centres of political and social life, and many of the cities have a considerable historical significance reflecting the standard of culture and civilization of the state.

The development of municipalities was particularly rapid in the early 1960s. This was the result of the concentration of production and the development of large new residential complexes, some of which were built outside the previous built-up area and form relatively independent housing estates. Others complement the existing built-up area. Partly as a result of these developments the size and population of the districts has been affected by amalgamation. Between 1970–80, 1,567 communes (1,302 in the CSR and 265 in the SSR) have been amalgamated with towns.

These developments combine with the influence of economic restructuring to bring new tasks and demands to the administration of towns. The challenge is to satisfy and shape the conditions for more efficient production, for a healthy and harmonious environment and for both physical and cultural regeneration of the work force. The complexity of these administrative tasks increases in proportion to the size of the towns. Recognizing the importance of size differences, the municipalities in Czechoslovakia are divided into five groups. Both size and social and economic importance are used as classification criteria.

The first group, as shown in the lower half of Table 11.2, contains only Prague and Bratislava which are the capitals laid down by law. At the top of their management is a National Committee for each city. These national committees are directly supervised by the national government. The status of the national committees of the capital cities of Prague and Slovakia-Bratislava correspond in principle to the status of a regional-level national committee, except for some specific features.

The second group of cities includes the so-called 'statutory cities', for example Brno, Ostrava, Plzeň, and Košice. They are called statutory because of the distribution of powers among their national committees, their organization, their competence and the division of their work is settled by statute. This special legal regulation arises from their historical position and from their particular significance.

The third group consists of the domiciles of the other regional-level national committees and other important towns pursuing the higher-level economic, political, cultural, social and administrative activities, including prominent spas. Some towns which are not domiciles of the regional-level national committees are part of this group. They are designated by the national governments following the proposals of the regional-level national committees.

The fourth group is formed by the district-towns. These have importance

Table 11.2 The distribution of national committees in towns and cities (1 Jan. 1987)

	CSSR	CSR	SSR
Category I: Town national committees	31	22	9
Category II: Town national committees	265	185	80
Category III: Town national committees	254	221	33
Total	550	428	122
1 National committees of the capital cities	2	1	1
2 City-district national committees in capital cities	15	10	5
3 Local-level national committees in capitals	55	46	9
4 National committees of the largest statutory cities	5	4	1
5 Town-district national committees in the largest statutory cities	24	19	5

as settlement centres which are endowed with facilities, business establishments and services with a recognizable and specific hinterland. As a rule these towns exceed 10,000 in population. They are designated by the regional-level national committees except for the domiciles of district national committees. The town national committees of the third and the fourth groups also exercise the competence that is otherwise vested in the district-level national committees.

The fifth group covers the remaining towns which have local importance as settlement centres. The competence of their town national committees does not greatly differ from that of local-level national committees in the central communes of rural areas.

Town national committees operate in the third, fourth and fifth groups. Their competence is laid down by the 1983 'great amendment' of the Law on National Committees mentioned earlier. The widest competence applies to the town national committees of the third group (see Table 11.2, lower half), that is in the towns that are the domiciles of regional-level national committees, or have a major importance or are spas. The competence of the town national committees of the different categories is graded to their status, which is summarized in three categories in the upper half of Table 11.2. For instance, there are important differences between categories in the spheres of planning, investment activity and in the exercise of state administration with respect to the sectors of supply, trade, transport and road management, public order, etc. Certain rights are differentiated among categories in the fields of promoting comprehensive economic and social development of towns (these are rights which town national committees exercise towards centrally controlled organizations, other non-subordinated organizations and state organs). These powers differ in categories I, II and III. There are also local powers to create organizations and establishments designed to satisfy the service needs of the population which are differentiated among categories. The purpose of these differentiated rights is to respond to the differentiated needs of the inhabitants of the towns, that is to their different demands for transport, services, supply and other needs which are related to the different sizes and social and economic importance of the towns.

There are some difficulties which arise from inevitable discrepancies between the territorial-administrative division of the state and the agglomerations which develop from the social and economic structure. One special case is the city of Ústí and Labem, where its national committee, which is supervised by the regional-level national committees, administers both the city and district. This solution may well be adopted by other towns in order to align administration and the economy better.

The reforms implemented since the late 1970s have sought a new approach to some aspects of agglomerations which emphasize a conception based on more effective use of resources and economic development. This has not, however, solved the problems of aligning territorial-administrative districts and agglomerations. The system of basic-level national committees in the central communes has not yet been fully implemented, while difficulties arise from the administrative separation of large towns from their hinterlands. Legal regulations do not yet enable sufficient co-operation among the relevant national committees and nor is there sufficient scope for handling the problems or benefits of agglomerations.

The character and structure of national committees

National committees are local organs of state power and administration as well as self-governing units. As representative authorities they consist of deputies elected in general, secret and direct elections from lists prepared by the National Front, which bring together all political parties and social organizations, for example trade unions, the women's union, the Socialist Union of Youth etc. The number of deputies varies, ranging from a minimum of eighty members at regional level, to sixty in the smaller districts and eighty in the larger districts, and from nine to eighty-five at the municipal level. The variation in numbers is related to the number of inhabitants, the size of the territory and the range of competence of the committee. All deputies serve five-year concurrent terms of office.

The deputies act as the plenary body of the national committee. This handles the fundamental tasks of economy, culture, health and social development, especially with respect to the provision and quality of services, housing construction, house property maintenance, necessities of life and further important interests and needs of the population. All the tasks are fully enumerated in the law. The other representative organs of the national committee are the board and various standing committees. The number of these is determined by the plenary body of deputies. The standing committees consist of deputies as well as outside experts whose duty is to submit proposals to the plenary body and to the board, as well as initiating and supervising the activities of the administrative department relevant to their particular field of concern. The committees of the plenary sessions in rural and urban municipalities often do not establish administrative departments at all, or establish only a few; they function as executive organs, as well as administrative departments.

In the recent amendments to the Act on National Committees in 1982 the direct responsibility of the deputies to their electorate has been increased. Among other things, there is now an obligation laid down by law for the deputies to report to their voters on their actions. At least twice a year the deputies of the basic-level national committees must meet their voters at public meetings and inform them on how they have asserted and defended local interests and carried out their duties as deputies.

The law enables the national committees to apply resources for a more effective and efficient accomplishment of tasks. It is in the competence of the plenary body to approve the basic trends of combining means (or financial resources) and action. The board of the national committee is responsible, in its turn, for submitting proposals and for co-ordinating the combining of financial means and actions. Even though no nation-wide data on this co-operation between communal authorities are available, it may be said that the combining of financial means and actions most frequently takes place either between the national committee and an economic organization, or between individual organizations at the initiative and with the co-ordination of the national committee, rather than between national committees themselves.

There are also regional national committees and district national committees as organs of both state power and administration. The local-level and town national committees (with the exception of the national committees operating in the capitals of the Republics and the five largest cities) are governed by the district national committees which, in their turn, are governed by the regional national committees. Under the principle of 'dual subordination' the board and the administrative departments at one level are responsible to the plenary session at that level, as well as to their counterparts at the higher levels of government, up to the central level. This principle, however, does not apply to plenary sessions nor to the standing committees which are not subordinated in this way. This inevitably leads to possible tensions between the subordinated administrative board and departments and the representative deputies.

The co-operation between the districts and regional national committees is laid down by the Act on National Committees and in many special laws. There is, however, no fixed organizational pattern defined. The way in which the co-operation is realized rests with the national committees themselves.

There are also many administrative bodies which operate outside the system of national committees, some within the same geographical boundaries as the district or regional national committees, some within other areas, depending upon their functions and activities. At the request of the national committee at any level, the state organs are obliged to report to it about their activities concerning the interests and needs of the citizens of the territory and to remedy any failures which are pointed out by the national committee.

About 70 per cent of the financial resources for carrying out the work of the national committees has come from the state budgets. The rest derive from local sources. The budgets of the local units are incorporated within the budgets of the next higher level, and all form part of the overall national budget. Decisions of major economic and social importance are made at the national level. A step towards increased horizontal control was taken with the passage of the 1983 legislation. This gave local authorities greater powers of supervision over the activities of state economic, co-operative and social organizations operating within their territory. However major changes are now occurring which affect these financial relationships.

Conclusion

The administrative reform of 1983 carried out by the so-called 'minor' and 'great amendments' to the Law on National Committees was particularly directed toward three chief goals: (i) the promotion of comprehensive economic and social development of the territory administered by national committees at each hierarchical level; (ii) towards decentralization in the exercise of state administration; and (iii) towards a further development of democracy. To achieve this, the powers and competences of the most basic-level national committees were strengthened. In the rural areas a system of central communes was created and was almost complete by 1988. A categorization of town national committees has been carried out and their powers and competences have been widened and differentiated to give a level of local autonomy (or 'competence differentiation'). The role played by the elected organs of the national committees has increased, the rights of the deputies have been broadened and their authority has been strengthened.

The broadening of the powers and competence of national committees has aimed at the promotion of comprehensive economic and social development of the relevant territory. In particular it has sought a rational development of the territory with an effective administration and management of economic, natural and social resources. This rationality has aimed particularly at increasing the conformity of general society-wide needs to the needs and interests of the local communities and their inhabitants as articulated by the new administrative powers.

The particular objective of the new legislation was to improve the relationship between the basic local-level national committees and the centrally controlled economic, co-operative and social organizations. So far the partnership of the basic-level national committees and the centrally controlled organizations has not always been on an equal footing, especially where the development of the local territory to meet local needs, and to promote local interests and rights of the citizens is at stake. This has been a key factor behind the strengthening of the legal position of the national committees which has led to the extension of their powers with regard to those centrally controlled organizations which conduct activities in their territory, especially concerning economic development. The competence of the national committees was also extended in relation to the organs operating in the fields of social and economic information, financial administration, administration of agriculture and forestry, water management, transport, trade and communications, etc.

The creation of central communes in rural areas and the categorization of town national committees in more urban areas has made it possible to develop adequate responses to the different needs of the inhabitants of urban and rural areas and to promote suitable economic and social development in these settlements.

Decentralization of state administration has been pursued in accordance with the principle that most needs of the citizens could be satisfied by the basic-level national committee. This gives new powers to the basic-level national committees that are closest to the citizen and are in the best position to judge the legitimacy of citizens' needs and interests, as well as enforcing and defending these.

The strengthening of the role of the elected organs, the increased direct responsibility of the deputies to their voters and the broadening of their rights together with the increases in the powers of the basic-level national committees has sought particularly to bring the administration of public matters closer to the citizen, to broaden the possibility for direct supervision by public decision-makers in the fields of economic and social development of towns and communes and to stimulate the citizens' interest and participation in the administration of their affairs and those of the commune or town where they live.

That the 1983 administrative national reform was well founded has been proved especially by the new trends and tendencies in Czechoslovak state administration which have led to a general improvement in efficiency, effectiveness and participation and have stimulated the ensuing proposals for restructuring of the economic mechanism. At the same time, however, this development of economic reforms confirms that not all the objectives of administrative reform have been fully achieved. The main impediment is still perceived to be the highly centralized system of management of the national economy which has limited the full implementation of the administrative reform of 1983.

Notes

1. These consisted of Bohemia, Moravia and Slovakia.
2. Sčítání lidu, domů a bytů 1980-ČSR, Population Census 1980, (1982) Czech Statistical Office, Prague.

12 Bulgaria: administrative division and territorial management

P. Popov and Z. Demerdjiev

Introduction

The history of economic development and administrative division in Bulgaria demonstrates strong interdependence. In earlier periods the functions of the administrative units promoted the formation of consolidated territorial systems which gradually developed into clearly defined regions with specific socio-economic characteristics. In later periods an opposite tendency developed. As a result the administrative boundaries have been reformed with the primary aim of bringing together the administrative division and the economic regionalization of the country. Thus, for example, the former counties (*okolii*), which existed prior to World War II, served as the basis for the present-day micro-regions, while the districts, established in 1959, shaped the meso-regions, which were groups of counties. This process was rooted in economic and social events and was by no means accidental.

The counties emerged around markets and economic and cultural centres with a related hinterland of other smaller settlements. With increases in economic prosperity the relation of the hinterlands' settlements to the core became closer. This was the result of collectivization in agriculture, active migration flows and accelerated industrialization and urbanization. Above the county level the districts concentrated the main administrative, political and economic potential. This strongly affected the territorial structure and organization of industrial production on a nationwide scale. Owing to the expansion of economic interdependence within hinterlands, each district incorporated several micro-regions, which were primarily interlinked with the district centre. Hence clear-cut taxonomic units, called 'integral territorial systems' could be discerned in the regional economic structure, and these were subdivided into micro- and meso-regions. These regional systems differed from one another in terms of their environmental and economic characteristics and specific problems. The territorial systems are identified and described in the regional monograph by the Institute of Geography; Vol. 3, 1989.

At a higher level of territorial organization were the economic regions, comprised of several meso-regions. Until 1987, these were not relied upon as a primary element for the purposes of economic planning and administrative management. The regional scheme was mainly co-ordinative and hypothetical. It is now mainly used for forecasting, as a statistical division and for teaching purposes.

It is widely accepted by most scientists that it is desirable for administrative areas to be drawn up in conformity with economic regions. This idea was launched by Beshkov (1934), who was the founder of the economic geography regionalization of Bulgaria. According to Beshkov economic territories should provide the basis for administrative areas. However, it was not until the end of 1987 that the newly outlined administrative regions almost completely coincided with economic regions. The regions proposed derive from the Bulgarian Academy of Sciences and Research Planning Centre. The coincidence which has now been achieved is the result of a consistent and scientific policy aimed at achieving better territorial management and regional development. The ultimate goal of the 1987 territorial reform is to replace some centralized planning methods with local self-management capacities. It is thus sought to decentralize some administrative and economic functions and to hand them over to local government bodies and to new economic associations and units. As a result the economic and territorial structure of Bulgaria has been completely reformed with major and fundamental consequences for both regional administrative and economic management.

A further key aspect of the reforms of early 1987 was that those ministries responsible for the development of the economy were reorganized so that their management activities could be taken over by new associations. These associations were given the right to control the economy. Territorially this resulted in the twenty-eight former districts being merged into nine new administrative regions. The lower-level administrative units (the settlement systems) were transformed into municipalities. The general goal of this reform was to bring the interests of the state into closer correspondence with the management of the enterprises and the economy, as well as with the interests of the municipalities and the administrative regions.

Principles of spatial planning prior to the 1987 reform

The geographical distribution of economic enterprises has two aspects in centralized planning: sectoral and spatial.

Spatial planning is undertaken at several different levels: national, regional and local. The national level allows the completion of complex programmes which apply the results of new scientific developments to the economy. As a result the spatial organization of production is improved, demographic forecasts of population change at the national and regional scale are accommodated and socio-economic policies are implemented. Spatial planning applies a unified system of central control at the regional scale. It completely reflects central state policy by applying at regional level the plans for development and implementation of short-, medium- and

long-term projects which are concerned with the spatial organization of the
national economy. The term 'spatial organization' refers to the location of
new production facilities and their accompanying infrastructure. Also
included in this planning is the concentration of activities in a hierarchy
of territorial units, and the formation of economic links between and within
regions which seek to increase the effectiveness of production.

Sectoral economic plans are subordinate to the national strategy. They
seek to reflect the distinctiveness and development possibilities of individual
regions. The chief aim is to produce an optimum spatial location of new
production bearing in mind the various economic, social and ecological
constraints which exist. Sectoral plans are also concerned with the
reconstruction of existing facilities and with innovations which might
improve the spatial organization of production.

Regional planning goals are restricted to the *implementation* of complex
territorial programmes concerned with the socio-economic development of
a hierarchy of administrative units, consisting of regions, administrative
districts, municipalities and inhabited localities where the strict application
of economic, social, ecological and spatial organization policies are needed.
Regional policy, as it is conceived here, is used for the redistribution of
resources, for the formation of enterprises from which socio-economic
development is organized and for the delimitation of territorial-production
complexes. Territorial-production complexes are the economic structures
which underpin the spatial organization of the economies of the regions.
These complexes are formed from the combination of various specialist
sectors of the economy in particular regions. They are planned with respect
to the economy, society and ecology of the region. In certain areas, specific
regional programmes are introduced. These relate to special cases such as
the regulation of population migration or the exploitation of new natural
resources. Such programmes are important in south-eastern Bulgaria,
particularly in the Strandja and Sakar regions.

Finally it should be stressed that a paramount goal for regional spatial
planning is to reduce differences in the socio-economic levels of the population of the various territorial units and to equalize regional incomes. Each
of these goals seeks to improve sectoral and regional resource allocation.

Prior to 1987 the aim was to combine the principles of both centralization and decentralization in the development and implementation of the
plan. This methodology required that the territorial structure of the
economy should conform with national interests. At the same time the
territorial structure of the economy was not to contradict the local interests
which were considered to be the primary constructive elements of the
national optimum. The national overall interests were co-ordinated by the
optimization of the territorial production structures within the nation and
by the unified socio-economic plan which was developed by the central
planning agencies. The plan for an individual territory was a component
part of the general plan for the socio-economic development of the country.
It embraced the sectoral, regional and local plans worked out by the
respective organizations and reflected the main indicators and guidelines
laid down in the national plan. Thus it was hoped that the principles of

centralized democracy were observed in planning. The central planning agencies suggested guidelines which tied in with national totals, outlined expected trends in socio-economic development and pursued an overall optimum, while the sectoral and local administrative bodies created the working plans in which the local optimum was fixed in the light of national interests. These local plans aimed at involving all potential resources.

Under this system the state policy for the regions was carried out by the Planning Committee which co-ordinated the activities of all ministries. Territorial planning was under the authority of a special department at the Planning Committee for the development of territorial plans. The State Planning Committee controlled plan implementation, requiring the ministries and local agencies to present their own projects for new developments and for the reconstruction, reorganization and enlargement of facilities. The planning departments in the ministries and in the largest administrative districts generalized the local proposals and sent them on to the State Planning Committee. The latter co-ordinated them, using totals of available raw materials, labour resources and capital investment, information on the income and expenditure of the population and on the likely consumption of goods in the home market. Having been generalized by its administrative units, the territorial plan was then brought into line with the general socio-economic plan for the country as a whole and became its component part. It was then adopted by the Parliament and grants were made from the state's budget, or from the budgets of the individual enterprises.

Changes in the administrative and territorial management and their roots

Up to 1959 Bulgaria was divided into thirteen administrative districts and 105 counties (*okolii*). The counties were relatively small and, because of their significant position as economic centres, they formed the basis for the structure of the micro-regions. This was scientifically substantiated by Penkov *et al.*, (1976). Although the micro-regions were still a hypothesis without practical application, it was believed that in the future a well-grounded micro-regional scheme could be employed as a key instrument for solving socio-economic problems at the local level. This might be achieved if several municipalities joined efforts to tackle their most important problems, for example the construction of a unified infrastructure network in their territory.

In 1959 the counties were abolished. Abolition was based on arguments that they were expensive to administer, that they fragmented the territory, which it was argued, resulted in difficulties in territorial management. In their place twenty-eight new districts were defined (see Figure 12.1). These were the principal territorial units until the end of 1987. The main production capacities were located with respect to their boundaries and modern facilities were planned and built in accordance with defined political, cultural and social requirements. The districts played a positive role in

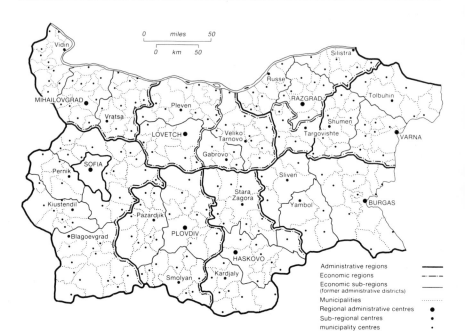

Figure 12.1 Administrative regions, economic regions and sub-regions since 1987

seeking ways to disperse the productive forces territorially. Before their formation industries had been concentrated into ten settlements situated around the main transport axes. Significant economic and social gaps became apparent between the individual regions, and gradually the district centres attracted considerable economic potential. Inside the districts the spatial organization was ill-balanced: usually there was a highly developed district centre but the periphery lagged behind. The local authorities in these old settlement systems (the present-day municipalities) had neither enough power nor financial resources available to solve their problems. Hence they entered a period of stagnation. In particular the rural regions began to suffer from depopulation. At the same time the district centres concentrated a large number of administrative bodies and population.

As a result of this development, experts in spatial planning and management, together with the government organizations, concluded that the old districts, if confined to their boundaries, would have slowed down the rate of economic growth. The situation was further aggravated by a rather complicated district administration and by highly centralized management and planning. Therefore a major governmental reform policy was initiated. This has been directed, first, at restructuring the primary economic sectors, and second, at restructuring territorial management on new principles. As a result a new territorial administrative structure was established in 1988. This seeks to combine the traditional links between the districts and the integral territorial complexes, but has led to the formation of new administrative regions whose boundaries almost fully coincide with the economic regions. This reorganization is concerned primarily with macro-economic objectives, and is based primarily on the existing territorial production complexes. As a result it is sought to guide regions and regional government agencies in their development decisions in compliance with the national territorial complex. This administrative, territorial and economic reform has tended to create a qualitatively new situation which seeks to create a transition from centralized management to decentralized self-management. Under such circumstances the former districts no longer conform to the mechanism of territorial management. Hence they have given way to more flexible units and have ceased to perform managerial functions.

At regional level these reforms have also modified the regional planning structure in Bulgaria, and its relationship to state economic planning. Regional analysts distinguish three levels: macro-, meso- and micro-regions. Bulgarian scientists are not unanimous in their conceptions about the pattern of regional classification schemes and have propounded several alternative approaches, each one leading to different regions (see for example Naidenova, 1986).

The new administrative regions and the former administrative districts are shown in Figure 12.1. Here it can be seen that the new regions coincide with the large economic regions, and former administrative districts relate to the meso-regions. There are also slight differences in the territorial extent of the administrative and economic regions which are marked on the map.

For the implementation of the economic and administrative reforms two instruments are to be employed: first, new economic associations, and second, changes to the role and responsibilities of the new administrative units, particularly the municipalities. Each is discussed in turn below.

The role of the new economic associations and their territorial distribution

The new economic associations created in 1987 are primarily economic agencies. They are vested with extensive duties for the implementation of the national economy. Their chief task is to overcome the previously rather narrow departmental approach to economic management. In addition administrative management principles are being replaced by economic incentives. Thus the associations are expected to stimulate the following changes:

— a rapid development of new production capacity linked to the scientific and technological progress of Bulgaria;
— the development of advanced technologies which will allow producers to participate more actively in the international division of labour;
— stimulate the transition to various forms of local self-management by converting the state production property into the property of the new autonomous economic establishments.

Irrespective of the specific nature of the activity, the new associations will perform some more general functions. They are also faced with a number of common tasks. Key examples are:

— to attempt to align the interests of the state with the interests of the new economically independent organizations and enterprises;
— to pursue a general technological, financial and market policy;
— to co-ordinate the activities of the self-managing organizations with the help of integration of technology and production methods, thus contributing to the formation of multi-sectoral economic complexes;
— to organize such activities which are in the interests of all their subordinates;
— to exercise a level of freedom over the allocation of their own funds and resources to provide modern technical equipment.

Both the government authorities and the self-managing organizations exercise control over the new associations. However, apart from their common functions and goals, each association has its own characteristics predetermined by its organizational structure and specific tasks determined by its role in its territorial production complex. The new associations embrace various other economic units as their chief subordinates which in turn include a number of different enterprises, industrial plants and other economic establishments. Half of all the economic units in these new associations are located in the main economic and administrative centre of Bulgaria, in Sofia. The population of this area has risen rapidly and is creating serious economic, transport, ecological and social problems. The location of the new economic units which have been given a new status of self-management is shown in Figure 12.2.

Tasks of the new administrative units since 1987

Government statements of administrative objectives lay emphasis on the fact that the administrative districts that existed up to 1987 were primarily organs of the supreme state power (the central representative bodies). In contrast the aim of the new administrative units established in 1987 is to realize decentralized management policy at three hierarchical levels: a mayorship (an individual settlement); a municipality (a single inhabited locality or a group of settlements); and nine administrative regions (those of Sofia, Plovdiv, Haskovo, Bourgas, Varna, Razgrad, Lovetch, Mihailovgrad and the agglomeration of Sofia which is delineated as an independent urban region). At each of these administrative levels local problems are to be solved by the principle of self-management. The municipalities are vested with the chief responsibilities. They have extensive duties and have been given all rights of control in both the production and non-production spheres. At the same time they are responsible for any failures, that is they function as autonomous integrated territorial systems. A few municipalities can amalgamate with each other in order to find

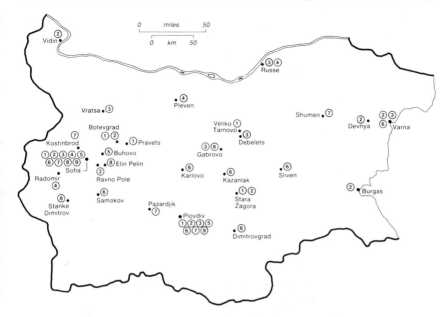

Figure 12.2   Territorial distribution of economic units and economic associations. Key to economic units affiliated to the following associations: 1. Electronics; 2. Biotechnology and high-technology industry; 3. Transport, agricultural and building facilities; 4. Engineering; 5. Metallurgy and mineral resources; 6. Light and food industry; 7. National Agro-Industrial Union; 8. Forestry and wood processing; 9. Construction and building industry

efficient solutions to local problems. These are the so-called 'associated municipalities'. They concern mainly new economic activities initiated with regard to the specific features of the territory, the creation of new jobs, the construction of a unified social and technical infrastructure, the establishment of a common service system, measures to limit depopulation of the rural districts, environmental protection and regeneration and the improvement of the conditions of living, work and recreation, etc. Research on these problems is a major task of geography which allows application of its methods to the scientific solution of major administrative and economic problems (see for example Popov, 1985; Donchev, 1985).

A special law has been passed by the National Assembly which, together with other normative documents adopted by the supreme state authorities, has laid down the main principles of administrative management. According to these principles the municipality is defined as the fundamental administrative territorial unit and is an autonomous system. A municipality includes all the settlements in its adjacent territory, the local productions plants, technical facilities, social infrastructure and public utilities owned and managed by the population. The municipality is also required to take care of social property (land, buildings, infrastructure, etc.). Its population directly participates in the management by means of referendums and open sessions, sponsored by the People's Council, and hence, in decision-making procedures. This decision-making is contexted within the following objectives:

1. The basic perspectives for socio-economic and cultural development, for territorial organization and for environmental protection. These can be converted into reality if the municipalities operate on the principle of self-sufficiency and self-financing, and if they maintain and expand their production links with the enterprises which belong to other municipalities;

2. Determination of the structure and location of public facilities, planning self-sufficiency in farm products, implementing the necessary changes in administrative and territorial division and the naming and renaming of certain local entities;

3. A policy devised by the municipality council and aimed at central, scientific, technical, territorial-organizational, social and cultural development of the municipality. This also determines the structure of production capacities as well as balancing, co-ordinating and regulating the use of municipal resources (labour resources, land, forests, pastures, water, jobs, houses and other buildings) and elaborating plans to meet the demand for workers and specialists;

4. Five-year and one-year plans which envisage: the boosting of local production, the setting up of a system for comprehensive services, the extension of infrastructure and the development of links with other municipalities;

5. The norms fixed by the municipality are compulsory for all enterprises. Also compulsory are the regulations which influence the all-around development in the production and non-production sphere which emphasizes environment controls and standards of goods and services. Each municipality specifies the objects of local-level services, approves the territorial structures and town-planning projects which are to be carried out within its boundaries and gives its consent for new planning and buildings belonging to the basic, technical or social infrastructure. The municipality is to take the role of a single investor in the course of planning, designing and financing the unified infrastructure. It is to co-ordinate and control the activities of all organizations which are concerned with municipal investments. It also is responsible for stimulating enterprises and organizations to enter into contracts; and it periodically is to monitor developments to ensure that contractual terms are strictly adhered to. It also plans and regulates the scope and range of products produced within the system of self-sufficient agriculture, their purchases and marketing; it allocates that land which remains unused by co-operative farms, or land under forests, both fit for growing crops or for being converted into grassland, which has to be cultivated on a family or collective basis, thus giving impetus to self-sufficiency in agricultural activities;

6. Each municipality has the right to design its transport network, to

implement functional management in the sphere of education, to supervise nurseries and kindergartens, to make provisions for cultural entertainments, to distribute houses, to improve ecological and working conditions, to define environmental control norms and labour safety regulations, and to levy sanctions on all who fail to protect the environment from pollution;

7. The municipality also has the right to build industrial plants and food-processing enterprises, to initiate construction works and maintenance services for the upkeep of buildings, etc.

The administrative regions are also autonomous, but of a higher rank. Besides their managerial functions they have to be advocates of government regional policy. A fundamental principle laid down in the new administrative regionalization is the creation of a simple, flexible and efficient administration which allows self-management to be effected at a municipal level. Hence the administrative regions are to operate only as co-ordinating bodies. In addition, they direct and co-ordinate the functions executed by municipalities for solving managerial problems and defining regional strategic goals.

The councils of the administrative regions are involved in drafting the guidelines for national socio-economic development, the general plan for the distribution of production and the unified territorial-structuring plan. The councils are to outline the regional socio-economic strategy and its spatial organization. The council should carefully consider the territory and population and assess their potential with regard to economic and cultural development, the solution of multi-attribute problems, the achievement of comprehensive services, the equalization of the standard of living at municipal level and the invention of advanced technologies using the technical and scientific potential of the region.

The regional councils organize and conduct the work of the municipalities in order to carry out and fulfil the state policy tasks set by the government. The regions also reflect the objectives of the municipalities: to maintain integral links between the sphere of economy, science, technology and socio-cultural events; to unfetter the individual and collective labour creativity in producing goods and services; to satisfy local needs for agricultural products and foodstuffs on a self-sufficient basis; to build integrated enterprises, run by several municipalities; to undertake a mutual construction work; and to take measures for environment protection and regeneration.

The regional councils seek to define the priorities given to different branches of activity to ensure a profit-making economy and rapid technical, scientific, social and cultural progress by using the resources available in the municipalities and by levelling out the conditions of living between them.

It is intended that the territorial management of Bulgaria should develop in line with central government regional policy. Its goals are defined in sectoral and territorial five-year plans, as discussed earlier, are elaborated and updated each year and are adopted by the National Assembly. After the 1987 administrative reform these plans should begin to reflect only strategic development trends. General goals are translated into concrete targets, clearly formulated in the production programmes which have to be carried out by the respective associations and economic units so as to meet the demands of home and foreign markets. This reform has led to changes in the way that sectoral and territorial planning are combined and co-ordinated. Responsibility for co-ordination is now mainly held by the associations and the new integral territorial complexes (the municipalities and their administrative regions) within whose boundaries the production process is going on. New approaches will be needed in order to correctly balance the sectoral and territorial plans under this new system of decentralized planning and self-management. The restructuring of the national and regional economy depends upon the successful implementation of this new balance of planning and administration.

References

Asótsàtsiite ot nov tip i preustroistvoto na bankovata sistema, (1987), *Prilozhenie na vestnik 'Rabotnichesko delo'*, br. 114 ot, 24 April.

Beshkov, A. (1934), *Stopansko-geografsko podelenie na Bulgaria*, Bulgarian Academy of Sciences, Sofia.

Donchev, D. (1985), 'Goals of spatial planning for the small settlement systems of Bulgaria', in J.H. Johnson (ed.), *Geography Applied to Practical Problems*, Geobooks, Norwich, 27–36.

Institute of Geography, (1989), *Geografia na Bulgaria, Vol. 3, Fizikogeografsko i sotsialno-ikonomichesko raionirane* (Physio-geographic and Socio-economic Regionalization), Bulgarian Academy of Sciences, Sofia.

Naidenova, R. and Nikolov, F. (1974), Po vaprosa za ikonomicheskite raioni v Bulgaria; *Trudove na Nauchnia Tsentar po teritorialno planirane i razpolozhenie na proiz-voditelnite sili*, Vol. I, Bulgarian Academy of Sciences, Sofia.

Naidenova, R. (1986), *Teritorialno-proizvodstveni komplexi i sotsialno-ikonomichesko raionirane — sb. Geografiata v savremenna Bulgaria*, Bulgarian Academy of Sciences, Sofia.

Penkov, I., Dinev, L., Kanchev, H. and Donchev, D. (1976), *Schema na ikonomicheskite mikroraioni v Bulgaria — sb. Problemi na geografsko i ikonomgeografsko raionirane na Bulgaria*, Nauka i Izkustvo, Sofia.

Popov, P. (1985), 'Principles of spatial planning in Bulgaria', in J. Johnson (ed.), *Geography Applied to Practical Problems*, Geobooks, Norwich, 19–26.

Ukaz No. 3005 na Darzhavnia Savet za administrativno-teritorialni promeni v stranata, (1987), *Darzhaven vestnik*, br. 78, 9 October.

Zakon za sazdavane na administrativno-teritorialnite edinitsi — oblastite, *Darzhaven vestnik*, br. 65, 21 August.

13 The German Democratic Republic

Joachim Bräuniger

Introduction

The administration of territory in the GDR takes place within a framework which defines the fundamental aims of all public policies. These can be divided into a set of political and economic assumptions.

Political assumptions

It is assumed that social ownership of the means of production ensures the possibility of developing productive activities and services in line with the requirements of all elements of society. As a result the key objectives of all administrative activities are: first to provide the conditions in which the continuing increase of the national product can be secured, and second to transform this increase into an improvement of living standards in all parts of the country. The term 'living standards' is to be understood in its widest sense. It covers not only the immediate material needs of the population but also the protection of the environment and securing conditions propitious to further economic growth. A continuing improvement in the standard of living must be perceptible to the population in all parts of the country, including those areas where conditions are already superior to the national average, while every effort must also be made to raise the standards in other regions to the level of the favoured regions.

Within population there is no fundamental distinction made between the various groups such as between dwellers in town and country, inhabitants of different parts of the country, members of different social strata or occupational groups, although clearly some contrasting characteristics remain. Thus, the administration of the state is regarded as a unity, although there is a division of responsibilities and duties between its various levels.

Economic and geographic assumptions

A free choice of workplace and place of residence is guaranteed by the constitution of the GDR. In earlier years there was considerable internal migration, influenced by the location of employment opportunities and the construction of new housing. Today, however, the only interregional migration flow is to the capital, Berlin. In all parts of the country there is now a sufficient choice of work. Naturally the detailed selection of jobs available will vary from place to place, but everyone is assured of employment and an adequate income. Rural areas are not exceptions to this rule: the net income of the population is also high. As a result special development schemes for particular parts of the country are no longer necessary.

At a time when there is no population growth, even occasional decline, the migration of people into the big cities and into the larger middle-sized towns has necessarily involved the decline of population in the small towns and in the villages. However, a particular problem is presented by the older industrial agglomerations in the south of the GDR. History has left these settlements with a housing stock and urban infrastructure that are badly in need of modernization. They cannot be neglected, for they are still highly important to the economy because of their endowment with industrial plant and accumulation of productive experience.

The system of public administration in the GDR

The GDR is divided into fifteen administrative divisions or intermediate-level units (*Bezirke*). This division dates from 1952. The *Bezirke* vary in population from 0.5 to 1.9 million. The term '*Bezirk*' is simply a 'district' mainly used for administrative and statistical functions. However, since 1952 the *Bezirke* have also been transformed into functioning economic regions, used for spatial economic planning. Below *Bezirk* level there is a lower-tier unit, the *Kreis* (county). There are twenty-eight urban units (*Stadtkreise*) and 191 rural units (*Landkreise*). The capital, Berlin, has the administrative structure of a *Bezirk*. Berlin, like the capitals of other states, is integrated into the central planning process.

Economic development in the *Bezirke* and *Kreise* is achieved through improvements in productive activities and in infrastructure. With regard to the latter, the urban hierarchy is particularly important, as the higher-level functions in fields such as science, culture and health care are predominantly concentrated in the larger cities, which also tend to receive most additional investment in these fields. Particular functions are allocated according to the threshold population achieved by a city and its hinterland. Examples of functions which require large populations include TV studios, symphony orchestras, comprehensive facilities for fundamental scientific research or facilities for advanced medical treatment. The hierarchical principle enables two requirements to be satisfied: a minimum threshold population to support a service, and optimum public access in terms of travel distance minimization (defined to be a forty-minute isochrone on public transport).

The capital of the *Bezirk* is always its largest town. This is largely because the *Bezirke*, from their creation, were centred in the large cities whose name they bear. However, this degree of primacy has been reinforced by subsequent industrial development and their role in delivering the higher urban functions. The combination of functions (administration, infrastructure and, as a rule, industry) is used as an advantage for planning the economy and the population using the city-region as a basic unit. As a result 13.8 million people, 83 per cent of the inhabitants of the GDR, can reach either a *Bezirk* capital or a *Kreis* capital by a journey of not more than forty minutes by public transport.

This ease of access to the points of supply of higher-level services is facilitated by a closely meshed road network, a well-developed urban network, the short distance involved and the high degree of vehicle ownership (50 per cent of all households own a car; for households of economically active persons the proportion rises to over 70 per cent). At the same time, the appropriate administrative bodies are required to ensure that services in everyday demand such as day nurseries, kindergartens, schools for the lowest four classes, doctors' surgeries, shops, inns or clubs, are made available even in the smallest villages. There is an inevitable problem, however, that the services that are provided in small villages cannot always be fully used.

Sectoral and territorial plans

A major aim of planning in the GDR is to combine the sectoral and territorial principles of administration. The economy, which is planned and organized within sectors, and the territorially arranged organization of the state, must be co-ordinated. The economy is managed at the highest level by ministries which are guided by the decisions of the party. In the economic fields the ministries are subdivided into *Kombinate* (trusts) which are themselves composed of a varying number of enterprises. There are ten ministries for industry, including mining and energy production. There are also ministries for construction, transport, post and telecommunications, water and environmental protection and geology. These are organized like the economic sectors, but always have closer ties with the institutions for territorial development than the industrial ministries.

Ministries concerned with social infrastructure (for example culture, health, education, trade) link with the relevant local government at the level of the *Bezirke* or *Kreise*. Only a few activities are directly controlled by the ministries. Apart from certain aspects of trade, there is no sectoral structure at this territorial level. Otherwise, the departments responsible for these fields of infrastructure are parts of the local government structure of the *Bezirk* and *Kreis* and are responsible to the councils of these bodies. However, the local government departments also operate according to instructions from their ministries to which they are subordinate. Hence they have a double responsibility. This is a general principle of the state's organization and applies also to agriculture, planning and other fields. In general, this principle is reflected in a corresponding structure of administration at the level of the state, *Bezirk* and *Kreis*. On the basis of directives from the State Planning Commission the ministries determine the targets for the development of their output and capacity. This in turn provides the targets for the departments of the *Bezirke* and *Kreise*. For industry the process is rather different: the linkage is to the *Kombinate*, is subdivided between them and is then provided to the enterprise. However, the linkage is not one way since each of these levels prepares its own plans with regard to its needs, but co-ordinates with the targets derived from the state economic plan. Thus there is a co-ordination in which the plans for the *Kreise* and *Bezirke* are harmonized with the targets of the higher planning levels. This is a general principle which is used repeatedly in each annual planning cycle.

The *Bezirke* and *Kreise* have Planning Commissions (BPC, KPC) which are responsible for the integrated development of all sectors of the economy and infrastructure of their territories. This is the horizontal side of their contributions. Parallel to this they have to subdivide the planning targets derived from the State Planning Commission (vertical co-ordination). This means that the BPC has to adjust the targets for the *Kreis* derived from the state PC in such a way as to bring into line the development of the economic sectors and the comprehensive territorial plan for the *Kreise*. This is not always readily accomplished since it is necessary to make central tasks conform with local possibilities.

The elaboration of the plans is regulated in a uniform way with respect to their content, methods, organization, termination, responsibilities and targets. This yields an obligatory 'order of planning' which is elaborated and defined for each five-year plan period, and may give the impression that there is a strong centralization in the GDR. This is indeed the case in respect of fundamental principles and the main tasks of development. However, in the detailed fulfilment of the plans there is a broad local capacity for initiatives at the lower levels. This capacity has been continuously broadened in the last fifteen to twenty years. A second aspect is that the elaboration of plans does not end with the *Kreise* and enterprises. Working teams (*Brigaden*) in the enterprises and drawn from the towns and villages are also engaged in preparing plans for their particular needs and developments, as well as contributing to the plans of the *Kreise* and enterprises.

There is thus a uniformity in the planning process and administration at all levels of the state and in all fields of economic and social activities. As a result the planning institutions have the right and the duty of supervision. Information on 'plan implementation' derives mainly from the consultations which take place in elaborating the next annual plan between, on the one hand the Planning Commission, and on the other hand, the sectoral management institutions and the local government departments for sectoral infrastructure.

Planning objectives

The objective of each plan is defined within the requirements of the comprehensive development of the whole of society. A key starting point for both the enterprise or territory is what tasks the plan provided in the previous year. In the productive sphere, concerned with increasing national income, the plan for the following years usually includes an allowance for increases. In the non-productive sphere the so-called 'attained level of provision' is decisive. This means that indicators are compared between territories: for example doctors, or beds in hospitals per 1,000 inhabitants, provision of schools and colleges per 1,000 pupils, places in nurseries per 1,000 children in the ages between one and three years, etc. Comparisons are drawn between the *Kreise* in a given *Bezirk*, and between *Bezirke* in the country as a whole. This is done by the relevant ministry together with the State Planning Commissions. The method of allocating finance and the targets for allocating material resources (construction capacity, equipment, labour) are generally characterized by an intention of favouring areas with lower standards of living, but in each case other special aspects are taken into consideration.

— Ongoing projects have priority;
— Infrastructure is mainly provided in association with 'housing complexes' — thus a specified number of houses (dwelling units) has to include certain infrastructure facilities;
— Industrial development is often allowed preferential provision of associated housing and infrastructure (not for resettlement, but for the existing workforce).

A further general characteristic of planning and administration is that *all* measurements are taken into the plans in order to minimize disturbances caused by exceptional activities outside the scope of the plan; and that the implementation of plan aims is ensured by 'plan orders' and/or by contracts. 'Plan orders' are issued from the immediately higher level of planning or administration to the subordinate level (for example from the *Kombinate* to the enterprise, or from the *Bezirk* to the *Kreis*). Horizontal co-operation is carried out by use of economic contracts, for example between towns, between an enterprise and a town, between enterprises subordinated to different *Kombinates*, and so on.

The role of territorial planning in administration

Territorial planning acts as the core of all spatially oriented activities in the administration of the GDR at all three levels: state, *Bezirke* and *Kreis*. Territorial planning strictly binds the administrative units to their territory. In the GDR it is accepted that regions exist as spaces distinguished by physical indicators or defined by common historical development, but territories are the administrative units. Planning concerns these latter units. Hence we speak of 'territorial' and not of 'regional' planning. Planning for the region is rarely undertaken explicitly or separately. It is the objective of central comprehensive planning to take into consideration aspects of regional development, while developments which concern the *Kreise* or *Bezirke* are co-ordinated by the next higher level (that is by the *Bezirke* of SPC).

Planning starts from the supposition that all investments and developments take place within administrative units. Thus plan orders address economic development. This is not the case with physically demarcated regions which have no separate powers. Similarly, there is no separate regional development planning for achievement of either increased or more equal development between regions of places of work or infrastructure.

Territorial planning in the GDR has a high level of authority in relation to planning as a whole and administration. The main aspects are:

(1) The integration of the management process into the implementation of plans.
(2) The balancing character, not so much involving 'programmes' and 'studies' as planning of the economy and infrastructure, as well as the equal provision of resources within the respective territory and co-ordination of sectoral developments.
(3) The conservation of resources. Within the GDR resources such as space, water and manpower, but also the output of the construction sector and of infrastructure, are balanced between the territories of the administrative units. The starting point is that developments must correspond with the output of resources in a given territory. A spatial transformation of manpower or construction capacities is either impossible or inefficient. Because of this limitation of resources, there must be very exact balances between territories and over time. Growth of the economic sectors, linked with a higher demand for resources, can be initiated only if the resources are sufficient at a given time or location. This fine-tuning is achieved either by territorial planning, especially for manpower itself, or through the strong influence of the many sectoral investments.
(4) The role of territorial planning derives from its objective of co-ordinating the planning of living conditions (especially housing construction) and all sectoral planning into one comprehensive plan for the *Bezirk* or *Kreis*. Of course, in the comprehensive plan, important developments in the field of production are included only for plan information or as a target for the territory in order to ensure production increases in line with the capacity of the territory. Important economic investments are prepared in the State Planning Commission, decided in the Council of Ministers (cabinet), and implemented by the ministry of the relevant industrial sector or the appropriate *Kombinate*. It would be too much to expect a *Kreis* to decide on developments in the field of high technology. But this does not mean that a *Kreis* has no responsibility or capacity for the support of this type of production.

The main approach to planning thus makes use of local balancing combined with comprehensive calculation of sectoral developments for each territory. This operates well when the territorial consequences and inter-linkages are taken into consideration at the outset. This should occur directly because the plan framed by the State Planning Commission is already territorially founded. This means that already it takes into consideration the conditions in each *Bezirk*, *Kreis* and city as well as industrial locations. The planning commission in each *Bezirk* (BPC) receives the targets from the industry ministries for their *Bezirk*. Additionally, the BPC receives further information from the consultations and co-ordination with the *Kombinate*. This defines the capacities and needs for each economic sector and its output in the *Bezirk*. The same situation applies to the planning commission in the *Kreis* and also to the enterprises located there.

The co-ordination of the economic leaders in sectoral management with the *Bezirke* and *Kreise* is based on equality of provision and calculations of planning targets derived from the superior level. The common aim is to ensure the planned increase in output and efficiency (especially concerning national income) and the improvement of living conditions.

The tools for Territorial Planning (TP) for implementing plan decisions are as follows:

(1) The TP has to provide decisions on important factors such as manpower, construction, training capacities and housing development which lay down the foundation for the plans at all levels and which strongly influence sectoral developments.

(2) The TP generates economic and social benefit by organizing co-operation among enterprises in a given location which are organized in different sectors. For example, the spare capacity of one partner can be used by another. This is formally based on contracts and involves payment for mutual benefit. Normally, this involves manufacturing activities, but the social field can also be involved, for example enterprises like food preparation for employees, or heating for rooms. This type of co-ordination is called 'territorial rationalization'. The chief possibilities of such co-ordination are components of the future plans, but their preparation is a continuous process.

(3) Territorial Planning must give its approval for all new investment locations: the 'permission for location'. For large projects this may require approval by the TP at all three levels. For medium-sized or smaller projects, only the *Bezirk* or *Kreis* is concerned. The final permission is granted by the local authority (town or village). This ensures that local interests are taken into consideration. Before this approval all questions must first be clarified by the planning institutions: for example a village would be overworked and unable to decide the location aspects of a nuclear power station in its area. The approval by the TP is linked with other consents (water, energy, transport or environmental protection) which require prior approval. The territorial approval is the precondition for the delivery of permission for any developments.

(4) Planning in the GDR is not only concerned with elaboration of a formal document, but is a process which includes a permanent and detailed adjustment. This process may be of equal importance to the plan itself.

The comprehensive duties of local government

In addition to the planning system outlined above local government has many duties and responsibilities where specific local conditions are taken into consideration. Chief among these are:

(1) The councils of the *Bezirke*, *Kreis* or local community support, within the Territorial Plan, local economic development of production facilities by directing the application of scientific and technical facilities among the enterprises. Local councils help to plan the full use of resources and organize the priorities for use among the enterprises: for example, where their local enterprises have to make major increases in output, or where they have special problems with their labour force.

(2) The local councils seek to ensure that energy, water and transport are made available according to the demands of the population and production facilities. This also includes the provision of transport for shift-workers.

(3) Local councils pay particular attention to the conditions of shift-workers (transport, meals, opening hours of shops) in order to promote the readiness for shift-work and so make full use of the fixed capital in the enterprises.

(4) The local councils seek to influence the capacity of the enterprises for vocational training according to the changing labour conditions. They control and support firms by retraining redundant workers. This ensures that most displaced workers are re-employed in the same enterprise.

(5) Special attention is paid to housing construction. The local authorities not only influence housing through their planning regulations, but also are involved in housing enterprises. The volume, location, construction period, type of house, site-clearance and facilities for the new residential areas are all fields which require the participation of the local councils. For the maintenance of buildings and for small projects, the local construction enterprises organized by the construction development in the *Kreis* play the dominant role. It follows that the local administration is responsible for the capacity and efficiency of the local construction sector.

(6) Housing provision is an important and comprehensive field for local government. This includes responding to applications from the inhabitants, as well as the control of the housing stock and its use.

(7) The local governments are also responsible for the steady increase in agricultural production. In order to do this they support not only the

agricultural enterprises and co-operatives in their territories but also horticultural enterprises, fishing co-operatives, the association of small gardeners and private livestock and breeding by individual co-operative farmers. This latter support concerns the purchasing of products, provision of fodder, supply of equipment, and so on.

(8) The provision of consumer goods to the population is also a task for local government. The trading organizations have to report regularly on supplies and local authorities must ensure that adequate decisions are made. Many enterprises in the food industry, and small enterprises producing consumer goods, are organized by a council of the *Bezirk*. The *Bezirke* have an important role in this area, although most consumer goods are produced in enterprises which are centrally organized and subordinated to the industrial-sector ministries.

(9) Other important fields of work for local governments are of course those which directly serve the inhabitants: for example building repairs and services, culture, trade and leisure facilities. Trade, culture and leisure facilities are almost completely autonomous to the *Kreis* for the local administrations. This is particularly true of sports and recreation facilities, most restaurants, clubs and provision of allotments.

New developments influencing the work of local government

A series of recent reforms has affected the GDR with the aim of decentralizing more powers to the local authorities.

Formation of Kombinates *(Trusts)*

The *Kombinates* have recently been charged with the chief responsibility for developing new products, for training and retraining workers and, in some cases, for exporting. These functions have been transferred from the ministries and hence there has been a degree of economic decentralization. As a result of this reform, decisions, especially in production, can be made earlier and can be better related to the specific demand conditions. It is not expected that independence will be give to individual enterprises, as they are judged to be too small. The independence of the *Kombinates* represents a new set of conditions for the councils (and Planning Commissions) in the *Bezirke* and *Kreise*. Since more decisions are now made at the place of management of the *Kombinate*, the *Bezirke* now need information on enterprises which are located in *Bezirke* than that in which the management of the *Kombinate* is situated. Hence increased efforts are required from the *Kombinates* as well as the *Bezirke* and *Kreise* to ensure that co-ordination is achieved.

Increasing industrial output

Following these developments in the national economy the enterprises are now being forced to increase their output by switching to new products with a higher value. Increases have to be achieved without substantial increases in the use of energy, labour force or raw material: for example increases in efficiency and productivity are required. This makes co-ordination between the industrial sectors and *Bezirke* or *Kreise* easier and should allow the release of local resources.

Changes in housing construction

The construction of new houses is being increasingly accompanied by modernization of old houses so that new construction is going on mainly within the cities and is no longer taking place on the outskirts. Parallel to this trend is a tendency to shift development from the big cities to the medium-sized and smaller towns. Associated with these changes the size of residential complexes is being reduced. At the same time, the construction of single houses, based on individual family initiatives has also increased. All these changes have strengthened the role of local government since they are occurring within the areas of local administrative competence.

Reductions in the scale of agricultural producers

After the establishment of large, modern agricultural producers in the 1960s and 1970s more attention is now being paid to the production conditions which exist within the villages. This involves the size of fields, modernization of older buildings and the improvement of *all* villages for housing those employees in agriculture. As a result, increased responsibilities are being given to local government in the rural *Kreise* and in the villages.

Promoting private initiatives

Various developments have occurred to promote private initiatives. The main fields are private handicrafts, shops, inns, horticulture, livestock (in the villages), trade in the markets, crafts and home production, services from freelance activities (such as translation, typing, consultancy in architecture and tax affairs) and private health facilities (such as physiotherapy and stomatology). Local authorities are now able to promote a wide range of these initiatives, for example by easier granting of licenses, by support for such items as rooms, credits, construction work and equipment.

Increasing interactions between city and hinterland

Many factors are leading to the increase in the linkage; for example:

— the growing needs and opportunities of the urban population for
  activities and recreation related to the natural environment;
— the increasing level of car ownership;
— the increasing demand by the population of the hinterland for goods
  (technical goods, modern clothes and high-quality food), services and
  cultural events which can be obtained only in the central places for
  service provision.

In the case of the largest cities, the co-operation between the city and
its hinterland also concerns technical infrastructure. The administration of
local areas has to ensure that the requirements of both city and hinterland
inhabitants are developed. Sometimes the *Kreis* councils fulfil this task of
co-ordination.

Increasing financial independence of Bezirke, Kreise *and communal administrations*

Since 1980, some of the targets (indices) of the plan have been transmitted
to local administrations as a lump sum. This gives them direct access to
the financial resources derived from the economic enterprises in their
localities. It allows the localities to be more efficient with the same amount
of money, for example by constructing more dwelling units than was
planned for these financial resources in the original plan. Of course, there
is still central control of quality. Another source of local financial flexibility
is the freedom to use part of the surplus earnings derived from community
facilities, or from improvements in efficiency at the local level, particularly
through 'territorial rationalization' as discussed earlier. These resources
can then be spent on additional improvements in the locality.

Overall, the responsibilities of local government have increased in recent
years. More facilities are now provided and organized at the local levels.
More decisions are made in those situations where local knowledge can be
best applied. The work of the representatives of the local councils has
become more important and more comprehensive. The State Council
receives regular reports from the councils of the *Bezirke, Kreise* and cities.
These reports, as well as decisions, are published. The State Council and
the ministries have also sought to ensure that the rights of the local councils are not limited by the bureaucratic decisions of the upper levels.

The description of developments given here shows only the main direction of recent innovations in territorial administration. Similar processes of
development are going on in many other countries. But the decentralization of economic and administrative decision-making in the GDR is now
recognized as having achieved a high level of success in improved efficiency
of both services and economic decision-making.

Part 4 Present and futures: case studies in liberal democracies

14 Spain: developments in regional and local government

Joaquim Solé-Vilanova *

Introduction

In the last thirty years, economic and social changes have significantly affected the territorial structure of government and public administration in Spain. However, it is political factors and, in particular, the approval of a new democratic constitution in 1978, that have generated the major transformations of Spanish subcentral government. The aim of this chapter is to describe the recent developments of the Spanish territorial governments, with particular attention to those derived from constitutional reform, and to analyse the economic and social factors which have caused the different changes, or have obstructed or delayed what the author believes would be the necessary reforms.

Background

Spain has traditionally been a monarchy, but in 1931 when the majority of Spaniards revealed a preference for the republican idea in municipal elections, King Alfonso XIII abandoned the country. A republican regime was immediately proclaimed, but in 1936 a *coup d'état* led by General Franco meant a three-year civil war and the burial of the republican system. The victory of General Franco involved a dictatorial regime that lasted till his death in 1975. His successor, King Juan Carlos I — grandson of Alfonso XIII — rapidly proved to be a man firmly committed to leading the country to a parliamentary monarchy. This goal was achieved in 1978 with the approval of a new democratic constitution, which defines the powers of the king as head of state, the legislative body (congress and senate), the executive government and the judiciary.[1]

After twenty years of autarky, Spain enjoyed a period of rapid economic growth during the 1960's and 1970's. This growth was accompanied by

* The author is grateful to some university colleagues — Núria Bosch (Barcelona), Antoni Castells (Barcelona), Luís Caramés (Santiago), Angel Melguizo (Madrid), Miquel Roig (Valencia), Javier Suárez-Pandiello (Oviedo) and Ignacio Zubiri (Bilbao) — for their helpful comments on an earlier draft.

strong migration from most rural regions to the traditional industrial regions (Catalonia and the Basque Country) to the new industrial areas of Madrid and Valencia and to European countries like Germany, France and Switzerland. Simultaneously, the production of the agricultural sector declined from generating 18.4 per cent of total GDP in 1964 to 10.1 per cent in 1974, and 6.1 per cent in 1986. During the same years, the production of the industrial sector was 37.4 per cent, 40.8 per cent and 35.5 per cent, and the production of the service sector was 44.2 per cent, 49.1 per cent and 58.4 per cent, respectively. Economic disparities between regions have always been significant and the economic growth of the sixties and seventies has tended to reduce them slightly but not sufficiently.[2]

The dimension of the public sector has increased significantly in the last fifteen years. Public expenditure represented 24.7 per cent of GDP in 1975 (the year General Franco died), but rose to 37.2 per cent in 1982 and to about 42 per cent in 1987. On the one hand, the rapid growth of the public sector was caused by an increasing demand for public services, redistributive territorial policies, unemployment and industrial subsidies and interest payments. This demand for public services was particularly high at the time when political parties, trade unions and local associations were legalized and began their lobbying activities. On the other hand, the financing of the expenditure generated was made possible thanks to two successful tax reforms (the reform of personal and corporation income taxes in 1978, and the substitution of a value-added tax for a turnover tax in January 1986 at the time of Spain joining the European Community) and by incurring in large deficits (up to 6.7 per cent of GDP in 1985) which have recently been reduced (to 3.3 per cent of GDP in 1988).

Spain is outstanding in the variety of its regions, despite the fact that its effective political unification took place nearly three hundred years ago. Besides the traditional differences in income and economic activity, there is strong diversity in culture between regions. The different languages spoken by the Basques, Catalans and Galicians, the political institutions that some regions (Catalonia, Aragon, Valencia and Mallorca) retained till the eighteenth century or the fiscal charters the Basque Country and Navarre benefited from till the twentieth century have always induced in their citizens a special sense of political identity.[3]

Regional and local government before 1978

Regional and provincial governments

Since the beginning of the eighteenth century, Spain had not had any regional government, though there was one significant exception. During the Second Republic (1931–9), Catalonia in 1932 and the Basque Country in 1936 were granted a regional statute of political autonomy. Galicia was also in the legal process of receiving a statute, but the civil war made its final approval impossible and the actual outcome of the war put an end to the whole experience of regional government.

Table 14.1 Levels of government in Spain

Before 1978 constitution	After 1978 constitution
Central government	— Central government — Regional government[a]: Autonomous communities: 17 ● AC with 'high' responsibilities $\left\{\begin{array}{l}\text{multi-province: 6}\\[1em]\text{single-province: 1}\end{array}\right.$ ● AC with 'low' responsibilities $\left\{\begin{array}{l}\text{multi-province: 4}\\[1em]\text{single-province: 6}\end{array}\right.$
Local government[a]: ● Provinces: 50; Island Councils[b]: 7 ● Municipalities: 8,022 ● Metropolitan Counties[d]: 1 ● *Mancomunidades*[f]: 124 ● Parishes and other sub-units: 3.486	— Local government:[a] ● Provinces 43; Island Councils[c]: 10 ● Municipalities: 8,022 ● Metropolitan Counties[d]: 2; Counties[e]: 41 ● *Mancomunidades*[f]: 287 ● Parishes and other sub-units: 3,486

Notes: a. Autonomous Communities, provinces and municipalities cover the whole Spanish territory. However, since the approval of the constitution seven provincial governments have become regional governments, undertaking the provincial responsibilities as well.

b. In the Canary Isles, seven island councils replace the two formal provincial units.

c. In the Canary Isles and the Balearic Isles, seven and three island councils replace the provincial units, respectively.

d. One metropolitan county is in the area of Barcelona and was created in 1974 and reformed in 1987. Another metropolitan county was created in the area of Valencia in 1987.

e. All forty-one counties or *comarcas* were established as a new tier in the region of Catalonia in 1987.

f. *Mancomunidades* are multipurpose associations of municipalities. In other countries they are known as *syndicats* (France), *consortia* (Italy), *Zweckwerbände* (Germany), or councils of government (USA).

Provincial administration was established throughout Spanish territory in 1823, under the influence of French territorial reform. In 1833 Spain was divided into forty-nine provinces, rising to fifty in 1927. The division was easily accepted in many areas, but was found rather artificial in regions like Catalonia, Valencia and Aragon. For about one hundred years, provinces acted as agents of central government and the controllers of municipalities. However in 1925 provincial administration was reformed.

Provinces, though with very limited autonomy, strengthened their local government profile and changed their dominating relations with the municipalities. Since then, provincial governments have been responsible, in conjunction with central government, for highways, hospitals, cultural and social activities and technical and economic assistance to municipalities.

All provincial governments (*Diputaciones*) had equal powers and responsibilities. The exceptions were the three provinces of the Basque Country and the province of Navarre. These provinces retained advantageous historical charters on fiscal and economic matters, though only one Basque province (Alava) and Navarre retained the historical charters during Franco's regime. Another exception was made in the 1970s, when the government of the two provinces of the Canary Isles was replaced by seven island councils. (Table 14.1 offers a full picture of the structure of government as it was just before the approval of the constitution in 1978.)

Municipal government

The present structure and conception of the Spanish municipalities date back to 1812. The prevailing political philosophy was that each village, no matter what size, should have its municipal government (*Ayuntamiento*). The outcome of that policy was that more than 9,200 came into being. The municipal division was well accepted in most parts of the country, but was not necessarily the best political solution in regions like Galicia and Asturias where the population was, and still is, extremely scattered.

During the nineteenth century, municipalities were tightly controlled by provincial governments, but in 1924 municipal governments gained some degree of autonomy, although they continued being aided by provincial governments. In later years, municipal governments had progressively taken responsibility for town planning and urban development, sanitation and recreation activities. Some large municipalities also found themselves involved in educational activities, urban transport and in the provision of health and social services. Financial resources have always been scarce at local level, but political life and interest in local affairs have usually been significant.

Spain had 9,267 municipalities in 1900. The number of municipalities did not drop till the mid-60's when a realistic but timid policy of merging or amalgamating municipalities was implemented. By 1975, when this policy was interrupted, more than one thousand municipalities had disappeared (mainly because many villages which had lost most of their population were forced to amalgamate) and the total number of municipalities had dropped to 8,194. Nevertheless, almost 6,000 municipalities (73 per cent) still had fewer than 2,000 inhabitants and only 523 (6.4 per cent) had more than 10,000 inhabitants. Ten years later the number of municipalities tended to increase slightly (8,056 in 1986), after falling to 8,022 municipalities in 1981.

Before 1978, the level of responsibilities of municipal government was the same throughout the country. A consequence of this was that the large municipalities wanted more responsibilities, whereas the small municipalities were unable to provide a minimum level of services. This situation worsened in the 1960's and 1970's.

In 1975 the number of *mancomunidades* or multi-purpose voluntary municipal associations (joint boards) was only 124. This is quite in accordance with the low intermunicipal relation or co-operation that has always prevailed among Spanish municipalities. Parishes and other submunicipal units of government number 3,486. They are common in the northwest of Spain (Galicia, Asturias, Cantabria and Castile-Leon) where population is scattered, and are more scarce in the rest of the country.

In 1960 the municipality of Barcelona and in 1963 the municipality of Madrid were given special charters which meant additional fiscal powers and responsibilities. In 1974, the first multi-purpose metropolitan authority was created in the area of Barcelona. This metropolitan authority was a new tier over twenty-seven municipalities, and its government had responsibilities for urban planning, transport, water and sanitation. In the area of Madrid a metropolitan government was not created because a different policy had been applied. Between 1947 and 1954 Madrid absorbed thirteen neighbouring municipalities. This merger provided the municipal government of Madrid with a much larger area in which to act.[4] Moreover, in 1963 an autonomous agency (COPLACO) with the responsibility of urban planning in the conurbation of Madrid (twenty-three municipalities) was created by central government and kept under the control of the ministries.[5] Hence the metropolitan government became unnecessary for the conurbation of Madrid.

Regional government after 1978[6]

The approval of a new constitution in 1978 meant not only the restoration of parliamentary democracy, but also the viability of regional government in Spain. However, the constitution does not list the regional jurisdictions, nor does it state that this new level of government has to be established throughout the country. The constitution simply offers two procedures by which the parliamentary representatives of a single province or a group of provinces can initiate the process of the creation of a regional government or autonomous community.

The first procedure was intended for those historical regions (Catalonia, the Basque Country and Galicia) that had been in the legal process of devolution in the 1930s. The procedure was also open to other regions or provinces provided that they went through a more complicated legal process. The second procedure was much easier to follow for any province or group of provinces that wanted to form a regional government. The final result was, in many cases, similar because both procedures ended with the approval of a regional statute and the creation of an autonomous community, but it was not equal, because the level of responsibilities that the autonomous community can exercise is different. Those statutes that

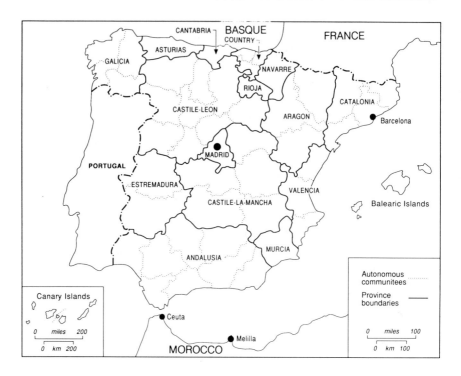

Figure 14.1 The Regions (Autonomous Communities) and Provinces.

were achieved by some autonomous communities through the final procedure — via Article 151 of the constitution — contained a 'high' level of responsibilities. Those statutes obtained through the second procedure — via Article 143 — entitled them to a 'low' level of responsibilities, at least for several years.[7]

In 1978, when the constitution was being written, the regions which were expected to claim political autonomy were the more conflictive nationalist regions of the Basque Country and Catalonia, and Galicia. It was also supposed that a further two or three regions would demand some degree of autonomy. However, when the statutes of the Basque Country and Catalonia received their final approval in 1979, a kind of 'demonstration effect', as economists would call it, took place, and the claims for autonomy proliferated. Between 1981 and 1983 fifteen new statutes were approved and the same number of autonomous communities were created.[8] At the end of the process of devolution the entire Spanish territory had a new level of government. The only exceptions were the two towns situated in northern Africa. See Figure 14.1 and Tables 14.2 and 14.3 for details of the seventeen autonomous communities that now constitute the new regional level of government in Spain.[9]

Table 14.2 Regional government in Spain: general and economic factors

Autonomous Community	Population (1986)		Area		Income per capita (1985)[b]		Net migration[c] People (thousands)		
	People	%	Km²	%	US$	Mean: 100	1961–75	1976–80	1981–5
Andalusia	6,789,772	17.6	87,268	17.3	4.5	77.5	−1,041.6	−53.9	162.9
Aragon	1,184,295	3.1	47,669	9.4	6.6	112.4	−48.1	9.9	7.4
Asturias	1,112,186	2.9	10,565	2.1	6.5	111.9	−17.4	−4.0	−23.3
Balearic I.	680,933	1.8	5,014	1.0	8.2	140.3	−28.3	28.3	90.1
Canary I.	1,466,391	3.8	7,273	1.4	5.2	88.7	137.4	−39.6	108.9
Cantabria	522,664	1.4	5,289	1.0	6.3	108.5	−12.7	−1.9	0.6
Castile-Leon	2,582,327	6.7	94,147	18.6	5.8	100.0	−627.2	−25.4	−15.7
Castile-La Mancha	1,675,715	4.4	79,226	15.7	4.6	79.4	−904.6	−57.9	−15.8
Catalonia	5,978,638	15.5	31,930	6.3	6.7	114.4	947.1	39.2	−72.9
Estremadura	1,086,420	2.8	41,602	8.2	4.0	69.2	−494.1	−45.3	1.7
Galacia	2,844,472	7.4	29,434	5.8	5.0	86.5	−220.1	−12.7	−56.1
Madrid	4,780,572	12.4	7,995	1.6	6.8	116.2	996.7	31.9	8.6
Murcia	1,006,788	2.6	11,317	2.2	4.9	84.9	−109.1	17.4	18.9
Rioja	260,024	0.7	5,034	1.0	7.6	130.6	−14.9	4.6	3.3
Valencia	3,732,682	9.7	23,305	4.6	5.8	99.9	476.9	72.7	40.5
Navarre	515,900	1.3	10,421	2.1	7.0	120.3	15.8	4.8	−4.4
Basque Country	2,136,100	5.6	7,261	1.4	7.2	123.7	320.3	−40.8	−53.9
Ceuta and Melilla[a]	117,539	0.3	32	0.0	4.0	68.0	n.a.	n.a.	n.a.
Spain	38,473,418	100.0	504,782	100.0	5.8	100.0	−623.9	−72.7	200.8

Notes: a. Ceuta and Melilla are territories in northern Africa
b. 1 US$ = 115 pta
c. The Spanish totals represent net migration with respect to foreign countries

Sources: Instituto Naçional de Estadistica and Ministerio de Economia y Hacienda

Table 14.3 Regional government in Spain: political indicators

Autonomous community	Self-government statute Year	Expenditure functions[b] Level	Education	Health	Police	System of finance[c]	Regional taxes[e]	Senators in central parliament[f] Direct	Reg. parl.	Provinces No.	Municipalities No. (1986)	Other local tiers (potential)[g]
Andalusia	1981	H	D	D		C	LT	32	7	8	764	CO
Aragon	1982	L	D			C		12	2	3	727	CO
Asturias	1981	L				C-P		4	2	1	78	CO, MET, PA
Balearic I.	1983	H				C-d		5	1	1	66	IC[h]
Canary I.	1982	H	D		E	C	OT	11	2	2	87	IC[h]
Cantabria	1981	L				C-P		4	1	1	102	CO
Castile-Leon	1983	L				C		36	3	9	2,248	CO
Castile-La Mancha	1982	L				C		20	2	5	916	CO
Catalonia	1979	H	D	D		C	GT, GS	16	6	4	940	CO[h], MET[h]
Estremadura	1983	L				C		8	2	2	380	CO
Galacia	1981	H		E		C		16	3	4	312	CO, PA
Madrid	1983	L				C-P		4	5	1	178	SM
Murcia	1982	L				C-P	GT, GS	4	2	1	45	CO, MET
Rioja	1982	H				C-P		4	1	1	174	CO
Valencia	1982	H	D	D		C	GT, GS	12	4	3	536	CO, MET
Navarre	1982	H				S-P		4	1	1	265	–
Basque Country	1979	H	D	D	D	S	IS	12	3	3	236	SM
Ceuta and Melilla[a]	–	–				–	–	4	–	–	2	–
Spain	–	–				–	–	208	47	50	8,056	–

Notes: a. Ceuta and Melilla are territories in northern Africa.
b. H = High; L = Low; D = Decentralized; E = Expected in the near future. Regional police concurs with central police.
c. C = Common; S = Special; P = Provincial revenues.
d. Formally, the Balearic Isles constitute one province, but provincial revenues are used to finance insular councils and not the regional government.
e. LT = Land Tax; OT = Oil Tax; GT = Gambling tax; GS = Gambling Surcharge; IS = Income Surcharge (levied in the Basque Country in 1984 only).
f. Senators are elected by direct voting of people of each province, or by the regional parliaments.
g. CO = Counties; MET = Metropolitan councils; PA = Parishes; IC = Insular Councils; SM = Supra-municipalities (not specified).
h These tiers have already been created by the regional parliament.

Each statute defines the regional institutions including the president, the parliament and the executive government of the autonomous community.[10] The statute also lays down the responsibilities and the taxing powers devolved to the autonomous community. Seven communities have a 'high' level of responsibilities and the other ten have a 'low' level of responsibilities. In terms of expenditure the main differences between the communities with a 'high' level and the communities with a 'low' level can be found in the areas of education and health. The power to tax is the same in fifteen autonomous communities, and conspicuously different in the Basque Country and Navarre.[11] Finally, seven autonomous communities have formed from only one province. This means that the old provincial institutions and resources are now integrated in the new regional statutory institutions and budgets, respectively.[12] (See Tables 14.1 and 14.3.)

Regional parliaments can pass laws and their level of political autonomy is quite considerable. However, the power of the government of an autonomous community is subordinated in many ways to the power of the central government, despite the faculties guaranteed to the regional governments by the statutes and the constitution. The senate, for instance, is known as the house of territorial representation, but its role as protector of the interests of the autonomous communities has been nil. The first explanation of this is the prevailing role — stated in the constitution — of the congress over the senate on any subject, which results on an upper house performing a subsidiary and not very active role as a legislative power. A second explanation is the way senators are elected: four by direct election for each province (not for the autonomous community!),[13] and one elected by the regional parliament of each autonomous community, plus one for each million of the population elected in the same way. The result is that less than a fifth of the senators have a regional basis, a situation that is clearly reflected in the present attitudes expressed in the Spanish senate. (See Table 14.3 for the distribution of senators among the autonomous communities.)

Local government after 1978

The 1978 constitution did not lay down any specific reform of the existing system of local government. It merely stated that provinces and municipalities will be the two tiers of local government that will have to be retained throughout Spain.

From a political perspective, the changes in the system of local government that have taken place since the approval of the constitution are due to several different factors: first, the creation of the regional level of government that inevitably affected the allocation of responsibilities to the different territorial governments; second, the approval of the 1985 Local Government Act by central parliament which regulates basic aspects of provincial and municipal government; third, the power possessed by regional parliaments to reform local administration which some autonomous communities have already exercised. Finally, one has to stress that the rapid economic and social transformation of the country required important reforms in local administration that would have been undertaken whatever the political circumstances because they were urgently needed, irrespective of any future constitutional change.

Local government has a double dependence and relationship. Both central and regional governments can regulate different aspects of local administration, and also both levels of government are supposed to provide local authorities with tax power and financial resources.[14]

Provincial government

The provincial division is well rooted in most autonomous communities, so that provincial governments are likely to have an important role in most parts of Spain even with the new presence of the regional government. However, regions like Catalonia, which has never completely accepted the provincial division, would have preferred the provincial level to be optional. Technically, this stance is quite correct once the regional tier has been created.

Formally the number of provincial authorities (*Diputaciones*) has been reduced by seven since the approval of the constitution. This is so because those single provinces which became autonomous communities had their provincial institutions absorbed by the regional government.

Municipal government

According to the constitution and the statutes, most regional governments are vested with the power to alter municipal boundaries and create new municipalities or amalgamate others. In recent years, some regional governments have had difficulties in containing the demands of some localities which have sought separation from their municipality so as to form a new and independent municipality of their own. The result of this has been that the tendency in the last thirty years for the total number of Spanish municipalities to decrease has now been reversed. A minimum of 8,022 municipalities was reached in 1981, but by 1986 the number of municipalities had already risen to 8,056.

Since the first democratic municipal elections of April 1979, co-operation between municipalities has improved considerably. The number of *man-comunidades* or multi-purpose voluntary associations of municipalities (joint boards) rose from 124 in 1975 to 287 in 1987.

The parliaments of most autonomous communities have the power to create supramunicipal units of government (counties and metropolitan councils) or inframunicipal jurisdictions (parishes). (See Table 14.3.) The government of Catalonia, for example, has been the first to undertake an important territorial reform with the creation of a new supramunicipal level of government. In 1987 forty-one counties or *comarcas* were created, covering the whole Catalan territory. Their responsibility is to provide the small municipalities with the supramunicipal services and basic municipal services that they cannot provide themselves. The intention of the present government of Catalonia is to substitute the county tier for the provincial tier in the medium term.

The metropolitan county of Barcelona, created in 1974 by the central government and covering an area of twenty-seven municipalities, has recently been transformed by the regional government of Catalonia into two single-purpose metropolitan districts. One metropolitan district, which covers eighteen municipalities, is now responsible for transport and the other metropolitan district, which covers thirty-two municipalities, is responsible for water and refuse disposal. The real causes of the reform have been political and not technical, and one can see some parallel between the transformation of the metropolitan county of Barcelona and the abolition of the Greater London Council in 1986. A return to a multi-purpose metropolitan authority can be expected in the future.

Madrid — with a very large municipality since 1954 — has, with the creation of the single-province autonomous community, virtually rejected the creation of a metropolitan county. Since the 1960s there has been an autonomous agency (COPLACO) responsible for urban planning and developments which was initially dependent on the ministry of highways but which in 1983 shifted its responsibilities to the new autonomous community. However, the so-called 'metropolitan area' of Madrid now covers an area of twenty-six municipalities.

In the area of Valencia, a new multi-purpose metropolitan county covering forty-four municipalities was created by its regional government in 1987. However, in the Basque Country in 1980 the regional government abolished the inactive autonomous agency created in 1946 without bringing in any alternative to the nineteen municipalities that it covered.[15]

Assignment of responsibilities between levels of government

During the dictatorship of General Franco, Spanish public administration was highly centralized. Education, health services and public housing, for instance, were mainly provided by central government. Provincial governments provided some minor health and educational services, and shared the responsibility for highways with central government. The main concern of municipalities was town planning and urban development.

In the mid-seventies there was increasing pressure for decentralization. It is quite likely that, even without constitutional reform, sooner or later the provision of some services would have been transferred to lower levels of administration. Thus one is inclined to believe that the claims for devolution from most parts of Spain would have been less vociferous or even non-existent if a much higher degree of decentralization and participation had already been in operation at the time of approval of the constitution.[16] This does not apply to the Basque Country and Catalonia which had persistently claimed self-government in addition to administrative decentralization.

The approval of the constitution (1978), the regional statutes (1979–83), and the Local Government Act (1985) have brought about the reallocation of expenditure responsibilities between the different levels of government. Defence, foreign affairs, economic stabilization, and pensions and unemployment subsidies are functions of central government. Law and order are also a responsibility of central government, but policing is shared with the regional government in the Basque Country, and to some extent in Catalonia.

Education and health services are provided regionally in those autonomous communities with a 'high' level of responsibilities, and provided centrally in the autonomous communities with a 'low' level of responsibilities. Highways and transport, housing and social services and development incentives are provided by central and regional governments, and to a certain extent by provincial and municipal governments. Community services, sports facilities and cultural activities are the responsibility of regional, provincial and municipal administrations. Town planning and urban development, parks and recreation activities, sanitation and water are the task of municipal governments. Large towns are also involved in minor educational activities and in welfare services.

The allocation of responsibilities between levels of government is not clear-cut. Some are duplicated particularly at regional and provincial level. Large municipalities are also involved in activities which are normally allocated to higher levels of government.[17] The 1985 Local Government Act was quite flexible about the allocation of responsibilities to the municipalities. The level of compulsory responsibilities depends now on the size of the municipality. Beginning with a minimum of responsibilities for all municipalities including those with fewer than 5,000 inhabitants, the larger the municipality the higher the level of compulsory responsibilities. However, the law was intentionally ambiguous about the additional areas in which municipalities could become involved. This ambiguity possibly meant the loss of a good opportunity to reduce the present overlap between some municipal activities and provincial and regional activities.

The degree of decentralization generated by the constitutional reform is quite significant and it is expected to increase in the coming years. In terms of public expenditure, central government dropped from 90.2 per cent in 1978 to 76.3 per cent in 1986; regional government rose from nil in 1978 to 12.0 per cent in 1986; and local government has increased from 9.8 per cent in 1978 to 11.7 per cent in 1986. These variations took place while the Spanish public sector was rising from 27.5 per cent of GDP in 1978 to 42.0 per cent of GDP in 1987.[18]

Nevertheless, the allocation of expenditure responsibilities and the degree of decentralization do not reflect the effective distribution of power between levels of government. The distribution of power depends on multiple legal, financial and administrative factors. Central and regional parliaments can approve ordinary laws, which are of equal rank. However, central government has the right to set the 'basic legislation', which ranks higher, in areas like education, health, law and order, the civil service, etc., and also on any topic that may be of 'general concern', or may affect basic rights such as liberty and equality or the unity of the economic market.[19]

Other factors which determine the effective distribution of power are the allocation of taxes among levels of government and the resulting financial dependencies or autonomy of each of them. It will be seen below that the autonomous communities depend, to a great extent, on granted revenue because the regionally collected taxes are not very significant and the actual capacity to levy new taxes is very limited. This situation is aggravated by the network of specific grants, set by central government when the public administration was highly centralized, and which has not been completely dismantled.

Regional and local finance[20]

Before the 1978 constitution local government had a very limited tax power. After the constitutional reform and establishment of regional government, most of the taxing power has remained in the hands of central government. This is so because the constitution states that the power to tax is initially vested in central government. Customs duties are the only taxes which are specifically allocated to central government by the constitution, and any other tax field could be assigned to other levels of government. However, any regional or local power to levy a tax on a particular tax base has to be transferred by central government. Therefore, any specific tax assignment depends on central parliament's decision.

Central government has so far retained the most important tax bases, and levies personal income tax, corporation income tax, payroll tax, value-added tax, excise taxes and customs duties. Table 14.4 shows the relative weight of each tax in the financing of central government and other levels of government.

Regional finance

The main sources of regional finance are regulated by the statutes and the Basic Financial Act of the Autonomous Communities (LOFCA, 1980). However, there are two systems of finance operating in Spain: the common regime and the special regime. The common regime applies to fifteen autonomous communities, while the special regime operates only in the Basque Country and Navarre.[21]

In the common regime the main sources of revenue are a tax-sharing grant, ceded taxes and several specific grants. Ceded taxes are death and gift duties, wealth (net worth) tax, immovable property transfer tax, stamp duties (since 1988) and gambling taxes. These taxes are collected by regional governments but are entirely regulated by central government. However, regional governments can levy a surcharge on every ceded tax and also on central personal income tax. Besides this, regions can levy their own taxes on areas not used by central government. Table 14.4 shows the taxes levied by regional governments in recent years.

Table 14.4 The structure of government revenue in Spain, 1987 (in percentages)

Revenue item	Central government[a]	Autonomous communities[b]			Provinces[c]	Municipalities (1986)	
		'High' level	'Low' level multiprovincial	'Low' level uniprovincial		20,000–50,000 pop.	100,000–500,000 pop.
Own revenues	95.92	23.07[d]	28.33	27.2	15.75	61.28	61.08
Taxes	86.00	18.03	20.48	10.1	6.22	29.67	33.91
Personal income tax	17.45	—	—	—	—	—	—
Corporation income tax	5.14	—	—	—	—	—	—
Payroll taxes	34.71	—	—	—	—	—	—
Other income taxes	0.66	0.01	—	—	—	—	—
Custom duties	2.17	—	—	—	—	—	—
Value-added tax	16.85	—	—	—	—	—	—
Alcohol, beverages & sugar t.	0.62	—	—	—	—	—	—
Motor fuel & oil products t.	5.20	1.84	—	—	—	—	—
Other excise taxes	1.75	0.21[e]	0.07[e]	0.2[e]	—	0.62[f]	0.28[f]
Death & gift duties	0.06	2.07[e]	4.09[e]	2.0[e]	—	—	—
Stamp duties	0.73	—	—	—	—	—	—
Property transfer tax	0.27	5.06[e]	6.94[e]	2.9[e]	—	—	—
Wealth (net worth) tax	0.09	1.58[e]	1.93[e]	0.7[e]	—	—	—
Property taxes	—	—	—	—	—	17.87[f]	19.27[f]
Vehicle tax	—	—	—	—	—	4.70[f]	5.14[f]
Business taxes	—	—	—	1.3[e]	6.22[e]	6.48[f]	9.22[f]
Gambling taxes	0.28	7.26	7.45	3.0	—	—	—

Fees, charges & fines	3.19	3.97	4.43	14.5	5.45	28.90	24.52
Other own revenues	6.73	1.07	3.42	2.6	4.08	2.71	2.65
Grants	4.07	76.93[d]	71.67	72.8	84.25	38.72	38.91
Current grants	2.86	66.33	44.31	57.1	84.14	29.80	34.63
Unconditional grants		49.68	35.15	45.7	78.95		
Specific grants		14.73	9.16	11.4	5.20		
Capital grants	1.21	10.60	27.36	15.7	0.11	8.92	4.28
Total revenue	100.00	100.00	100.00	100.0	100.00	100.00	100.00

Notes:
a. Includes autonomous agencies and Social Security funds.
b. Only ACs of the common financial regime are considered. 'High' level multiprovincial ACs contain data from the 5 ACs with a high level of responsibilities. 'Low' level multiprovincial ACs contain the data from the 5 ACs with a low level of responsibilities and with no provincial revenues because provincial governments have independent budgets. 'Low' level uniprovincial contains data from the remaining 5 uniprovincial ACs who possess regional and provincial revenues in one single budget. Pass-through grants from central to local government have been discounted.
c. Sample of the four provinces of the region of Catalonia.
d. In 1987 health services had only been decentralized to Catalonia and Andalusia. In order to standardize data, the health grant has been discounted. However, its inclusion would increase the grant revenue percentage to up to 83.49%, and reduce own revenue down to 16.51%. If the health grant were to be received by all five ACs the grant revenue might rise to 86% and revenue might drop to 14%. See Table 4 for an estimation of this.
e. These taxes are entirely regulated by central government.
f. Tax bases are regulated by central government, but tax rates, with limits, are a local decision.

Sources: Calculated by the author from budget estimates, except municipal figures which are derived from statistics from the Banco de Crédito Local de España.

The tax-sharing grant transferred annually to every autonomous community depends on some objective parameters (population, area, per capita income, income tax effort, etc.) and on the potential collection of ceded taxes. This regional tax-sharing is based on the whole set of central taxes, and in order to calculate each grant a sharing rate is previously calculated for each autonomous community. The tax-sharing grant rises when central tax receipts increase. However, for the period 1987–91 certain limits, based on the variation of GDP and 'relevant' central expenditure, have been established to restrain the increase or decrease of the tax-sharing grant.[22]

A block grant for health and social services is transferred to those autonomous communities (Catalonia, Andalusia and Valencia) that have the responsibility for their provision. The grant is distributed according to population and represents between 35 per cent and 45 per cent of total revenue in each community.

Another important grant comes from the Interterritorial Compensation Fund, the only source of revenue specifically regulated by the constitution. The original objective of this fund was to compensate for territorial economic imbalance, but, since its implementation in 1982, it has also been used to finance 'new' regional capital expenditure because no other specific resources were available for this purpose till 1987. For this reason, all autonomous communities receive the capital grant. The fund is distributed according to some objective parameters (population, per capita income, size, net migration, and unemployment) and the grant received by each community has to be spent in capital projects in agreement with central government.[23]

The two autonomous communities with a special regime of finance receive no tax-sharing grant. They finance their own services with the revenue raised from so-called 'contracted taxes'. The 'contracted taxes' are personal income tax, corporation tax, value-added tax (the Basque Country only), and the above mentioned ceded taxes.[24] In compensation for the services provided by central government, each autonomous community pays an annual quota to central government. In the case of the Basque Country the annual quota, agreed in 1981 and revised in 1987, is calculated according to the value of central services to be financed and regional income in relation to national income. In the case of Navarre the annual quota is a fixed amount, agreed in 1969, and for an indefinite number of years! The two special regimes are archaic, fiscally advantageous, and very unsatisfactory from the perspective of horizontal equalization, which the other fifteen autonomous communities do attempt to achieve. Moreover, since 1988 the Basque Country is also responsible for the provision of health and social services. Surprisingly, these services are financed with a block grant related to regional income and not to population as in the regions of Catalonia, Andalusia and Valencia.

Provincial finance

Provincial finance is in transition: first, because provincial governments are still in the process of adapting to the new regional government. This adaptation differs significantly among the single-province autonomous communities which have absorbed the provincial administration, the Basque Country where provinces have a predominant role, Catalonia where the regional government is attempting to reduce the level of responsibilities of the provincial administration to a minimum, the island autonomous communities where provincial administration is run by the island councils, and the remaining six autonomous communities where, in some cases, provincial governments rival their regional government.

A second cause of the transitional situation of provincial finance is that for many years provincial governments were mainly financed by a share of a turnover tax. This tax was abolished in 1986 at the time of implementing the value-added tax, and the provincial share was provisionally replaced by an unconditional grant. Provinces receive another unconditional grant also from central government which is distributed according to population. In 1989 the two unconditional grants will be reduced to one, according to the Local Finance Bill, which parliament passed in December 1988. Provinces also receive capital grants which are distributed among municipalities as project grants.

The only tax assigned to provincial governments is a surcharge on the municipal business tax. The rate of the surcharge is fixed by central government, but from 1990 onwards it will be left to provincial discretion.

Municipal finance

The main sources of municipal finance are taxes on immovable property and on business, fees and charges, an unconditional grant and project grants. The Local Finance Act approved by central parliament at the end of 1988 is not expected to vary the basic structure of finance. Taxes on immovable property are on urban and rural property. Since 1988, municipal governments have been able to fix the property tax rates freely between certain limits. A local business tax is levied on all types of business activity. Central government fixes its tax base and the tax rates, and municipal governments can levy a surcharge of up to 100 per cent, which will be increased to 300 per cent from 1990. Other municipal taxes are vehicle tax, land value increment tax (to be optional in 1990), vacant site tax, business location tax, luxury consumption tax and outdoor publicity tax. The last four will be abolished at the end of 1989.

Fees and charges have traditionally been very important at municipal level in Spain. They provided the minimum fiscal autonomy when taxes used to have fixed rates. The main fees and charges are on refuse collection, water, sewerage and building permission. Some fees are, in some respects, concealed taxes. This is possibly the reason why the fees on building permission will be converted into an optional tax in 1990.

Betterment levies (or special assessments) have often been used in Spain, particularly in the 1960's and 1970's, to finance urban development.

Municipalities get an annual unconditional grant from central government through the regional government. The total grant is decided annually by central parliament, but from 1990 onwards it will be indexed in the same way that the regional tax-sharing grant is now indexed. The total grant is distributed according to (adjusted) population (70 per cent), municipal tax effort (25 per cent) and number of public school units (5 per cent). Project grants are also very important, particularly among municipalities with fewer than 20,000 inhabitants. They are usually transferred by provincial governments, but also by regional governments.

The metropolitan county of Barcelona is financed by an unconditional grant from central government and a share in the revenues of the municipalities which it comprises and the province to which it belongs. Specific grants are received from the regional government. The metropolitan county can levy a surcharge on the municipal urban property tax.

Economic assessment

Tax power is centralized and the financial dependence of regional and provincial governments is very high. Table 14.4 shows that the financial dependence of autonomous communities is more than 70 per cent of total revenue, and the dependence of provinces is more than 80 per cent. However, at municipal level granted money is less than 40 per cent of total revenue. Paradoxically, municipal governments with less political power than regional governments are less dependent in financial terms. As discussed in a previous article[25] financial dependence is one of the main economic problems of regional finance, and implies a lack of accountability and fiscal responsibility and, consequently, less efficient decisions on public spending.

At municipal level, one of the main problems is the lack of horizontal equity, simply because the unconditional grant is wrongly designed. This situation contrasts with the high level of equalization that exists at regional level, with the exception of the Basque Country and Navarre which enjoy separate special regimes, fiscally advantageous only for rich regions. These special systems of finance have no equalizing mechanisms connected to the other fifteen autonomous communities.

Another important problem at municipal level is the lack of efficiency in financial management in most of the 7,000 municipalities (82.2 per cent) that have fewer than 5,000 inhabitants. This makes the transfer of additional responsibilities and tax power to *all* municipal governments very debatable. Moreover, the traditional and persistent claims of Spanish municipalities for more financial aid are difficult to meet unless a policy of discrimination or one of comprehensive amalgamation has not previously been implemented, as will be discussed below.

Causes of change in regional and local government

Changes in territorial government may be of different types. Some of the most significant are those relating to the number of tiers and territorial boundaries, the allocation of responsibilities with varying forms of autonomy or control and the assignment of tax powers and other financial resources. In the last decade, the developments of the Spanish territorial administration have been to some extent generated by constitutional factors, but economic, political and social influences should not be ignored.

The two main constitutional factors affecting territorial government were the approval of the new Spanish constitution in 1978, and the signing of the Rome Agreement whereby Spain joined the European Community in 1986. The first of these implied the creation of a regional level of government and the consequent reallocation of responsibilities and tax power. The second meant the acceptance of certain rules on tax harmonization and the opening of the Spanish economy to the European market. These two conditions have negatively affected the potential degree of decentralization of tax power to regional governments.

Some economic factors have produce changes in territorial administration and others have prevented changes taking place. On the one hand, the rapid economic growth of the 1960's and 1970's increased the level of personal income and the demand for public services, particularly those that now are provided at regional and local levels. This 'income effect' has obviously affected the degree of decentralization of public expenditure. Moreover, the large concentration of population in industrial areas has increased the demand for some local services (urban development, public transport, community services) and has brought about the implementation of new forms of administration (for example the metropolitan government of Barcelona and Valencia, and the municipal amalgamation of Madrid).

On the other hand, economic disparities between territories have clearly prevented central government from transferring more tax power to the newly created autonomous communities.[26] Nevertheless, this central attitude is in sharp contrast to the one adopted towards municipal governments which, having traditionally relied on local resources, differ enormously at the level of fiscal capacity and revenues — a situation which is aggravated by the present grant scheme and causes undesirable disparities in the level of provision of basic services.

Some of the developments or rigidities in territorial government have been caused by social and political factors. In the last thirty years, the formation of a large, more wealthy and better educated Spanish middle class has increased the interest in participating in public affairs and, therefore, has also increased the demand for public decisions being taken more at grass-roots level. This implies that there has been and there will continue to be pressure to move towards the decentralization of additional public responsibilities to regional and local levels.

However, this desire for participation in local affairs plus the strong identification of people with their localities and the relatively low geographical mobility of the Spanish population have prevented any serious consideration of a comprehensive policy of amalgamating municipalities. The absence of any strong tradition of co-operation among municipal governments for the collective provision of services makes any proposal for amalgamation even more problematical. The consequences are that the managerial capacity of the majority of the 7,000 Spanish municipalities with fewer than 5,000 inhabitants is quite inadequate. Obviously, additional transfers of responsibilities to municipal governments are not feasible, unless further discrimination is introduced in favour of large municipalities.

Politicians are obviously the makers of any move towards decentralization or towards centralization. Moreover, politicians always find decentralization more popular than centralization. In Spain, where a solution to the small municipalities is needed in most autonomous communities, regional politicians, whose parliaments are now responsible for policies of amalgamation, seem to find it easy to campaign for decentralization when central–regional relations are under discussion, but seem less prepared to propose that some 'centralization' is needed at municipal level, if a more efficient provision of services has to be made for the citizens of the autonomous community.

Future developments

In the last ten years the move towards decentralization has been very significant in Spain. In the next decade, additional changes in territorial government are expected to take place not only as a final development of constitutional reform, but also because some of the problems of local administration — now that regional government is a reality — will need to be solved.

Negotiations started in 1988 between central government and the autonomous communities with a 'low' level of expenditure responsibilities in order to raise their responsibilities to as 'high' a level as the rest of the communities. However, for at least some years, differences are likely to persist between the autonomous communities, particularly with the Basque Country and Catalonia.

Suggestions for decentralizing additional taxing power have also been made from both the centre and the regions in order to increase the fiscal responsibility of the autonomous communities. In this connection, central government could in the near future reduce the rates of its personal income tax and press regional governments to levy a regional surcharge on the central income tax.

Since the approval of the constitution in 1978 the role of the senate as the house of territorial representation has been insignificant. In future years it is likely that attempts will be made to improve its credibility on issues related to regional government.

Provincial administration needs to have its responsibilities clarified to avoid overlapping of functions. Its future is going to be different in every autonomous community. Some regional governments may employ provincial administrations as territorial agents and others may attempt to reduce their activity to that of assisting municipalities. The double dependence that provinces have on central and regional governments make predictions for any autonomous community very difficult.

The Local Finance Act approved at the end of 1988 will imply a simplification of municipal taxes and an increase in aid from central government. The latter will help to reduce the recurrent financial deficits of some large municipalities, though these deficits are, to some extent, due to the involvement of their governments in all manner of expenditure responsibilities not specifically allocated to the municipal tier.

One of the problems that sooner or later will have to be faced together by central and regional governments is related to the municipal structure. The extreme variety of municipalities and the large number of them with fewer than 5,000 inhabitants in most autonomous communities make decentralization of service provision and managerial efficiency difficult goals to achieve. There are three main alternatives for resolving this problem. One alternative is to adopt the policy of discriminating in the allocation of tax and expenditure responsibilities between large and small municipalities. Large municipalities would provide many services for which they would receive financial support, whereas small municipalities would have some of these services provided by the higher tiers of government. A second alternative would be to implement a policy of amalgamation of small municipalities in order for there to be a minimum number of people in each municipal jurisdiction. A third alternative would be to create a supramunicipal level of government to which municipal responsibilities would be progressively transferred, especially from small municipalities but also from larger ones.[27]

The first and third alternatives seem to have a lower political cost than the second one, but in order to be successful they need to be accompanied by a reasonable policy of financial assistance. The possible formation of metropolitan governments in different autonomous communities and the recent creation of counties in Catalonia could be interpreted as policies in the direction of the first and third alternatives.[28] Different regions are likely to adopt different solutions. The variety of regional experiences that are expected to emerge in the next decade will help each regional government to find the most appropriate solution to a problem which is common to all autonomous communities.

A final conclusion must be that the process of decentralization implemented in Spain in the last ten years has been very positive and significant, but new and important developments should be expected in the next decade, during which policies of decentralization and centralization are likely to be combined.

Notes

1. See Carr and Fusi (1979) and Preston (1986) for a description of the political transition. See also McDonough, *et al.*, (1986) for an analysis of the change in

popular attitudes towards dictatorship and democracy in Spain.

2. See Alcaide-Inchausti (1988) who analyses the economic and demographic tendencies of what he defines as the four different Spains. See also Hebbert (1982) and Table 14.2.

3. See Carr (1980), Díaz-López (1986) and Hebbert (1987) for an analysis of the history of regional nationalism in Spain.

4. The size of the new municipality of Madrid happens to be larger than the metropolitan jurisdiction of Barcelona. In 1986, the municipality of Madrid with an area of 607 square kilometres had a population of 3,058,182 inhabitants. In the same year, the municipality of Barcelona with an area of ninety-one square kilometres registered a population of 1,701,812, whereas the metropolitan county with an area of 478 square kilometres had a population of 3,025,666 inhabitants.

5. Less powerful institutions with similar functions were created for the area of Bilbao (1946) and for the area of Valencia (1949), but both were very inactive until their abolition thirty years later.

6. For a more detailed description of the process of devolution and the so-called 'State of the Autonomies' see Tamames and Clegg (1984), Díaz-López (1986), Monreal (1986), Vallès and Cuchillo-Foix (1988) and Brassloff (1989).

7. The statutes of the first type were passed by referendum by the people in the region and had to be ratified in full by central parliament. The statutes of the second type were not approved by referendum, but were discussed in detail by central parliament. A statute is like an internal constitution, but it is less powerful than the constitution of any of the states of a classical federal country.

8. In February 1981 a *coup d'état* carried out by a group of the military failed. However that event affected the process of decentralization. First, central parliament passed a basic law (LOAPA) in July 1982 which attempted to harmonize and reduce the political powers of the autonomous communities already created, but it was considered *ultra vires* by the Constitutional Court in August 1983. Second, all regional statutes approved after the attempted *coup d'état* were standardized or levelled down according to the spirit of the unsuccessful and strongly opposed LOAPA.

9. See Alvira-Martin and García-López (1988) for an interesting analysis of the changing attitudes and expectations of citizens in relation to self-government, and of how the autonomous communities operate.

10. See Bayona (1987) and Hebbert (1985).

11. The political life of the Basque Country and Navarre and their relations with the central government have been strongly affected by terrorism. Some of the solutions provided for some political and financial claims can only be understood bearing in mind the special situation of violence that has existed in those regions since the beginning of the 1970's.

12. The Balearic Isles which were formed by one province and the Canary Isles which were made up of two provinces have had their provincial responsibilities and resources transferred to three and seven insular councils, respectively.

13. At the time of writing the constitution it was not expected that the regional tier would be established throughout the Spanish territory. This explains why the province is the electoral district for the direct election of senators. One expects this issue to be one of the most likely to be considered for reform in any future amendment of the constitution.

14. See Clegg (1987) for a comprehensive alternative analysis of Spanish local government.

15. See Martín-Mateo (1987) for a useful description of the existing

supramunicipal authorities and a critical comment on the recent transformation of the metropolitan government of Barcelona.

16. At the time of discussion of the constitution and the first statutes in Spain, the United Kingdom was also debating devolution for Scotland and Wales. The devolution proposal might have had more chance of success if the degree of decentralization of the British public sector had been as low as it was in Spain.

17. Such involvement began in the 1970's when grave deficits in public services were not covered by other administrations and municipal governments decided to intervene, often without sufficient financial resources to implement their projects.

18. See Castells (1988) who offers a quantitative and rigorous analysis on the degree of decentralization of the public sector in Spain in comparison with other federal countries.

19. Martín Mateo (1985) offers a serious and illuminating discussion of the criteria that have been followed in the distribution of responsibilities at the time of interpreting the constitution. For some services the legislative power and the executive power are vested either in central government or in regional government, but for certain matters legislative power is central and executive power is regional. However, in other services, legislative power which may affect basic principles is vested in central government and the enactment of detailed legislation and executive powers is vested in regional government. Moreover, in some areas, like housing, tourism, and culture, both central and regional governments have legislative and executive powers that can be exercised co-operatively or independently. It is obvious that most responsibilities are concurrent and few are exclusive to regional government.

20. See Solé-Vilanova (1989) for a more detailed analysis of regional and local finance in Spain.

21. Strictly speaking, the special regime of finance is regulated by the 'Economic Contracts' pacted between central government and each of the two governments of the Basque Country and Navarre. This system of finance is an adaptation of the historical fiscal charters kept by both regions since the nineteenth century.

22. There was a transitional period of regional finance between 1981 and 1986. During this period the tax-sharing grant was based on the 'effective cost' of the services which had been devolved to the autonomous communities. See a more detailed explanation in Solé-Vilanova (1989) and Castells (1987, 1988).

23. Much attention has been paid by some Spanish economists to the Interterritorial Compensation Fund as if it was the only instrument of horizontal equalization at regional level. This fund is specially mentioned by the constitution (art. 158.2), as an instrument of regional development, but it would be wrong to believe that is the only resource that brings horizontal equity to the system because the present tax-sharing grant is by far the most important mechanism of territorial redistribution between autonomous communities.

24. In strict terms, in the Basque Country the 'contracted taxes' are raised by each of the three provinces. A share of their tax collection is then transferred to the regional government, which administrates no tax.

25. See Solé-Vilanova (1989).

26. The existing 'regional divorce of economic and political power' — that is economic power at the periphery and political power at the centre — is interpreted by Lasuen (1987) as an unusual inverted centre-periphery that reduces the possibilities for economic growth in the country. Lasuen suggests greater decentralized powers to the regions, 'but with more effective integration of the

nationalist parties of the Autonomous Communities into national policies'.
27. Another alternative would be to promote the voluntary association of municipalities for the provision of services. Historically, policies of this kind have not been very successful in Spain. Moreover, they solve only a small part of the problem.
28. Catalonia's reasons for creating the county tier were historical and political, although this new tier may prove also to be technically satisfactory in the future.

References

Alcaide-Inchausti, J. (1988), 'Las Cuatro Españas Económicas y la Solidaridad Regional', *Papeles de Economía Española*, 34, 62–81.

Alvira-Martin, F. and García-López, J. (1988), 'Los Españoles y las Autonomías', *Papeles de Economía Española*, 34, 402–21.

Bayona, A. (1987), 'The autonomous government of Catalonia', *Environment and Planning C: Government and Policy*, 5, 309–26.

Brassloff, A. (1989), 'Spain: the state of the autonomies', in M. Forsyth (ed.), *Federalism and Nationalism*, Leicester University Press, Leicester.

Carr, R. (1980), 'The regional problem in Spain', in J.C. Boogman and G.N. van der Plaat (eds), *Federalism, History and Current Significance of a Form of Government*, Martinus Nijhoff, The Hague, 267–87.

Carr, R. and Fusi, P. (1979), *Spain: From Dictatorship to Democracy*, Allen and Unwin, London.

Castells, A. (1987), 'Financing regional government in Spain: main trends and a comparative perspective', *Environment and Planning C: Government and Policy*, 5, 257–66.

Castells, A. (1988), *Hacienda Autonómica: Una Perspectiva de Federalismo Fiscal*, Ariel, Barcelona.

Clegg, T. (1987), 'Spain', in E.C. Page and M.J. Goldsmith (eds), *Central and Local Government Relations*, Sage, London, 130–55.

Díaz-López, C. (1986), 'Centre-periphery structures in Spain: from historical conflict to territorial-constitutional accommodations?', in Y. Meny and V. Wright (eds), *Centre Periphery Relations in Western Europe*, Allen and Unwin, London, 236–72.

Hebbert, M. (1982), 'Regional policy in Spain', *Geoforum*, 13, No. 2, 107–20.

Hebbert, M. (1985), 'Regional autonomy and economic action in the first Catalan government, 1980–1984', *Regional Studies*, 19, No. 5, 433–45.

Hebbert, M. (1987), 'Regionalism: a reform concept and its application to Spain', *Environment and Planning C: Government and Policy*, 5, 239–50.

Lasuen, J.R. (1987), 'The autonomous communities: politics and economics', *Environment and Planning C: Government and Policy*, 5, 251–6.

Martin-Mateo, R. (1985), 'Los Estados de las Autonomías', in F. Fernandez Rodriguez (ed.), *La España de las Autonomías*, Instituto de Estudios de Administración Local, Madrid. 345–446.

Martin-Mateo, R. (1987), Entes Locales Complejos, Trivium, Madrid.

McDonough, P., Barnes, S.H. and López-Pina, A. (1986), 'The growth of democracy in Spain', *American Political Science Review*, 80, No. 3, 735–60.

Monreal, A. (1986), 'The new Spanish state structure', in M. Burgess (ed.), *Federalism and Federation in Western Europe*, Croom Helm, London, 59–75.

Preston, P. (1986), *The Triumph of Democracy in Spain*, Methuen, London.

Solé-Vilanova, J. (1989), 'Regional and local finance in Spain: is fiscal responsibility the missing element?', in R.J. Bennett (ed.), *Decentralization, local governments and markets: setting a post-welfare agenda*, Oxford University Press, Oxford.

Tamames, R. and Clegg, T. (1984), 'Spain: regional autonomy and the democratic transition', in M. Hebbert and H. Machin (eds), *Regionalisation in France, Italy and Spain*, ST ICERD, London School of Economics, London, 31–54.

Vallès, J.M. and Cuchillo-Foix, M. (1988), 'Decentralisation in Spain: a review', *European Journal of Political Research*, 16, 395–407.

15 The Netherlands: changing administrative structures

Hans Blaas and Petr Dostál

Introduction

In discussing the changing character of the system of public administration in The Netherlands it is appropriate to examine both the small gradual and the major changes of the system. The Netherlands is a small and highly urbanized country covering an area (including inland waters) of 42,000 square kilometres and containing 14.5 million inhabitants in 1986. The relatively high population density of 425 inhabitants per square kilometre of the land area indicates the very basic fact that many small and gradual changes within the country's territory and the activities of the population must often have far-reaching implications for the organization and functioning of the public administration of the nation.

However, looking back over the long evolution of the public administration of The Netherlands there are also a number of moments of major changes to the system. This historical heritage is considered briefly in the next section because it is still indispensable for the understanding of the contemporary character of the country's local and regional administration and its functioning. After considering the historical heritage the main objective is to describe some small yet important cumulative changes in the system of public administration. These are usually conceived as the main process of a continuous reform of the system. Attention is devoted to three interconnected processes: (i) the amalgamation of municipalities, (ii) the financial rearrangements within the system, and (iii) the arrangements for co-operation among municipalities. In a separate section the post-war attempts to find an adequate solution to the problems of a seemingly missing regional link in the system are summarized. The character of the contemporary system of public administration in the 1980s is examined in the last section in order to provide an outlook on the country's public administration at the regional and the local levels in the future.

A look back: the historical heritage

During the existence of the Dutch Republic of Seven United Provinces the far-reaching competences of the provinces were most decisive as regards the administration of the country's territory and the government of the national population and its activities. In the eighteenth century, the provincial councils of regents and influential urban aristocracy dominated the system at the regional level. At the local level towns enjoyed considerable independence, but communities in the countryside lacked a well-articulated administration and were dominated by the urban councils (see Kocken, 1973). In spite of the formal democratic nature of the republic, the government and administration at both the local and the regional levels had an oligarchic character. The important positions within the system of government and administration were divided among the influential families and their relatives. The same applied also to the administrative tasks connected with water control management and the continuous process of land reclamation and the division of space in the new polders. A radical change took place in 1795 when the country came under the rule of Napoleonic France. First, the governmental and administrative competences were centralized at the national level and the powers of the provinces reduced considerably. Second, a uniform structure of munici-palities was established at the local level which covered both urban and rural areas. Yet, the municipalities were endowed with very limited administrative competences in accordance with the Napoleonic centraliza-tion of the powers at the national level.

After the end of the French occupation in 1813 the country became the Kingdom of The Netherlands. This was a constitutional monarchy but there were also restricted powers for a parliament which was elected by a narrow property suffrage. Despite proposals at that time to endow the municipalities with differential competences in accordance with their differences in size and urban and rural conditions at the local levels, the Napoleonic principle of fundamental uniformity of powers at the basic tier of the administration was maintained (see Toonen, 1982). This principle of uniformity remained to play an important role in the 1850s when the liberal prime minister Thorbecke took the successful initiative of reforming the Dutch governmental and administrative system. Thorbecke's reform was based upon two fundamental institutional principles which still appear to dominate the discussions concerning some possible step-wise or more radical reforms of the system of public administration today.

First, there is the principle of creating a balance of competences between the central government and the municipalities. As a reaction to the far-reaching federalism of the United Provinces in the eighteenth century and to the centralistic administration during the Napoleonic period, both the authorities of the central state and those of the municipalities have been given considerable rights and obligations and accompanying competences and tasks. An intermediate tier of relatively large provinces has been given less power. Consequently, the country's system of administration and govern-ment has been given a decentralized character and the authorities at the three levels have always been elected ones. Second, there is the above-mentioned principle of the unity or uniformity of the legal means of power and competences. The rights, obligations and tasks given to the municipalities have been basically uniform in accordance with the unitary character of the state despite differences in the size and character of each area. The same uniformity has applied to the competences and tasks which has been given to the eleven provinces. Consequently, Thorbecke's notion of a uniformity of powers within the Dutch institutional arrangement of the 'decentralized unitary state' has been, since his successful reform in 1851, an important fact in the discussions concerning possible reforms of the systems of public administration.

In addition to the Napoleonic and Thorbeckian reforms there were the numerous small but significant changes both outside and within the system of public administration: first, there have been territorially unequal and place-specific impacts resulting from the enlargement of the scale of societal activities; and second, population redistribution and increasing societal and material interdependences have involved impacts which cross the boundaries of the more than 1,200 municipalities and eleven provinces. These impacts have forced the central authorities to adapt the system in a quite continuous way to new emerging conditions of an industrializing and urbanized society.

Already in 1865 an additional important step was made towards the uniformity of administration at the local level. The right of municipalities to levy tolls was abolished in order to make national market unification easier. Furthermore, the right to levy taxes at the municipal level was limited considerably in order to redistribute financial resources in favour of the poorer municipalities. In compensation, the municipalities obtained the right to keep four-fifths of the personal taxes collected by the central authorities within their respective territories. Since the 1870s the provision of public services has become increasingly more important and pressed the central authorities to redistribute financial resources in a more equitable way both at the local and the regional level (Brasz, 1969). Among other things, the importance was recognized of a nation-wide and more uniform educational system (Knippenberg, 1986) and a reliable public supply of gas, electricity, water, etc. As a consequence of these changes, the financial arrangements and their changing institutional structure among the central, regional and local authorities have become one of the basic issues which it has been sought to resolve in a more or less continuous process of the administrative reform. After the reform of 1865 major changes in intergovernmental financial relations took place in 1897 and 1929. This new legislation changed the financial rights of municipalities considerably. The new laws were inspired by the idea that the substantial inter-municipal differences in income must be further reduced (Goedhart, 1975). Therefore, a nation-wide Municipal Fund was established by the central government, from which municipalities received annually the overwhelming share of their financial resources. The redistribution of finances from the fund has been based since 1929 on a number of objective criteria indicating local needs. In this the size of a municipality's population plays a decisive part. In addition a number of very small municipalities have amalgamated with neighbouring urbanized ones in order to secure, to some extent, the increasing scale economies of public services provision.

A continuous administrative reform

The historical changes summarized above illustrate the fact that the past radical reforms of the Dutch system of public administration have always been connected with the cumulation of small changes both in the arrangement and functioning of the system and in the societal and material circumstances which characterized the country's development and its differentiation at regional and local levels (Blaas and Dostál, 1981). In order to unravel both the major and minor changes it can be claimed that the system of public administration in The Netherlands has been involved, during the post-war period, in a continuous process of reform in which three distinguishable yet interconnected processes have played a decisive role.

First, there is the step-wise process of amalgamation of municipalities. The increasing necessity of the public provision of an adequate range of services has led to recurring problems of achieving scale economies of provision. In particular, since 1945 the primary redistributive institutions of the welfare state were developed (Schuyt and van der Veen, 1986). Recurring attempts have been made at central level to achieve increasing scale economies, both in the provision of services and in the necessary administrative apparatus, by increasing the territorial scale and the population size of municipalities. In Thorbecke's time there were 1,209 municipalities. During the time span of one century the number was reduced by incidental amalgamations to 1,014 in 1948. However, the option of reforming the local level of the administrative system by small steps gained considerably in importance during the post-war period. In 1976 there were 840 municipalities and in 1987 their number had been reduced to 714 (see Figure 15.1). Yet, the gradual process of amalgamation is still a time-consuming procedure which takes on average about seven years (Rombouts, 1986) mainly because local plebiscites can be organized by the municipal councils or local interest groups, and these usually have considerable power to retard the procedure. The amalgamation must also be approved both by the provincial and the national authorities.

Second, there is the process of the rearrangement of financial relations between the central government authorities, the municipalities and the eleven provinces. In addition to the mechanism of reallocating the revenues derived from the Municipal Fund after 1929, its counterpart for the eleven provinces was created in 1948 in the form of a Provincial Fund. During the post-war period the incomes from the provincial taxes have been highly constrained, and consequently the Provincial Fund has supplied the major share of the eleven provinces' financial resources. In 1960 new legislation on the Municipal Fund re-emphasized the importance of population size as the major distribution criterion and reduced further the importance of the remaining local and regional taxes. At the local level, the municipal taxes (mainly the taxes on immovable items) and local fees supplied the municipalities in 1980 with only about 8 per cent of their financial resources. The step-wise changes in the financial relation between the central authorities and the local and regional authorities have had, over a

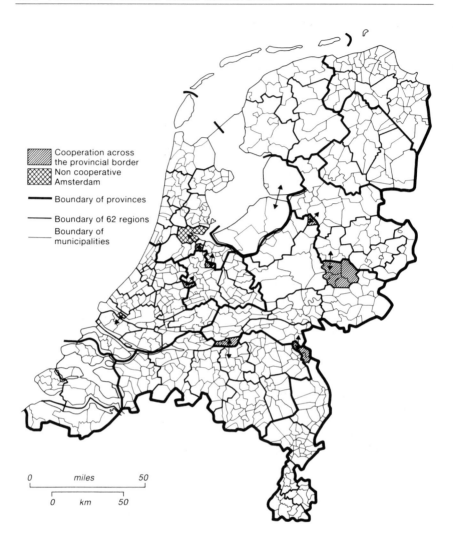

Figure 15.1 The administrative division of The Netherlands

long period, a very important consequence for the Thorbeckian doctrine of the decentralized unitary state: a *de facto* increase of the centralization of the decision-making in public administration at the national level by a gradual curtailment of the financial autonomy of both municipalities and provinces. In addition the share of general grants has decreased continuously in favour of an increasing variety of so-called 'specific grants' from the central authorities. The former can be allocated by the local and regional authorities in principle freely in accordance with their own policies. Importantly, the finances from the general part of the Municipal Fund are distributed among municipalities in accordance with a number of criteria (until 1984 especially according to the population size).

However, the increasing share of specific grants has to be allocated by the local and the regional authorities in accordance with the increasing number of fields of the policy delineated and evaluated by the central authorities (van der Dussen, 1987). In 1980 there was a very complex maze of 532 different specific grants at the local level (about 50 per cent of the total financial resources of municipalities). During the post-war period specific grants have financed an increasing share of the central government's policies and express the financial implications of the nationwide legislation at the local and the regional level.

Third, other important gradual changes in a continuous reform of the country's administrative system have been connected with the necessity of achieving some co-operation among municipalities at the subregional level within or between individual provinces (Doeschot *et al.*, 1987). Inter-municipal co-operation in The Netherlands is in fact concerned with the attempts to find an appropriate 'missing regional link' in the country's system of administration which can match a variety of problems at the intermediate scale between municipalities and relatively large provinces (Blaas and Dostál, 1985). Since Thorbecke's reform in 1851, inter-municipal co-operation has been allowed in order to fulfil a limited task more efficiently and effectively by means of a joint effort of two or more municipalities. By an innovation of the Municipality Law in 1931 the municipalities were allowed to create a supra-municipal apparatus to achieve this end. However, this new legislation was framed within the context of the concept that co-operation among municipalities must have the organizational form of an 'aim corporation', instead of a far more comprehensive one of a 'territorial corporation'. This emphasis gave the policy a facet-like form of co-operation and was an attempt to prevent the formation of a fourth tier of administration from 'below'. Yet, in the highly urbanized Netherlands, which had reached an average population density of 296 inhabitants per square kilometre in 1947 which was fast increasing, a variety of problems of co-ordination and planning were pressing at the supra-municipal level yet below the provincial one. New housing, expanding infrastructure and the expansion and maintenance of the public services' provision at the local level have forced many municipalities to establish quite comprehensive supra-municipal apparatuses in order to co-ordinate and plan in a more effective way and to suppress the increasing per unit costs of the public services' provision. By a separate Law on Inter-Municipal Co-operation in 1950 the municipalities were allowed to establish incorporations (that is legal personalities) in their joint efforts to solve the pressing problem of the 'missing regional link' in the country's system of administration. Their proposals for such (often comprehensive) co-operation were usually accepted by the provincial and the national authorities. In the beginning of the 1980s there were about 1,500 joint agreements for mutual co-operation chosen more or less freely from 'below' by the elected councils of the municipalities involved. The co-operation covers a wide range of sectors of service provision, production and planning in fields like education, social welfare, cultural and recreational facilities, basic health services, transport and traffic, physical planning and allocation of housing, police and fire-brigades. Yet, the municipalities participated often simultaneously in different areas of inter-municipal co-operation. In their attempts to combine the benefits of scale economies with effective internalization of external effects (particularly regarding the allocation and planning of housing, infrastructure and recreational facilities) the area of inter-municipal co-operation crossed, in many cases, even the boundaries of the eleven provinces. In short, it can be claimed that the post-war gradual introduction of the inter-municipal co-operation from 'below' has been another important reform by both the small and the large municipalities which attempts to match the (increasing) differentiation at the subregional level in a more effective and efficient way.

The missing regional link

The gradual process of increasing inter-municipal co-operation during the post-war period has inevitably been connected with a variety of regional reform proposals which seek the seemingly 'missing regional link' in the country's public administration. Reviewing the whole post-war period three distinct stages in the discussion can be distinguished.

First, during the 1950s and the 1960s, the facet-orientated co-operation among municipalities was considered to be a temporary solution of the issue. Given the increasing importance of the specific financial grants from the central government and the increasing variety of public services in the mature welfare state, the authorities of the central government established at the regional and subregional level an increasing number of inspection and advisory offices often accompanied by territorially very different *rayons* or districts of their operation (VWRR, 1975). Below the level of the eleven provinces there were at least fifty-four such *rayons* and districts at the beginning of the 1970s. In some cases the maze of the centrally constituted *rayons* or districts influenced the municipalities in their choice of areas for inter-municipal co-operation. At the same time there were about fifty areas of (often quite comprehensive) inter-municipal co-operation covering the major part of the territory in both the highly urbanized and the rural provinces. During the 1960s the new field of urban and physical planning claimed a lot of attention at all three tiers of the administrative system. The economy flourished, so did building activities, and consequently, urban regions were expanding. Town and country grew out of its jacket and the 'channelling' of a variety of suburbanization processes was a time-consuming field of decision-making and planning. At that time, the Liberal–Confessional cabinet supported the independent and influential spokesman of municipalities — the Organisation of Dutch Municipalities founded in 1912 — in its call for the formation of regions of administration from 'below' based upon the existing patterns of the inter-municipal co-operation. The then minister of interior made a proposal for such an upgrading of the Law on Inter-Municipal Co-operation. However, he was called back by the parliament because the majority of MPs wanted a procedure which must be initiated and sanctioned from 'above', that is by the central authorities.

A second stage of regional reform proposals was connected with the initiative of the only post-war cabinet dominated by the Labour Party (the cabinet Den Uyl, 1973–7). The cabinet's proposals followed the option of the establishment of more powerful yet smaller provinces. The proposals involved both a shift of tasks and competences from the municipalities and a decentralization of decision-making from the central level to that of new smaller provinces. Given the emphasis put upon the proposed far-reaching powers at the regional level the then minister of interior attempted to match the proposals with the existing urban hierarchy of the country described by the geographers Keuning (1971) and Buursink (1971). Initially, the minister proposed the establishment of forty-four regional units of public administration which could match territorially with the forty functional areas, or city-regions, of secondary and primary urban centres of the country (Concept-Structuurschets, 1974). Moreover, this proposal had also the aim of matching the then most comprehensive regions of inter-municipal co-operation such as the Public Authority Rijmond of the inter-municipal co-operation in Rotterdam area (Joolen, 1971) which had been created from 'above' by a unique separate law in 1964, or the Joint Authority of the Eindhoven Agglomeration (van Laarhoven, 1971) established from 'below'. In order to match also the heavy protests against this proposal coming from both the spokesmen of the municipalities and the provinces the minister modified it by raising the population threshold from about 100,000 to 200,000 inhabitants. The new scheme proposed twenty-four 'mini-provinces' (Tweede Kamer, 1976). This time, the proposal followed the functional areas of the country's twenty-one primary cities. Importantly it also implied the abolition of the eleven large and heterogeneous provinces. Consequently, the opposition from both the provincial and the municipal levels was considerable. The fall of this cabinet in 1977 appeared to be the end of proposals which were primarily based upon the results of geographical and regional-economic research and the interest of physical planning.

A third stage started at the end of the 1970s when the Liberal–confessional cabinets came to power again. And again, the solution of the missing regional link was sought at the local level. The option of so-called 'extended local administration' was taken as the starting point. In a note to the parliament the liberal prime minister of the interior stressed this time the following points: (i) that inter-municipal co-operation must be amended in order to strengthen subregional co-operation and planning among municipalities, (ii) a fourth administrative tier must be foregone, (iii) the tier of eleven provinces must be endowed with some new tasks by decentralization, (iv) the provinces must fulfil the surveillance of inter-municipal co-operation in order to solve possible conflicts at the local level, and finally, (v) the process of amalgamation of municipalities must be continued (Nota, 1983). However, the old liberal–technocratic option for the establishment of the missing regional link from 'above' led in 1985 to a new Law of Inter-Municipal Co-operation which is adding to the Dutch system of public administration sixty-two regions of inter-municipal co-operation as one of its basic features (see Figure 15.1).

The contemporary system of public administration: an outlook

In spite of the changes which have determined the character of the Dutch system of public administration, especially during the post-war period, the historical heritage of the three-tier hierarchical system has been maintained since the Napoleonic time and the successful establishment of the Thorbecke's decentralized unitary state of three levels of elected authorities.

First, at the local level there are now 714 municipalities. Municipalities are still governed by directly elected councils and these are chaired by burgomasters appointed by the crown: that is by the cabinet, for the queen does not have any legal responsibilities. Second, there are now twelve provinces (see Figure 15.1). A new province was established in 1986 to cover the new polders which had been reclaimed since the 1930s in the central Ijsselmeer. The provincial councils are chaired by the queen's provincial commissioners who are also appointed by the crown.

The relative strength of the two levels can be indicated by the number of public servants. In 1985 there were 170,000 full-time positions at the municipal level and only 17,000 at the provincial level (de Groot, 1987). These numbers indicate the great differences between the two tiers as regards the respective packages of public services they traditionally provide. Since the beginning of the economic stagnation in 1980 and the subsequent substantial economizing on public expenditure by the central government, the numbers have increased recently only very slightly. The only substantial increase took place in the provision of welfare services. The specific grants for social welfare from the central government and the Municipal Fund have been increased, yet compensated by economizing on other elements of the municipal package of services. In order to match the differences among municipalities in local socio-economic, housing and other conditions, and the accompanying needs of the population, a new law on the Municipal Fund was introduced in 1984 (Ministerie van Financien, 1984). Its primary aim was to reduce the importance of the municipality's population size from 57 per cent to 17 per cent in the distribution of the general grants compared with the law from 1960, and to increase the importance of the number of dwellings in the municipality from 10 per cent to 54 per cent. Considering specific grants, the emphasis is shifting towards the matched compensation of the municipal expenditures on social welfare, education and public housing provision. At the provincial level the criteria for the distribution of the general grants of the Provincial Fund has changed only slightly. The relative importance of population size has decreased from 40 per cent to 35 per cent, and that of land and water areas from 22.5 per cent to 17 per cent. The weight of the equal grant to all twelve provinces rose from 35 per cent to 42 per cent.

These small, yet important, changes in financial relations within the Dutch system of public administration indicate the continuous efforts made at all three levels of public administration to match the ever emerging differentiations in socio-economic and other circumstances at both the local and the regional levels by appropriate adaptations of the system. Unfortunately, it can be claimed that the delineation in 1985 of the sixty-two regions for inter-municipal co-operation, at the interstitial level between the municipality and the province, undermined such efforts importantly. In spite of the formal emphasis put by the central government upon the principle of 'extended local government' the regionalization procedure accompanying the new legislation was a procedure from 'above'. The central government demanded a procedure for dividing The Netherlands into new regions of inter-municipal co-operation abolishing the existing ones which had been formed since the 1950s from 'below'. The new regions were proposed by the provincial authorities after obligatory consultations with municipalities involved and finally sanctioned by the minister of interior in the Hague. A closer look at this new administrative pattern makes clear that the new regions will constrain the flexibility of inter-municipal co-operation considerably (Dostál, 1988). First, large municipalities like Groningen, Utrecht, or the Hague have been robbed to a large extent of their functional hinterlands. Second, areas showing socio-economic coherence (commuting, regional services provision, etc.) that cross provincial borders are hard to find. The area of Midden-Ijssel is the only important exception (see Figure 15.1). Third, it can be claimed that the new regions will also constrain the flexibility of municipalities because the regions are too small to be able to participate in future developments. The municipalities are obliged to co-operate only within the regions delineated. Co-operative intentions crossing the boundaries of the sixty-two regions can be allowed only exceptionally (VNG, 1984). It seems that because of the establishment of the new small regions, future attempts at a more flexible future-orientated inter-municipal co-operation will be considerably constrained. It can be argued that the areas of inter-municipal co-operation created since the 1950s, which numbered more than fifty, were approaching after a long and often difficult process of joint efforts the targets of both scale economies in the public services provision and the effectiveness of internalizing a variety of external effects, such changes could seldom have an identical spatial pattern coinciding with the new sixty-two regions delineated from 'above' (Snellen, 1986). Moreover, the municipalities are now forced to dissolve the former joint agreements and dismantle the accompanying apparatuses, and this exercise implies considerable extra costs for the implementation of the new legislation.

Recently, Kreukels (1987) has emphasized the tensions occurring between the scale-increasing and scale-decreasing processes. Today, the option of forming a variety of public–private partnerships is increasingly popular. Yet, in order to be able to take appropriate initiatives the local and the regional authorities have to co-ordinate their actions in a flexible way which matches the variable differentiation within the local and regional units of public administration. The Thorbeckian tradition of emphasizing the uniformity of the organizational pattern of the Dutch system of public administration had always been connected with the distributive principles of social justice (Dostál, 1984). However, in order to enable the local and regional authorities to contribute effectively both to the generation of national economic growth and the maintenance of locally and regionally bounded welfare situations, it seems to be necessary to extend the options for a more decentralized operation of the country's system of public administration. The comments made in the preceding sections suggest already that this aim must still be realized in the future. The recent developments in Amsterdam municipality are interesting in this respect (van Englesdorp Gastelaars and Heinemeijer, 1985). The city-centred region of Amsterdam does *not* form one of the sixty-two regions for inter-municipal co-operation (see Figure 15.1). The surrounding regions of Amsterdam municipality formalize the continuing administrative fragmentation at the subregional level and could lead to a further widening of the disparities of living and physical conditions between the municipalities involved. The council of Amsterdam municipality complicated the situation considerably by initiating in 1982 a far-reaching experiment of inter-municipal decentralization of both the decision-making and the financial resources towards sixteen neighbourhoods of the city (Bours, 1987). The establishment of sub-municipalities is allowed according to the Law on Municipal Government and nowadays there are in Amsterdam five sub-municipalities already established which have both councils and executives elected at the sub-municipal level. Yet, it seems that the successes of this experiment in local decentralization will depend in the future on the success of co-operation of Amsterdam with the surrounding municipalities which belong to its natural functional area. It can be claimed that both scale enlargement and scale diminution, in the future Dutch system of public administration, will be the inevitable processes of the system's attempt to match the emerging conditions of a highly urbanized society and its fast-changing economic circumstances. The outcome of the two processes will depend on the extent to which the authorities at the local and the regional tiers of the system will be able flexibly to anticipate the changes implied for the adaptation of public administration.

References

Blaas, H. and Dostál, P. (1981), 'De bestuurlijke indeling van Nederland', in J.M.M. van Amersfoort, W.F. Heinemeijer and H.H. van der Wusten (eds), *Een Wereld van Staten*, Samson, Alphen ad/R, 92–104.

Blaas, H. and Dostál, P. (1985), 'Het regionale gat van Nederland', *Planologische Diskussiebijdragen*, Deel 1, Delft, 131–44.

Bours, A. (1987), *Regional Divisions and the Machinery of Government in the Netherlands*, Paper, IGU Conference on Administrative Reforms in Europe, Pécs, Hungary.

Brasz, H.A. (1969), *Varanderingen in het Nederlandse Communalisme*, VUGA, Arnhem.

Buursink, J. (1971), *Centraliteit en Hierarchie*, Van Gorcum, Assen.

Concept-Structuurschets (1975), *Voor de Bestuurlijke Indeling*, Ministerie van Binnenlandse Zaken, The Hague.

Doeschot, R.G.P. (1987), *Intergemeentelijke Samenwerking*, Kluwer, Deventer.

Dostál, P. (1984), 'Regional policy and corporate organization forms: some questions of interregional social justice', in M. de Smidt and E. Wever (eds), *A Profile of Dutch Economic Geography*, Van Gorcum, Assen, 12–38.

Dostál, P. (1988), *On Flexibility of the Inter-Municipal Co-operation in the Netherlands: Some Institutional and Geographical Comments*, Paper, Seminar on Local Development and Planning, International Union of Local Authorities, The Hague.

Dussen, J.W. van der (1987), 'Vijenzeventig jaar financiële verhouding rijkgemeenten', *Economisch-Statistische Berichten*, 492–6.

Englesdorp Gastelaars, R. van and Heinemeijer, W.F. (1985), 'Stedelijk beleid en de ruimtelijke organisatie van stadsgewesten: het geval Amsterdam', *Geografisch Tijdschift*, 19, 95–104.

Goedhart, C. (1975), *Hoofdlijen van de Leer der Openbare Financiën*, S. Kroese, Leiden.

Groot, H. de (1987), 'De rol van gemeentelijke uitgaven in de collectieve sector', *Economisch-Statistische Berichten*, 497–500.

Joolen, A.W. (1971), 'Regional government in the Rotterdam area', in E. Kalk (ed.), *Regional Planning and Regional Government in Europe*, IULA, The Hague, 125–33.

Keuning, H.J. (1971), 'Spreiding en hiërarchie van de Nederlandse verzorgingscentra op grondslag van hun winkelapparaat', *Tijschrift voor Economische en Sociale Geografie*, 62, No. 1.

Knippenberg, H. (1986), *Deelname aan het Lager Onderwijs in Nederland Gendurende de Negentiende Eeuw*, Nederlandse Geografische Studies, No. 9, Free University, Amsterdam.

Kocken, M.J.A.V. (1973), 'Van stads-en plattelandsbestuur naar gemeentebestuur', *Stichting Gemeentelijk Cultuurfonds*, Mouton, The Hague.

Kreukels, A. (1987), *Public–Private Partnerships: een Vergelijking van Ervaringen in de Verenigde Staten en Nederland*, RUU, Utrecht.

Laarhoven, J.B.A. van (1971), 'Outline of the regional administrative unit', in E. Kalk (ed.), *Regional Planning and Regional Government in Europe*, IULA, The Hague, 247–51.

Ministerie van Financiën (1984), *Financiële Verhouding Rijk-lagere Overheden*, The Hague.

Nota, (1983), *Organisatie Binnenlands Bestuur*, Ministerie Binnenlandse Zaken, The Hague.

Rombouts, A.G.J.M. (1986), *Gemeenten zonder Garanties, een Onderzoek naar de Procedure voor Gemeentelijke Herindeling in Nederland, Belgie, Denemarken en Zweden*, Raad Binnenlands Bestuur, The Hague.

Schuyt, K. and Veen, R. van der (1986), *De Verdeelde Samenleving*, S. Kroese, Leiden.

Snellen, J.T.M. (1986), 'De regio: een vreemd vacuum?', *Bestuur*, 2, 16–19.

Toonen, T. (1982), *De Pluriformiteitsgedachte in het Openbaar Bestuur*, Raad Binnenlands Bestuur, The Hague.

Tweede Kamer (1976), *Wet to Wijziging van de Provinciale Indeling*, 14, 323, nrs, 1–3, The Hague.

Vereniging van Nederlandse Gemeeten (VNG) (1984), De regio gelokaliseerd, eindrapport van de Commissie intergemeentelijke samenwerking, *Blauwe Reeks*, 71, The Hague.

Voorlopige Wetenschappelijke Raad Voor Het Regeringsbeleid (1975), *De Organisatie van het Openbaar Bestuur*, Staatsuitgeverij, The Hague.

16 France: shifts in local authority finance

Guy Gilbert and Alain Guengant

The territorial administrative structure

The structure of French local government was established following the 1789 Revolution which was codified into a uniform structure of ninety-five mainland *départements* by Napoleon, headed by a central government official. Above the *départements* are twenty-two administrative regions used until 1982 by the central government for its own administrative purposes. Below the *départements* in 1982 were 325 sub-departments (*arrondissements*), 3,075 districts (*cantons*), and 36,433 municipalities (*communes*). The *communes* and *départements* have the most significance for our discussions here. The result is a highly centralized system of a 'unitary and indivisible nation'. In 1963 an attempt at governmental reform established regional economic planning councils (CODER) and in 1972 regional councils. In the 1970s under a conservative government an attempt was made to give more power to the *communes* if they amalgamated into larger units, but little practical change occurred. Major changes have awaited the socialist government, which, since 1982, has instituted a number of administrative reforms, but mainly affecting the financial structure. These are outlined in the main body of this chapter.

Communes

The powers of the *communes* derive from the 1884 basic law that gives them a constitutional status, which was incorporated in the Municipal Administration Code of 1957 and amended in 1979 and 1982 to increase the rights and freedom of *commune* action. A law of January 1983 instituted a division of competences between the central and local state authorities as well as effecting changes to regions, local authority personnel, local elections, inter-*commune* co-operation and citizen participation.

The major characteristics of French local government are the smallness of most *communes*, and the range of their sizes. Over 90 per cent of *communes* have a population of less than 2,000, but a few *communes* have over 500,000. The councils are elected with a number of members varying between nine and 109 depending on *commune* size. The council elects a mayor and may elect up to five deputies who together act as the executive in a fused system of administration. The mayor also has the dual role of being a representative of the state as well as chief executive of the council. The election of the mayor, and often the council, is a political choice and this can considerably affect expenditure and other policy decisions.

Because of the small size of so many *communes* inter-municipal co-operation is essential in certain fields. There were nearly 2,000 multi-purpose joint councils, and over 11,600 single-purpose councils in 1986. These *syndicat* are corporate bodies with their own taxation system. In addition there are approximately 150 urban districts which cover small- and medium-sized towns and have powers over housing, fire-fighting, other services, and also have their own taxes. For the large metropolitan areas, there are special authorities (*communautés urbaines*) which have been established since 1961. Originally co-operation with these bodies was mandatory for the immediate surroundings of these areas (Bordeaux, Lille, Lyon, and Strasbourg), but since then a number of voluntary councils have been set up.

Départements

Since 1982 these have the dual function of acting as both a deconcentrated division of the state, and as a decentralized unit of government. These also have elected councils from which a president is elected. Since 1982 the president is the chief executive of the council. This is a significant step towards increased local autonomy since previously the state-appointed prefect commissioner was the chief executive. The president, however, has still to work closely with the prefect commissioner. They are jointly charged with co-ordinating many state functions and the prefect still retains many of the most important powers, including supervising the exercise of power by both *départements* and *communes*. The decentralization law of 1982, therefore, represents only a modest increase in local autonomy.

Régions

Régions were first established in 1960 with the primary purpose of formulating and implementing a regional framework for national economic planning. In 1972 they became public bodies with a council of national deputies and senators as well as representatives of the *départements* and *communes*. The regional prefect commissioner was the head. Since 1982 they have become units of decentralized government with an elected council. Their main competences are in the fields of economic development planning and implementation; provision of vocational training; arts, cultural and leisure facilities; tourism; and preservation of heritage. Since 1982 an elected chief executive (president) has replaced the prefect commissioner. It is expected by some commentators that *régions* will play a significant role in economic development policy in the future. However, although significant increases in scope at regional level have now occurred, the prefect remains and the extent of true autonomy is still an open question.

Towards the consolidation of the grant system

At the same time as initiating reforms of the administrative and representative system France has, during the last twenty years, been experimenting with a change from a piecemeal block-grant system towards a more consolidated one. This has affected the financial autonomy of local public administration in two ways. On the one hand, the withdrawal of legal rules, especially those related to the assignment of specific resources for capital expenditures, has widened the budgetary choice of the local communities; it has thus reinforced the financial decentralization process. On the other hand, the emergence of block-grants induced the 'crowding out' of some local taxes. As a result the taxing power of the local communities has tended to be reduced by erosion of their local tax bases and this has lowered the level of financial decentralization. Each element is discussed in turn below.

Grants for capital expenditures

Before the recent reforms, and since the 1960s and early 1970s, the central government has contributed to the financing of local public investment jointly with other public entities through a piecemeal network of matching and categorical grants defined independently by central government, and compulsorily linked to central expenditure. (The local authorities had to set up a separate investment file for every new project for which they tried to obtain a subsidy.) Each project was examined first by the relevant government agencies in each *région* and *département*. Thus, the capital expenditure programmes were managed both by the central government and by the relevant local authorities. The grant system was primarily based upon the concept of 'subsidized expenditure' (a capital expenditure eligible for subsidy), which is essentially different from the actual amount of capital outlays charged to the local community.

Furthermore, the rates of subsidy varied sharply from one type of expenditure to another with the hierarchy of subsidy rates reflecting the priorities set by the central government. The 'rating' of capital outlays, the level and the scale of the rates of subsidy were voted in the early 1950s. They remained virtually unchanged since then despite a shift of capital outlays from some former priority sectors (schools, rural infrastructure) to new sectors where demand and needs were greater, but where the rates of subsidy remained low (roads and transport, recreation equipment, social services). Unfortunately these latter sectors became of prime importance to the growth of urban areas, which rapidly expanded over this period. Thus, the constant rate of subsidy applied to a changing local capital expenditure

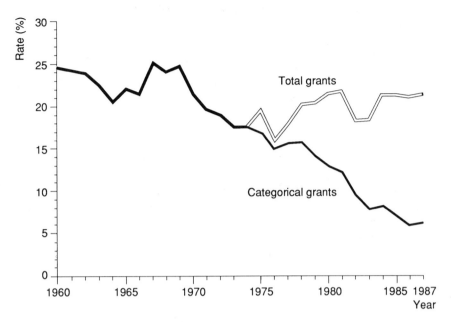

Figure 16.1 Average rate of subsidy from central government to local authorities 1959–1987 (% of local investment expenditure)

structure gave a decreasing average subsidy rate over time with level of local capital outlay (see Figure 16.1). This feature was one of the key aspects of the local financial situation in France before the reform of capital subsidies in the late 1970s.

Despite the decreasing level of financial support from central public agencies in local investment, this by no means reduced the discretionary control by the central government. At this time capital outlays were mainly financed by borrowing rather than by self-financing. The access by local government to loans at preferential rates (in fact at negative rates of interest in real terms) depended strictly upon the promise of a subsidy from the central government (see Derycke and Gilbert, 1985). Thus the linking of loans and subsidies to central action retained the subordination of local public investment power to the central bureau (both in a technical and in a financial way).

The tight indirect control exerted by the central bureaus was less and less tolerated by the local authorities. The main restrictive conditions to the eligibility for loans became so onerous that central government grants were reduced in value. As a result local politicians called for a reform based upon the implementation of a new block-grant to be exclusively devoted to local capital outlays and where the amount of grant was to be directly computed according to a set of objective criteria stated by law and not subject to central discretion. The political debate rapidly reached a general agreement on fundamental principles in 1972. This favoured the creation of a Block Grant for Public Capital Outlays (*Dotation Globale d'Equipment*, or DGE). Faced with the threat of a substantial loss of power of control (particularly since, at this time, local capital outlays amounted to 75 per cent of the whole capital expenditure of all public authorities), the central bureaux successfully challenged the political decision, preventing the project from being effective.

The issue arose again in 1978 within the more general debate on value-added tax (VAT). Local authorities are liable to VAT on their capital outlays. But, unlike other taxpayers, they are not allowed to pass on the tax burden (by reimputation) to local taxpayers or to local public-services users. In the meantime, the average rate of central subsidy on capital outlays declined to 16 per cent (tax included) which was close to the standard rate of VAT on capital expenditure. Thus with one hand the central government was taking back (through the VAT) the subsidy that it gave with its other hand. After hard political debate, the French senate voted in 1978 a payment-back bill of the VAT of local capital expenditure (FCTVA: *Fonds de Compensation de la TVA*). The FCTVA truly represents a block-grant on local capital expenditure: it is open-ended, proportional to capital outlays registered two years previously and at the flat rate of 15.682 per cent.

A further step towards the consolidation of the grant system was made in 1983 with the setting up of a 'new' block-grant, the DGE. The principle of this grant had been adopted ten years before but in 1983 it was possible to consolidate the majority (if not the totality) of the remaining selective grants on capital expenditures. However, local politicians and officers became quickly disillusioned with this new-born DGE, mainly because it induced a sharp decrease in the amount of selective grants to capital. Thus, the total amount of DGE remained much lower than expected by the local authorities. In addition, the investment behaviour of many local authorities, particularly the very small *communes* in rural areas, which is very irregular, did not fit well with an annual subsidy calculated on actual capital expenditures. For this reason, the smallest communities ($<$ 2,000 inhabitants) have been made eligible for categorical grants on capital outlays since 1987.

In summary, a globalization process (that is, the consolidation of the grants-in-aid system of the central government) has encouraged a political movement of emancipation of the local governments from central government. This can be termed a decentralization process. In fact, the consequences of the consolidation/globalization process have gone beyond these financial issues. The reform has also induced a true shift of political power from the central public authorities to local politicians and officers. The abolition of categorical grants resulted in the disappearance of the 'loan-subsidy link'. Consequently, central public agencies have been deprived of much of their control power on borrowing decisions at local level.[1] Thus in the late 1970s France, a centralized state *par excellence*, has experienced a shift towards decentralization in its public decision processes. The basic reform of 1982 (*Lois de Décentralisation*) led to the disappearance of the main part of the controls, regulations and tutelage imposed on the local public sector. However, it is perhaps best to interpret this reform process more

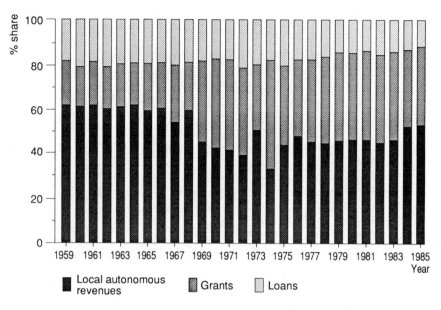

Figure 16.2 Structure of total resources of local authorities in France 1959–85 (%)

as a temporary achievement of a process started ten years previously than as a definitive breaking point in the evolution of the organizational network of the local public administration, since it is not yet clear that central government will allow the decentralization to continue indefinitely.

Tax subsidies

In the meantime, the central government also 'deregulated' its relations with the local authorities and increased its budgetary commitments towards them. The level of subsidies originating from the central state as a proportion of the total current resources of local governments has continuously increased. Conversely the share of the resources under the direct control of the local government (direct taxes, user charges, etc.) has diminished (see Figure 16.2). These trends resulted first from the reform in central government taxes and subsequently from the endogenous evolution of local taxation.

French local taxes consist approximately of: 50 per cent the *Taxe Professionnelle*; 25 per cent property tax and 25 per cent habitation tax. The recent evolution of local taxation in France began in 1968 when the VAT system was extended to the retail trade. VAT was enforced in lieu of the *Taxe Locale sur le Chiffre d'Affaires* (a local turnover tax) which formerly benefited the local communities. This loss in tax receipts was then compensated by a general-purpose-grant (VRTS). The VRTS was reformed once again in 1979 and became the DGF. The DGF is now indexed, on a

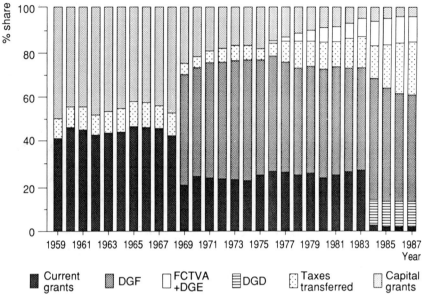

Figure 16.3 Structure of grants from central government to local authorities (APUL) 1959–87 (%)

national basis, to the net receipts of the VAT. The subsidy is shared between *Communes* and *Départements*. The level of allocation to each authority depends upon a set of indicators relating to the local tax resources and the 'fiscal needs' of each community. The set of criteria is laid down by law. The first objective of the DGF is to compensate local tax disparities. Secondly, the DGF aims at the redistribution of public resources. The allocation is supposed to benefit mainly those localities which are less endowed in tax base (measured through a 'tax capacity index') or have large 'fiscal needs' (measured by a set of variables such as population, number of pupils, road mileage, stock of social housing, etc). The DGF has now become the major part of the grants originating from the central government (see Figure 16.3). The DGF does largely correct local fiscal disparities. According to the most recent and reliable estimates, the DGF is supposed to reduce fiscal disparities among local authorities by up to 40 per cent (see Guengant, 1985a). Compared to a full equalization target, the latter result should appear relatively small. Nevertheless, is is far from being negligible in the French context if one considers: (i) the very large magnitude of the fiscal disparities due to the large number and wide range of sizes of local communities in France (there are 36,000 *communes*), and (ii) the unevenness of the spatial distribution of the tax bases especially concerning the main local tax, the *Taxe Professionnelle*.

It is possible to regard the setting up of the DGF as a by-product of the modernization of the tax system at the central level. Conversely, since the first oil crisis in 1973, we can explain the growth of subsidies as the outcome of local taxation. Strong reactions (even if they have not led to

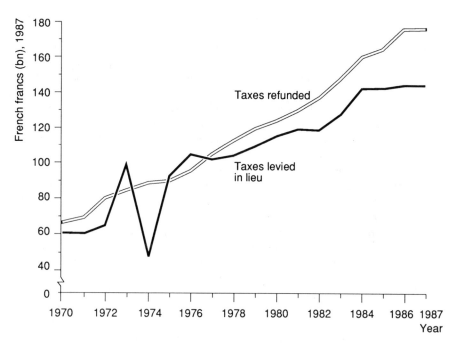

Figure 16.4 Taxes refunded to local authorities and taxes levied in lieu of local authorities by central government (Billions of French francs 1987 [in real terms])

'tax revolts') came from firms and large companies as local tax burdens increased in a period of macro-economic stagnation. Then, political power allowed local taxpayers several tax rebates and reductions without reducing the amount of the tax payments transferred to local communities. (The local taxes are collected by tax officers appointed by the central state tax administration; the *Trésor* repays the collected taxes to local governments.) So, the central state compensates explicitly the 'tax loss' due to tax expenditures (via a categorical grant: the *Fonds National de Compensation pour la Taxe Professionnelle*) or implicitly (via the pre-financing of the local tax receipts which result from the fact that taxes are provisionally paid to local governments by the *Trésor* before they are actually levied on taxpayers). These tax rebates amount to 25 per cent of the *Taxe Professionnelle* liabilities of firms, and 15 per cent of the property taxes paid by households.

The 'disconnection' between the tax receipts benefiting local communities and the taxes actually borne by the taxpayers has expanded over time and has led to increasing problems for the Treasury (see Figure 16.4). First, the increase in the level of fiscal compensations has weighed down the overall burdens of the central state and enlarged the fiscal deficit. The deficit has thus been shifted from the local sector (where it is strictly forbidden, by law) to the central level. This illustrates how far the trend of the fiscal requirements at local level has diverged from the marginal ability of that level to pay. The potential local public deficit is thus hidden by the grants system. Second, the tax rebates to local taxpayers threaten the fiscal autonomy of local governments. This arises because 'tax transfers' (indexed on national aggregates or even fixed in nominal terms) increase less rapidly than the local tax receipts (the DGF for example). Thus, local communities suffer from a 'lack of financial resources' while nevertheless receiving a strengthened local tax base.

Finally, increasing the level of subsidies (and especially tax subsidies) to local government has weakened the central political control over local budgets. The true evaluation of the actual needs of local public services requires full information from the local taxpayers who are, in addition, supposed not to be subject to tax illusion. If this is so, they are fully aware of the true marginal cost of the additional public services. Now, the central state contributes, via grants, to a distortion of the link between local outlays and local tax receipts, and this lowers the visible cost of local public services for the local politicians, officers and voters. In doing so, it conceals the additional tax burden imposed on both national and local taxpayers. In these conditions, one would expect a tendency to overspending behaviour in local communities. If this is so, an increase in subsidy (including 'cross subsidization' between local communities) clearly induces a decrease in the level of political responsibility by the local authorities. It also introduces more confusion into the assignment issue (the development of the co-management of public projects) and a deeper confusion into finance (where the co-financing of local projects induces the spreading of charges among communities).

The cut in the incentives to overspending

The effect of central subsidies on local spending behaviour depends heavily upon the characteristics of the grant system. To determine the effects which have arisen, we have to keep in mind both the multiple revisions and amendments of the grants framework in France since the early 1980s which affect behaviour, and the expectations of economic theory which support a number of a priori expectations on theoretical grounds.

The development of lump-sum subsidies

Matching grants are usually interpreted as strong incentives to 'over-spend'. Indexing the amount of grants to the level of outlays (or the volume of taxes) leads to expenditures which are greater than those which would have occurred with a lump-sum grant, the amount of which is independent of the level of expenditures.

If the objective of the economic policy is to decrease the level of matching of local public finance, suppressing matching grants is surely the major task. This seems to have been the effect in France, especially for expenditures related to social services (*Aide sociale départementale*) since the 'Decentralization Laws'. The sharp increase in these expenditures came from:

— the deterioration of the macro-economic environment;
— the ageing of the population;
— the upheaval of responsibilities between central and local public services; and chiefly,
— the network of matching-grants originating from the central state distributed at high average rates (for example 85 per cent for childhood care aid, 70 per cent for medical aid, 40 per cent for elderly programmes) and on an open-ended basis.

The *Lois de Décentralisation* re-mapped this system in 1982. It enacted a reallocation of responsibilities between the different levels (medical aid is assigned to the centre, social aid to *départements*), even if in some limited cases co-responsibilities remained in place. In line with these changes the former open-ended matching-grants were abolished and compensated by transferring taxes from central to *département* level (car licence tax, taxes on transfer of property). These transferred taxes represent roughly 50 per cent of the total of the expenditures at the local level. The remaining 50 per cent are financed by a new block-grant, DGD (*Dotation Globale de Décentralisation*). The DGD does not depend on the level of outlays devoted to social services; it grows at the same rate as the DGF, that is at the net rate of growth of the VAT. Thus the volume of the newly transferred tax liabilities depends on the free budgetary decisions of the local communities.

Since the enactment of the Reform Laws a dramatic decrease in the rate of growth of the expenditures in social services has occurred. Local politicians seemed fully aware of the financial and political consequences of any *laisser-faire* on these matters, especially in terms of tax burden, and asked the central bureaux to strengthen the eligibility criteria for grants. Certainly, it is too early to assert that the administrative reforms were entirely responsible for this change since the situation may have resulted from a temporary effect. However, the present situation does illustrate the effect of the termination of the former grant system.

Another example of the same 'dis-overspending policy' is the 1986 reform of the *Taxe Professionnelle* exemptions. The tax liabilities that the local communities were no longer able to levy, owing to the special tax rules imposed by the central government, were formerly fully compensated by a tax subsidy. The amount of this subsidy was calculated from the volume of the local tax liabilities actually levied by local governments. Thus the more that the local governments taxed the firms under the regime of *Taxe Professionnelle*, the higher became the potential loss in tax liabilities and the more the central state had to compensate. The 1986 reform removed this incentive to increase local tax rates, and its total amount became indexed to the level of the DGF, that is to VAT tax receipts. In other words, the local communities are not rationally induced to 'exploit' the central taxpayer. A new Reform Act of the DGF took place in 1986. This followed the same guidelines as discussed above and aimed at reducing the incentive to overspend in the local communities. The former DGF was partly (and positively) linked to the level of local taxes levied on households in the previous year (this part of the DGF was named the

Dotation Ménages). Thus, the local government received a strong incentive to increase tax rates. Nevertheless, this sub-grant was closed-ended; therefore what some local governments gained in increasing tax rates was exactly equal to what other governments lost, that is the amount of grant received in a given community depended both on its own tax effort and on the tax level in other localities. Hence a municipality which overspent was subsidized in a rather random way and the 'under-spending' communities were slightly penalized.

This situation was clearly inconsistent, but the 1986 Reform Act only partially removed this tax incentive: the sub-grant *Dotation Ménages* was abolished but a part of the DGF remained which was indexed to the tax borne by the households. This disposal is presently being challenged. Some politicians ask for the removal of any indexation of grants to the outcomes of the local fiscal choices: they seek a move towards a pure lump-sum system of grants. Others seek a system similar to the British one which has existed since 1981 where grants are negatively linked to the increments in local taxes or spending, so as to penalize overtaxing/overspending communities.

Rather oddly, the present debates on the future of local taxation in France focus more on seeking to decrease the growth of local taxes as a whole rather than on the inefficiency of the control of local budgets via central state subsidies. From this observation the question arises of the magnitude of the 'spending effect' attached to different grant formulae. Below we outline what we know about the elasticity of local public outlays to proportional or to lump-sum grants in France.

The effect of subsidies on local public spending: an econometric estimate

The estimation of the empirical magnitude of the spending-effect of different types of subsidies can be tested using various theoretical assumptions. Gilbert and Derycke (1988) and Guengant (1985b) provide an approach based on the median voter model. They suppose that a local community supplies a composite local public good. As it has been pointed out by the literature dealing with the 'fly-paper effect', a crucial point is how the individual perceives the additional resource resulting from the subsidy. If he considers an increase in the subsidy as equivalent to an increase of his personal income (that is he is not subject to fiscal illusion) his demand for the public good and the following expenditure function will be given by one theoretical specification. If alternatively he perceives the difference between the two income sources, his demand for the public good will be governed by another specification. Finally, if the local government receives a 'matching grant', a third type of expenditure function results. Except for the case where the local public good is free, a proportional grant reduces the relative price of the public good in comparison with private goods. This substitution effect causes an increase in the demand for the public good, and this finally causes an increase in local tax rates.

The key-point of the so-called 'fly-paper effect' is that the greater the extra-spending resulting from an additional lump-sum grant, compared to the 'rational' extra-spending depending only on the income-elasticity of the individual demand and the individual tax price, the more likely is the fly-paper effect to occur. To date, the existence and the empirical magnitude of the fly-paper effect is questioned. Following Fisher (1982) the gap between the 'rational' grant-elasticity of demand and the actual one is statistically different from zero, and ranges between 0.2 and 1. Following other authors, the fly-paper effect is unlikely if the local communities are able to convert the subsidies into 'fungible resources' which accrue to the total financial budget; in this case, the municipalities can reduce tax rates as well as increasing expenditures (see Gilbert and Derycke, 1988).

A test of the median-voter model described above by Guengant (1985b) illustrates the selective effects of different types of grants on the local public expenditures in the French context. His econometric estimates relate to the *communes* (about 300) of one *département*, Ille et Vilaine in the west of France. The estimated elasticities are fully consistent with the theoretical assumptions:

(i)   The price-elasticity of matching grants is significantly different and higher than the lump-sum elasticity; and the latter is significantly different and higher than the income elasticity.

(ii) These results require some qualifications if we consider the cases of *communes* of different sizes and with different wealth; the more wealthy the *commune* is, the more likely (and the higher) the overspending behaviour which results from an increase in the *Dotation Ménages* of the DGF. In contrast, the poorest *communes* do not discriminate among different types of grants. They simply increase their expenditures at the same rate whichever type of subsidy they receive. In this case the efficiency of the replacements of lump-sum grants in lieu of matching-categorical or proportional grants must be seriously questioned.

Summary and conclusions

France has recently experienced major changes in the assignment of responsibilities and financial resources among the central state and the local governments. Among other consequences, the Reform Act has induced a move from a financial system with an open-ended matching grant system to a more closed-ended grant system. Undoubtedly, the system has gained in clarity, simplicity and (perhaps) in efficiency. But, in the meantime, cross-subsidization between local governments has been reintroduced by the back-door and categorical grants remain important for the smallest communities. In the present context of fiscal pressure and reductions in overall levels of finance, the economic consequences of the recent reforms are important. The discussion presented in this chapter provides some insights into the effects of different types of grants on local spending behaviour. The hypothesis of overspending cannot be rejected and hence the 'expenditure-effects' of grants are likely to be of very different magnitudes with respect to the type of grant, since block-grants or lump-sum grants do not necessarily differ in elasticity. It is clear that, as yet, the local financial regime in France has not developed all the desired features of a decentralized system. In particular local fiscal decisions are not independent of the form of central grants received.

Notes

1. The institutional framework of the French borrowing system was entirely dominated until recent years by a central public agency, the *Caisse des Dépôts et Consignations*, or more precisely by the network CDC, *Caisses d'Épargne, Caisse d'Aide à l'Equipement des Collectivités Locales* (*Crédit Local de France* since 1987). The resources of the CDC derive mainly from the savings of households (for further details, see Derycke and Gilbert, 1985).

References

Derycke, P.H. and Gilbert, G. (1985), 'The public debt of French local government', *Journal of Public Policy*, 5, 387–99.

Fisher, R.C. (1982), 'Income and grant effects on local expenditure: the fly-paper effect and other difficulties', *Journal of Urban Economics*, 12, 324–43.

Gilbert, G. and Derycke, P.H. (1988), *Economie Publique Locale*, Economica, Paris.

Guengant, A. (1983), *Equité territoriale et inégalités*, LITEC, Paris.

Guengant, A. (1985a), 'Le pouvoir redistributif de la DGF', *Revue d'Economie Urbaine et Régionale*, 1, 31–71.

Guengant, A. (1985b), 'L'influence des subventions sur la demande de services publics locaux', *Journées de microéconomie appliquée*, (mimeo), University of Rennes I, CREFAUR, Paris.

17 West Germany: from decentralization in theory to centralization in practice
Gerhard Bahrenberg

Introduction

The Federal Republic of Germany (FRG) has a structure of political power and responsibilities which is decentralized and fragmented to a far greater extent than almost any other European state. This is mainly because of the historical experiences, particularly with the Nazi regime. The German Reich was founded in 1871 when twenty-five German states formed a federation (not all of them joined voluntarily) with a substantial concentration of political power in Prussia. Nevertheless the traditional strength of local government (community) and regional self-government (the *Länder* or states) was preserved until the end of the Weimar Republic. But the self-government by the states and local communities was destroyed by the Nazis who established a highly centralized system. For example, community self-government was abolished through the Municipal Government Act (1935). Officials at the local level were no longer elected but appointed by the higher-level state and party authorities.

During the reconstruction period after World War II there was a strong consensus among West German politicians in favour of a federal system with weak federal government powers. This was aimed at making impossible the resurgence of a totalitarian state. The idea was reinforced by the western allies (especially by the French and Americans) and led to the establishment of a very complex and complicated political system. Its basic principles were laid down in the Basic Law of 1949 which defines the constitution of the FRG. The Basic Law especially strengthened the position of the states (*Länder*) as a counterbalance to the centralized power of the federation. Their distribution and characteristics are shown in Figure 17.1.

These developments are mirrored to some extent in the proportion of the expenditure being made by the three principal levels of government: central (federal or national), states and local communities (see Table 17.1.)

Because of the relatively weak position of the federal government in comparison to other European states, the development over most of the period since the establishment of the Basic Law has tended to grant more competence and power to the federal government. Indeed, until the end of

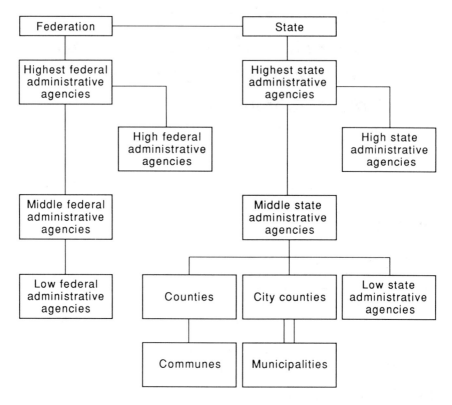

Figure 17.1 The structure of West German government and administration
Source: Berzing *et al.* (1978, p. 183)

Table 17.1 Expenditure of Reich states and local communities 1913–60

	1913	1928	1933	1938	1951	1955	1960
Reich (federal government)	33.1	40.3	41.0	74.9	55.4	47.9	50.3
States (Länder)	28.1	23.1	22.5	6.4	26.5	30.1	28.5
Communities	38.8	36.6	36.5	18.7	18.1	22.1	21.2
Total	100.0	100.0	100.0	100.0	100.0	100.0	100.0

Source: Hunxe, 1982

the 1970s, the political debate in West Germany was not on decentralization but on centralization. In broad outline, there was a request for more central power in order to enable the federal level to fulfil its responsibilities. A major question of current debate has been whether this process should continue or whether it has gone too far already. The rise of regional movements is one indicator that this question has gained greater attention at the moment. In order to analyse the question of the appropriate level of decentralization one has to look at the aims, functions and responsibilities of the different territorial authorities, their economic power (revenues), and their degree of independence (from the other authorities) as well as other issues.

The political and administrative system: responsibilities of the territorial authorities[1]

Federal–state relations

There exist four levels of territorial government with the right of self-government in West Germany: the federal government, the states (*Länder*), the counties (*Kreise*) and the communities (*Gemeinden*): see Figure 17.2. The counties and communities represent the level of local government which is regulated by state laws (*Ländergesetz*). Therefore there are differences at this level because of the differing constitutions of the states. However, the responsibilities of local government are virtually the same in all states.

A key characteristic of the West German constitution is the relation between the two constitutional parts: the federal government (*Bund*) and the states. It is important to note that the *Länder* do not merely execute federal law (for example as high or middle federal administrative agencies) but also have their own legislation which gives them the character of independent states. The division of responsibilities between the *Bund* and *Länder* (and the related allocation of political powers) is based on the division of legislative powers determined by the Basic Law,[2] and this determines the allocation of expenditures between the different policy areas (see Table 17.2). The Basic Law from the point of view of the *Bund*, distinguishes between exclusive, concurrent and residual legislation. The *Bund* has the right of exclusive legislation in matters such as foreign affairs, defence, nationality, currency, federal railways, air traffic, postal and telecommunications services. These are fields that lie well beyond the possible responsibility of a single state and concern the republic as a whole (see Article 73 of the Basic Law, and Table 17.2).

The most important fields of concurrent legislation (Article 74) are civil and criminal law; economic law; labour law; the production and utilization of nuclear energy for peaceful purposes, protection against hazards arising from the release of nuclear energy or from ionizing radiation, and the disposal of radioactive substances; protection standards in the fields of marketing of food, drink and tobacco, of the necessities of life, fodder; preservation of the natural environment; and road traffic.

Residual legislation (that is those subjects that are not defined as belonging to exclusive or concurrent legislation in the Basic Law) is the responsibility of the *Länder*. The main areas included are education, police and internal security, mass communication media which are a prominent part of interior politics and in the process of forming public opinion (see Table 17.2).

It is essential to note that the role of the *Länder* in concurrent legislation

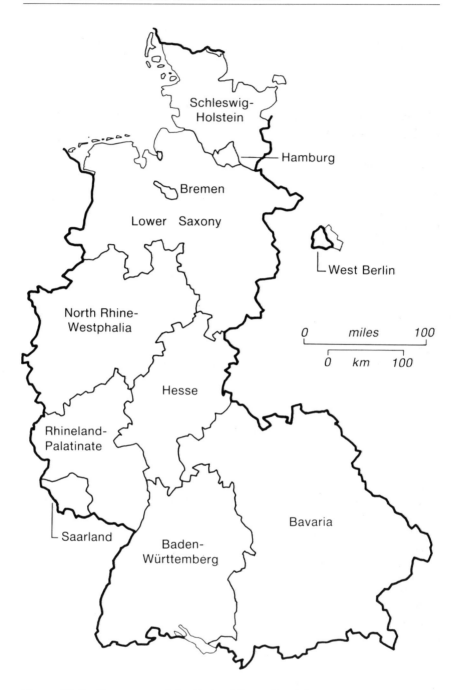

Figure 17.2 The states of the Federal Republic of Germany

Population size and area of states in West Germany as shown in Figure
17.2 on page 258

State	Area (km²)	Population (000)	Population density (number per km²)
Schleswig-Holstein	15,728	2,613	166
Hamburg	755	1,571	2,082
Lower Saxony	47,439	7,196	152
Bremen	404	654	1,618
North Rhine-Westphalia	34,067	16,677	490
Hesse	21,114	5,544	263
Rhineland-Palatinate	19,848	3,611	182
Baden-Württemberg	35,751	9,327	261
Bavaria	70,553	11,026	156
Saarland	2,569	1,042	406
West Berlin	480	1,879	3,914
Federation	248,709	61,140	246

Source: Statistiches Bundesamt, 1987

was never very strong and has steadily declined. The reason is that the
federal government has the right to legislate in concurrent matters if 'the
maintenance of legal or economic unity especially the maintenance of the
uniformity of living conditions beyond the territory of any one *Land*,
necessitates such regulation' (Basic Law Article 72 (3)). Thus in political
practice concurrent matters are exclusively regulated by federal law. This
loss of political power by the *Länder* is to some degree balanced by (i) the
participation of the *Länder* in the process of federal legislation; and (ii) the
fact that the *Länder* are the main executors and administrators of federal
laws and decrees.

In addition to the federal parliament (*Bundestag*) the federal council
(*Bundesrat*), the second legislative chamber, is responsible for enacting
federal laws. The members of the *Bundesrat* are delegates from the respective state governments. The delegates of each state vote *en bloc* according
to the instructions from their state government. All laws that affect the
constitutional interests of the states must be approved by the *Bundesrat*. All
other laws have to pass the *Bundesrat* whose possible veto may be overruled
by the *Bundestag*. The vast majority of laws belong to the first group
because of the administrative functions of the *Länder* regarding federal law.
This gives them a potentially strong position in the legislation process.[3]

Because of their executive and administrative functions the *Länder* can
circumvent or retard the application of federal law for formal reasons. This
sometimes means a direct influence on federal policy. An example has been
the refusal, in 1987–8, of the state government of North Rhine–Westphalia
to allow the operation of the plutonium-producing nuclear power plant at
Kalkar.[4]

While the influence of the *Länder* on the policy of the federal government
has steadily increased since 1949, the degree of autonomy of the *Länder* has

Table 17.2 Net expenditures of territorial authorities by policy area in West Germany, 1984

Policy areas	Federation		States		Communities	
	Absolute in 10⁶ DM	%	Absolute in 10⁶ DM	%	Absolute in 10⁶ DM	%
General administration	6,404	2.5	11,963	6.0	12,978	11.4
Foreign affairs	9,045	3.6	58	0		
Defence	49,542	19.7				
Public security and administration of justice	1,789	0.7	19,559	9.9	4,077	3.6
Education (primary and secondary level)	20	0	37,547	19.0	11,283	10.0
Education (tertiary level), research	12,666	5.0	25,234	12.7	2,316	2.0
Culture	128	0.1	2,826	1.4	3,032	2.7
Social security	81,480	32.3	15,191	7.7	24,127	21.3
— family, social and youth-aid	17,285	6.9	9,765	4.9	21,255	18.7
Health, sports,	1,387	0.6	8,844	4.5	25,462	22.5
recreation, hospitals	919	0.4	6,316	3.2	18,945	16.7
Housing, urban and regional planning	1,896	0.8	9,144	4.6	4,013	3.5
Communal services	118	0	1,589	0.8	15,752	13.9
Assistance to the economy	9,458	3.8	9,272	4.7	1,580	1.4
Transportation, communication	12,629	5.0	8,690	4.4	6,341	5.6
Others (incl. economic enterprises and general finance)	65,378	26.0	48,089	24.3	2,409	2.2
Total	251,940	100.0	198,006	100.0	113,370	100.0

Source: Statistisches Bundesamt (1987)

decreased. The strengthening of all kinds of distant, interregional functional ties within West Germany since World War II has necessarily led to policy adjustments between the various *Länder*, and between the *Länder* and the federal government — even in those fields that were formerly the sole domain of the *Länder* (that is the 'residual' matters in the sense outlined above). The best example is perhaps education. With the increasing mobility of the population between states, the different regulations of each state with regard to the curriculum of secondary schools (for example, the order of foreign languages) posed severe problems and created a concern for unification. Adjustments between the *Länder* have been taken care of by 'conferences of the state ministers' (*Ministerkonferenzen der Länder*). Where such conferences have been established they continue to meet regularly. In addition to inter-*Land* co-operation several commissions between *Bund* and *Länder* have been founded in order to facilitate co-operation.

A particular interesting form of co-operation of the *Bund* and *Länder* has been so-called 'joint tasks' (*Gemeinschaftsaufgaben*), which were included in the Basic Law (Article 91a). The 'joint tasks' concern political fields which originally belonged exclusively to the responsibilities of the *Länder*, but were 'important to society as a whole and [make] . . . federal participation . . . necessary for the improvement of living conditions' (Article 91a (1)). Three 'joint tasks' have been established (see Article 91a (1)):

— expansion and construction of institutions of higher education including university clinics (tertiary level of education);
— improvement of regional economic structure;
— improvement of the agrarian structure and coast protection.

These tasks were obviously too large to be solved by the states concerned — at least in terms of finance. By meeting one-half of the expenditures the federal government has helped to improve regional development but at the same time it has gained significant influence.

Further co-operation derives from contracts between the states and the federal government. These have been used as a means of developing initiatives on specific topics. Finally, the objective of maintaining the uniformity of living conditions in the federal republic has been used to motivate so-called 'frame legislation' (*Rahmengesetzgebung*) by the federal government in areas of state responsibility (for example in the field of 'regional planning' (*Raumordnung*), protection of nature and the countryside). Although this frame legislation has been opposed by some states it has been effective in diminishing the competence of the states.

In summary, it may be said that at the upper level territorial policy has become more centralized (that is *Länder* autonomy has decreased), but centralization has been accompanied by the more powerful participation of the *Länder*. This development corresponds to the functional requirements of a 'modern' industrial and urban society with a high degree of short- and long-term horizontal mobility.

Local government

Article 28 of the Basic Law guarantees the self-government of the communities and counties. The constitutional framework of local government is determined by the respective state laws. Differences between the states mainly result from the way in which the former occupying powers after the war framed the different state constitutions. Nevertheless the responsibilities of local government are fairly uniform throughout West Germany:

(1) In the same way that the *Länder* execute federal law, the local

governments carry out actions which are determined by federal and/or state laws (for example in tax collection, health care, housing, social aid).

(2) Local government's responsibilities include physical and social infrastructure such as school construction and maintenance; public transport; provision of gas, water, electricity; cultural activities; refuse disposal; land use and zoning. For these purposes they own and run various public utility enterprises (see Table 17.2). If the communities are too small to perform these functions several of them may constitute a county which performs local government functions. Some large and important cities perform all county functions themselves and are called 'city-counties' (*Kreisfreie Städte*) (see Figure 17.1). But there is no general rule for the threshold size necessary to become a city-county.

In addition the communes can build 'common purposes associations' (*Zweckverbände*) for specific purposes (for example transportation or sewage disposal). These associations are an important aspect of German local government and there are about 2,000 for different purposes.

In summary local government plays an important role in the daily life of its citizens. It has a large degree of autonomy in theory since the supervisory powers of the *Länder* are mainly restricted to controlling the legality of actions. Limits to autonomy exist because of the insufficient financial resources of the local authorities.

Interactions

There are many interactions between the different levels of territorial authority. As a result, particularly for the state and federal level, the decision process in many areas of public services is rather complex and not easy to understand (see Figure 17.1).[5] In addition, decisions may not be very efficient in terms of time and money, and sometimes the political responsibility for decisions is concealed. To give one example, the following list exhibits the range of institutions engaged in the provision of roads in Niedersachen (see Benzing *et al.*, 1978):

— Federal ministry of transportation: planning and financing, preparation of laws concerning the federal long-distance highways (*Bundesfern-strassen*).
— Federal research institute for roads: technical guidelines for road construction.
— State minister of transportation: participation in the planning of the federal long-distance highways, planning of state roads, construction of federal long-distance highways as an agent of the federation.
— State office of administration: formal procedures of plan identifications (*Planfeststellungsverfahren*).
— Road construction office of the respective district: detailed planning,

road construction and maintenance.

— Counties: regional planning of roads as part of regional infrastructure planning (in Niedersachen the counties perform the task of regional planning), construction and maintenance of county roads.

— Cities with a population of more than 80,000: planning, construction and maintenance of the local city section of federal long-distance highways and state roads.

— Communities: construction and maintenance of local community roads.

The financial system: the material base for self-government of the territorial authorities

In order to fulfil their responsibilities, the different levels of government need financial resources. They receive these mainly in the form of taxes. A major question is whether the system of revenue collection and distribution is appropriate to maintaining the strength of self-government of the states and local authorities, and leaves them enough freedom to exercise political discretions.

The revenues of the different administrative authorities derive from fees and charges (for services at the local level) and from taxes. The tax system is regulated by federal law but the taxes are levied by the states and collected at the county level. The rules for the allocation of taxes to the territorial authorities and the sharing system have changed several times since the Basic Law was formulated. At the moment it works as follows (see Table 17.3). There exist four different types of taxes. Three of these, federal taxes, state taxes and community taxes go exclusively to their respective levels of government. A fourth category, of common taxes or shared revenues, is distributed to the different authorities according to specific formulae (see Table 17.3). Shared revenues make up three-quarters of all tax revenues. It should be noted that 50 per cent of all tax revenues go to the *Bund*, but only 45 per cent of all expenditures are made by the *Bund*. The states receive 35 per cent of tax revenues and make 35 per cent of expenditures; the community and community associations receive 14 per cent of tax revenues and make 20 per cent of expenditures. The residual 3 per cent of tax revenues go to the European Community. These data can be directly derived by comparing Tables 17.2 and 17.3.

The sharing of revenue already demonstrates the dependence of local government on upper level authorities. The financial gap on the side of the communities is closed mainly by grants from their respective states. The states derive the resources for these grants from the federal government. Grants are part of the complex revenue sharing system. Before this system is described it should be borne in mind that the federal government receives about 95 per cent of its income from taxes, while taxes account for only about 70 per cent of state and 40 per cent of local government revenues; the residual percentage is paid by grants, fees, charges and other sources. The importance of grants indicates the potentially strong influence

Table 17.3   Tax revenues of territorial authorities in West Germany, 1986

	Federation		States		Communities	
	Absolute in 10^6 DM	%	Absolute in 10^6 DM	%	Absolute in 10^6 DM	%
Federal taxes	56,350	24.9				
Customs	5,239	2.3				
Oil and petrol tax	25,644	11.3				
Tobacco tax	14,480	6.4				
Other consumption taxes (coffee, spirits etc.)	6,565	2.9				
Others	4,422	2.0				
State taxes			21,255	13.4		
Automobile tax			9,356	5.9		
Capital and inheritance tax			6,286	4.0		
Beer tax			1,263	0.6		
Others			4,350	2.8		
Commune taxes					41,156	60.1
Property tax					7,637	11.2
Business tax					31,987	46.7
'Bagatelle' taxes					1,532	2.2
Common taxes	169,849	75.1	136,508	86.5	27,317	39.9
Individual income taxes	77,398	34.2	77,398	49.1	27,317	39.9
Corporate income taxes	20,211	8.9	20,211	12.8		
Value-added taxes	72,240	31.9	38,899	24.7		
Total	226,199	100.0	157,763	100.0	68,473	100.0

Source: Statistisches Bundesamt, 1987

of the federal government on state and local politics.

The tax revenues of a single state or of a single community depend mostly on its population size and its economic strength. As a result revenue sharing is necessary in order to maintain the uniformity of living conditions with the republic. The sharing system includes:

(1) 'Vertical sharing' (payments of the federal government to the poorer states — *Ergänzungszuweisungen*).
(2) 'Horizontal sharing' between richer and poorer states (*Länderfinanzausgleich*).
(3) Grants and subsidies from the federal government to the states within the framework of 'joint tasks' or for special purposes. These do not formally belong to the sharing system but may play an important role in specific cases. Since they are appropriated, they reinforce the influence of the federal government on the states. These

payments vary from year to year and it is almost impossible to study their regional impact systematically. The payments accounted for 8,328 million DM in 1983 and 9,363 million DM in 1985. In 1983 the states of Hamburg, Bremen, Rhineland-Pfalz and Saarland received transfers closely in line with their population share (see Bundesminister für Raumordnung, Bauwesen und Städtebau, 1986, pp. 86–7). It should be noted that grants and subsidies are significantly higher than the combined volume of the vertical and horizontal sharing. Sharing in 1986 amounted to only about 4,400 million DM. This represents about 2 per cent of the expenditures of the states and less than 1 per cent of the expenditures of all authorities. Therefore the recent controversial discussion on changes of these two components of the sharing system seems to be ridiculous. But one has to remember that a major part of the transfers contributes significantly to the budget of the small states such as Bremen which had a budget of about 3,800 million DM (including the community budgets of the city of Bremen and city of Bremerhaven).

(4) The revenues shared with the communities: involving grants from the states to their communities and transfers of taxes between *Bund* and *Gemeinden*.

In general the financial situation of the states is satisfactory. The chief problems for the states have resulted from the poor revenue base of the communities. A further important problem is the disparity between small and/or economically weak states and large, economically strong states. The question is whether the differences between the states should be equalized in the future (as in the past) by procedures of tax sharing, or by a territorial reorganization of the states. The first alternative would have the disadvantage of dependency by the smaller states on their fellow larger ones and on the federation. Second, it would make necessary rather complicated and contested formulae for computation of the resource transfers required.

In my view a territorial reorganization represents a better alternative. Article 29 of the Basic Law allows for a territorial reorganization and the so-called 'Ernst-Commission' presented some proposals (see Bundesminister des Innern, 1973). This proposed reducing the number of states by integrating the smaller ones (for example Hamburg, Bremen, Schleswig-Holstein, Saarland) into the larger units. This would provide units which are large enough for self-government at this level, and that have roughly the same size and economic resources as each other. However, the chances of realizing these proposals are not high because a major loss of political power would be required by some political groups.

The disparities between the *Länder* are overshadowed by the more severe financial problems existing at the level of local government. These have recently received a lot of attention (see for example Akademie für Raumforschung und Landesplanung, 1985; Bennett, 1984; Bennett and Krebs, 1987; Bunderministerium für Raumordnung, Bauwesen und

Table 17.4 Revenues of communities, 1983

	Billion DM	%
Tax revenues	48.61	38.46
among which		
— Community share of income tax	21.73	17.19
— Business tax	19.94	15.78
— Property tax	6.18	4.9
Fees and charges	18.22	14.42
Grants from states	22.05	17.45
('communal revenue sharing')		
— General grants	13.10	10.37
— Specific purpose grants*	8.95	7.08
Credits	10.88	8.61
Other income	26.62	21.06
Total	126.38	100.00

*Including a small proportion of federal payments
Source: Sander (1987, p. 385)

Städtebau, 1984; Sander, 1987; Zimmerman, 1981). The financial problems derive from the composition of the revenues of the communities (see Table 17.4). They can be summarized as follows:

(1) Those tax revenues which are autonomous local taxes account for a mere 20 per cent of all revenues. Together with fees and charges, which are collected for local services, only 35 per cent of all revenues are locally autonomous. This means that almost two-thirds of total community revenues rely on other levels of government. Under these circumstances the term 'self-government' can hardly be applied to local authorities.

(2) Fees and charges are too small in order to cover the expenditures of the communities for the provision of the services they support. This low level of cost coverage is a result of the 'social welfare state-principle'. Covering of the costs of service provision by grants has tended to lead to an economically ineffective provision of services, a confusion of lines of accountability and a dependency on higher levels of government which have not produced adequate resources.

(3) The main local tax is the business tax. This consists of two elements; a profits tax (*Gewerbeertragssteuer*) and a capital or assets tax (*Gewerbekapitalsteuer*).[6] The problem with the business tax is that it follows the location of business and thus produces strong disparities between areas. It is pro-cyclical while local expenditures are constant, and it also often shows a counter-cyclical tendency. This creates considerable problems for the communities. A major example is the increase in the need for 'social aid' expenditures in recent years. These support welfare payments and have moved in the

opposite direction to the yield of revenues. Because of these disadvantages the *Bund* has sought to reduce the level of business tax through several changes in tax legislation since the end of 1969. However, it is still the major local tax and many researchers argue for a replacement by other taxes (see Bennett and Krebs, 1987 for a summary of new proposals; Sander 1987). A problem remains, however, that under most proposals the principal dilemma would continue to exist, namely that every autonomous local tax is in some way dependent upon the size and economic strength of the community.

(3) The system of grants (see Table 17.4) has also been criticized. General grants depend on the tax potential of a community and its local 'need'. The main measure of need takes into account population size and other factors. Therefore, the general grants mainly take the form of a 'per-capita-grant' which favours the larger communities. In addition richer states can pay higher grants to their communities than poorer states. Specific-purpose grants are composed of current-expenditure grants and of capital-investment grants. The last type, used for example for urban transportation and urban renewal programmes, undermines local autonomy directly but in practice has favoured the older and larger cities (Bennett, 1984, p. 20). In addition, it had a social bias towards middle- and higher-income groups (see Zimmerman, 1981). As with general grants, tax potential and population size are the most important determinants affecting the level of current-expenditure specific grants received by a community.

At the moment there is widespread feeling of financial crisis in the communities. This is based on the continuing high unemployment rate, especially in the older industrial areas. Long-term unemployment increases community expenditures for social services and, in particular, for social-aid payments to the long-term jobless. In Germany it is important to be aware that there is an unusual arrangement by which the federal government pays for the short-term unemployed. However, after a specified time of being jobless (depending on the duration of preceding employment) the communities are obliged to take over the burden of payment. The resulting situation is so critical that some state governments are pressing the *Bundesrat* for a law that places the burden of social-aid payments in the poorer states on the federal government. Apart from these current problems a general reform of community finances is required if the autonomy of local government is to be secured.

A further continuing problem is the dependency of local revenues on population size. In the case of the states a territorial reorganization has been recommended (see above). This strategy cannot be applied to solve the resource problems of communities and counties. As a matter of fact the population size distribution of communities and counties or city-counties was extremely skewed, with a large number of rather small communities. Prior to 1967 some local governments had a population of less than 100

Table 17.5 Results of the territorial reform of local government

	1967	1980
Number of communities	24,235	8,409
Number of city-counties (municipalities)	137	91
Number of counties	425	236
Average population of communities and municipalities	2,469	7,226
Average population of counties and city-counties	107,056	187,829

while other communities had more than one million inhabitants; in total there were more than 24,000 communities. Between 1967 and 1977 a territorial reform took place which reduced the number of communities to 8,409 (see Table 17.5). The goals of the reform were (see Wagener, 1969; Kommunale Gebietsreform, 1973) to integrate the very small communities and counties into larger units in order:

(1) To reduce the costs of administration by realizing economies of scale;
(2) To provide better and more differentiated services and thereby increase the attractiveness of the former small communities for business and population (because many service facilities have to meet specific threshold requirements);
(3) To diminish the differences in living conditions between rural areas (with a lot of small communities) and the rich communities in the agglomerations.

As a result of the reform the number of counties and communities was drastically reduced and their average population size increased. In particular the very small communities disappeared. In addition many of the 8,409 independent communities merged into specific 'associations' which became the real decision units for the main local government activities. Sometimes the population of the new communities and 'associations' had difficulties in indentifying with the new units and some of them had to be dissolved. But in general the reform was accepted since the territorial reorganization of local government executed what had already become a reality for most people: the expansion of human activity spaces.

One might argue that the small communities are still too small and that the discrepancies in population size between the communities are still too large to allow a uniformity of living conditions to be reached in West Germany. But more important is the establishment of a base for local self-government. Such a base should allow for local solutions to local problems instead of central solutions — not because of irrational and romantic feelings for home (*Heimat*), smallness and a 'life-world easy to survey', but because local (small) solutions are in most cases better than central (big) solutions — even in functional terms. In order to improve local self-government and the degree of local autonomy the creeping decline induced by state and central government policy has to be stopped. An appropriate measure would be to increase the communities' share of common taxes and state grants. Necessary for such a financial reform is a political will at all levels of government which rests on the confidence that small (local) problems are better solved by local people. The fathers of the West German constitution had this confidence. I don't see any reason why they should have been wrong.

Notes

1. For general introductions to the political and government system of the Federal Republic of Germany see Ellwein (1983) and Sontheimer (1984). Brief English introductions are offered by Conradt (1978), Goldman (1974), Johnson (1973) and Neumann (1966).
2. For a brief introduction to the Basic Law in English, see Goldman, (1974).
3. In case of a conflict between *Bundestag* and *Bundesrat* the Committee for the Joint Consideration of Bills (*Vermittlungsausschuss*) is asked for a solution. Both chambers have the same number of members on this committee.
4. Although nuclear politics belongs to concurrent legislation (see above) and is regulated by federal law which allowed the construction of the power plant.
5. For instance expenditures for primary and secondary education are to be made by the states (mainly for salaries of teachers) and by the communities (mainly for construction of buildings). But the responsibility for school provision lies at the state level. Similarly, as can be seen from Table 17.2, all territorial authorities spend some money of transportation.
6. Until 1979 there was a third element, the payroll tax. This is also a minor local property tax (*Grundsteuer*).

References

Akademie für Raumforschung und Landesplanung (1985), *Räumliche Aspekte des kommunalen Finanzausgleichs*, Vincentz, (Veröffentlichungen der Akademie für Raumforschung und Landesplanung, Forschungs- und Sitzungsberichte No. 159), Hanover.

Bennett, R.J. (1984), 'The finance of cities in West Germany', *Progress in Planning*, 21, 1–62.

Bennett, R.J. and Krebs, G. (1987), 'Local business taxes in Britain and Germany: assessment of comparative burdens 1960–84 by use of the "costs of capital" methodology', *Government and Policy: Environment and Planning C*, 5, 25–41.

Benzing, A. (1978), *Verwaltungsgeographie. Grundlagen, Aufgaben und Wirkungen der Verwaltung im Raum*, Heymanns, Cologne.

Bundesminister des Innern (ed.) (1973), *Bericht der Sachverständigenkommission für die Neugliederung des Bundesgebietes. Vorschläge zur Neugliederung des Bundesgebietes gemäs Art. 29 des Grundgesetzes*, Heymanns, Cologne.

Bundesminister für Raumordnung, Bauwesen und Städtebau (1984), *Kommunaler*

Finanzausgleich und zentralörtliches System, Selbstverlag (Schriftenreihe 06 'Raumord-nung' des Bundesministers für Raumordnung, Bauwesen and Städtebau 06.052), Bonn.

Bundesminister für Raumordnung, Bauwesen und Städtebau (1986), *Raumord-nungsbericht 1986*, Selbstverlag (Schriftenreihe 'Raumordnung' des Bundesministers für Raumordnung, Bauwesen and Städtebau, Sonderheft), Bonn.

Conradt, D.P. (1978), *The German Polity*, Longman, New York and London.

Ellwein, T. (1983), *Das Regierungssystem der Bundesrepublik Deutschland*, Westdeutscher Verlag, Opladen.

Goldman, G. (1974), *The German Political System*, Random House, New York.

Hunke, H. (1982), 'Die Gestaltung des Finanzsystems zur Verwirklichung der Ziele von Raumordnung und Landesplanung', in Akademie für Raumforschung und Landesplanung (eds), *Grundriss der Raumordnung*, Vincentz, Hanover, 426–52.

Johnson, N. (1973), *Government in the Federal Republic of Germany: The Executive at Work*, Pergamon Press, Oxford.

Kommunale Gebietsreform in den Ländern der Bundesrepublik Deutschland (1973), Berichte zur Deutschen Landeskunde 47, 5–147.

Neumann, R.G. (1966), *The Government of the German Federal Republic*, Harper and Row, New York.

Sander, L. (1987), *Aufgaben und Einnahmen der Kommunen in der Bundesrepublik Deutschland. Eine ökonomische und rechtliche Analyse in Lichte der Kollektivgütertheorie*, Lit (Empirische Wirtschaftsforschung 4), Münster.

Sontheimer, K. (1984), *Grundzüge des politischen Systems der Bundesrepublik Deutschland*, Piper, Munich.

Statistisches Bundesamt (1987), *Statistiches Jahrbuch für die Bundesrepublik Deutschland 1987*, W. Kohlhammer, Wiesbaden.

Wagener, F. (1969), *Neubau der Verwaltung. Gliederung der öffentlichen Aufgaben und ihrer Träger nach Effektivatät und Integrationswert*, Duncker and Humboldt (Schriftenreihe der Hochschule Speyer 41), Berlin.

Zimmermann, H. (1981), *Fiscal Policy vis-à-vis Communities in the Federal Republic of Germany*, Abteilung für Finanzwirtschaft, Research Report No. 1, University of Marburg.

18 Finland: present and futures in local government

Eero Nurminen

The forms of public administration in Finland

Finland has a parliamentary, democratic system of government based upon the tripartite division of powers. The legislative power of the country is vested in parliament and the president. The highest executive power is held by the president, elected for a period of six years. The most essential organ of state power is parliament because of its legislative and budget powers. The administration of the country is directed by the Council of State, that is the ministers and the twelve ministries. Under each ministry, there are twenty-two national boards which carry out the tasks that fall within their respective administrative sectors. The mixed system of ministries and national boards is the result of an historical development which has gone through a number of stages, traces of it deriving from both Swedish and Russian rule (Nousiainen, 1971, p. 283).

Figure 18.1 shows that the three-tier hierarchy of public administration comprises at the intermediate level the provincial governments, state agencies and joint authorities (municipal federations). Finland's system of self-government is different from comparable systems in many other nations in that territorial self-government has gone no further than the municipal level; a higher type of self-government, within a broader territorial framework, has not been organized (Nousiainen, 1971). The matter has been discussed several times and proposals to this effect have been made recently. This has in turn meant that certain important functions of municipal administration requiring broadly based regional co-operation have been handled by large, statutory joint authorities; some of them may include all municipalities in one of Finland's twelve administrative provinces (Finnish Local Government 1983, p. 17).

The provincial governments are regional agencies of the central government headed by governors appointed by the president of the republic. The provincial government looks after the province's needs and promotes its development and the welfare of its inhabitants. Municipal authorities are supervised by the provincial government which in turn is responsible to the ministry of the interior. The position of Aland (*Ahvenanmaa*) as a semi-autonomous province is safeguarded by the Self-Government Act of 1951.

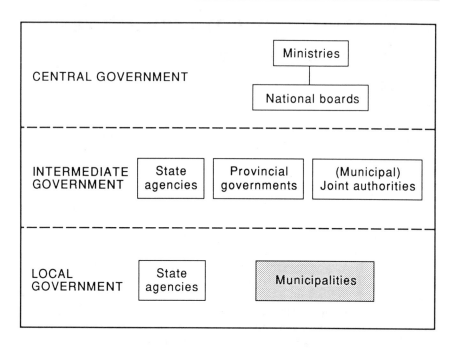

Figure 18.1 The three-tier hierarchy of public administration in Finland

In addition to provincial governments intermediate-level administration includes separate district organizations of state agencies. These authorities are not subordinated to provincial governments but report directly to ministries or national boards. In order to guarantee a similar level of services to all citizens, many of these districts are divided into smaller units (from two to five municipalities which have an office common to all these municipalities. This applies especially to services directly to people (for example health and social services, taxation) or which need special local personnel to take care of the duties (public roads and waterways). There are no local-level state authorities of a truly general character.

The Finnish constitution states that municipal administration must be based on self-government by the citizens, but this is not defined in greater detail. However, it is generally agreed that the most important features of local government are the following: (i) municipal authority is general and broadly based, (ii) the power of decision resides with persons elected by direct ballot, (iii) the state can assign new functions to the municipalities or take others away solely on the basis of law, and (iv) the municipalities have the right to levy taxes (Finnish Local Government, 1983, p. 7). The term 'municipal democracy' is often used to refer to the Finnish system of local government. This term is used to indicate that local government is democratic and also it depicts the close relationship between municipal residents and the local government bodies which administer their affairs.

The present system of local government in Finland is the result of a long historical development. Earlier, a special institution, the parish *Thing*, which was a combination of local assembly and law court, was created to deal with matters of public interest. By the beginning of the fifteenth century, the *Things* had evolved into a network of district councils. Administrative responsibility was gradually transferred to the church authorities which undertook important local government functions such as the care of the poor and education (Finnish Local Government, 1983). The Finnish municipality, in the modern sense of the word, was created in the nineteenth century. A statute enacted in 1865 made Finnish rural municipalities self-governing by separating ecclesiastical and secular administration at the local level. In cities a system of local government, in the present sense of the expression, was implemented by statute in 1873. In principle, this transferred power in the cities from a single estate, the burghers, to all inhabitants.

The fundamental regional units

The fundamental regional unit in Finland is a municipality (*kunta*). Each municipality has its own boundaries, which are fixed by the Council of State (government). With the exception of certain sea areas, the whole of the country is divided into municipalities, which currently number 461. The functions and powers of each municipality are limited to its area, although this does not prevent intermunicipal co-operation. A new Municipal Boundaries Act, in force since 1977, permits changes in boundaries to be made by ruling of the Council of State. Municipalities can be reduced or expanded in area, they can be merged or new ones created (Finnish Local Government, 1983).

It should be noted that the municipalities are units of administrative self-government and that the distinction between urban and other municipalities does not depend on their size or density. Many rural municipalities have a greater population than the smallest urban municipalities and, on the other hand, there are regions of rural character inside the boundaries of several urban municipalities (STV, 1985/86, XXVII). The land area of the municipalities varies from 15,172 square kilometres (*Inari*) to 6 square kilometres (*Kauniainen*). The largest municipality is 1.5 times larger by area than the Province of Uusimaa (STV, 1985/86, Table 16). As a result of historical development, local government legislation has contained different regulations for urban and rural areas. An additional intermediate form between urban and rural municipalities was the incorporated urban district. The first such units were created after the middle of the nineteenth century. The aim was to form regional centres (city-regions) where urban means of livelihood could be practised, above all trade. The 1976 Local Government Act abolished incorporated urban districts as an independent form of municipality. All twenty-one then in existence were made cities by law. It should be noted that the Finnish language makes no distinction between 'town' and 'city' (Finnish Local Government, 1983).

Although the present act preserves towns and cities as an independent type of municipality in Finland, it is interesting to note that it no longer contains special regulations for them. The regulations are the same for all municipalities. Nowadays town or city is merely a term indicating a particular kind of municipal structure. In special legislation, however, a difference continues to be made between cities and other municipalities. This applies to building laws, for instance, and also to other regulations governing the contributions made by the state to municipal finances. In general, differences between municipal forms, particularly with respect to legislation concerning financial aid from the state, are disappearing. However, these differences do continue to exist in certain important fields. In most such instances cities have greater responsibilities than other municipalities. In earlier times cities had to maintain special functions, for example a city court, or a police department, but these special responsibilities of the cities were abolished by legislation in 1978. This legislation, together with the present Local Government Act, largely means that the city as a legal entity is disappearing in Finland. On the other hand, the concept will be preserved, as in other parts of the work, to indicate a specific type of urban regional unit and a functional centre (Finnish Local Government, 1983, p. 10).

The Finnish system of local government operates with the concept of a municipality having 'members'. It should be emphasized that the 'members' of the municipality include not only persons living there, but also companies, associations and other bodies located within its territory. Membership in a municipality is legally based on one of several of the following factors: (i) domicile, (ii) ownership or possession of real estate in the municipality, (iii) a business or professional practice there. The rights and responsibilities of a member of a municipality depend on the conditions under which such membership was acquired. Physical persons, whose membership is by virtue of domicile, are in a special position. Both their rights and their responsibilities are considerably more extensive than those of other members. They alone are eligible to vote and hold elective office. They also pay municipal tax on their personal incomes (wage income). Real estate owners and many corporations are also members. Moreover, entitlement to membership may, as was stated above, stem from running a business or practising a profession. Thus a person (physical or juridical) can be a member of more than one municipality at the same time. Indeed, many companies with nation-wide operations are members of a great many. Corporate income is also subject to municipal taxation.

The machinery of local administration

In each municipality in Finland there is a representative council (municipal council) and Board, and an administration authority (office) qualified as a fundamental machinery of administration. The highest decision-making powers in the municipality are held by the municipal council (see Figure 18.2) chosen every four years in direct elections. At the elections, each municipality constitutes an electoral district. The electoral districts are divided into polling districts. The population of a polling district must not

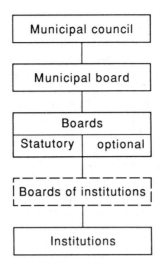

Figure 18.2 The representative machinery of local administration in Finland

exceed 3,000 inhabitants. The number of municipal councillors elected in a municipality depends on the number of inhabitants registered in a municipality for census purposes, as shown in the table below. Deputies who serve when regular council members are unable to be present or are disqualified from participation are chosen in the same elections.

Number of inhabitants	Number of councillors
less than 2,000	17
2,001–4,000	21
4,001–8,000	27
8,001–15,000	35
15,001–30,000	43
30,001–60,000	51
60,001–120,000	59
120,001–250,000	67
250,001–400,000	75
over 400,000	85

(Source: Kunnallislaki, 1976, para. 38)

The municipal board (in cities the city board) is set up by the council. It has at least seven members and their personal deputies appointed for two-year terms. In administering the municipality, the municipal board is responsible for: planning; finances and accounting; supervising the work of committees, local government officers and employees; monitoring the liquidity of the municipality and implementing its budget; and in general seeing to the daily administrative routines. In addition to those separately required by law, the council can also set up committees to carry out specific tasks under the supervision of the municipal boards. There are, in fact, two kinds of committees: statutory and optional. The former are required by law, while the latter are established at the council's discretion (Finnish Local Government, 1983).

Even though the number of full-time local government officials has steadily increased as administration has developed, the significance of elected municipal representatives in local government in Finland is still central. Indeed, decision-making power at all levels of the municipal organization rests with politically elected representatives (the council, the boards, committees, and the boards of various institutions). Only in minor matters does the law permit decision-making power to be transferred to local government officials, and even then such matters must be carefully specified in the municipal regulations approved by the council (Finnish Local Government, 1983). The number of elected representatives in all municipal councils in Finland has increased from 12,408 in 1960 to 12,881 in 1984. About 3,900 representatives are members of town councils, but the number of persons in all representative authorities in towns and cities is about 36,600 (Soumen Kunnalliskalenteri, 1961, p. 525; Soumen Kaupunkiliitto, 1987a, p. 75).

In 1983 the largest groups of the municipal personnel consisted of persons who worked in health care (35 per cent), education (29 per cent) and social services (20 per cent). Only 4 per cent of the full-time employees worked in general administration (Soumen Kunnalliskalenteri, 1985-8, p. 19). Earlier, in 1964, almost 70 per cent of the full-time officials in rural municipalities were primary school teachers (Soumen Kunnalliskalenteri, 1965, p. 38).

It is natural that municipalities in Finland co-operate in many ways. There are many different kinds of joint functions. Two municipalities may have a single fire chief or building inspector, or several municipalities may jointly maintain an institution, etc. When, for example, a joint post is established, or when one municipality performs a function on behalf of another, co-operation is generally fairly easy to arrange. The municipalities conclude an agreement, and then proceed on that basis. Co-operation can also be based on identical resolutions passed by two or more municipal councils. When one municipality carries out a particular function on behalf of another, it can be agreed that the latter municipality appoints some of the members to the administrative body (committee or boards of an institution) set up by the former to execute the function in question (Finnish Local Government, 1983).

Intermunicipal pooling arrangements are a typical form of co-operation in Finnish local and intermediate government. Under these arrangements two or more municipalities (towns or other municipalities) establish joint authorities with responsibility for various functions within the municipalities' combined territory. These joint authorities are corporate persons under Finnish law, and their assets are clearly separated from the general assets of the municipalities in question. When a joint authority is set up under a pooling arrangement, the municipalities involved draft a basic charter stipulating its organizational structure, administration and the allocation of costs and revenues. The highest decision-making body in a joint authority is its council, to which the councils of the municipalities involved elect their representatives. The executive body in a joint authority is its boards. There may also be committees and boards of various institutions under a joint authority.

The Helsinki Metropolitan Area Council is a joint administrative body set up by special legislation. The Council is responsible for the four municipalities of Helsinki, Espoo, Kauniainen and Vantaa. It is charged with handling matters of common interest. The council can, provided the member municipalities consent, perform certain joint administrative tasks as well (Finnish Local Government, 1983).

Resources and autonomy

Finnish municipalities have many functions which can be divided into two main categories: general and specific. The Local Government Act states that it is the responsibility of municipalities to carry out local government functions and other functions entrusted to it separately by law. Within the limits of their financial resources, they can voluntarily assume activities to meet the needs of citizens. Consequently, one municipality may offer services which its neighbour does not.

The division of functions between the state and municipalities has been arrived at, for the most part, by chance. Over a long period of development it is difficult to discern a leading principle in this matter. Also the borderline between the general and the specific appears to be constantly changing as the municipalities continually assume new responsibilities belonging to the general sector, while the state provides for functions formerly included in the general category but now placed in the specific category through legislation. In addition, over the last two decades, the state has been steadily increasing the number of matters to be included in the specific category; for example some very important groups of functions, such as education, health care, social welfare, and building and housing. Consequently, municipal operations have greatly expanded, and municipal finances have been stretched in a number of cases (Finnish Local Government, 1983).

In general, most municipalities have largely the same responsibilities and provide a uniform standard of service. This is because they have a statutory duty to provide basic services and the standard of service to be maintained in various sectors is in many cases stipulated in the relevant statutes. In the course of the past few decades, statutory services have come to account for an increasing proportion of all municipal services. Statutory functions already account for 80 to 90 per cent of the services provided by those municipalities with below average population and financial resources (Finnish Local Government, 1983).

Municipal finance

The corner-stone of municipal self-government in Finland is municipal taxation. The municipal income taxes are the chief source of municipal revenue. Since 1960 both the state and municipal taxes have been levied together. The municipal sector (municipalities and joint authorities) accounted for 6.9 per cent of the gross national product in 1960 and for 9.3 per cent in 1983 (Koivukoski, 1985, p. 29). Municipal finance supplies about two-thirds of public-sector consumption — in practice this means a higher proportion of public spending than by the state. Municipal finance accounts for about 9 per cent of all capital investment in the economy. The proportion of total borrowing by municipalities and their joint authorities is about 7 per cent. Unlike some other countries, Finland has no municipal bank — municipalities must therefore secure their loans on the open market like other prospective borrowers. Local authorities employ about 415,000 people which is almost twice as many as are in state service (Soumen Kaupunkiliitto, 1987b, p. 9).

Taxes and revenue-sharing payments by the state are among the municipalities' most important sources of income. Against the background of steadily rising municipal expenditure, state payments have been increasing annually in both absolute and relative terms. Nevertheless, total municipal expenditure has increased faster than state expenditure since the beginning of the 1970s (see Figure 18.3). In 1985 municipal income taxes accounted for 39 per cent and state revenues for 20 per cent of the total municipal revenue (Soumen Kaupunkiliitto, 1987a, p. 76). The remainder was covered with loans, charges, fees and other sources of income.

Municipal joint authorities differ from municipalities in that they do not enjoy the right to levy taxes. Therefore municipalities proper contribute their respective proportional shares to the budgets of the joint authorities in which they are involved. In examining the revenues of joint authorities attention should also be paid to the high proportion of state payments — approaching half of all revenues.

Present problems of small municipalities

The total number of municipalities in Finland has been decreasing since World War II. The most dramatic change occurred in the 1970s when fifty-four municipalities lost their independence. This represented 10 per cent of all municipalities in 1970. The present number of municipalities is 461: ninety-four urban and 367 rural. Settlements in Finland do not lose their status of municipality (*kunta*) or town (*kaupunki*) as a result of depopulation. Consequently, the population of the smallest municipalities is under 200 inhabitants.

The migratory movement from the countryside to towns and cities has impaired the economic situation of small municipalities by causing a decline in their tax receipts at the same time as the per capita expenditure fixed by legislation has increased. In this situation it has been difficult for a small municipality to create, or to maintain, communal services of a high standard. This has led to mergers of small municipalities into their greater

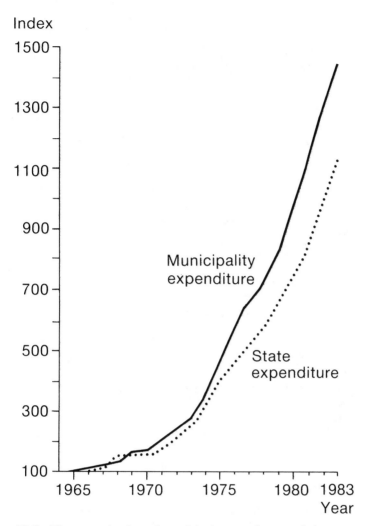

Figure 18.3 The growth of total municipal expenditure and the state
expenditure 1965–83 (1965 = 100)

Source: Koivukoski (1985, p. 30)

and richer neighbours. Lack of potential land for housing and industries
in urban municipalities has also been a factor in their willingness to unite.
Some urban municipalities (small in area) have had problems with
neighbouring rural municipalities when trying to expand by merger (see
Figure 18.4). It must be noted that municipal self-government in Finland
includes the right to decide about unification of two municipalities or a
rural municipality and a town. Sometimes these negotiations take dozens
of years and a local plebiscite may be arranged in the status-losing
municipality. The problem of incorporation mainly exists in regions where
there is a large town surrounded by one rural municipality — a situation

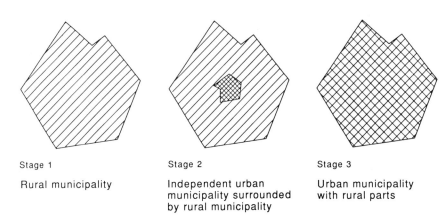

Stage 1

Rural municipality

Stage 2

Independent urban
municipality surrounded
by rural municipality

Stage 3

Urban municipality
with rural parts

Figure 18.4   The evolution of a special type of municipal territorial division

which has been given the figurative name accorded to the round quoit
shape of Finnish rye bread. Urban settlement has been expanding into
rural parts where commuting is on the increase. Young and wealthy
taxpayers have left the town but remain dependent on jobs in the town.
It has been debated whether in such cases town and rural municipality
should be forced to merge.

According to the Municipal Boundaries Act (1977), there are general
and special criteria to be applied to reducing, expanding or merging
municipalities. The general criteria deal with the opinion of the municipal
council and the local population in question, geographical factors, trade
and transport factors and public efforts to arrange an appropriate regional
division. The special criteria include the idea of public advantage. This
would allow, for example, a densely populated community divided by a
municipal boundary to be united with one of the municipalities, in spite
of its opposition (*Laki kuntajaosta*).

The Act on Certain Measures to Develop the Municipal Division and
the Co-operation between Municipalities, enacted in 1967, made it
necessary for the provincial governments to make plans showing which
municipalities should be united and how the municipal divisions should be
changed in other respects. The objective of the plan was to ensure that the
municipalities would be large enough; each municipality should, if possible, have at least 8,000 inhabitants. The legislation necessary for carrying
through this municipal administrative reform has not been passed because
of stiff opposition, but municipalities have in any case been extensively
united on a joint application (Atlas of Finland, Appendix, 1979). The total
number of small municipalities (with fewer than 2,000 inhabitants) was
sixty-three at the end of 1985. This number does not include the Aland
Islands. A closer examination of these small municipalities reveals some
typical characteristics such as (see Table 18.1) the high proportion of
primary industries (agriculture, forestry and fishing); the ageing population; and the low percentage of secondary industries.

Table 18.1   Small municipalities (less than 2,000 inhabitants) compared
with the average figures of Finland

Feature	Small municipalities n = 63 %	The whole country n = 461 %
Municipalities with over 50% in primary industries (1980)	24	3
Municipalities with over 30% in secondary industries (1980)	1	41
Municipalities with over 30% in tertiary industries (1980)	51	71
Population over 65 years of age (1985)	18	13
Municipalities losing population in 1985	44	43

Source: STV 1987, table 23

In many ways the story of small municipalities is the story of local
political inertia. These municipalities have persisted for a long period in
areas with traditional primary industries with small or zero investments
into modern activities. In addition, they are usually remote or located far
away from highways and other traffic flows. As a result, it has been
difficult for them to create or to maintain the necessary services and a high
proportion of municipal revenue is therefore directed to the municipal joint
authorities, especially for health care and education. A large number of
small municipalities (38 per cent) are located in south-western Finland.
These are the smallest by population (average 1,215 inhabitants), but they
have passed their worst period; the majority of them are now gaining
population. The regions with the highest losses of population among small
municipalities are now to be found in central Finland and in the south-
eastern parts of the country. It seems that, notwithstanding the efforts of
the small municipalities to maintain their independence, the majority of
these municipalities will be obliged to join their larger neighbours by the
end of this century. They will be forced to accept this solution by the
realities of their municipal finance.

Futures in local government

The rapid evolution of the Finnish welfare state since the 1960s has greatly
expanded local services. Simultaneously the local government has not been
able to answer all the growing needs. During the 1970s the major aspect
of change was a rapid expansion in the number of the local government
personnel. In the period from 1965 to 1985 the major feature and benefits
of the welfare state were created. The development of administrative
organization went through a boom in the late 1960s and early 1970s. To

a great extent, this development meant an expansion and increased resources. All this has occurred under strict state supervision. Subsequently, when economic growth slowed down and partly even stopped, efforts have instead been concentrated on minimizing the growth of administration. However, the main problems of resource allocation and the redistribution of benefits are now finding a solution. Finland is a welfare state, but this does not mean that there are no problems in personal well-being. From now on it is clear that the resources will have to be targeted on individuals instead of expecting social groups or regions to diagnose and cure the ill-health of the communities.

The future development of local government in Finland is at present based on a dual vision of innovation needs: first, the relations between the state and the municipalities must be reorganized which means the decentralization of administration at all levels. Second, the municipalities have to be capable of developing their services and administration in order to meet the modern needs and changing requirements of the citizens.

A committee on decentralization of administration in Finland, recently set up by the Council of State, has defined the methods of decentralization in the following way (Komiteanmietintö, 1986, 12, pp. 1–20):

— to shift duties and decision-making downwards in the administrative machinery;
— to transfer administration in the regional hierarchy;
— to modernize and implement duties;
— to improve services giving special importance to bringing the administration closer to the people;
— to reduce the number of norms issued by central government to allow greater flexibility;
— to create new levels of administration.

The central government in Finland also needs to be reorganized, an alteration which will have its effects on all levels of administration. It is especially important to contain the dispersion of the intermediate-level government. The relatively strict control by central government should be loosened and the system of state subsidies and grants to local authorities should be made substantially simpler. The aim is to group the present very large number of separate payments into larger categories of state contributions based on population size, output performance and other measurement criteria: that is to shift from specific to general grants. This restructuring will strengthen the local authorities' powers to decide independently how their tasks are to be performed, thus greatly strengthening their autonomous status.

One of the major demands by local administration has been the claim for legislation of pilot 'free-municipalities'. This involves greater self-government for municipalities and a decrease in state and intermediate government control. In addition it will allow more decision-making powers by the municipalities. This pilot-plan also includes decentralizing actions within local administrations such as cancelling 'duplicate organizations' and decreasing the level of scrutiny of decisions inside a given municipality (Soumen Kaupunkiliitto, 1987b, p. 45).

Future developments of local administration require greater emphasis on general goal-setting, effectiveness, a new employees' policy and better budgeting as a stronger part of the municipal planning system. The overall organization of administration should be reformed in such a way as to improve its efficiency, democratic control and legal safeguards and to bring administration closer to the citizens.

References

Atlas of Finland (1979), Appendix 311, Public Administration, National Board of Survey and the Geographical Society of Finland, Helsinki.

Finnish Local Government (1983), Association of Finnish Cities and the Finnish Municipal Association, Helsinki.

Koivukoski, E. (1985), *Kunnallistalouden tietoa*, Kunnallispaino Oy, Vantaa.

Komiteanmietintö, (1986:12) *Hallinnon hajauttaminen* (Committee on the Decentralization of administration), Valtion painatuskeskus, Helsinki.

Kunnallislaki (1976), 10.12.1976/953, *Local Government Act*, Helsinki.

Laki kuntajaosta (1977), 21.1.1977/73, *Municipal Boundaries Act*, Helsinki.

Nousiainen, J. (1971), *The Finnish Political System*, Harvard University Press, Cambridge, Mass.

STV (1985/86/87), *Soumen Tilastollinen vuosikirja*, (Statistical Yearbook of Finland), Central Statistical Office of Finland, Helsinki.

Soumen Kaupunkiliitto (1987a), *Tietoja kaupungeista ja Kaupunkiliitosta*, Kouvola.

Soumen Kaupunkiliitto (1987b), *Uudistuva kunta*, Lahti.

Soumen Kunnalliskalenteri (1961/65), Finnish Municipal Calendar, Finnish Municipal Association, Helsinki.

Soumen Kunnalliskalenteri (1985–8), Finnish Municipal Calendar, Finnish Municipal Association and the Association of Finland's Swedish-speaking Municipalities, Helsinki.

19 Belgium[1]
Robert Sevrin

Introduction

The administrative structure of Belgium is relatively complex and fluid. Belgium has an area of 30,513 square kilometres and a population of 9.9 million. It has sub-national governments of regions, provinces and communes. The communes, the 'Agglomeration' of Brussels, and the provinces have an elected assembly and a college or standing deputation (the government of the area). In general the three assemblies of the communities and regions are made up of deputies and senators elected nationally, but they now have their own government, the Executive. However, the German cultural community has an elected assembly and an Executive. The Executive of Brussels is made up of ministers and secretaries of state from the national government. Since 1977, the amalgamation of communes has reduced their number to 589 with an average size of 51.80 square kilometres and 2,540 inhabitants.

The regional structure of Belgium

Description of the intermediate regional units

Since the revision of the constitution (1967–71), Belgium has been a regionalized state. There are four linguistic regions (French, Dutch, German and bilingual), three cultural communities (French, Dutch and German), and three regions (Wallonia, Flanders and Brussels) which contain the nine provinces. These are subdivided into forty-three administrative districts with thirty constituencies for the House of Representatives, twenty-one constituencies for the Senate (see Figure 19.1). There is also, for the judicial organization, 225 cantons with Justices of the Peace at the lowest level. The other levels are: twenty-six judicial districts within the jurisdiction of Tribunals of First Instance, Labour Tribunals and Tribunals of Commerce; nine provinces within the jurisdiction of

1. With acknowledgement to Mrs Sue Garrod, for correction of my translation.

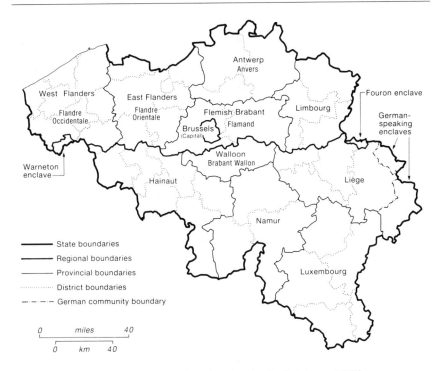

Figure 19.1 The boundaries of regional units in Belgium, 1988

Assize Courts; five provinces or groups of provinces within that of Courts of Appeal; and nationally the Supreme Court of Appeal. The Roman Catholic Church, predominant in Belgium, has eight dioceses: the archdiocese of Mechelen-Brussels, and seven other dioceses which correspond with the territory of the provinces (except for the diocese of Namur, which includes Namur and Luxembourg); Tournai is in the bishopric for Hainaut.

As early as the annexation of Belgium to France in 1795 nine departments were created which are the precursors of the present provinces. The departmental boundaries were independent of the linguistic frontier and in several departments part of the population was Walloon, in others Flemish and in a few, German. An enclave of the north department (Barbençon) continued to exist within the area of Jemappes. The departments were created using the travel time of a horse coach: the administrative authorities had to be able to reach all the localities in the area between sunrise and sunset.

After 1800, some of the departmental boundaries were called into question. However, no change occurred. The *Grand Juge*, the minister of justice, emphasized on the '15 ventose an VII' that the government would change the district boundaries, or the choice of their chief town, only if it was proved that substantial mistakes had been made in their demarcation. The *Grand Juge* stated that 'the fixing of the new cantons has been made after making close inquiries of the Prefects, Justices of the Peace, etc; the most important thing to avoid in government service is the appearance of instability'; most of the requests for changes 'are dictated by the interests of some communes and will immediately provoke requests from other communes if the proposed changes are accepted'. This desire for administrative stability is understandable during these early stages of economic development. Under the period of the Dutch domination, after 1815, the departments were termed provinces and a number of changes to boundaries occurred. The northern part of the departments of the Escaut and of Deux-Nethes was united to the Dutch provinces of Zealand and North-Brabant; the area of Landen passed from the department of the Dyle into the province of Liège; some parts of the departments of the Ourthe and of Les Forets were transferred to Prussia, while several cantons of the department of the Ardennes and the Barbençon-enclave (north) were annexed. Near the north-eastern confines of Wallonia, the neutral territory of Moresnet (the present commune of Kelmis) was created by the border Treaty of Aix-la-Chapelle (26 June 1816), in consequence of a mistake in the drafting of the Act of Vienna (9 June 1815).

Between 1831 and 1961 the most important changes in the provincial boundaries were linked to the changes made to the eastern borders of Belgium. By the Treaty of London in 1939, Belgium gave up the eastern part of the provinces of Limburg and Luxembourg to The Netherlands; in consequence of the Treaty of Versailles, the province of Liège extended eastwards with the annexation of neutral Moresnet in 1919 and of the cantons of Eupen, Malmedy and Sankt Vith, including thirty German communes in 1925. The other changes in provincial boundaries were more limited: in 1923, the province of Antwerp increased by two communes on the left bank of the Scheldt, transferred from East Flanders, and at various times there were minor changes of communal boundaries.

The 1960s' reforms

A law of 8 November 1962 reformed administrative boundaries, and another law of 2 August 1963 concerned the use of language in administrative matters. These had two objectives:

(1) To bring about territorial changes in most provinces and districts. (Only the provinces of Antwerp, Luxembourg and Namur went untouched.) Three new districts were created: Brussels (capital), Brussels (peripheral communes), Mouscron and fifteen districts: eight in Wallonia, seven in the Flemish region underwent territorial changes.

(2) To demarcate four linguistic regions, the boundaries of which would be fixed definitively. The Flemish-speaking region included the provinces of Antwerp, Limburg, West and East Flanders, as well as the districts of Brussels (peripheral communes abolished in 1970), of Halle-Vilvoorde (to which the preceding was attached in 1970) and of Leuven. The commune of Fourons, summarily attached to

Limburg in 1963, forms an enclave in the province of Liège, at the border with The Netherlands. The French-speaking region includes the provinces of Hainaut, Namur and Luxembourg, that of Liège (except for the German-speaking region) and the district of Nivelles. Comines-Warneton is a Hainaut enclave in West Flanders, at the French border on the Lys (see Figure 19.1). The bilingual region of Brussels (capital) is limited to the district comprising nineteen communes of the central part of the Brussels urban area. This is not a very defensible region geographically speaking; its delimitation is based on purely political considerations, which are not necessarily rational or appropriate. The German-speaking region includes twenty-five of the thirty-one communes attached to Belgium after the Treaty of Versailles (1919), grouped around the towns of Eupen in the north and Sankt Vith in the south which are the two main poles of attraction.

This new subdivision acts as the territorial framework for the administrative pyramid of regionalized Belgium:

— three cultural communities (Dutch, French and German);
— three regions (Flemish, Walloon and Brussels; the German community being included in the Walloon region);
— nine provinces;
— 589 communes.

Table 19.1 shows the variations of the areas and population of provinces and districts after the reform of 1962–3. These territorial changes, the most important since the independence of the state, have led to the exchange of 64,176 inhabitants and of 5,306 hectares, as well as the division of Brussels into three new districts. As of 1 January 1987, the 9.86 million inhabitants of Belgium were distributed as follows: 973,499 in the region of Brussels, 5,685,601 in the Flemish region and 3,205,651 in the Walloon region (including 66,473 in the German-speaking region). The province of Brabant, the most populated with 2,219,272 people, covers the three linguistic regions (bilingual, Dutch, French). With 225,563 inhabitants, the province of Luxembourg is the least populated. If we exclude Brussels (capital), the population of the other districts ranges from 36,690 (Bastogne) to 919,453 (Antwerp).

Administrative relationships

The first intermediate level above the commune is the *administrative district*, the only public authority of which is the district commissioner, who is subordinate to the governor of the province. In the instance of the German-speaking cantons (subdivision of a district) to the east of the district of Verviers and in the Fourons enclave of the Tongeren district in Liège, the district commissioner is assisted by a deputy commissioner. In

Table 19.1 Population and area (ha) of the provinces and districts in Belgium before and after the reforms of 1962–3

	Before Reforms (000s)		After Reforms (000s)		Difference	
	Inhabitants	Hectares	Inhabitants	Hectares	Inhabitants	Hectares
Provinces						
Hainaut	1,248	372	1,317	379	+68,644	+7,414
Liège	1,003	394	991	387	−11,633	−7,032
Brabant	1,992	328	2,009	336	+17,050	+8,570
West Flanders	1,068	325	997	313	−71,070	−10,260
East Flanders	1,272	297	1,271	297	−460	−61
Limburg	574	240	572	242	−2,531	+1,376
Districts						
Nivelles	200	104	207	109	+7,165	+4,924
Ath	78	50	77	49	−1,914	−1,349
Soignies	165	53	162	51	−2,886	−2,915
Tournai	146	60	148	61	+2,374	+1,410
Mouscron	–	–	71	10	+71,070	+10,267
Liège	604	75	607	77	+3,448	+1,376
Verviers	235	204	233	201	−2,243	+3,393
Waremme	70	41	57	36	−12,838	−5,015
Brussels	1,439	110	(1,438)	(110)	−747	+294
Brussels (capital)	–	–	1,022	16	–	–
Brussels (peripheral)	–	–	45	5	–	–
Halle-Vilvoorde	–	–	370	89	–	–
Leuven	352	112	363	116	+10,632	+3,349
Ieper	122	61	104	54	−18,135	−6,295
Kortrijk	299	44	246	110	−52,935	−3,972
Oudenaarde	114	41	113	41	−460	−61
Hasselt	279	90	278	90	−984	−448
Tongeren	158	63	156	65	−1,547	+1,824

addition to tutelage over communes with fewer than 5,000 inhabitants (which are much less numerous since the amalgamation of communes), the district carries out missions of public interest such as the compilation of statistics, responsibility for the rural police (in all communes with fewer than 5,000 inhabitants and in some communes with fewer than 10,000 inhabitants), and for regional tax collection for those communes with fewer than 10,000 inhabitants. The district centralizes information concerning young men aged sixteen and resident in the communes of the district, with a view to military service and it grants deferment for studies. In addition, the district commissioner is responsible for daily checks of conscientious objectors during their unarmed service. He also issues shooting licences. There is no elected assembly at district level.

The second intermediate level is the *province*, the bodies and responsibilities of which are clearly defined by the law of 30 April 1836 which has repeatedly been amended. The bodies are:

— the *provincial council* with from fifty to ninety members, depending on the population size (Luxembourg fifty, Namur sixty, Limburg seventy, West Flanders eighty, Liège eighty-six, Brabant, Antwerp, East Flanders, Hainaut ninety), elected by citizens over twenty-one years of age. There are 706 provincial councillors;
— the *standing deputation*, with six members elected within the council;
— the *governor*, appointed by the central authority, presiding over the provincial council and the standing deputation.

The responsibilities of the provincial council cover all matters of provincial interest: it can create public charitable organizations and schools, administrative posts, take the initiative in creating societies for regional development (SDR), and elects forty-eight provincial senators (the Belgian senate consists of 179 members).

The standing deputation is the executive body, which exercises the responsibilities of the council between its sittings. It is responsible for enforcing laws and general decrees, supervises the provincial administration and proposes to the king the nomination of the provincial registrar, who comes under the governor's authority. It also plays the role of an administrative jurisdiction. It appoints representatives to the national commission for territorial planning. Since 1972, the nine standing deputations have shared a common technical design office.

The governor is appointed and removed from office by the king. He directs the administration, examines cases, presides over the council and the deputation and exercises tutelage over these institutions. He also has to enforce the laws and decrees concerning general administration, the community and regional decrees, and is responsible for the maintenance of law and order. In Brabant, the vice-governor has responsibility for observance of the linguistic laws and has competence concerning territorial planning and development of the international role of Brussels.

The provinces play an important part in national life though they only have some 15,000 officials and their budgets are equivalent to one-eighth of the communal budgets.

The third intermediate level consists of the *cultural communities* and the *regions*. In Flanders, the Flemish Council, made up of the members of the Dutch linguistic group of the House of Representatives and the directly elected members of the Dutch linguistic group of the senate (Special Law on Institutional Reforms, 8 August 1980, 29) has resulted from the amalgamation of the Council of the Flemish Community and the Flemish Regional Council; the Regional Executive (the regional government) is formed from the regional ministers and a presiding minister of the Flemish executive. In Wallonia, there is a distinction between (a) the Council of the French Community (members of the French linguistic group of the Houses of Parliament); the Executive of the French Community is formed from the ministers and a presiding minister of the French community; and the Walloon Regional Council (members of the French linguistic group [except those of Brussels] of the Houses of Parliament); the Executive of the Walloon region is also formed from the ministers and a presiding minister of the Walloon region. In the German-speaking commune, the Council of the German Cultural Community is formed from the twenty-five members who, since 1985, have been elected by the legislative electors of the German-speaking region; the Executive of the German Community is formed from the community ministers and a presiding minister of the German community.

Before the parliamentary elections of 13 October 1985, the members of the Executives were ministers of the national government. This is still the case for the Executive of the region of Brussels (which does not have a regional council, but an Executive which may have to work with the 'Agglomeration' Council, a supracommunal body). The competence of the cultural councils covers cultural matters, teaching, international co-operation and co-operation between Belgian cultural communities themselves. The competence of the regions includes so-called 'personal matters'. The councils issue decrees with the power of law.

Co-operation between the communities and regions and the provinces is self-evident since the governors of the provinces are responsible for the enforcement of the decrees of the Council of Communities and Regions. Some politicians (especially the Liberals) would like the councils and Executives of the French community to amalgamate with those of the Walloon region, as in Flanders.

The government is now preparing an extension of the competences of the communities and regions; the members of the councils will be directly elected; the Region of Brussels (capital) will be formed from a bilingual Regional Council and a bilingual Executive composed of two Dutch-speaking and two French-speaking ministers and a presiding minister elected by the council.

The law of 15 July 1970 set up three regional economic councils, under public law: one for the Flemish region, one for Wallonia and the third (that will be suppressed) for the Province of Brabant, the monolingual districts of which thus having double membership. The councils have consultative status. This law has also created the Societies for Regional Development (SDR): one for the whole of Wallonia, one for Brussels and five for the Flemish region. They provide an institutional framework for the intercommunal societies for economic development. This complex and as yet incomplete system is in no way a federal one, but with the modifications of the constitution which have occurred in 1988, Belgium has now become a federal state. The competence of the state now covers:

— residual powers;
— exceptions to the powers of the regions and communities, especially to protect the economic and monetary unity.

Competence for the Regions:

— town and country planning;
— environment;
— economic policy, including foreign trade with the exception of what concerns economic and monetary unity;
— some control of energy;
— public works and transport;
— subordinated authorities (tutelage and financing);
— job policy;
— scientific research.

Competence of the Communities:

— cultural matters including the publicity on radio and television and the support to the written press;
— personal matters (health, aid to people, research, etc.) including henceforth youth welfare.

The freezing of the linguistic boundary has been accompanied by a system called 'protection of the minorities' thanks to the establishment of the 'communes with facilities' which can be broken down into five groups:

— twelve communes of the Dutch-speaking region with a protected French-speaking minority. It is, however, necessary to draw attention to the communes of Fourons and of the periphery of Brussels, in which the French-speaking population is in the majority, but encounters difficulties created by the Flemish region. The French-speaking majority is respectively: 63 per cent in Fourons and 59 per cent in the six communes of the periphery of Brussels taken as a whole (50 per cent in Wemmel, 51 per cent in Rhode-Saint-Genese, 54 per cent in Drogenbos, 60 per cent in Wezembeek-Oppem, 75 per cent in Linkebeek and in Kraainem) (see Figure 19.1); in the other five communes, including the cities of Mesen and Renaix, the French-speaking population really is in a minority;
— four communes of the French-speaking region with a protected Flemish-speaking minority (towns of Comines-Warneton, Mouscron and Enghien as well as Flobecq);

— two communes of the French-speaking region with a protected German-speaking minority (towns of Malmedy and Waimes);
— three communes of the French-speaking region with the possibility of protecting the German-speaking and/or Flemish-speaking minorities (Plombières, Welkenraedt and Baelen);
— the nine communes of the German-speaking community with a protected French-speaking minority (towns of Eupen and Sankt Vith, Kelmis, Lontzen, Raeren, Butgenbach, Bullingen, Amel and Burg-Reuland).

The communes

The basic regional units

Every locality of Belgium forms part of the territory of a commune which is the cellular territorial division, administered by a burgomaster, assisted by a college of deputy mayors and by the communal council. In pursuance of the communal law of 30 March 1836, the commune is 'a piece of the political and administrative life of the state. It has its own existence, magistrates whom it elects, particular interests which it administers. Bringing together local interests, it is a body within the state' (Houet, undated).

The decree of the National Convention (2 brumaire an II), issued in 1795 under French domination, abolished the difference of legal status between towns and villages. However, the decree of 30 March 1825, issued under Dutch domination, authorized eighty-eight communes to bear the honorary title of 'town' which the royal decree of 17 September 1875 confirmed for eighty-four of them. Eupen, Malmedy and Sankt Vith were transferred from Rhenish Prussia to Belgium under the Treaty of Versailles (1919). Since the amalgamation of the communes in 1977, the title of 'town' has conferred by the law on several other communes. In 1987 125 communes were authorized as 'towns' (sixty-three in Wallonia, sixty-one in Flanders, as well as Brussels). On the other hand, a few small urban communes, as well as the eighteen communes surrounding Brussels, are not allowed to call themselves 'towns',

The decree of 14 December 1789 established all the communes of France on a uniform and regular basis. This was also applied to the Belgian territories immediately after the installation of French domination in October 1795. According to the *principle of immutability* the 'territory of the present communes, with a few exceptions, is identical to that of the former parishes' (Du Moreau, 1948), or again: 'the most usual boundaries of the present rural communes are the same as those which, under the old regime, were determined, to use the expression of the time, for the extent of spiritual jurisdiction' (Sevrin, 1961). This principle is, moreover, confirmed by the official map of Ferraris (prepared 1771–8), which has enabled the map of the parishes of Hainaut at the end of the old regime to be drawn up: outside the towns, with a few exceptions, the communal boundaries coincide with the parochial boundaries since they pre-date the changes which occurred during the nineteenth century (Sevrin, 1961).

The shape of the communal territory, heir of the parochial territory, varies considerably and reflects the diversity of physical geography. Changes in communal boundaries and the creation or elimination of communes are decided by law without any prior local referendum. There is no population limit below which an inhabited area, even if it is becoming depopulated, loses its legal status as a commune.

The communal boundaries have been a matter of concern since the period of French domination. As far back as Year V of the French period, and more particularly in the circular of prairial 22th Year VIII sent by L. Bonaparte, Minister of the Interior, to the Prefects of Departments, proposals are mentioned that 'suburbs should be joined onto the town which they surround or small communes onto other larger communes' (Sevrin, 1961). Between 1795 and 1813, twenty-two amalgamations of communes are reported as against the creation of nine new communes. During the period of Dutch domination between 1819 and 1828 there were twenty-six amalgamations of communes and two communes were created, with the result that in 1830, at the beginning of Belgian independence, there were 2,492 communes.

From independence (1830–1) until 1961, in addition to numerous changes of communal boundaries, 153 communes were created (the last in 1928) and thirty former German communes, incorporated into Belgian territory under the Treaty of Versailles in 1925, were annexed, but there were only twelve amalgamations (involving thirty communes). The number of communes increased to 2,675 in 1928 but reduced to 2,663 in 1961. Between 1880 and 1961, the percentage of communes with fewer than 2,000 inhabitants decreased from 75.6 per cent to 64.7 per cent, while the number of those with more than 2,000 inhabitants increased. However, if we consider an important threshold to be 5,000 inhabitants, above which the communes are free from the tutelage of the district commissioner, the percentage of communes with more than 5,000 inhabitants modestly increased from 6.5 per cent to 15 per cent. The distribution of the population among the communes, classified according to the number of inhabitants, presents a different structure and evolution. Indeed, the proportion of the population in communes with fewer than 2,000 inhabitants decreased from 31.6 per cent to 15 per cent 1880–1961 and the population in communes with 2,000 to 5,000 inhabitants decreased from 25.4 per cent to 18.5 per cent. Thus, for all the communes with fewer than 5,000 inhabitants there was a diminution of population from 57 per cent to 33.5 per cent. On the other hand, the proportion of the population in communes with 5,000 to 10,000 inhabitants increased from 32.5 per cent to 57.1 per cent. After an increase from 10.6 per cent in 1880 to 12 per cent in 1920, the proportion of the population in communes with at least 100,000 inhabitants fell to 9.2 per cent in 1961 because of the 'city' phenomenon (the decreasing population of the centre of the city.)

Between 1964 and 1971, the first waves of amalgamations reduced the number of communes to 2,359; 304 communes were eliminated, 218 in Flanders and eighty-six in Wallonia. The greatest number of amalgamations took place in 1964 (seventy-seven communes eliminated) and 1970 (214 eliminated) with a few other amalgamations in 1969 and 1971. The percentage of communes with fewer than 5,000 inhabitants slightly decreased from 85 per cent in 1961 to 81.1 per cent in 1974 (Malvoz and Verbist, 1976). These amalgamations affected only part of Belgium and several districts remained untouched. The reforms were insufficient. They left more than 80 per cent of the communes with fewer than 5,000 inhabitants and with inappropriate boundaries in several places, often unconnected with the spread of the built-up areas in urban centres.

At the beginning of the seventies, successive ministers of the interior examined proposals to amalgamate communes but no further proposals for reforms could be agreed. However, numerous discussions took place, particularly concerning the minimum population limit for a viable commune. The agreed limit has varied at different times: 400 inhabitants in 1829, 1,000 in 1958 (Sevrin, 1961), 2,500 to 3,000 in 1968, 5,000 in 1972-4 (Sevrin, 1972, 1974). But it was necessary to legislate to allow either amalgamation (law of 28 July 1971) or the organization of associations, 'agglomerations' and federations of communes (law of 26 July 1971). The 1975 decree amalgamating communes and changing their boundaries (Moniteur belge, 25 September 1975) came into effect on 1 January 1977 (1983 for the amalgamation of Antwerp with seven other communes) and was in two parts: (i) the report to the king from the Minister of the Interior, J. Michel, (ii) the royal decree itself.

The report to the king stated that the recent extension and diversification of the responsibilities of the local authorities confined the communes within boundaries which were nearly two centuries old. The communes could not as a result provide all the services required by the inhabitants, they could not attract qualified staff and had insufficient finances and population and territory. The intercommunal associations could not meet these demands because of their fragmented nature.

The inadequacy of the local structure had already been pointed out in 1937 by the Study Centre for State Reform and in 1959 by the Central Economic Council. The laws of 14 February 1961 and 23 July 1971 enabled a general and systematic reform of municipal territories to be carried out. Prepared by successive governments, the proposed amalgamation of communes was evoked in the investiture declaration of the Tindemans government of 12 June 1974 which stated a firm intention to institute a maximum of amalgamations of communes before the communal elections of 1976 in accordance with a general plan. Additionally, the amalgamation of communes had an effect on the boundaries of provinces, administrative districts and peripheral federations. These proposals placed before the communal council, the federation councils, as well as before the standing deputations of the provinces, were passionately discussed and also contested by burgomasters who organized in their communes an 'anti-amalgamation referendum' as well as protest demonstrations. Much of this resistance stemmed from considerations of self-interest or party interest.

The plan to amalgamate communes, introduced by the royal decree, was based on the following criteria:

1. Care was taken to amalgamate into the same commune all urban areas which were adjacent or virtually adjacent to each other (either whole communes or parts of communes), as well as territories which, although a certain distance away, came within the hinterland of the urban areas.
2. Geographic factors played a considerable part: distance from a municipal centre, lines of communication, means of transport, relief, river basins, wooded areas as well as recent features marking the landscape, such as motorways and waterways.
3. Service centres were, logically, used as poles of attraction for amalgamation.
4. Economic data were used as important criteria; as a result the setting up of industrial areas and the flows of trade were taken into consideration.
5. Particular importance was attached to affinities: since people should remain the central concern, the sense of community and the way of life were decisive in the choice of amalgamations.
6. Care was taken to ensure that the new communes were viable in having a sufficient number of inhabitants, covered an adequate surface area and had appropriate financial resources.

The law reduced the number of communes to 589. There was also the non-amalgamation of 118 former communes, some with changes in boundaries. Thus the amalgamation, with or without changes in boundaries, produced 471 communes: 223 in the Flemish region, 239 in Wallonia and nine in the German-speaking region. Since the law of 23 July 1971 prohibited the amalgamation of communes with different official languages, only communes with the same official language could be amalgamated; this reduced from 880 to 296 the number of monolingual Dutch-speaking communes; from 1,386 to 244 the number of monolingual French-speaking communes; and from seventy-one to thirty the number of multilingual communes (excluding the nineteen communes of the capital, Brussels). The amalgamation of communes involved a change of district in the same province for some forty-eight communes.

The 471 new communes involved amalgamation of between two and thirty former communes but more than 10 per cent involved two to five former communes (Figure 19.2). Two Walloon cities involved the largest number of amalgamations: Tournai resulted from the amalgamation of thirty communes and Namur from twenty-five. A few amalgamations in 1977 were an extension of previous groupings, as for example Hannut, resulting from the amalgamation in three stages (1964, 1970 and 1977) of eighteen former communes. Out of the 141 communes resulting from the two earlier stages, thirteen underwent no change, three simply had their boundaries changed, fifty-eight were the central commune in the amalgamation and sixty-seven were joined onto a larger commune.

While 85 per cent of the· 470 'legally new' communes (Malvoz and Verbist, 1976) took the name of one of the former communes (often the most populated, but sometimes the one with the most well-known name or

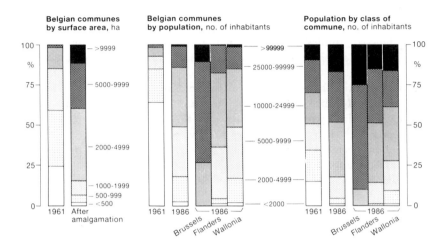

Figure 19.2 The distribution by size of communes in Belgium, 1961 and 1986

that with the most central position), sixty-eight communes were given a new name. The royal decree of 1975 makes it clear that the new commune may be known as a town in eighty-seven cases. More significant is the classification of the communes according to the extent of their urbanization (Van Waelvelde and Van der Haegen, 1967). There are now 116 *rural* communes (19.7 per cent of the total) instead of the former 1,109 (or 47 per cent); there are now 165 towns and *urban areas* (or 28 per cent) instead of the former 208 (8.8 per cent). It is necessary, therefore, to emphasize that the amalgamation of many communes around a central town (for example, Tournai, Namur) included former communes in the new entity so that it might have much of its surface area devoted to farming, for example 66 per cent of the surface area of the commune of Tournai.

The amalgamation of communes increased the average surface area and population of the Belgian communes: from 1,300 to 5,200 hectares, and from 4,136 to 16,512 inhabitants. Previously, the great majority of Belgian communes had fewer than 5,000 inhabitants and about 66 per cent had fewer than 2,000. They were consequently not free of the tutelage of the district commissioners. After the reform, only 18 per cent of the communes have fewer than 5,000 inhabitants, while 66 per cent of the communes fall into the category of 5,000 to 25,000 inhabitants. However, the commune sizes differ among the three regions. In Brussels (capital), more than 66 per cent of the nineteen communes have from 25,000 to 100,000 inhabitants; in Flanders only 5 per cent of the communes have fewer than 5,000 inhabitants, compared with 36 per cent in Wallonia; while communes with more than 10,000 inhabitants account for 62 per cent of the Flemish communes but only 34 per cent of the Walloon communes (Sevrin, 1980).

The amalgamation of communes has had other results. Although the first criterion was to insure the amalgamation into the same commune of all adjacent or virtually adjacent urban areas, it should be noted that the urban centres of Liège, Charleroi, La Louviere and Antwerp remain split up (Sevrin, 1978).

Some surprising amalgamations can be associated with party electoral motives; this is all the more regrettable in that it would have been possible to form communes with more than 5,000 inhabitants on the basis of geographical criteria (Sevrin, 1972, 1974). Nevertheless, extensive amalgamations have been made to good effect around those towns which have a regional role so that the population of the town is balanced by the addition of the population of the other communes. This is the case in particular of Namur, Ath, Lessines and even Tournai where, however, the amalgamation could have been different and more extensive.

Sometimes there was considerable opposition to the Michel plan, emanating principally from burgomasters, deputy mayors and communal councillors in danger of losing their office in consequence of the amalgamations. However this did not cause any major political difficulties since the decision was voted on by the Belgian legislative assembly.

The sudden increase in size of communes has undeniably posed problems. For example, the most extensive commune of Belgium, Tournai, increased from 1,550 to 21,500 hectares and from 33,000 to 67,000 inhabitants and extends over 25 kilometres from east to west and over 15 kilometres from north to south. The number of communal officers was considerably reduced: one burgomaster instead of thirty, eight deputy mayors instead of sixty-five and thirty communal councillors instead of 360. The territory of the commune has been divided into five administrative areas, each of which has its basic maintenance allocated with appropriate equipment. The associations to promote cultural and sports activities are federated and have contacts with representatives of the communal council (Dumortier, 1979).

The communities associated with the former communes which have lost their legal identity have often developed their individuality by, for example, reviving interest in local schools or through the activity of their associations and the success of their festivities (Mory and Sevrin, 1978). Even if some amalgamations aggravated financial problems, they nevertheless gave the former small communes access to a social and technical infrastructure of which they were previously deprived. The quality of the communal politicians also generally improved, especially in the rural areas, mainly as a result of the rise of the better educated and a decline of the role of local leading citizens. This has led to a greater interchange and continuity between national and regional political life (Mory et al., 1977).

At the time of the census of population and housing in December 1970, the 2,585 communes were divided into 14,844 statistical areas. Each commune included a maximum of ten divisions and each division a maximum of ten statistical areas (Brulard, 1970; Van Waelvelde and Liekens-Rousseau, 1972). For the census subsequent to the amalgamations and for the general census of population and housing in March 1981, it was found convenient to maintain, with adaptations, the division into statistical areas. The amalgamated communes included several villages or small towns, the demographic and economic evolution of which was important to follow (Sevrin, 1974). The new communes were divided into their former communes and these into divisions and statistical areas; in comparison with 1970, a few areas had to be subdivided, more particularly in the case of residential suburbs becoming urbanized. On the other hand, the yearly population statistics are available only for the amalgamated communes.

The law of 26 July 1971 established *Agglomerations* and federations of communes, a supracommunal level and district from the intermediate level regional units. In fact, only the *Agglomeration* of Brussels and the five peripheral federations of Halle, Asse, Vilvoorde, Zaventem and Tervuren have been established. The *Agglomeration* of Brussels consists of the nineteen bilingual communes of Brussels (capital) which were not amalgamated in 1977.

Administrative relationships

In each of the 589 communes of Belgium, voters elect, by proportional representation, an odd number of communal councillors which varies depending on the population of the commune, from seven for communes with fewer than 1,000 inhabitants (only Herstappe) to fifty-five for communes with 300,000 inhabitants and more (only Antwerp).

From its members the *communal council* appoints the college of the burgomaster and deputy mayors. Their number varies from two for communes with fewer than 1,000 inhabitants to ten for communes with a population of 200,000 and more (law of 30 March 1976). The burgomaster is nominated by the king, usually from within the communal council but occasionally from outside. Apart from these political bodies, the communal administration is composed of the mayor's secretarial assistant (or town clerk) and a number of communal employees and workers, depending on the number of inhabitants.

The *college of the burgomaster and deputy mayors* is the political government of the commune. Its responsibilities are numerous and varied (for example population statistics, the registry office, education, social services, administration of infrastructure and collective services, town and country planning, economic growth). The paid staff are appointed by the politicians. In addition, the communes are able to encourage political participation by citizens, especially by organizing advisory commissions (young people's council, immigrant council, commission for arts, town planning, etc).

If decisions in communal affairs are taken autonomously as a part of communal self-government, their legality and advisability are supervised by the province or ministry of the interior. However, communes with fewer than 5,000 inhabitants remain under the tutelage of the district commissioner (ninety-three communes: seventy-eight in Wallonia, fifteen in Flanders).

Long-term co-operation has been set up among communal authorities for performing certain duties. This takes three forms:

1. *Agglomerations*: The law of 26 July 1971 lists the five *agglomerations* to be created: Antwerp, Charleroi, Ghent, Liège and Brussels. Only the *Agglomeration* of Brussels was set up in June 1972, and it constitutes the only democratic representative assembly of the population of Brussels as a whole. The draft bill of 6 March 1987 transfers competence to the *Agglomeration* for removal and treatment of refuse, public transport, fire-fighting (the *Agglomeration* concluded some agreements with communes on the outskirts), emergency medical assistance, administration and maintenance of the *Agglomeration* road system, the water supply and data processing.

   The *Agglomeration* Council includes eighty-three members chosen by the electors of the nineteen communes. It elects the president of the council and the Executive College. This includes, besides the president, four deputy mayors, (two French-speaking, two Dutch-speaking, instead of the former twelve). The council also selects the members of both Brussels' Cultural Committees (one French-speaking, the other Dutch-speaking).

   The only subdivisions possible within a town are technical or administrative and not political (for example, the areas in Tournai). Apart from the *Agglomeration* of Brussels and the five peripheral federations, discussed below, there is no special organizational unit for the administration of urban areas.

2. *The Peripheral Federations* of Halle, Asse, Vilvoorde, Zaventem and Tervuren have the same competence as the *Agglomeration* of Brussels. The number of members of the Federation council depends on the population figures (twenty-three in Tervuren and Zaventem, twenty-seven in Halle and Vilvoorde, thirty-five in Asse); it chooses the deputy mayors in the Executive College which, with the president, consist of five members in Tervuren and Zaventem and seven members in the other federations.

3. *The intercommunal societies*. Article 108 of the Constitution gives the communes authority to agree among themselves or to enter in partnership in order to settle or jointly administer matters of communal interest. The law of 1 March 1922 specified the limits for the development of intercommunal societies. The law of 18 July 1959 gives the communes authority to set up intercommunal societies for regional equipment. Endowed with a legal status, the intercommunal societies can take out loans and receive grants from the state. There are more than 200 intercommunal societies set up to provide varied services: gas, electricity and water supply, administration of public transport, removal of refuse, medical and social services, land management, education, public works, housing and regional development. The majority take the form of a co-operative and the rest are limited companies.

In addition the communes have authority to conclude agreements among themselves concerning supplies or services of common interest or take part with other authorities, in *co-operative societies of public authorities* (National Water Society, National Housing Society, National Land Society etc).

References

Brulard, T. (1970), 'Les recensements généraux au 31 Décembre 1970 et la division des communes en secteurs statistiques', *Le Mouvement communal*, No. 10.

Du Moreau, S.J.E. (1948), *Histoire de l'Enlise en Belgique*, (Tome complementaire I), Brussels.

Dumortier, P. (1979), 'Fusion des communes formant l'actuelle ville de Tournai. Aspects', *Note dactylographiée du cabinet du Secrétaire communal*.

Houet, A. (undated), *Dictionnaire moderne géographique, administratif, statistique des communes belges*, Geographical Association of Belgium, Brussels.

Malvoz, L. and Verbist, C. (1976), 'Une Belgique de 589 communes. Les fusions de communes vués sous l'angle de la géographie administrative', *Bull. trim. du Crédit Communal de Belgique*, No. 15, January.

Mory, P., Got, P and Sevrin, R. (1977), 'Fusions de communes en Belgique. Un exemple de commune rurale fusionnée, Brunehaut dans le Tournaisis', *Communic. au Congrès de l'Ass. des Ruralistes Français*, Rennes.

Mory, P. and Sevrin, R. (1978), 'Vie associative et types d'animation dans la commune rurale de Brunehaut', *Ass. des Ruralistes Français, Table ronde de Lille*.

Sevrin, R. (1961), 'Contribution à la géographie administrative du Hainaut', *Le Hainaut Economique*, No. 3.

Sevrin, R. (1972), 'Un essai de géographie administrative appliquée: la fusion des communes hennuyères', *Cahiers marxistes*, No. 14, Brussels.

Sevrin, R. (1974), 'Vers la fusion des communes de Wallonie', *Fondation Jacquèmotte*, Brussels.

Sevrin, R. (1976), 'La réforme de l'Etat belge. Une nouvelle géographie administrative', *La Wallonie le Pays et les Hommes*, Tome II, Brussels, 367–85.

Sevrin, R. (1978), 'Les fusions de communes en Belgique: une nouvelle géographie administrative', *Actes du 101e Congrès National des Societés Savantes Lille 1976*, Bibliothèque Nationale, Paris, 77-8.

Sevrin, R. (1980), 'Les fusions de communes en Belgique', *Hommes et Terres du Nord*, Lille, 4, 1–8.

Sevrin, R. (1987), 'Le contrôle par la région néerlandophone d'un petit espace à population francophone majoritaire: Fouron, périphérie bruxelloise', *Communication au symposium de Paris de Groupe de Travail de Géo. Politique de Comité National de Géographie*.

Van Waelvelde, M. and Van der Haegen, H. (1967), 'Typologie des communes belges d'après le degré d'urbanisation au 31 Décembre 1961', *Bull. de Statistique*, INS, Brussels, No. 9, 722–75.

Van Waelvelde, M. and Liekens-Rousseau, S. (1972), 'La division des communes belges en secteurs statistiques', *Bull. de Statistique*, INS, No. 4, 89–102.

Part 5 Future agendas

20 Territory and administration: towards a future research agenda
Robert Bennett

The argument

This book has argued that administrative obsolescence is an inevitable consequence of the rapid rate of economic and technological development. The discussion of the historical development of European administrative systems has served to emphasize not only the continuities of structures from the past, but the political and other difficulties of changing those structures. Administrative reforms of territory take years to approve; because of political compromise reforms seldom fully satisfy any of the criteria on which the demand for reform was pressed, and by the time they are implemented have been superseded by new demands for different reforms. No political or administrative reform process can keep up with this type of development. Hence disjunctures are inevitable. Moreover, the review of the theories and practice of allocation of competences and financial resources (in Chapter 4) has served to demonstrate that no single principle offers a fully satisfactory solution.

In view of these characteristics the early chapters of the book have argued for a flexible approach: *flexible decentralization* to the most basic and smallest units where the demands of participation, legitimacy, representation and community identity can be met; and *flexible aggregation* of basic units into collectives, co-operatives and associations for which efficient sizes of administration can be achieved which allow internalization of externalities and technical-bureaucratic efficiency. This suggestion, however, opens more questions than it answers. Hence this chapter outlines the chief questions as a research agenda which is subdivided into five areas: representation, accountability, participation, economic development and administrative rationality. These are outlined briefly below as a means of projecting the future research needs in the fields of territory and administration.

Conceptual underpinnings: towards a research agenda

It has been argued, in Chapter 2, that there is an inevitable tension in

European administrative institutions which is characterized by a duality: between direct or 'popular' representation and institutional representation. Although applied to liberal democracies, a similar tension of representation also characterizes socialist democracies, although within a very different institutional framework. The tension is maintained by the three processes identified by Almond and Powell (1966): of interest *articulation*, interest *aggregation* and interest *communication* through social and administrative institutions. The outcome is the process which maintains and develops the institutional and political systems of Europe: the *conversion* process. Each of these processes contains within it a further tension between modes of approach to resolving tensions between people, areas and sectors. Hence, articulation, aggregation, communication and conversion processes will normally evolve with aspects which fall across each level of aggregation/disaggregation: of people, communities and fields of administration.

A number of conceptual approaches have been developed to resolve these tensions at a practical level. However, the discussion in this book has emphasized a further set of questions which are challenging traditional practice as a result of the impact of rapid economic and technological change. As a consequence, new practical solutions are required and these in turn require new conceptual development. These are briefly outlined here in terms of an agenda for new research.

Representation

This produces the links between the administrative state and the individual: how are interests articulated and mediated by the system of representation? Such an issue arises only in state administrative systems: it is unnecessary in direct exchange between individuals such as market transactions. Representation is seen in liberal democracies as a question of infrequent mass participation in agreements on broad political agendas during elections to legitimize a strategy for day-to-day administrative action. In socialist democracies pluralist political party representation has been argued to be irrelevant but this assumption has been increasingly questioned. Territory is very important within both concepts. As argued by Agnew (1987), 'place politics' plays a crucial role in the form of mediation between state and society: as interdependence with the society and its politics. Taylor (1985) following Wallerstein (1979) uses this as a means of integrating concepts of international, national, regional and local representative structures. Representation, therefore, becomes an outcome of a complex set of processes within places at various scales. The main aspects of this are captured in Figure 20.1. As Brustein (1981) argues, voters from their own social position act strategically to vote for those candidates who maximize their benefits.

However, there is a strong fracture between those political and sociological accounts of representation that emphasize general social and structural contexts, and economic theories of representation that emphasize voting as a signal of preferences. The economic theory leads to competition

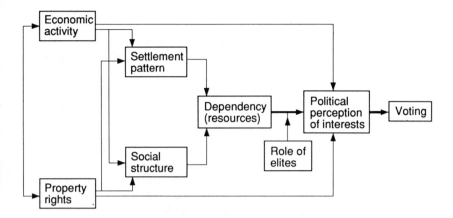

Figure 20.1 The relations of voting to economic structures

Source: Brustein (1981)

between areas for people, businesses and tax revenues, with improved efficiency as an outcome (the Tiebout and Oates argument; see Chapter 4). The economic theory has formed the basis of many of the public choice accounts which are now finding considerable political support in western Europe. Resolution of the economic with the political and sociological notions of representation within the context of territory is, therefore, a major research question. Galeotti (1987, 1988) suggests one useful way forward by seeking to use the concept of politician's 'rent'. He argues that preference revelation is an issue that can be resolved only within multi-party systems, while the formation of government requires (and therefore stimulates) a two-party system. Galeotti argues that 10 to 15 per cent of votes support the 'opinion' market (30 per cent in non-compulsory voting systems) while the remainder of votes support 'political effectiveness' — a government to deliver goods and services. In addition, there are voters which substitute between preference and effectiveness depending upon the election issues concerned. This suggests a mechanism beyond the simple utility or income-maximizing models of political party behaviour (see for example Riker, 1962; Wittman, 1973) in which politicians are constrained by a safety net of voters' support: their 'rent' is achieved whenever they obtain more votes than they deserve based on their behaviour and performance. Galeotti argues this rent will be greater the lower is the level of information and the greater is the span of issues. Hence, political 'rents' will be greater the larger the population concerned, the greater the territorial scale and the more highly centralized the two-party system. Decentralized systems, therefore, should minimize political 'rents' with the consequence that government is more effective. This, in turn, he suggests, requires the emergence of stronger executives at local level in order to mediate more effectively the spread of local preferences.

The issues raised by Galeotti's analysis, and a related argument by Stigler (1972), are challenging for research on the issue of representation and how it interrelates with territorial administration at different government levels. Clearly further theoretical and empirical work is required. Additionally, the concepts need to be expanded to analysis of one-party socialist democracies in order to determine their theoretical and practical limits to effectiveness.

Accountability

This has become a key concept in discussions of west European administrative development, particularly in Britain and is interrelated with the question of representation. There are two levels of debate concerning accountability: internal or external to the administrative unit. The issues involved are usefully highlighted by Foster (1988), whose classification is followed below. *Internal accountability* is essentially a concern of managerial structure and financial control. The basis of discussions is the requirement of administration for others: if someone is spending the resources of others then they must be accountable to someone else; if they are spending their own resources then accountability does not arise. This internal accountability is an issue which arises because there is an administrative state. Foster argues that four principles must be observed in order to achieve a workable system of accountability:

(a) the activities of an accountable unit must be freely available to view in appropriate management or financial accounts;
(b) managerial and financial links between units should be minimized to make clear who is responsible for what;
(c) at the head of each 'unit' must be a single individual;
(d) inter-unit transfers should operate as closely as possible in relation to 'real' costs.

These characteristics have rarely applied to public administration and there are some arguments that their application should be limited: for example because of the needs of social policy, the 'synergy' between units, etc. However, it is also clear, as Foster argues, that the absence of application of these four principles has given rise to considerable problems of maintaining and improving administrative efficiency. Hence in Britain the Audit Commission has been established, as an independent body, to apply these accountancy principles and thus to improve local government efficiency. The commission has identified a range of difficulties, and their findings, although specific to Britain, can be argued to be typical of the administrative problems of both liberal and socialist democracies:

(a) interdependence of decisions is too high with no clarity as to who is accountable for which service in quality or finance;
(b) financial and management accounts are usually inadequate and not widely enough available, thus undermining the possibility of scrutiny and checks;

(c) there is insufficient distinction between current account and capital investment activities and the appropriate financial and management distinctions that should apply;

(d) management and financial policy are often unclear in relation to declared political agenda;

(e) administrators and politicians have insufficient constraints to ensure their performance.

External accountability interacts with and compounds the complexity of the links between administrative receivers, financers and administrative managers. Foster (1988) identifies four issues in external accountability:

(a) *Accountability to tax payers.* This is the issue on 'no taxation without representation'. However, the question is complex since tax payers are often only a small proportion of the electorate. Reforms in Britain in 1989 and 1990 to a local poll tax are dominated by this concern.

(b) *Accountability to local business.* Local administrations provide services to businesses as well as people: how is their interest to be represented and accountability to be resolved?

(c) *Accountability to higher level government.* In all European countries central government, or federal plus state/regional governments, are a dominant force in providing financial resources and in laying down statutory requirements for local administrators. How is this wider state or national interest to be maintained within local administrative decisions?

(d) *Accountability to the electorate.* Although the focus for much writing, this form of accountability is almost a residual, after taking account of the restrictions under which administrators must act as well as other forms of accountability. Hence, there is usually limited scope to follow particular strategies developed from local community desires and political priorities.

Considerable discussion has usually been accorded to the relation of administrative decisions to local electorates: this is the problem of representation outlined above. However, it is far from clear that representation of interests is the dominant concern of administrators. Interest articulation, aggregation and communication pressures may be only imperfectly, and certainly only infrequently, represented by political agendas. More frequent representation is through tax and fee payments, and any individual or business choices that these represent, as responses to central and regional level directives, and to internal administrative pressures. What is clear, therefore, is that the issue of accountability raises numerous questions which concern the relations of territory and administration to people and community. Within these questions are major research agendas at both the level of theory and practice.

Participation

This concerns the relationship between administrative outcomes and involvement of individuals or groups: hence, how far administrative outcomes conform to individual or group desires and needs. In Chapter 3, and in the case studies in this book, the issue has been addressed at three levels: (i) as a question of regionalized ethnic-nationalism; (ii) as a question of alienation of individuals from large administrative units and the reassertion of 'basic' territorial levels; and (iii) as a question of the relation of individuals' basic rights to needs and desires. In these terms, participation is largely a regulatory question, of how best to link administrative outcome to personal and group requirements. This can be viewed from two points of view: how to seek a method of more effective government, and how to find a means of better relating government to needs? This is classified by Verba (1971) and Binder *et al.*, (1971) into four issues within a development process from which participation derives:

(a) *Identity*: the maintenance of community interest and mutual support between individuals and groups within areas;
(b) *Legitimacy*: the extent to which administrative decisions are accepted as 'right' by individuals or groups;
(c) *Penetration*: the extent and effectiveness of administrative effects on individuals or groups;
(d) *Distribution*: the extent of social transfers which mediate between those who depend upon state administrative support and those who provide the financial and other means to support social needs.

Participation is affected by each of these. Normally it will be greater, the closer the identity of interests and the legitimacy of administrative actions; arguably participation should also increase the greater the penetration of state administration and the larger its role in distribution. However, here is a tension, or irony, of modern developments. That, as the scale of the administrative state has expanded in both liberal and socialist democracies, the lower has been the enthusiasm of people to participate. Especially in socialist democracies this has been an increasing problem. As a result of low levels of participation, or disillusionment with its benefits, the legitimacy and identity of interests may be radically impaired. Thus, participation is at the core of the tensions in the administrative state: to rethink its structure (as in western Europe) or to stimulate its economic efficiency (as in eastern Europe).

Participation, like representation and accountability, is an issue which arises solely in administrative systems. In a private-sector (market) transaction, individual choice delivers full participation in a decision, and also no question of representation or accountability arises. It is natural, therefore, that ineffective or disillusioned participation is leading in western Europe to questions of the 'privatizing' of the state, contracting out services or otherwise modifying administrative practice. In eastern Europe it is argued that greater decentralization of responsibility to economic enterprises and to local administrative units will reinvigorate participation. The contributions to this volume see important benefits to be gained by such developments, although the benefits are by no means guaranteed. Clearly, a research agenda exists to establish ways of improving the links between the individual and the state and to reassert the significance of the local territorial dimension. Some guidance can be found in Sack's (1986, p. 10) concept of territory as the area within which individuals or groups seek 'to affect, influence or control people, phenomena and relationships, by determining and asserting control over a geographic area'. He argues that administrative territory sits at the intersection of tendencies of territoriality such as classification, communication and enforcement of access with combinations of behaviour such as hierarchy, bureaucracy and planning. Such a 'behavioural' approach to unravelling the human significance and use of territory as a concept is a key aspect underlying the legitimacy of, and participation in, administrative systems. It is interesting that Sack should use as an example the territories of the church which still underlie the rationality of the vast majority of local governments (at commune level) in Europe. The re-emergence of the importance of this 'primitive' level seems to offer some pointers for satisfying Sack's observation of the need for human territorial dimensions.

Economic development

Economic development is frequently ignored as an issue to be included within discussions of territory and administration. Yet the economic basis of the state determines its national income and hence scope for fulfilling people's needs and the extent of possible welfare provision. From one perspective the interaction of administration with economic development should be minimalist: to reduce compliance costs and administrative barriers to investment to a minimum. The liberal democracies of western Europe are, however, moving towards a position in which local as well as regional and central government actions are seen as critical in laying the foundations for economic development — even if these foundations are being increasingly seen as primarily facilitating business investment, rather than as direct interventionist strategies (see for example Bennett, 1989). In socialist democracies, however, the issue has an enhanced prominence since economic development has been treated as largely an administrative question.

As a result of these issues we can define a number of possible research agendas. In western Europe these issues centre on the appropriate roles of government administrations as opposed to market forces, and the appropriate level of government (Bennett, 1988):

Governmental
  (a) What economic development functions should government perform?
  (b) Within the public sector at what level of government (federal/central, state, local) is economic support most appropriate

and what actions are most effective at each level? How local should economic development policy be?

(c) To what extent are new agencies required in the public sector (for example enterprise agencies at regional level for groupings or localities; or at local level to focus activities within a given locality)?

(d) What is the most appropriate governmental management agency: *sectoral* (for example ministerial/departmental) and vertical divisions; *functional*; or *horizontal* (for example integrated area bases and inter-agency collaboration)?

(e) What are the most appropriate public sector instruments: initiatives, management expenditure policy, fiscal policy?

Private sector

(a) What is the scope for economic development, activities internal to the firm (for example employment policy, purchasing policy, trading policy)?

(b) What is the scope and extent of the private sector's external interest in collective action?

(c) What is the appropriate level and form of corporate social responsibility (for example donations, secondment of staff, membership of local bodies funding enterprise and community agencies, etc.)?

(d) How should business respond to society's expectations; should this be carried 'on the sleeve' as mainly a public relations exercise, or should it imbue the corporate and management culture?

(e) What is the most appropriate *mechanism* for delivering the private sector's collective needs (Chambers of Commerce, trading associations, enterprise agencies, etc.)?

Public-private targets and questions of mechanisms
There are considerable overlaps between the potential public- and private-sector positions, although within each are specific and unique positions. From each, however, derive a further set of questions of the key *targets* for action and the most appropriate *mechanisms* to achieve those targets:

(a) What is the relative weight to be given to the targets of wealth creation or distribution?

(b) Deriving from this, what is the relative importance to be attached to use of different factors of production (labour, land efficiency and productivity)?

(c) What is the relative weight to be given to different incentives to use of the returns to different factors including the ownership and use?

(d) What is the most appropriate scale of action: small firm and 'seed corn' or a large firm and restructuring of capital access?

(e) What is the most appropriate agency or means of initiating, managing, monitoring, evaluating and feeding back experience to innovate new forms of development initiatives?

For each set of questions we are confronted with issues internal and external to the organization, and with questions to be resolved on the best weight to be placed on growth or distribution, the scale of action and the appropriate mechanism or agency to ensure effective activity. Some of these questions can be resolved by recourse to theory, some by appraisal of effectiveness in practice and some remain issues of political choice.

In socialist democracies major research questions to be resolved relate to how to improve the overall economic efficiency of the economy through administration reform. As noted by Kuklinski (1987) it is now being accepted that socialist economic planning has over-emphasized the role of scale economics and has suffered from the liquidation of many small-scale plants. Kuklinski argues that the important developments that are required are:

(a) how to combine the advantages of large-scale and small enterprises;
(b) how to modernize agriculture through greater use of individual farms;
(c) how to improve housing by ensuring better supplies of building materials;
(d) how to stimulate greater local government efficiency through local self-government rather than workers' self-government;
(e) how to create and diffuse innovations by allowing local development which induces 'others to close ranks in the upward direction' (op. cit. p. 10);
(f) how to use the power of the economic 'demonstration effects' of experiments to stimulate overall reforms.

These question represent major challenges for socialist democracies and suggest the need to move to a new balance with less administrative power and greater individual opportunities. Whether such changes can be achieved will remain one of the major issues for the rest of this century.

Administrative rationality

Administrative (or technical) efficiency has been used by a number of authors as the chief criterion for the organization of the appropriate territorial basis of governance. This dominated the geographical market principle of Christaller's (1936) central place theory applied to administrative organization of space which has underlain the rationale for the city-region administrative structure. And this approach has been developed by more recent writers into a general approach to 'districting' for public services (see for example Morrill, 1974; Massam, 1975). For services which require travel to a distribution point, or which must be distributed from a limited network of distribution points, Lea (1979) has developed a general theoretical approach applying the Lindahl-Pareto ideas to yield optimal allocations of travelled-for public goods using the concept of internalizing externalities. Hägerstrand's concepts, outlined in Chapter 3, of action spaces developed within spatial and time constraints is also a development of this approach.

The rationale of the efficiency approach to administrative design, however, leaves many unresolved questions which require further research. First, is the question of adaptation of districts in periods of rapid change. Second, is the problem that the 'natural' area of an administrative function may conflict with existing political units (see for example Fesler, 1973; Jackson and Bergman, 1973). Third, it is seldom the case that different services cover the same natural areas. Forth, technically efficient areas do not necessarily have any relation to identities of community interests (see Chapter 4 and Bennett, 1980). Fifth, it is not at all clear in socialist democracies that attempts to improve administrative efficiency through changes in the extent of party control, or the territorial scope of decentralized policies will change present administrative behaviour. Indeed, Bendix (1968, pp. 335–51) argues that the level of collusion and joint decision-making in the Soviet system will prevent radical change. However, Smith (1985) argues, as earlier chapters have done, that the resolution of this and the other problems may be found in more flexible approaches in which the more basic local level finds a greater place.

It is now clear that while administrative rationality must, where possible, be enhanced and associated efficiency gains achieved, the dominance of this criterion over others will also lead to losses of efficiency because it will undermine community identity and the requirements of representation, accountability and participation. A set of joint criteria is therefore required. This suggests a difficult and complex research agenda in which both centralized and sub-national bureaucratic solutions are required in order to gain both greater economic efficiency as well as the benefits to be derived from aligning administration better to preferences.

References

Agnew, J.A. (1987), *Place and Politics: the Geographical Mediation of State and Society*, Allen and Unwin, Boston.

Almond, G.A. and Powell, G.B. (1966), *Comparative Politics: a Developmental Approach*, Little, Brown, Boston.

Bendix, R. (ed.) (1968), *State and Society: a Reader in Comparative Political Sociology*, Little, Brown, Boston.

Bennett, R.J. (1980), *The Geography of Public Finance*, Methuen, London.

Bennett, R.J. (ed.) (1988), *Local Economic Development: Identifying the Research Priorities*, ESRC, London.

Bennett, R.J. (1989), 'Local economic development: the possibilities and limitations of decentralized policy', in R.J. Bennett (ed.), *Decentralization: local governments and markets: setting a post-welfare agenda?*, Oxford University Press, Oxford.

Binder, L., Coleman, J.S., La Palombera, J., Pye, L.W., Verba, S. and Wiener, M. (1971), *Crises and Sequences in Political Development*, Princetown University Press, Princetown, NJ.

Brustein, W. (1981), 'A regional mode-of-production analysis of political behaviour: the cases of Mediterranean and western France', *Politics and Society*, 10, 355–98.

Christaller, W. (1933), *Die zentralen Orte in Süddentschland: Eine ökonomisch-geographische*

Untersuchung über die Gesetzmässigkeit der Verbeitung und Entwicklung der Siedlungen mit Städtischen Funktionen, G. Fischer, Jena.

Fesler, J.W. (1973), *Public Administration Theory and Practice*, Prentice-Hall, Englewood Cliffs, NJ.

Foster, C.D. (1988), 'Accountability in the development of policy for local taxation of people and business,' in R.J. Bennett (ed.), 'Local fiscal crises: the policy imperative', *Regional Studies*, 22, 13–8.

Galeotti, G. (1987), 'Political exchanges and decentralisation', *European Journal of Political Economy*, 3, 111–30.

Galeotti, G. (1988), *Decentralisation and Political Rents*, paper presented at international seminar on local government finance, Ferrara, Italy.

Jackson, W. and Bergman, E. (1973), *A Geography of Politics*, Brown, Dubuque, Iowa.

Kuklinski, A. (1987), 'Local studies in Poland: experiences and prospects', in P. Dutkiewicz and G. Gorzelak (eds), *Local Studies in Poland*, Institute of Space Economy, University of Warsaw.

Lea, A.C. (1979), 'Welfare theory, public goods and public facility location', *Geographical Analysis*, 11, 217–39.

Massam, B. (1975), *Location and Space in Social Administration*, Methuen, London.

Morrill, R.L. (1974), *The Spatial Organization of Society*, 2nd ed., Duxbury, N. Scituate, Mass.

Riker, W. (1962), *The Theory of Political Coalitions*, New Haven, Conn.

Sack, R.D. (1986), *Human Territoriality: its Theory and History*, Cambridge University Press, Cambridge.

Stigler, G.J. (1972), 'Economic competition and political competition', *Public Choice*, 13, 91–106.

Smith, B.C. (1985), *Decentralisation: the Territorial Dimension of the State*, George Allen and Unwin, London.

Taylor, P. (1985), *Political Geography: World Economy, Nation-state and Locality*, Longmans, Harlow.

Verba, S. (1971), 'Sequences and developments', in L. Binder *et al.*, *Crises and Sequences in Political Development*, Princetown University Press, Princetown, NJ.

Wallerstein, I. (1979), *The Capitalist World Economy*, Cambridge University Press, Cambridge.

Wittman, D.A. (1973), 'Parties as utility maximizers', *American Political Science Review*, 67, 490–8.

Index